HASTINGS AND THE ROHILLA WAR

HASTINGS AND THE ROHILLA WAR

JOHN STRACHEY

Published by

Gyan Publishing House
5, Ansari Road
Daryaganj, New Delhi-110002
Phone: 011-47034999, 9811692060
E-mail: books@gyanbooks.com

Distribution Network
gyanbooks.com
India, USA, Canada, UK, Australia

ISBN: 978-93-7447-182-1 (PB)

First Published, 1892

2nd Impression 2025

Printed at: Gyan Press, Delhi.

HASTINGS AND THE ROHILLA WAR
Author: JOHN STRACHEY

HASTINGS

AND

THE ROHILLA WAR

SIR J. STRACHEY

HASTINGS

AND

THE ROHILLA WAR

BY

SIR JOHN STRACHEY, G.C.S.I.

Oxford
AT THE CLARENDON PRESS
1892

PREFACE

I CANNOT more clearly explain the reasons for which this history has been written than by making the following quotation from a book of my own, published three years ago:—

'Sir Henry Maine has pointed out with admirable truth the consequences in India of the fact that English Classical literature towards the end of the last century was "saturated with party politics."

'"This," he says, "would have been a less serious fact if, at this epoch, one chief topic of the great writers and rhetoricians, of Burke and Sheridan, of Fox and Francis, had not been India itself. I have no doubt that the view of Indian government taken at the end of the century by Englishmen whose works and speeches are held to be models of English style has had deep effect on the mind of the educated Indian of this day. We are only now beginning to see how excessively inaccurate were their statements of fact and how one-sided were their judgments [1]."

'These remarks of Sir Henry Maine point to what I have long believed to be a serious misfortune to our Indian Government—the non-existence of any history of British India, which is trustworthy and complete in its facts, and which at the same time possesses the essential quality of literary excellence. Since the earlier part of the present century the old stories of the crimes by which the establishment of our power in India was attended have been passed on from one author to another. A few students know that for the most part these stories are false, and (to use the words of Sir

[1] The Reign of Queen Victoria, 'India,' vol. i. p. 508.

Alfred Lyall) that "the hardihood and endurance of the men who won for England an empire were equalled only by the general justice and patience with which they pacified and administered it." These calumnies have caused and still are causing no little mischief both in England and in India. Thousands of excellent people are filled with righteous indignation when they read of the atrocious acts of Clive and Hastings, the judicial murder of Nandkumar, the extermination of the Rohillas, the plunder of the Begums. No suspicion of the truth reaches them that these horrors never occurred, and the fear can hardly be repressed that there may be some foundation even now for the charges of Indian misgovernment and oppression. Disparagement of their own countrymen has always been one of the common failings of unwise Englishmen, those "birds of evil presage who at all times have grated our ears with their melancholy song." They find in the supposed crimes of the founders of our Indian Empire an unfailing source of invective and obloquy. This false history is systematically taught by ourselves, and believed by the educated natives of India to be true. It is impossible that this should not have a serious effect on their feelings towards their English rulers.

'We owe to Sir James Stephen, to whom India owes many other debts for good service, "the first attempt" (I am quoting the words of Sir Henry Maine) "to apply robust, careful, and dispassionate criticism to this period of history." One at least of the imaginary crimes to which I have referred—the judicial murder of Nandkumar by Impey and Hastings—will hardly again appear in sober history.

'The great criminal in this matter was James Mill, whose history, "saturated," if history was ever so saturated, "with party politics," is ordinarily accepted to this day as the standard and veritable history of British India. His "excessive dryness and severity of style" (Sir James Stephen says) "produce an impression of accuracy and labour which a study of original authorities does not by any means confirm. . . . His want of accuracy is nothing to his bad faith. My experience is that, when he makes imputations, especially on lawyers, he ought always to be carefully confronted with the original authorities [1]."

'I should have hesitated, even on such authority as that of Sir

[1] The Story of Nuncomar and the Impeachment of Sir Elijah Impey, vol. ii. pp. 149 and 198.

James Stephen, to accuse an historian not only of inaccuracy but of bad faith, if I did not feel that I had qualified myself to form an independent opinion on the subject. I have personally had occasion to investigate the facts of perhaps the worst of the crimes of which Hastings has been accused, the sale and extermination of the Rohillas. Several years of my Indian service were passed in the province of Rohilkhand. When I was first sent there, old men were still living who remembered having heard in their childhood the story of Hafiz Rahmat, the great Rohilla Chief, of his defeat by the English, and his death. I went to Rohilkhand without a doubt of the truth of the terrible story told by Burke and Mill and by Lord Macaulay in his famous essay, but I soon changed my opinion. I found myself in the midst of a population by which the history of those times had not been forgotten, and of which an important and numerous section consisted of Rohillas, the children and grandchildren of the men whose race was supposed to have been almost exterminated. I was in frequent communication with a Rohilla Prince who ruled over a considerable territory which his ancestor owed to Warren Hastings, and which had been in the possession of his family ever since. No one had ever heard of the atrocities which to this day fill Englishmen with shame. Later in life I was able to undertake an examination of the original authorities on the Rohilla war, and I can hardly express in moderate language my indignation at the misrepresentations, the suppression of truth, the garbling of documents of which I found that Mill had been guilty. The English army was not hired out by Hastings for the destruction of the Rohillas; the Rohillas, described by Burke as belonging to "the bravest, the most honourable and generous nation on earth," were no nation at all, but a comparatively small body of cruel and rapacious Afghan adventurers who had imposed their foreign rule on an unwilling Hindu population, and the story of their destruction is fictitious. It was unfortunate that Lord Macaulay accepted Mill as an authority deserving the fullest confidence. There is not an important fact in his essay on Warren Hastings which is not taken from Mill's History. I share the admiration which Sir James Stephen has expressed for the great services rendered to India by Lord Macaulay, and of him I shall speak no word of disrespect. But it is a misfortune that he was thus misled. I fear that the time is distant when English people will cease to accept his brilliant essays as the chief sources of their knowledge regarding the establishment of our Empire in India[1].'

It has been my object in the present work to bring together all the materials necessary for enabling students of this period of Indian history to form an accurate judgment on the proceedings of Hastings in connection with the Rohilla war.

The original materials are very voluminous, of very unequal value, and not always easy of access. Among them the following are the more important:—

(1) The Proceedings or Consultations of the Bengal Government, and of the Secret Select Committee by which a very large part of the more important business was conducted. These Consultations, to which I have had free access, form a complete series of large manuscript volumes at the India Office. They are, as Sir James Stephen says, 'one of the most interesting, authentic, and curious collections in the world. It was the practice for a long series of years to enter minutes of all the proceedings at every meeting of the Council. . . . To the present day it is possible to follow with perfect clearness the progress of every measure—legislative, financial, military, or administrative—which occurred in the government of India during a long series of years.'

It is much to be regretted that little has hitherto been done to make this immense mass of invaluable records accessible to students of Indian history; but measures are now in progress which will, it may be hoped, remove this reproach.

(2) In 1781 a 'Committee of Secrecy' was appointed by the House of Commons 'to inquire into the causes of the war in the Carnatic, and of the condition of the British possessions in those parts.' It was also authorised to inquire into 'the general state of political connections and interests in India,' to sit in the India Office, and to call for

[1] 'India,' by Sir John Strachey, p. 194.

all papers that it desired to see. The Committee presented a number of Reports, but the only one of them that need be noticed here is the Fifth Report, printed in 1782. It contains an account of the relations of the Bengal Government with the Emperor, the Nawab Vizier, the Marathas, the Rohillas, and other powers, during the greater part of the period with which the present work is concerned. The Report itself is far less valuable than its numerous Appendices, which fill more than 800 pages of a huge folio volume. It will be seen, from the frequent references that I have made to them, that they contain a large proportion of the Consultations of the Bengal Government, and of the Secret Select Committee, relating to the Rohilla war and to other events between 1772 and 1776, letters to the Court of Directors, correspondence with civil and military officers, minutes by the members of the Government, and a multitude of other papers. They have been printed with no sort of arrangement, chronological or other, and it is often no easy matter to discover what they contain or what is omitted.

(3) In 1890 three volumes of 'Selections from the Letters, Despatches, and other State Papers preserved in the Foreign Department of the Government of India, 1772–1785' were published in Calcutta. They were edited by Mr. George W. Forrest, the accomplished officer now permanently appointed to the charge of the old records of the Government of India. 'His object,' he says in his Preface, 'is to trace the history of our Indian Empire from 1772, the year Warren Hastings became Governor of Bengal, to the 1st of February, 1785, the day on which he resigned the office of Governor-General. The story of the administration of Warren Hastings—one of the most important periods in the history of our Empire—is told by the letters and narratives, the dissents and discussions of the chief actors. These have been printed letter

by letter exactly as they were entered day by day in the Secret Proceedings of the Select Committee of Council.' The value of these Selections has been greatly increased by an admirable introduction by Mr. Forrest. It gives a careful and valuable summary of the principal facts connected with the administration of Hastings. The greater number, but not all, of the papers relating to the Rohilla war printed in Mr. Forrest's Selections, are to be found in the Appendices to the Fifth Report from the Committee of Secrecy above noticed.

(4) The Speeches and Charges of Burke. These, although I have frequently referred to them, throw little or no light on the questions with which the present volume deals. The House of Commons having rejected the first Charge relating to the Rohilla war, this did not form one of the Articles of Impeachment, and the other Charges to which I have had more particularly to refer were not gone into at the trial of Hastings. No one acquainted with Burke's Charges can doubt the justice of Sir James Stephen's description :—

'Instead of being short, full, pointed and precise, they are bulky pamphlets sprinkled over with imitations of legal phraseology. They are full of invective, oratorical matter, needless recitals, arguments, statements of evidence—everything in fact which can possibly seem to make an accusation difficult to understand and to meet. They are, moreover, extremely tricky, being full of insinuations, and covering, by their profusion of irrelevant matter, the total and no doubt designed absence of averments essential to the conclusion which they are meant to support. In short they are as shuffling and disingenuous in substance as they are clumsy, awkward and intricate in form [1].'

Hastings himself, in his Defence before the House of Commons in 1786, described these Charges in not dissimilar terms :—

'In truth they are not charges, but histories and comments. But

[1] 'Nuncomar and Impey,' vol. ii. p. 9.

they are yet more; they are made up of mutilated quotations; of facts which have no mutual relation, but are forced by false arrangement into connection; of principles of pernicious policy and false morality; assertions of guilt without proof or the attempt to prove them; interpretations of secret motives and designs which passed within my own breast, and which none but myself could know; actions of others imputed to me; and epithets and invectives affixed to acts ascribed to me, equally to those which in the construction are bad, as to those which are indifferent or even meritorious.'

It is not easy to understand how such a man as Burke can have used 'the almost insane language' which, as Mr. Lecky says, is often attributed to him in his published speeches. Some of this, but not much, may perhaps be due to the imperfect reporting of those days.

Burke's contemporaries often expressed their amazement at his language. For instance, in the Debate of the 20th June, 1794, when Pitt moved that the thanks of the House should be given to the Managers for their conduct in the Impeachment of Hastings, Law said that

'he could not suppress his surprise and astonishment at the conduct of gentlemen of character, whose talents he revered, in attempting to excuse the leading Manager by asserting that in some instances his expressions had been misrepresented. Mr. Law solemnly affirmed that they were not; that the English language did not afford expressions more gross, violent, abusive, and indecent than those which the Manager had used. If any passage in his speech could be called sublime and beautiful it was at best but sublime and beautiful nonsense; at other times his expressions were so vulgar and illiberal, that the lowest blackguard in a bear-garden would have been ashamed to utter them. . . . His expressions could not be mistaken, and he was confident that if the minutes of the short-hand writers were called for, it would appear that the terms he used were more illiberal, outrageous, and offensive than his Honourable friends had represented them to be. They were universally reprobated, from the first characters among the numerous audience that had heard them, down to the messengers, door-keepers, and guards.'

The 'History of the Trial of Warren Hastings' [Debrett, 1796, pp. 151–156] contains many illustrations of the extraordinary language applied by Burke to Hastings. I will quote a few examples :—

'For years he lay down upon that sty of disgrace, fattening in it, lying feeding upon that offal of disgrace and excrement, and everything that can be opprobrious to the human mind.'—'Such are the damned and damnable proceedings of a judge in hell, and such a judge was Warren Hastings.'—'A wild beast when his belly is full may be pleased and lick your hand. You might have a serene day under such a beast, but can you under that man Hastings?'—'A captain-general of iniquity, thief, tyrant, robber, cheat, sharper, swindler; we call him all these names, and are sorry that the English language does not afford terms adequate to the enormity of his offences.'—'Sir Walter Raleigh was called a spider of hell. This was foolish, indecent, in Lord Coke. Had he been a Manager on this trial, he would have been guilty of a neglect of duty had he not called the prisoner a spider of hell.'—'What! compare this man, a bullock-driver, with Tamerlane and those conquerors! When God punished Pharaoh and Egypt, he did not send armies but lice and locusts to lay the land waste[1].'

No one doubts that Burke's persecution of Hastings was prompted by pure and noble motives, but, in the words of Macaulay, 'his imagination and his passions, once excited, hurried him beyond the bounds of justice and good sense.' There can be no question that his animosity against Hastings had its origin in the vile malevolence of Francis, which he unfortunately mistook for virtue. Francis himself declared that he had been the chief mover in the

[1] Much that cannot be excused was said and written on behalf of Hastings, but none of his advocates before the Lords, or in the debates in the House of Commons, ever used language that could be compared in virulence and indecency to that of Burke. Hastings himself maintained at all times the dignity and equanimity by which he had through life been distinguished. It is true that Major Scott, thinking perhaps of the well-known epigram, called Burke a reptile, but Macaulay, when he tells the story, does not add that Burke had previously called him a jackal. The character of Scott, it may be added, although he was often an injudicious friend, has been very unjustly misrepresented. See 'Memoirs of Charles Reade,' vol. i. p. 8. Scott was Charles Reade's grandfather.

impeachment, that 'he supplied the information, furnished the materials, and prompted the prosecution.'

(5) The British Museum contains 264 volumes of the 'Official and private correspondence of Warren Hastings, with some additional correspondence of his family after his death.' The greater part of this collection, which is of inestimable value to the student of the life of Hastings, was left by his widow to her son Charles Imhoff. He in his turn left the papers to Mr. Winter, Rector of Daylesford, who married the niece of Mrs. Hastings. In 1872 they were purchased by the British Museum from Mrs. Winter, the widow of the Rector of Kingham, Chipping Norton. Many of these volumes contain duplicate copies of the Official Consultations of the Bengal Government while Hastings was at its head. The private letters and papers are often extremely interesting, and throw important light on the history of the time. Little or no use has hitherto been made of them. It will be seen that they have been frequently quoted in the present volume.

(6) Mill's History of British India. My own opinion, and that of Sir James Stephen, regarding this work, which is still usually accepted as the standard history of the foundation of our Indian Empire, has been already stated. The reader of the present book will be able to judge whether or not—so far as the Rohilla war is concerned—those opinions are justified. How we ought to explain the strange inaccuracies of Mill's history, his suppressions of the truth, his garbling of documents, his falsification of evidence, is a problem on the solution of which I shall not speculate.

I have now named the principal English sources of information for the history of the period with which this book is specially concerned. I have also consulted a multitude of works of which it is unnecessary to give a list, but which I have, in some cases, quoted. I will mention a few of them only, and there is one in particular which has become so famous that it must be specially noticed. I refer to Macaulay's Essay on Warren Hastings. My reasons have been given for considering his account of some of the transactions in which Hastings was concerned with the Vizier, the Rohillas, and the Emperor, totally undeserving of credit. His essay is a splendid tribute to the genius of Hastings, but when he wrote it the authority of Mill was undisputed, and Macaulay accepted that authority with no suspicion of its worthlessness.

Gleig's 'Memoirs of the Life of Warren Hastings,' published in 1841, deserved the small respect with which Macaulay treated them. It would be difficult to name a biography more unsatisfactory, from every point of view, than this. Its sole value lies in the extracts from the original papers of Hastings—now in the British Museum—to which Gleig had access.

A good article on the Rohillas in Northern India, by Mr. Whiteway of the Bengal Civil Service, will be found in the 'Calcutta Review,' 1875, and much information on the same subject is contained in the District Gazetteers of the North-western Provinces.

Several short biographies of Warren Hastings—the most important of them by Sir Alfred Lyall—have been published in the last few years; but I will not more particularly refer to them, because it did not fall within their scope to discuss in detail the subjects of which the present volume treats.

In addition to the materials which have been mentioned, and which are mostly of English origin, there are other sources from which valuable information can be obtained regarding the Afghans in Rohilkhand, and the war which ended their dominion.

(1) The most important of these is the 'Historical Relation of the Origin, Progress, and final dissolution of

the Government of the Rohilla Afghans in the Northern Provinces of Hindostan, compiled from a Persian manuscript and other original papers, by Charles Hamilton, Esq., an officer in the service of the Honourable East India Company on the Bengal Establishment,' published in 1787. Hamilton says in his Preface that the Persian Manuscript in question, which he had translated about ten years before, was given to him by 'a person of some consequence, who was an Afghan, then acting on the part of the Rohilla Chief, Faizullah Khan, in a confidential capacity'; that this person had been himself engaged in many of the events related, and that the Persian Manuscript had been written under his inspection. In some parts of the work specially referring to the proceedings of the English Government, Hamilton says that he had recourse to other sources of information. Although he does not conceal his sympathies with Hastings, he claims credit for having delayed the publication of the book until the charge against him in connection with the Rohilla war had been finally rejected by the House of Commons in 1786. He was, he says, 'deterred by an apprehension that were it to come forth at a period when the contest of opposite factions respecting the affairs of India had agitated men's minds to an uncommon degree of animosity, or whilst the decision of the legislature upon the most interesting part of its subject was yet pending, it might have been regarded as a frivolous farrago, vamped up merely to serve the purpose of the hour, and as such have drawn upon its author suspicions which he trusts cannot, with any support of probability, be imputed to him at present.' Although Hamilton does not say in his Preface that the actual author of the Manuscript was a Rohilla, he several times, in the body of the work, speaks of the 'Rohilla narrator,' or 'Rohilla historian.' The author, however, appears to have been a Hindu. A description of the original Persian work will be found in

Dr. C. Rieu's Catalogue of the Persian Manuscripts in the British Museum, vol. i. p. 306. It is called 'Tārikh-i-Faiz Baksh' (the History of the Bestower of favours or the Bountiful), a title evidently, as Dr. Ethé has observed to me, coined in honour of the author's patron Faizullah Khan. 'The author' (I am quoting from Dr. Rieu) 'was, as appears from the preface, in the service of the Rohilla Chief, Faizullah, who employed him as his agent in his negociations with the Colonel in command of the British force at Bilgrām. There he became acquainted with Mr. Kirkpatrick, at whose request he wrote the present work. He completed it in A.H. 1190 [A.D. 1776], and dedicated it to the Nawāb, to whom it was submitted for correction. . . . His name, Shīv Parshād, is a conclusive proof of Hindu nationality.' A full account of the contents of the Persian Manuscript, which is in the main identical with that used by Hamilton, is given in Sir H. M. Elliot's 'History of India, as told by its own historians,' vol. viii. pp. 175–179, but the editor of that work does not seem to have known of the English translation.

This is the most valuable of all the contributions made by native historians to our knowledge of the Rohillas in Rohilkhand, and wherever it is possible to check its statements, by comparing them with those of the official English authorities of the time, it is found to be remarkably accurate. There is, however, one respect in which it cannot be expected to be free from prejudice. It represents the views of Faizullah Khan; and although he had been treated by Hafiz Rahmat with greater consideration than that shown to the other sons of Ali Mohammad—for he had been left in possession of a considerable territory—it was hardly possible that his feelings should be friendly towards the man who had despoiled his family of the greater part of their inheritance.

(2) The life of Hafiz Rahmat Khan was written by his

son, Mohammad Mustajab Khan, under the title of 'Gulistan-i-Rahmat.' An abridged translation of this work, called 'The Life of Hafiz ool-Moolk,' was published by Mr. Charles Elliott in 1831. There is a description of the original Persian Manuscript in Dr. Rieu's Catalogue, vol. i. p. 307. Another life of Hafiz Rahmat, 'an expanded recension of the Gulistān-i-Rahmat,' was written by his grandson, Sadat Yar Khan of Bareilly. An account of both these works will be found in Sir H. M. Elliot's History. They have little historical value. The object of their authors was to eulogize Hafiz Rahmat; everything that seemed to throw discredit on him is suppressed, and in the narrative of the events which led to the Rohilla war the facts are often completely misrepresented. For instance, no reference, except one that is altogether misleading, is made to the treaty entered into in 1772 between the Rohillas and the Vizier, which was attested by the English Commander-in-Chief, and the non-fulfilment of which led to the ruin of the Rohilla Government.

(3) The only other work of an Indian historian that need be mentioned here is the 'Sair-ul-mutakherin' ('Review of Modern Times'), written by Ghulam Husain Khan, and completed in 1783. Although it does not throw any fresh light of importance on the history of the Rohilla war, of which it gives a description, it is worth consulting because the work is one of great interest and value. A full account of it will be found in Sir H. M. Elliot's History, vol. viii. pp. 194–198. 'It was translated into English by Mustafa, a French renegade, and published in Calcutta in 1789 in three quarto volumes. . . . His version is full of Gallicisms. A large portion of the impression of his work was lost on its way to England, and it has long been a rare book, only to be found here and there in public libraries.' An amended version of one volume was published by General Briggs. Ghulam Husain

b

is 'the Musulman historian of those times' whom Macaulay, in his Essay on Clive, has quoted with approval.

The reputation of Hastings has passed through remarkable vicissitudes. In India no Governor was so universally honoured, and no man possessed in a higher degree the faculty of making himself beloved by the people that he governed. He was beloved not only for his personal qualities, but for the happiness that he had brought into the homes of the people of Bengal. He gave to them, for the first time within their memory, security, imperfect though we should now think it, for their lives and property, and means, such as they had never possessed before, of obtaining justice against their oppressors. Before him there was virtually no government. Bengal was a sink of misrule and crime and official corruption. When he left India, a rare example of personal integrity and honourable poverty, our provinces had become 'the most flourishing of all the States in India.' 'It was I,' he said, with well-justified pride, 'who made them so. . . . The valour of others acquired, I enlarged and gave shape and consistency to the dominion which you hold there; I preserved it . . . I gave you all, and you have rewarded me with confiscation, disgrace, and a life of impeachment.[1]'

He was acquitted upon every charge, and the nation was practically and rightly unanimous in the conclusion that the judgment had been just. During the rest of his life that conclusion was not disturbed, and he was treated with constantly increasing honour. Lords and Commons, on a well-known occasion, 'rose with their heads uncovered, and stood in silence till he passed the door of their chamber.' When he died, he doubtless thought that he had outlived calumny, and it might have been confidently believed that he would be remembered not only

[1] Address to the House of Lords, June 2nd, 1791. 'History of the Trial of Warren Hastings,' Part iv. p. 103.

among the most wise and courageous of the founders of our Indian Empire—for that even his enemies could hardly deny—but as one of the most virtuous. This was not to happen. As time went on the truth became more and more forgotten, while the writings and speeches of Burke, his great accuser, were imperishable. 'We are only now beginning' (to repeat the words of Sir Henry Maine that I have already quoted) 'to see how excessively inaccurate were their statements of fact and how one-sided were their judgments.' There is no history of British India that deserves the name, and the task of writing a pretended history fell into the hands of James Mill, the most prejudiced of men. His work remains to this day our standard and often worthless authority. He repeated every falsehood that ignorance or folly or malice had invented against the great men who had built up our empire. After this came the crowning misfortune. Macaulay, obviously without independent inquiry, received as truth the baseless stories that had been recorded as history, and gave them fresh life in his glittering periods. Thus the fame of Hastings has become obscured. It is only in our own time that the work of reparation has begun. One of the imaginary crimes of Hastings, the judicial murder of Nandkumar, has been blotted out by Sir James Stephen. If I should help to satisfy the students of Indian history that the crime of selling the services of a British army for the extermination of a noble people is imaginary also, the object with which this book was written will have been gained.

JOHN STRACHEY.

CONTENTS

CHAPTER I.

CHAPTER II.

CHAPTER III.

CHAPTER IV.

CHAPTER V.

CHAPTER VI.

CHAPTER VII.

CHAPTER XI.

CHAPTER XII.

CHAPTER XIII.

CHAPTER XIV.

NOTE ON THE SPELLING OF INDIAN WORDS.

In the spelling of Indian words I have generally followed the system adopted for official purposes by the Government of India, and now in more or less common use. Accents, however, have been almost always omitted. Unless very sparingly employed they have, in a work like this, a disagreeable and somewhat pedantic appearance. Those who wish to know, approximately, how the principal proper names should be pronounced, can consult the Index, where, whenever it seemed necessary, accents have been inserted. The following, taken from Sir William Hunter, shows the sounds to be given to accented and non-accented vowels :—

a	has the	sound of	*a* in rural.
á	,,	,,	*a* in far.
e	,,	,,	*ey* in grey.
i	,,	,,	*i* in police.
í	,,	,,	*ie* in pier.
o	,,	,,	*o* in bone.
u	,,	,,	*u* in bull.
ú	,,	,,	*u* in sure.
ai	,,	,,	*y* in lyre.

Many Oriental words have become, with more or less alteration, part of the English language. No one need now attempt or wish to change the ordinary spelling of such words as Caliph, Vizier, Calcutta, Bombay, Oudh, Cawnpore. About many other words there is much greater room for doubt or dispute. No rule can be laid down. Strict accuracy in this matter of orthography is impossible, unless, as Sir William Hunter says, 'we resort to puzzling un-English devices of typography, such as dots under the consonants, curves above them, or italic letters in the middle of words.' Consistency is impossible also, and there will always be differences of opinion in regard to the compromises which an author may adopt.

HASTINGS

AND

THE ROHILLA WAR.

CHAPTER I.

THE RUIN OF THE MOGHAL EMPIRE.—THE GROWTH OF THE POWER OF THE MARATHAS.—THE AFGHANS IN INDIA.

The decay of the Empire before the death of Aurangzeb.—The rise of the Marathas.—Their mode of warfare and policy.—Immense extension of their power.—Destruction of their army at Panipat.—Recovery of their power.—Their aim at universal dominion over India.—Protection of the British provinces against the Marathas the key to the policy of Hastings.—The Rohillas or Afghans in India.

IN 1750, when Warren Hastings first landed in India, the ruin of the Moghal Empire was virtually complete. The last of the great Emperors had been Aurangzeb, but before his death, in 1707, his dominion, which had at one time been more extensive and undisputed than that of any of his predecessors, had begun to break up under the constant and exhausting attacks of the Marathas. During the next fifty years the growth of the Maratha power was such that it seemed destined to overwhelm the whole of India. There was hardly a province between the Himalaya and the southern extremity of the peninsula which had not been either occupied or invaded by its plundering hordes, or from which it had not exacted tribute. Throughout a tract hardly less extensive than the whole of civilised Europe, men for a long series of years lived in dread of the sudden

B

inroads of the Maratha horsemen, the rapidity of whose movements baffled all attempts at resistance or defence. It was no part of their policy to meet their enemies in the open field; plunder and ruthless destruction seemed usually to be their sole objects, and the only way of escape for the rulers of invaded countries was the payment of ransom or a formal engagement to make over annually to the Maratha authorities a fixed proportion of their revenues.

Instead of directly establishing their own government in the countries which they had conquered, the Marathas usually preferred an organised system of spoliation. Forty years before the death of Aurangzeb, Sivaji, the founder of their power, began to demand, under the name of *chauth*, an assignment to himself of one-fourth of the revenue of the countries in which he was strong enough to exact compliance. The system received afterwards an immense development, and it gave to the Marathas great and permanent resources. In 1717 their right to receive this tribute, as well as other payments, from the whole of the States of Southern India was formally recognised by Imperial grants. In 1741, and in the following years, they repeatedly overran and devastated great portions of Bengal. For several generations the people remembered the horrors of that time, and a record of it survives to the present day in the name of the Maratha ditch made by the English for the protection of their settlement of Calcutta. In 1751, only six years before the victory of Clive at Plassey, the Viceroy of Bengal was compelled to purchase peace by the engagement to pay to the Marathas an annual chauth or tribute, and by the cession of the southern part of the province of Orissa. In 1759 they occupied Delhi. They were in possession of the Punjab, and declared their intention of leaving no part of India unconquered. 'Their power,' writes Elphinstone, 'was at this time at its zenith. Their frontier extended on the north to the Indus and Himalaya, and on the south nearly to the extremity of the peninsula; all the territory within those limits that was not their own paid tribute. The whole of this great power was wielded by one hand. The establishments of the Maratha Government had increased with its power. Its force was no longer composed of predatory bands alone; it included an army of well-paid and well-mounted cavalry in the direct service of the State, and 10,000 disciplined infantry, who, though a very imperfect copy of that commanded by Europeans, were far superior to any infantry previously known in India. The Marathas had now also a train of artillery surpassing that of the Moguls, which they had so long regarded with awe and envy. They even endeavoured to assume the pomp which was characteristic of their rivals. Rich dresses, spacious tents, and splendid caparisons became common among them, and their courts and retinues were formed on the Mogul model[1].' Although titular Emperors remained, the dynasty of the Moghals had now virtually perished.

At the very time in which the power of the Marathas seemed to have become irresistible, they were on the brink of a tremendous catastrophe. The Afghan monarch Ahmad Shah Abdali had three times since 1748 invaded India, and in September 1759 he again entered the Punjab. During the following year he held possession of that province, and towards the end of the rainy season he marched towards Delhi, supported by Shuja-ud-daula the Nawab Vizier, and by large numbers of his Afghan countrymen who had settled or taken service in India. The Marathas met him, early in January 1761, at Panipat with an army said to number some 300,000 men. The result of the battle that followed was their almost total destruction. In the course of the campaign 200,000 men are said to have been killed, and few of the great Maratha chiefs escaped. Ahmad Shah made little use of his victory, and soon after the battle he returned to Kabul.

It seemed for a time that the Marathas could never recover from their defeat, but within a few years their

[1] 'History of India,' book xii. ch. 4.

power and the terror that they inspired were hardly less formidable than before. They returned to Northern India, possessed themselves of Delhi, and devastated the Doáb and Rohilkhand. Oudh narrowly escaped a similar fate, but the English, whose power was now rapidly extending, were strongly interested in the safety of that province which was contiguous to their own territories, and by their arms and influence it was saved from the ruin of a Maratha invasion.

It does not fall within my purpose to give in any detail the history of the Marathas, but it has been necessary at the outset of my work to remind the reader how nearly they achieved that universal dominion over India which they openly declared to be their aim. In the recognition of that fact, and of the peril with which in common with other Indian countries our own provinces were threatened, lies the key to the policy of Hastings throughout the events which it is the special object of this work to describe.

Before the establishment, in the middle of the sixteenth century, of the Moghal dynasty, a great part of India had been ruled for several centuries by princes of Afghan origin, and it was their practice to surround themselves with the hardy soldiers of their own religion and race. When Babar invaded India in 1526, and founded the empire which, under a succession of remarkable sovereigns, lasted for more than 150 years, there was scarcely a district of Northern India without its settlement of Afghans. The Peshawur valley and the country between the mountains and the Indus had been before that time conquered and permanently occupied by Afghan invaders, and in that tract men of Afghan race still constitute the most numerous section of the population. Further south in the Punjab, and in what are now called the North-Western Provinces, Afghan chiefs often obtained grants of land for military services, and settled in their new homes; neither they nor their followers were usually inclined to devote themselves to agricultural pursuits, and they remained for the most part, as their descendants often remain still, a small minority in the midst of a Hindu population. During the time of comparative prosperity between the accession of Akbar and the earlier part of the reign of Aurangzeb there was less room for Afghan adventurers, but after the death of Aurangzeb, when the empire was rapidly breaking up, they became more numerous than ever. Tempted by the certainty of military service and by the hope of finding distinction and wealth and plunder, they flocked from their mountains into India. In the words of the Sair-ul-mutakherin, 'they seemed to shoot up out of the ground like so many blades of grass.' 'The country,' writes Hamilton, 'swarmed with multitudes of vagrants, chiefly in search of employment, who were ready to enlist under any standard that might be raised, or to fight in any cause that might offer. Comparatively few of these men received regular pay; the horse and accoutrements of every trooper were his own property, and he often engaged with no other view than plunder [1].'

The history of India at this time is full of the contests in which bands of Afghan soldiers took an active part, of the terror they inspired, and the atrocities they committed. Even the Marathas who were then devastating India were less sanguinary and faithless than the Afghans. If the latter were less formidable and less destructive, it was only because they were less numerous, and because unlike the former, who had common interests and were obedient to their chiefs, the Afghan thought of little, as a rule, but his own personal advantage, and was ready at a moment's notice to transfer his services to a new master. Having no single purpose, there was no possibility that a new Mohammedan power should be raised by the Afghans on the ruins of the empire of the Moghals.

'Rohilla [2],' a word signifying 'Mountaineer' or 'Highlander,' was the name often given in India to these Afghan

[1] 'History of the Rohilla Afghans,' p. 38.

[2] I have retained the ordinary spelling 'Rohilla,' but 'Rohélah' would be more accurate. I quote the following from Colonel Yule:—' "Rohilla," a name by which Afghans, or more particularly Afghans settled in Hindustan, are sometimes known. The word appears to be Pushtu, *rōhēlah*, or *rōhēlai*, adj. formed from *rōhu*, "mountain," thus signifying "mountaineer of

adventurers or immigrants. Whether originally there were any differences of signification or not, the three terms Afghan, Rohilla, and Pathan, became practically synonymous.

Afghanistan." But a large part of Eastern Afghanistan specifically bore the name of *Roh*.' Colonel Yule gives a quotation from the Tárikh-i-Sháhi, written in the time of Akbar, which mentions the 'Afghans of Roh, who came, as is their wont, like ants and locusts to enter the king's service'; and another from Ferishta which says:—'Roh is the name of a particular mountain [-country] which extends in length from Swád and Bajaur to the town of Siwí belonging to Bhakar. In breadth it stretches from Hasan Abdál to Kábul. Kandahár is situated in this territory.' Yule's 'Glossary of Anglo-Indian Words,' p. 580. The term Rohilla is now seldom heard in Northern India, but in the Deccan, and especially in Hyderabad where Afghan immigrants are numerous, it is still in common use. The name by which Afghans settled in India are now more usually known is Pathan, a word of which, as Colonel Yule says, the derivation is obscure. According to some authorities, it is a name of Afghan origin, according to others it is Indian. Colonel Yule has given some of its fanciful derivations; another still more fanciful is found in Ferishta's Introduction to his History:—'The people of this country call their home in their own language Afghanistan and themselves Afghan. The people of India call them Pathan; but the reason for this is not known. But it seems to me that when under the rule of Mohammedan sovereigns, Mussulmans first came to the city of Patna and dwelt here, the people of India, for that reason, called them Patans,—but God knows!' Sir H. M. Elliot's 'History of India, as told by its own Historians,' vol. vi. p. 568.

CHAPTER II.

OUDH AND ROHILKHAND.—THE ESTABLISHMENT OF AFGHAN DOMINION IN ROHILKHAND.

Geographical features of Oudh and Rohilkhand.—Area and population.—Settlement of Afghans in Rohilkhand.—Ali Mohammad, the founder of the Rohilla power.—Hafiz Rahmat Khan.—Death of Ali Mohammad.—Appointment of Rahmat Khan and Dundi Khan as guardians of his sons.—Other Afghan chiefs in Northern India.—Conflicts between the Rohillas and Safdar Jang of Oudh.—The Marathas invade Rohilkhand.—Conditions of their retirement.—The guardians appropriate the greater part of Rohilkhand.—Shuja-ud-daula, Nawab Vizier of Oudh.—Third invasion of India by Ahmad Shah Abdali.—The Marathas again invade Rohilkhand and are expelled by Shuja-ud-daula.— Fourth invasion of India by Ahmad Shah Abdali.—He is joined by the Rohillas and Shuja-ud-daula.—Destruction of the Maratha army at Panipat.

THAT portion of the vast alluvial plain of Northern India which lies between the borders of the Punjab and of Bengal, and which now comprises the greater part of the North-Western Provinces and the whole of Oudh, includes two extensive tracts of country, separated from each other, through a distance of more than 400 miles, by the Ganges. The first of these tracts, situated between the right or western bank of that river and the Jumna, which joins the Ganges at Allahabad, contains the districts of the Doáb, and on the right bank of the Jumna are Delhi and Agra, the capitals of the Afghan and Moghal Sovereigns. The second of these tracts lies between the left or eastern bank of the Ganges and the lower ranges of the Himalaya. It comprises the whole of Rohilkhand and Oudh, with which my present narrative will mainly be concerned. Physically there are no important differences between these two provinces, nor are they separated by any natural boundaries. They form one continuous plain with hardly any undulation of surface except where it is broken by the rivers that intersect it. Owing to their position below the mountains, Oudh and Rohilkhand have a damper climate and a more luxuriant vegetation than the country on the other side of the Ganges, and their comparative greenness, the greater abundance of wood, and in many parts the views of the distant peaks of the snowy Himalaya, give them a more pleasant aspect.

Oudh, the larger of the two provinces, lying to the south-east of Rohilkhand, has an area of 24,000 square miles, and it contains at the present time a population of more than 11,000,000.

In the last century, during the time of which I am about to write, the people of Oudh had often to suffer from misgovernment and oppression, but their lot was in one respect comparatively fortunate. The province was in a great measure protected by its geographical position from foreign invasion. While the greater part of India was being devastated or subjected to tribute by the Marathas, Oudh, although the danger seemed sometimes imminent, escaped this crowning calamity. On its northern frontier, the Himalaya was an impassable barrier; on the south and east the unfordable Ganges or the British provinces gave sufficient protection, and the only frontier that was perilously weak was that on the north-west, on the side of Rohilkhand. During the winter months, when the floods of the rainy season have ceased, and the river has not yet been swollen by the melting of the snow in the Himalaya, the Ganges in the upper part of its course is often fordable. Rohilkhand was thus exposed to the attack of the Maratha hordes, and through that country the road into Oudh and towards our own provinces was open to them. They repeatedly crossed the river and carried destruction through Rohilkhand; they threatened, but, deterred by fear of the English, they never actually invaded Oudh.

Rohilkhand has an area of 12,000 square miles, about that of Belgium, and it has at the present time a population of nearly 6,000,000. It extends from Hardwar, where the Ganges enters the plains from the mountains, along the foot of the Garhwal and Kumáon Himalaya, to the frontiers of Oudh, a distance of nearly 200 miles. It is now one of the richest and most highly cultivated parts of the North-Western Provinces; it includes six British districts and many large towns, and in the middle of the province lies the small native state of Rampur, with about half a million people, ruled by a Mohammedan prince, the descendant and representative of one of the Rohilla chiefs of whose history I am about to write. We shall not find in the plains of Rohilkhand the 'fair valleys' of Macaulay's description; his 'snowy heights' at the sources of the Ramganga, the chief river of central Rohilkhand, are not quite so imaginary, but the beautiful hills from which it comes are hardly more snowy than those at the sources of the Thames[1].

One other geographical fact must be explained because, in the troubled times of which this narrative will treat, it often affected the fortunes of the people and the rulers of Rohilkhand. The whole of the province is not the rich and cultivated country of which I have spoken. Immediately below the mountains, which rise like a wall suddenly from the plains, lies a belt of forest, usually ten or twelve miles broad, locally known as the Bhábar. It is almost entirely without water, and the soil consists of a vast deposit of sand and boulders. The larger rivers struggle across this remarkable tract, but the smaller streams are absorbed as soon as they leave the mountains, and except during the rainy season they disappear from their shingly beds. Much of the forest has been destroyed, but parts may still be found where it retains its former splendour, and immediately below the hills scenes of extreme beauty are not uncommon. At a distance of ten or twelve miles from the mountains the waterless forest suddenly ceases; the streams that were absorbed in the great deposit of shingle come again to the surface, the water runs on sluggishly or collects in swamps, and in place of the forest we enter on a tract covered with tall reeds and grasses. This is the Tarái, well known for its tigers, and infamous during a portion of the year for its fevers. It

[1] Macaulay's Essays: Warren Hastings.

has usually a breadth of about ten miles, and gradually passes into the cultivated districts of the plains. Many parts of the Tarái were more populous and better cultivated a century ago than now. When anarchy prevailed, or when the country was threatened with savage invasion, the Tarái and forest afforded, in spite of their deadly climate, a comparatively safe asylum to the people of Rohilkhand. It was their established custom, in time of danger, to fly with their families, their cattle, and their valuables to these refuges where no enemy was usually disposed to follow, and on more than one critical occasion the rulers of the province were able to escape destruction by retreating to the fastnesses at the foot of the Himalaya. This was especially the case during the Rohilla dominion of which I propose to give the history.

The ancient name of Rohilkhand, and one still in common use by the people, was Katehr. The name Rohilkhand was first applied to it in the middle of the eighteenth century when it fell into the hands of the Rohillas. It had long been a rich province of the Moghal Empire, ruled by Mohammedan governors; many grants of land were from time to time given to Mohammedans, especially in the northern districts now known as Bijnor and Moradabad. The number of converts from Hinduism was unusually large. At the present time there is no part of the North-Western Provinces in which Mohammedans are so numerous, but they form less than one-fourth of the population, and the mass of the people is and has always been Hindu.

In the beginning of the eighteenth century Afghans had become numerous in Katehr. After the death of Aurangzeb the authority of the Emperor was often hardly recognised. The Hindu chiefs, who if they had been united under a common head might have freed themselves from Mohammedan dominion, thought only of their own quarrels and jealousies, and general confusion prevailed. It was at this time that an enterprising soldier, Ali Mohammad, rose rapidly to power, and became the founder of the short-lived rule of the Afghans in Rohilkhand.

According to accounts that have been usually accepted, this remarkable chief was not an Afghan by birth, but a Hindu, a Jat by caste. When a child he was forcibly seized by an Afghan adventurer called Dáud, who, beginning life as a slave, obtained by the murder of his master Shah Alam and by his own energy a position of importance in Katehr. Ali Mohammad was adopted by Dáud as his son, and was brought up as a Mohammedan. This is the account given in the Gulistán-i-Rahmat and by other authorities, but according to the Persian manuscript on which Hamilton's history is based, Dáud was the son of Shah Alam, and the brother of Hafiz Rahmat of whom I shall soon have to speak; Ali Mohammad is there stated to have been the son of Dáud, the story of his Hindu birth and adoption is denied, and nothing is said respecting the murder of Shah Alam. It is needless to enquire which of the two accounts is true. The author of the Gulistán-i-Rahmat and the friends of Hafiz Rahmat were interested in maintaining the low origin of Ali Mohammad and in disparaging a family whose rights Hafiz Rahmat had usurped. On the other hand, the work from which Hamilton mainly derived his history was written by an adherent of Faizullah Khan, the son of Ali Mohammad, and he desired to give as much honour as possible to his master.

Dáud, in his turn, was murdered, and Ali Mohammad, succeeding to his property and to the command of his retainers, soon became the most important personage in Katehr. He was a man of ability and courage, and his great reputation attracted large numbers of Afghan adventurers to his service. His power was chiefly established by the usual means, by violence, assassination, treachery and corruption, but he did not owe to them the whole of his success. 'He neglected,' writes Hamilton, in his History of the Rohilla Afghans, 'no means in his power to strengthen his interest and enlarge his connections, and the circumstances of the times afforded him ample scope for accomplishing these views by methods the most easy and obvious. The Court of Delhi being, at this time, torn to pieces by the struggles of contending nobles, had lost much of its power and influence, so that Ali Mohammad, conscious of his strength, showed little attention to the imperial mandates, and delayed or avoided, on various frivolous pretexts, any payment of revenue into the royal treasury, employing the income of his lands in raising troops, purchasing artillery and military stores, and, above all, in securing the friendship of many of the principal personages in the province, by a judicious and well-timed liberality; neither was he remiss in cultivating the attachment of the lower orders by the same practices as enabled him to succeed with their superiors, and he now only waited an opportunity to throw off the mask and openly assert his independence, as most of the governors in the more distant provinces had already done[1].'

The invasion of India by Nadir Shah in 1739 strengthened the power of Ali Mohammad by weakening that of the Emperor, and large numbers of Afghan soldiers took service with him. He further improved his position and guarded himself against future danger by attaching to his interests his uncle, Rahmat Khan, the man who was destined to become the most important of all the Afghan chiefs in Rohilkhand. He joined Ali Mohammad and received from him a large grant of land.

Rahmat Khan was born in Afghanistan about the year 1710. His father Shah Alam had settled in Katehr in the latter part of the seventeenth century, and obtained from the Moghal Government service in that province. He tells us, in a work which he wrote on the genealogy of the Afghans, that the whole of his tribe, the Kútah Khail, had emigrated from Afghanistan into India. His family originally belonged to the Baraich or Badalzái tribe in the province of Kandahar. His great-grandfather, he says, was Shaikh Shiháb-ud-din, 'but he liked to call himself the dog (Kútah) of the Prophet,' and from this was derived the name of his tribe, the Kútah Khail. His sons and grandsons lived, and became people of some import-

[1] Hamilton, p. 40.

ance, among the Yusufzáis on the Peshawar frontier. The greater number of the Rohillas settled in Rohilkhand were of Yusufzái origin, and Rahmat Khan afterwards gave evidence of his interest in that tribe by ordering an old history of their occupation of Kabul and of their subsequent movements into India to be translated from Pushtu into Persian[1].

In 1740 the greater part of the country now called Rohilkhand was in Ali Mohammad's possession, and he was recognised by the Emperor as its Governor. For five years his authority was almost undisputed, but in 1745 he quarrelled with Safdar Jang the Subahdar of Oudh. The retainers of Ali Mohammad had seized some property belonging to Safdar Jang's servants, and redress for the

[1] The work of Hafiz Rahmat Khan, mentioned on p. 12, is called the 'Khulásat ul-ansáb.' An account of it will be found in Dr. Rieu's Catalogue of Persian MSS. in the British Museum, vol. i. page 212, and in Dr. Ethé's Catalogue of MSS. in the India Office Library, No. 583. In the translation of the Gulistán-i-Rahmat (noticed in the Preface), the authorship of the Khulásat-ul-ansáb is erroneously ascribed to Shaikh Shiháb-ud-din. I have to thank Dr. Ethé for the information that he has given me regarding the contents of this work. Dorn, in the notes to his translation of Niámat Ullah's 'History of the Afghans,' has made numerous references to the 'Khulásat ul-ansáb.' See also Raverty, 'On the Origin of the Afghan People,' p. 571. I have been unable to discover anything further regarding the Kútah Khail tribe to which Hafiz Rahmat belonged. Dr. Bellew, to whom I am indebted for much interesting information, suggests that Kútah Khail may be the same as Kútazai, a sub-division of the Kúkúzai, a small section of the important tribe of the Mohmands, who occupy the mountainous country to the north-west of Peshawar. He tells me that *Kútah*, though not a Pushtu word, is commonly used by the Afghans on the Indian border, and represents the Pathan pronunciation of the Hindi *Kutta* (dog). The history of the Yusufzáis, referred to in the text, is the 'Tawárikh-i-Rahmat Kháni,' India Office MSS. Nos. 88, 581, 582. Dr. Ethé says in his Catalogue that this was an old Pushtu history written about A.D. 1622, which Hafiz Rahmat desired, about 1770, should be condensed and re-written in Persian in an easy and readable style. It is noticed by Dorn in his preface to the 'History of the Afghans,' and an abridged German translation of the work was given by him in the Bulletin Scientifique de l'Académie Impériale de St. Pétersbourg, 1838, vol. iv. p. 6. Regarding the settlements of Yusufzáis in Rohilkhand and elsewhere in India, see Elphinstone's 'Kingdom of Caubul,' vol. ii. p. 35, &c., and his 'History of India,' book xii. chap. 3; Dr. Bellew's 'General Report on the Yusufzáis,' and his 'Races of Afghanistan;' Mr. Ibbetson's 'Report on the Punjab Census of 1881;' 'Hayát-i-Afghan, or Afghanistan and its inhabitants, by Muhammad Hayát Khan, C.S.I., translated by H. Priestley.'

injury was refused. Safdar Jang, furious at the insults he had received, and jealous of the growing power of his neighbour, went to Delhi and induced the Emperor to order Ali Mohammad to make instant restitution of the property that had been seized and to deliver up the Rohillas who had been guilty of the outrage. Ali Mohammad refused in positive terms to obey the imperial mandate. The Emperor, Mohammad Shah, was easily persuaded to punish, if possible, this offence, and to endeavour to expel Ali Mohammad and his Afghan followers from Rohilkhand. With the help of Safdar Jang and others a considerable force was collected, and accompanied by the Emperor in person it crossed the Ganges. Ali Mohammad was deserted by his troops; he made his submission, and was taken to Delhi, where he received honourable treatment. His adherents were still so strong and turbulent that it was necessary to conciliate him, and he was soon entrusted with the government of Sirhind between the Jumna and the Sutlej.

In 1748, the invasion of India by Ahmad Shah Abdali gave to Ali Mohammad the opportunity of recovering his power. He returned to Rohilkhand, was joined by most of his old retainers, and was soon in virtually independent possession of nearly the whole country. Almost every military and civil post of importance was given to Afghans whom he could trust, and large numbers of his followers received grants of land.

Ali Mohammad's rule was by no means oppressive to the mass of the Hindu population, but he drove across the Ganges every one of whom he had any apprehension. Hindus of rank and influence were treated with cruel severity; Hindu zemindars were deprived of their lands, and public officers of their employments. 'In the space of a few weeks,' says Hamilton, 'the country was put completely under a Pathan government, and this decided mode of proceeding, although harsh and tyrannical, was certainly the only means of securing Ali Mohammad in that absolute independence at which he aimed. During the remainder of his life no attempt was made to disturb or subvert the despotic authority of the Afghans in Rohilkhand.' The historian goes on to express his belief that if Ali Mohammad had lived longer he would have raised the country to a high degree of prosperity, for, 'being altogether unmolested by other interference, he employed his whole time in making various wise and salutary regulations, placing his army on a respectable footing, and correcting and arranging the different departments of Government with a skill which distinguished his character as much for his policy and prudence in the exercise of power, as his preceding actions for the perseverance and enterprise by which that power was acquired [1].'

Ali Mohammad's capital was Áonla, in the district of Bareilly. His tomb is still to be seen there among the ruins of mosques and other relics of the time of the Rohillas.

In 1749, little more than a year after the re-establishment of Ali Mohammad's power, he died. He left six sons, of whom the two elder, Faizullah Khan and Abdullah Khan, were absent, having been taken by Ahmad Shah Abdali to Kandahar, and the other four were children. Before his death, he made arrangements for dividing the country among them, and he chose his uncle and trusted friend Rahmat Khan to be 'Hafiz,' or chief guardian of his sons during their minority. Dundi Khan, the cousin of Rahmat Khan and a distinguished soldier, was at the same time appointed Commander of the troops; he was to take part with Rahmat Khan in the guardianship of the children and in the supreme government of the country. These two men gave to Ali Mohammad solemn assurances of attachment to his sons, and they swore upon the Koran to observe their promises. Other chiefs were appointed by Ali Mohammad to administer, in subordination to the guardians, districts which were assigned to them, and to preside over some of the more important departments of

[1] Hamilton, p. 87.

the government. Ali Mohammad hoped in this way to establish checks on the power of Rahmat Khan and Dundi Khan and to guard the interests of his children. All the chiefs were to consult together when emergencies occurred; each of them was to pay his share towards the common expenses of the central government, and to contribute troops for the common defence. As might have been anticipated, these arrangements did not last long. The death of Ali Mohammad was soon followed by quarrels and intrigues among the chiefs, and by the attacks of foreign enemies.

While the Rohillas were establishing their power in Rohilkhand, other Afghan adventurers were possessing themselves of considerable territories on the other side of the Ganges. In the Central Doáb, an Afghan, Káim Jang, belonging to the Bangash tribe, established himself at Farukhabad, and became, by means very similar to those of Ali Mohammad, the ruler of a large district. Further north, Najib Khan, afterwards called Najib-ud-daula, had already begun a distinguished career. He was one of the bravest and most able of Ali Mohammad's adherents; he received from him a grant of land in Bijnor, the most northerly district of Rohilkhand, and married the daughter of Dundi Khan. A few years after Ali Mohammad's death, Najib-ud-daula became the First Minister of the Emperor and the master of a large tract in the upper Doáb between the Ganges and Jumna, extending southwards from the mountains almost as far as Delhi. By his ability and integrity he upheld for a time the falling fortunes of the empire.

Thus in the middle of the eighteenth century, Afghan chiefs were in possession not only of the whole of Rohilkhand, but of a large portion of the Doáb.

Safdar Jang, the Subahdar of Oudh, who had become Vizier of the empire, found in the death of Ali Mohammad a good opportunity for promoting his own interests, and he saw with anxiety the increasing power of the Rohillas on the borders of his own territories. Acting under his advice, Kutb-ud-din, whose father had formerly received from the Emperor Mohammad Shah the military command of the district of Moradabad, claimed the succession to that office. He invaded Rohilkhand, he was defeated by the Rohillas under Dundi Khan, and he himself was killed. Safdar Jang then encouraged the Afghan chief of Farukhabad, Káim Jang, to renew the attack, knowing that, whatever might be its result, war between the two Rohilla powers was likely to turn to his own advantage. In the winter of 1750, Káim Jang invaded Rohilkhand with a large force. He was met by Hafiz Rahmat and Dundi Khan, and after a battle near Budáon he was defeated and killed. The villagers, Mr. Whiteway tells us, still point out the battle-field, and tell how phantom armies fight by night in the skies [1].

Safdar Jang, thinking the opportunity favourable for his own aggrandisement, seized Farukhabad and the territories of his Afghan ally, but Ahmad Khan, the son of Káim Jang, soon succeeded in collecting his adherents, and defeated the troops of the Vizier. Enraged at this, Safdar Jang caused all the members of Káim Jang's family on whom he could lay hands to be put to death, and he marched in person with a numerous army to attack Ahmad Khan. He was totally routed, he himself was wounded, and escaped with difficulty, and the Rohillas overran the country as far as Allahabad, which they seized and plundered.

Safdar Jang was furious at his failure, and resolved, as the only means of destroying the power of the Rohillas, to call in the aid of the Marathas. Their chiefs, Malhar Ráo Holkar and Jaiapa Sindia, agreed, on receiving promises of large subsidies, to join him with their troops; he himself collected a large force, and the united armies marched with irresistible numbers towards Farukhabad. Ahmad Khan applied for assistance to Hafiz Rahmat and Dundi Khan, urging that all Rohillas should combine against a common danger. Although they refused the request, some of the chiefs were less prudent and joined Ahmad Khan. This fatal step involved the whole Rohilla confederacy in the

[1] 'Calcutta Review,' 1875.

C

quarrel; it brought the Marathas into Rohilkhand, and was the beginning of events which ended with the downfall of the Rohilla power.

Ahmad Khan was soon defeated; in 1751 the Marathas and Safdar Jang entered Rohilkhand; the Rohillas, unable to resist the attack, retreated to the wild forest tract below the mountains, and the province was soon overrun and devastated. The Marathas, we are told by a Mohammedan writer, 'ransacked the whole country, not allowing a single man to escape, and every article of money or property they carried off as booty[1].' In the following year, 1752, the alarm of a fresh invasion of India by Ahmad Shah made Safdar Jang and the Marathas anxious to leave Rohilkhand, and they agreed to evacuate the province on the condition that bonds for fifty lakhs of rupees should be given by the Rohillas to the Vizier, and that the Rohillas should pay every year a tribute of five lakhs to the Emperor. The bonds were made over by Safdar Jang to the Marathas in part payment of the subsidies that he had promised. They were never paid, and they afterwards formed the basis of Maratha claims on Rohilkhand. The ravages of the Marathas had reduced the country to a state from which it did not recover for years[2]. Ahmad Khan was allowed to re-establish himself in Farukhabad.

Soon after these events, violent quarrels broke out among the heirs of Ali Mohammad and their followers, and in 1754 Hafiz Rahmat and Dundi Khan resolved no longer to regard the pledges which they had given, and they appropriated to themselves the most valuable portions of Rohilkhand. The larger share was taken by Hafiz Rahmat, and he soon became by far the most important man in the province, and virtually its ruler. Small districts were assigned to Faizullah Khan and Abdullah Khan the two elder sons of Ali Mohammad, and to several influential

[1] Tárik-i-Ahmad Shah. Elliot, vol. viii. p. 119.

[2] Elphinstone, book xii. chap. 4. There are discrepancies in the dates assigned by Elphinstone, by Hamilton, and by other authorities, to the death of Ali Mohammad and to the events of the following two or three years. I have given those which seem most likely to be correct.

chiefs; a money allowance was given to Saidullah Khan, another son of Ali Mohammad, and the other sons received nothing. 'Thus,' writes the native historian, 'giving their honour to the winds, and suffering the tide of avarice and ambition to sweep away the dying injunctions of their benefactor into the ocean of oblivion, the guardians iniquitously deprived the children of Ali Mohammad of their birthright, and seized the reins of authority with the hand of ingratitude[1].'

It is needless to describe in detail the events of the next few years. Rohilkhand had suffered terribly from the devastations of the Marathas; great tracts of country had been almost deserted by their inhabitants, and fresh misfortunes were soon to follow.

In 1754, the Emperor Ahmad Shah was deposed and blinded by his unscrupulous Minister Ghazi-ud-din. Safdar Jang died soon afterwards, and was succeeded in the government of Oudh by his son Shuja-ud-daula, a man who during the next twenty years was to take a conspicuous part in the history not only of the Rohillas but of the English in Northern India. In 1756, Ahmad Shah Abdali invaded India for the third time, and captured Delhi. When in the following year he returned to his own dominions, he appointed the Afghan chief, Najib-ud-daula, of whom I have already spoken, to be First Minister and Commander-in-Chief to the nominal Emperor, Alamgir the Second. Immediately after the departure of Ahmad Shah, in 1757, Ghazi-ud-din, in the hope of restoring his own power, persuaded the Marathas to help him. With their assistance he marched on Delhi and occupied the city, and Najib-ud-daula was forced to retire to his own territory in the northern parts of the Doáb and Rohilkhand.

In 1758, the Marathas were in possession of the whole of the Punjab. In concert with Ghazi-ud-din they resolved to attack Najib-ud-daula and possess themselves of Rohilkhand and Oudh, and 'they talked (writes Elphinstone) without the least reserve of their intended conquest of the whole

[1] Quoted by Hamilton, p. 122.

C 2

of Hindostan.' Shuja-ud-daula had been on friendly terms with Najib-ud-daula, the relations between him and the other Rohilla chiefs had been more amicable than in the time of his father, and the common danger to which they were now exposed brought about an intimate alliance. He knew that if the Marathas established themselves in Rohilkhand the road to his own territories in Oudh would be open to them. No time was lost by the Marathas. In the autumn of 1759, after laying waste the country of Najib-ud-daula, who was forced to take refuge with the greater part of his forces in entrenchments on the western bank of the Ganges, they crossed the river into Rohilkhand. In the districts of Bijnor and Moradabad alone, in the course of a month, they destroyed 1300 villages and committed every conceivable atrocity. Hafiz Rahmat and the other Rohilla chiefs could offer no effectual resistance; they retreated with their troops to the forest below the mountains, and sent urgent messages to Shuja-ud-daula for assistance. He was not backward in affording it. He had already, on hearing of the Maratha invasion, marched rapidly with his army from Lucknow; he entered Rohilkhand, surprised the Marathas, and, in November, 1759, drove them with heavy loss across the Ganges.

The intervention of the Vizier had saved the Rohillas from destruction, but it would probably have been less successful if the Marathas had not been compelled by the approach of a more dangerous enemy to devote all their attention to other matters. Ahmad Shah Abdali was now beginning his fourth invasion of India; he had entered the Punjab in September, 1759, and there was nowhere any power except that of the Marathas, which had now reached its highest point, to oppose him. More than a year elapsed before the final trial of strength. Ahmad Shah was joined by Najib-ud-daula, by Hafiz Rahmat and by other Rohilla chiefs, with all the troops they could collect[1]. The co-

[1] Elphinstone, 'Kingdom of Caubul,' vol. ii. p. 296, says:—'I conjecture Ahmad Shah's force to have amounted to 40,000 of his own subjects, 30,000 Rohilla troops, and 10,000 belonging to the Indian chiefs.'

operation of Shuja-ud-daula was, for some time, doubtful, but he at last threw in his lot with the invader.

In October 1760, Ahmad Shah marched towards Delhi, and on the 6th January, 1761, the army of the Marathas was destroyed at the great battle of Panipat. Ahmad Shah remained only a short time in India after his victory; before his departure he acknowledged Shah Alam as Emperor, he restored Najib-ud-daula to the post of First Minister, he appointed Shuja-ud-daula to be Vizier, and gave to the Rohilla chiefs who had joined him the districts that he had occupied in the Doáb. Etawa and the country between Agra and Kalpi fell to the share of Hafiz Rahmat and Dundi Khan. For a few years after their terrible defeat, the Marathas did not actively interfere in the affairs of Northern India, and this was the most peaceful time of the Rohilla dominion.

CHAPTER III.

THE ROHILLAS.

Character of the Rohillas or Pathans.—The Yusufzáis.—The Rohillas in Rohilkhand.—Their true position.—Misrepresentations of Burke and Macaulay.—Hafiz Rahmat and the Poet Hafiz.—Number of Rohillas in Rohilkhand.—The Rohilla Government.—Hafiz Rahmat's administration.—Comparative prosperity after the battle of Panipat.

I HAVE already given some account of the origin and character of the Rohillas, but, although I may have to anticipate some of the facts belonging to a later period of my history, I wish before going further to show still more clearly what sort of people these Afghan adventurers were. Ignorance in regard to this matter has been at the root of much of the error and misrepresentation which, after the Rohilla war, began to prevail in England, and which even now continue to obscure the fame of Warren Hastings.

The Rohillas, or to give them the name by which they are now more commonly known, the Pathans, when they have been settled for several generations among a comparatively civilised people, lose in a great measure, but by no means entirely, their barbarous characteristics, but the Pathan when he first entered India was, as he still is in his native mountains, a ruthless and treacherous savage. The character which these people bore in the last century was so precisely that which they bear now, that a description of them at the present day is as applicable as it would have been in the time of Ali Mohammad or of Hastings. An account of the Pathans on the Punjab frontier has been given by Mr. Ibbetson in his 'Report on the Census of the Punjab' (1881), and I make from it the following quotation:—

'The true Pathán is perhaps the most barbarous of all the races with which we are brought into contact. He is bloodthirsty, cruel, and vindictive in the highest degree; he does not know what truth or faith is, insomuch that the saying *Afghán be imán*[1] has passed into a proverb among his neighbours; and though he is not without courage of a sort and is often curiously reckless of his life, he would scorn to face an enemy whom he could stab from behind, or to meet him on equal terms if it were possible to take advantage of him, however meanly. Here are some of his proverbs: "Keep a cousin poor, but use him." "When he is little play with him: when he is grown up he is an enemy; fight him." "Speak good words to an enemy very softly; gradually destroy him root and branch." At the same time he has his code of honour, which he observes strictly. It imposes upon him three obligations: the right of asylum, which compels him to shelter and protect even an enemy who comes as a suppliant; the necessity to revenge by retaliation; and open-handed hospitality to all who may demand it. And there is a sort of charm about him, especially about the leading men, which makes one forget his treacherous nature. As the proverb says, "The Pathán is one moment a saint, and the next a devil." There is an air of masculine independence about him which is refreshing in a country like India. He is a bigot of the most fanatical type, exceedingly proud and extraordinarily superstitious[2].'

The Rohillas who established themselves in Rohilkhand are said, as I have already mentioned, to have been for the most part Yusufzáis. The following passage, which, in a slightly abbreviated form, I quote from the work called Hayát-i-Afghan, describes the people of this tribe on the Punjab frontier:—

'The Yusufzáis are of somewhat robust build, of full stature, fair complexion, and high bearing. Highway robbery, cattle-lifting, house-breaking, and kindred forms of violence are familiar to all, and form the chief means of subsistence to some. Not a few of the young men find a charm in the career of a soldier of fortune, and enter the service of some independent state, or enlist in some of the British infantry regiments, where they are accounted good soldiers. Rarely indeed is any Yusufzái found engaged in trade or a handicraft, not because he has any especial contempt or aversion for trade, but rather because he feels himself to have no capacity for it. They are, on the whole, rather rigidly conformist to the external rites and discipline of Islam.

[1] *be imán*, 'without faith.'

[2] Report, p. 200.

They are well instructed in the obligations of their faith as to prayers, fasting, pilgrimages and almsgiving. Among a people so complacently and invincibly ignorant, whose best-born despise all learning as only becoming to the *mulla*, or clerical, no wonder that superstition is rife. But no scruple of religion nor fear of priest, strong as these may be, will avail to turn the Yusufzái from any course of action on which his self-willedness has once been set. Excessive self-esteem finds itself quite at home with excessive ignorance, and the Yusufzái is profoundly impressed with the conviction that everything in and about himself is matter of just and swelling pride. He is proud of his clan, of his own and his ancestors' prowess, and not least of his own ignorance and obstructiveness. Nor is his pride of the lofty kind that is satisfied with the rapt and silent contemplation of its own superiority. On the contrary, it loses no chance of finding expression in arrogant demeanour and blatant boastfulness. They are but too truly charged with being passionate, malignant, resentful, envious, covetous, avaricious, and implacably vindictive. The success or prosperity of their fellow they regard with an evil eye, and though courteous and conciliatory to the powerful, they have a heavy hand on the poor and the helpless. Their neighbours call them pitiless, without generous or chivalrous feeling, and devoid of all notion of gratitude. On the other hand, the Yusufzái is noted for a high sense of honour, allowance being made for his ideas as to what constitutes honour, and a scrupulous sensitiveness to whatever affects his fair name and fame. These traits are especially conspicuous in his rigid observance of the Afghan code of honour, and in his jealous regard for the reputation of his women. The Afghan code of honour, whose provisions are of such stringent obligations, has reference chiefly to three things: (1) Right of asylum, which every Afghan is bound to render, with all needed aid and protection, to any one, even a deadly enemy, who comes as a suppliant. This right, however, is limited to the boundaries of the premises, and if the fugitive step over them, he may be dealt with as may be thought proper. With reference to the sacredness of this right of asylum, a current Pushto proverb says that if even a pig, most unclean of creatures, come into one's house it must be protected. (2) The sacred duty of revenge for a wrong, of whatsoever kind, by retaliation on the wrong-doer. No efflux of time can cancel this obligation, and if circumstances should for a while baffle the desired revenge, it is bequeathed as a legacy from father to son, and may even run on for generations ere the favourable opportunity, patiently waited for, arrives, and the debt is paid in full. (3) Hospitality, or the duty of providing for the wants of the guest and the stranger. The guest is provided with food and a bed in the guest-house, and, if of rank, the chicken-broth, sweetmeats, and leavened bread, that will probably form his repast, will be prepared by the ladies of the host's family, and brought by the host himself or some member of his family. The poor friendless traveller repairs to the mosque, and makes a meal from the morsels begged from door to door. But all this cordiality of reception will not protect the traveller from being openly robbed by the host out of whose boundaries he has just passed, should his wealth and the probability of impunity tempt to the act[1].'

I am far from wishing it to be supposed that all the Rohillas were savages of this type. Some of them had been settled in India long enough to give them a tinge of civilization, and some of their chiefs were undoubtedly deserving of respect, but it is a matter of historical certainty that the descriptions which I have quoted would have been generally applicable to them.

Nothing could be further from the truth than the idea, still I suppose commonly believed, that the Rohillas were a nation inhabiting Rohilkhand. The term 'nation' was frequently applied to them by Burke and Francis and others during and before the trial of Hastings. 'To this man,' said Burke, referring to the Vizier and to Hastings, 'he sold this whole nation, whose country was cultivated like a garden,... the bravest, most honourable and generous nation upon earth.' In the same way, Macaulay writes of the Rohillas as 'an injured nation,' 'the finest population in India': he refers to them as if, though originally colonists from Afghanistan, they had become the inhabitants of the country; he calls them a people 'distinguished by skill in the arts of peace'; he says that during the Rohilla war, more than a hundred thousand people fled from their homes, and the reader supposes that these were Rohillas; he tells us that when the military resistance of the Rohillas ceased, their villages were burned, and it is inferred that the people of the villages were Rohillas. When Macaulay compares the actions of Shuja-ud-daula in Rohilkhand to those of Catherine in Poland and to those of the Bonapartes in Spain, the reader assumes that the position of the Rohillas was similar to that of the Poles and Spaniards, that of an injured people violently oppressed by foreign invaders. Every one who has lived, as I have done, in Rohilkhand, knows as a fact that re-

[1] Hayát-i-Afghan, p. 121.

quires no evidence of its truth that to apply such language to the Rohillas is nothing less than absurd. It would be less inaccurate to compare the position of the Rohillas in Rohilkhand with that of the Russians in Poland, or with that of the French in Spain in the time of Napoleon. The three cases had at least this in common, that in each of them a body of foreign soldiers was more or less successful in imposing, by violence and bloodshed, its rule over a large and unwilling population. The Rohillas were as much foreigners in Rohilkhand as Frenchmen in Spain or Russians in Poland[1].

These facts were repeatedly pointed out by Hastings and others. Thus, in a letter dated the 30th December, 1774, addressed to the Court of Directors by Francis and the majority of the Council, a month after their arrival in Calcutta, when their virulent opposition to Hastings had already begun, the Rohillas were described as 'a brave and independent, though from the nature of their constitution, a weak and divided nation'; and Hastings, replying to this, wrote as follows: 'Brave and independent are the epithets of declamation, and require no reply, but they are not very consistent with the description given of the Rohillas. I must beg to except to the word "nation" applied to the Rohillas. They are a tribe of Afghans or Pathans, freebooters, who conquered the country about sixty years ago[2], and have ever since lived upon the fruits of it, without contributing either to its cultivation or manufactures, or even mixing with the native inhabitants. The Rohillas are Mahometans, the Natives Hindus, and have only changed masters[3].' A little later, Hastings wrote again: 'The majority know, as well as myself, that the Rohillas are not the people of the country, but a military tribe who conquered it, and quartered themselves upon the

[1] In his Essay on Clive, published before that on Warren Hastings, Macaulay referred to the Rohillas in more accurate language: 'A band of mercenary soldiers occupied Rohilkhand.'

[2] Less than forty years would have been more correct.

[3] Minute by Hastings, 10 Jan. 1775, 5th Report, App. No. 45. Forrest's Selections, vol. i. p. 178.

people, without following any profession but that of arms, or mixing in any relation with the native inhabitants.'

'Agriculture and commerce,' Macaulay writes, 'flourished among them, nor were they negligent of rhetoric and poetry.' The connection of the Rohillas with agriculture was this, that they collected the rents and revenue of the land as zemindars or superior landlords, the land itself being left in the occupation of the Hindu cultivators. 'They added,' the Mohammedan historian tells us, 'to their own Afghan stubbornness all the perverseness and refractory behaviour inherent to the character of a zemindar[1].' Middleton, who was British Resident with the Vizier during the whole of the Rohilla war, speaking of what he had himself seen and learned by personal observation in Rohilkhand, stated in his evidence before the House of Commons, 'the Rohillas never applied themselves to any profession but arms, never to husbandry, manufactures, or mechanic arts[2].'

The 'rhetoric and poetry' of which Macaulay tells us the Rohillas were not negligent deserve a brief notice, for the apparent origin of this statement is curious. Throughout nearly the whole period of the rule of the Rohillas, their most prominent chief was Hafiz Rahmat Khan. The term 'Hafiz' was, as I have already said, a title, signifying 'Guardian,' given to him when he was made by Ali Mohammad the chief guardian of his children and of the state. By one of the many absurd mistakes of the time, Hafiz Rahmat was supposed by some of the enemies of Hastings to be Hafiz, the famous Persian poet of the fourteenth century. It was as if, in a history of the Irish Viceroyalty of Lord Spencer, he were credited with the authorship of the Faerie Queene. Law, in his opening speech in the Defence of Hastings, referred to this absurd blunder. 'Hafiz Rahmat,' he said, 'had been particularly lamented, not only as being a great prince, not only as an hereditary one, but on account of his gallantry, his soldier-like qualities, and also as a poet. I have read an ingenious publication on the

[1] Sair-ul-Mutakherin, vol. iii. p. 54. [2] Evidence, 22nd May, 1786.

subject, which states his being celebrated throughout the East on account, not only of his valour, but for the beauty of his poetic compositions. Hafiz is a great poet, but this man, so far from being a poet, if he had not signed this treaty, I should have doubted whether he could make his mark.'

Sometimes, although the identity of Hafiz Rahmat with the poet Hafiz was not asserted, he was spoken of as the worthy successor of his great name-sake. Thus, in his speech on Fox's East India Bill, on the 1st December, 1783, Burke referred to him as 'the most eminent of the Rohilla chiefs, one of the bravest men of his time, famous throughout the East for the elegance of his literature and the spirit of his poetical compositions, by which he supported the name of Hafiz.' Finally, the names of Hafiz and Hafiz Rahmat drop out, and the legend takes the form given to it in Macaulay's Essay,—'nor were the Rohillas negligent of rhetoric and poetry.'

These stories were, however, not so ridiculous and baseless as Law imagined. Hafiz Rahmat was far from being ignorant and uneducated. He was certainly a man of considerable literary attainments. I have already referred to the Persian work on the genealogy of the Afghans of which he was the author[1]. His son, in the Gulistan-i-Rahmat, tells us that 'in his fifth year he commenced the perusal of the Koran, and at the age of ten years he had, in addition to the Koran, read many learned works.' He was also, like many of the great Afghan chiefs of his time, something of a poet, and, no doubt, he and the Rohillas generally were as fond as the rest of their countrymen of the popular songs which have always been, and still are, so marked a characteristic of the Afghans[2]. Several of the members of Hafiz Rahmat's family were men of education. His son, Mustajab Khan, wrote the Gulistan-i-Rahmat, a life of his father. Another son, Ilahyar Khan, compiled a Hindustani and Pushtu Dictionary, with explanations

[1] P. 13.

[2] For a further account of Hafiz Rahmat as a poet, see Appendix A.

in Persian[1]; another, Muhabbat Khan, wrote an Afghan grammar and dictionary; and a grandson, Sádat Yar Khan, was the author of another life of Hafiz Rahmat, called the Gul-i-Rahmat[2].

There is not much evidence to show the number of Afghans in Rohilkhand when their power was at its height. Mr. Whiteway, who has given much attention to their history, thinks that there may have been about forty thousand of them in a population of about a million Hindus[3], and it is very improbable that this number was ever exceeded. According to Hamilton, the best authority on the subject, there were fifteen or twenty thousand Rohillas in Rohilkhand in the time of Ali Mohammad. In 1768, according to Verelst, who succeeded Clive as Governor in Bengal, the strength of the army of Hafiz Rahmat Khan was estimated at from fifteen to eighteen thousand horse and foot[4]. The number of men brought into the field by the Rohillas in their final struggle with the English and the Vizier is variously stated at forty and at twenty-eight thousand. These figures, however, are of little or no value as a guide towards the probable number of the Rohillas in Rohilkhand, because it is well known that their troops, like those of our own and other Indian armies, were composed, not only of their own people, but of any soldiers that the chiefs were able to engage, and they often included considerable numbers of Hindus[5].

[1] Dr. Rieu's Catalogue of Persian MSS. in the British Museum, vol. i. No. 399.

[2] For an account of the Gulistan-i-Rahmat and Gul-i-Rahmat, see Preface.

[3] 'Calcutta Review,' 1875.

[4] Letter to the Court of Directors, March 28, 1786; Verelst's 'View of the Rise, Progress, &c. of the English Government in Bengal,' 1772, App. No. IV.

[5] It is hardly worth while to give examples of the misstatements and exaggerations regarding the Rohillas put forth in Parliament and elsewhere by the enemies of Hastings; but I give the following quotation from a speech made by Francis in the House of Commons on June 2, 1786:—'The argument of Mr. Hastings that the Rohillas were not a nation is fallacious in the extreme. They were a people capable of sending 60,000 fighting men into the field. A body capable of doing that merited, in his mind, the name of a people. What must the number of that people be who, exclusive of the women, old men, and children, were capable of bringing 60,000 men into the field?' Mill says that 'the united force of all

It was frequently asserted by the enemies of Hastings that the government of the Rohillas in Rohilkhand had been one of remarkable excellence. It became part of their case to dwell in moving terms on the happiness of the people under their Rohilla rulers, and to contrast it with the misery that prevailed under the abominable administration of the Oudh authorities after the death of Shuja-ud-daula. Oriental historians seldom thought it worth while to describe the condition of the people, or to treat of matters other than those connected with the proceedings of chiefs and princes and the wars and disputes in which they were almost constantly engaged, and little is known of the state of Rohilkhand during the more prosperous times of Rohilla dominion. Although there can be no question that the accounts given by Burke and others of the extraordinary prosperity of the country were grossly exaggerated, we know that Hafiz Rahmat and several of the other chiefs were men of ability, and there is reason to believe that under their strong personal rule the mass of the Hindu population were treated with greater consideration and received better protection than was the case in any of the neighbouring provinces, excepting those in the possession of Najib-ud-daula. Elphinstone tells us, but without giving his authority, that 'their kindness to their Hindu subjects cannot be denied, and the state of improvement to which they had brought their country excited the admiration of our troops[1].'

Some of the few facts that are known regarding the administration of Hafiz Rahmat seem to show that he had greater intelligence than many of the rulers of his time. Thus, we are told by his son, in the Gulistan-i-Rahmat, that in the year 1769 'he gave orders that henceforth no

these leaders was estimated at 80,000 horse and foot.' This is taken from Verelst, but it was an estimate of the number of troops that all the Afghan chiefs, great and small, not only in Rohilkhand but throughout Northern India, might bring together if united, and it had no reference to the number of men at the disposal of the chiefs in Rohilkhand.

[1] 'Kingdom of Caubul,' vol. ii. p. 35. For a notice of Mill's statements regarding the Rohilla government see Appendix B.

duties should be levied on any article of merchandise throughout his dominions; his sirdars strongly objected to the measure, as depriving him of a large source of revenue, and consequently from keeping up such an army as the circumstances of the times required; but his object was to gain the affection of his subjects, and no persuasions could induce him to rescind the order. Throughout his dominions he abolished taxes of every denomination, whether on exports or imports, though those imposts had yielded many lakhs of rupees annually, nor would he revive this odious demand, even when his finances were at their lowest ebb.' Francklin, who visited Bareilly in 1795, says that it had become 'an emporium of commerce' through the 'discriminating foresight' of Hafiz Rahmat. Bareilly had long been, and still remains, the principal city in Rohilkhand, but the favourite place of residence of Hafiz Rahmat was Pilibhit, where he built himself a palace and a handsome mosque. The annual revenues of Hafiz Rahmat were said by Verelst to be fifty or sixty lakhs of rupees. Colonel Champion, who had good opportunities of learning the truth, stated, after the downfall of the Rohilla government, that he believed the revenues of the whole of Rohilkhand to have been between seventy and eighty lakhs [1].

The most peaceful and prosperous period of Rohilla

[1] See Evidence of Colonel Champion regarding the Rohilla war, MSS. Records, India Office, and Forrest's Selections, vol. i. p. 173. Major Hannay (Forrest's Selections, p. 171) gave evidence to the same effect. The Board of Commissioners in the Ceded and Conquered Provinces stated in a Report, dated April 13, 1808, that the province was said to have yielded in the time of the Rohillas an annual revenue of eighty-four lakhs, but they point out that the rupees then current in Rohilkhand were inferior in value to those of the Company. See 'Selections of Papers from the Records at the East India House,' vol. i. p. 19, A.D. 1820. Francklin, who went to Rohilkhand when the country had been ruined by the maladministration of the Oudh rulers, says that in the flourishing times of the empire the revenue of Katehr was five millions sterling, and 'under the Rohilla government, who paid unremitting attention to agriculture, the province might have yielded that sum.' Francklin's 'Shah Alam,' p. 59. These figures obviously deserve no credit. In 1889, the gross land revenue of Rohilkhand was (taking the rupee at the conventional rate of two shillings) nearly £690,000, and the revenue from all sources was a little more than £1,000,0000.

rule was that which followed the defeat of the Marathas at Panipat, but it was of short duration. Before that time, as the preceding narrative has shown, Rohilkhand had suffered almost constantly from war, from violent dissensions among the chiefs, or, worst of all, from the devastations of the Marathas, but between 1761 and 1768, it enjoyed comparative peace. During these seven years, Hamilton tells us—

> 'The Rohillas had no enemies to interrupt their tranquillity from without, and although the injustice of the guardians gave rise to frequent jealousies and disputes, yet the vigorous administration of the chiefs who had usurped the government preserved the country in a tolerable degree of internal harmony, but we have no documents from which we might enter into a more minute description of the domestic management or political intrigues which occupied their attention within this period, as all that the Rohilla narrator remarks upon it is, "The Afghan sirdars, being freed from the vexatious interruptions of the marauders of the Deccan by their chastisement at Panipat, and allaying the ferments of the discordant and the factious by the wisdom of their auspicious councils, passed seven years in harmony and ease"[1].'

Not only was Rohilkhand free at this time from Maratha invasion, but its frontiers on the north and west were kept in security by the wise administration of Najib-ud-daula. Shuja-ud-daula, although he had saved the Rohillas from destruction, might at any time have become a dangerous neighbour, but he was engaged in looking after his interests elsewhere.

[1] Hamilton. p. 161.

CHAPTER IV.

RETURN OF THE MARATHAS.—THE NAWAB VIZIER, THE EMPEROR, AND THE ENGLISH.

Return of the Marathas to Northern India.—Najib-ud-daula and Zabita Khan.—The Oudh dynasty.—Shuja-ud-daula, Nawab Vizier.—His character.—His conflicts with the English.—1764. Battle of Buxar.—1765. Meeting of Clive with Shuja-ud-daula and the Emperor.—Kora and Allahabad given to the Emperor.—The grant of the Diwáni.—Alliance between the English and Vizier.—Policy of Clive and Hastings.—Increase of the power of the Marathas.—Return of the Emperor to Delhi.

THE Marathas did not again enter Rohilkhand until the beginning of 1772, but they had returned to Northern India with hardly diminished force before that time. In 1765 and in the following years their constantly growing power was one of the chief anxieties of Clive and of his successors, and in 1769 they seized Etawa and the districts in the Doáb which had been given by Ahmad Shah Abdali to Hafiz Rahmat and Dundi Khan. In the following year, 1770, Najib-ud-daula died, and this was an irreparable loss to the Rohillas. He was succeeded in his territories by his son Zabita Khan. For a short time his administration seemed likely to be successful, and he exerted himself in bringing his unruly followers under control[1]. But the difficulties of his position soon proved too great for him, and he inherited few of the good qualities of his father. In the same year the Rohillas in Rohilkhand lost their most

[1] Even Najib-ud-daula found this a difficult task. 'Although,' says the Sair-ul-Mutakherin, 'he was attached to the rules of justice and equity, wished well to every one, and studied the repose and welfare of the people of God, almost all his people or even all of them were Rohillas; and after all the Rohillas are but the best of a race of men in whose blood it would be difficult to find one or two single individuals endowed with good-nature, and with sentiments of equity. In one word they are Afghans, and that

gallant soldier and perhaps the most respected of their chiefs by the death of Dundi Khan.

Early in 1771 the Marathas took possession of Delhi, Zabita Khan was obliged to flee, and it soon became clear that Rohilkhand would not long escape attack. Before, however, continuing the history of that country it is necessary to refer to events that had occurred in the neighbouring provinces of the Nawab Vizier of Oudh and of the Emperor.

Sádat Khan, the founder of the Oudh dynasty, became Subahdar or Governor of Oudh in 1720. Faithless and treacherous like most of the chiefs of his time, he was a good soldier and administrator, and Oudh flourished under his rule. Sir Henry Lawrence says that

> 'He respected the poor and restricted his exactions to the rich. He overthrew many lordlings, and established in their stead one stronger and therefore better rule. No questions of conscience stood in his way. The aggrandizement of his own family was his one object, in furtherance of which he was regardless alike of gratitude, loyalty, or patriotism. So long as his own territory escaped, he cared not that Persian or Maratha should ravage the empire and humble the monarch in whose weakness he found his own strength[1].'

He was succeeded in 1739 by his son Safdar Jang. His quarrel with Ali Mohammad, his invasions of Rohilkhand, and the devastation of that province with the help of the Marathas have been already noticed. Safdar Jang died in 1754, and was succeeded by his son Shuja-ud-daula.

'No public man,' Sir Henry Lawrence has observed, 'has ever been painted in more opposite colours than Shuja-ud-daula.' The close relations between him and Hastings caused him to be singled out by Hastings' opponents as the incarnation of all that was cruel, contemptible, and vile, and in India itself he had so

unbridled soldiery exerted upon the inhabitants of the capital, most of whom were gentlemen of character or noblemen of ancient race, such violences and such extortions, and they invented such new ways of tormenting them, that nothing like is to be imagined, nor is there any mentioning those violences with any decency, or even to any purpose; the sufferers have suffered, and past is what is past.'

[1] Sir H. Lawrence, Essays, 'The Kingdom of Oude,' p. 83.

many enemies that it was easy to quote contemporary authority for every epithet of blame. Some great crimes he undoubtedly committed. The one virtue which friend and foe alike attributed to him was personal courage. Even Dow, who calls him 'cruel, treacherous, unprincipled, deceitful,' allows that he possessed this redeeming quality. Francklin describes him as 'active and vigorous in his mind, bold, daring, and enterprising. His temper was irascible, which often led him to commit acts of cruelty, yet he was an excellent magistrate, a lover of justice, and anxiously desirous of the prosperity of his country[1].'

He is said to have been extremely handsome, active, and fond of field sports, 'so nervous and strong that with one stroke of the sabre he could cut off the head of a buffalo, . . . more fit for the manly exercises of the field than for deliberation in the closet[2].' Many stories were told of his personal intrepidity. The Sair-ul-Mutakherin gives an account of his reception by Ahmad Shah Abdali, which, whether true or not, serves to illustrate the character which he bore in India. He was welcomed, we are told, with the greatest distinction, and on his first interview with the Afghan monarch,

> 'He requested leave for his music and kettledrums to play in the Abdali's camp. The King answered mildly that it was unprecedented, and contrary to rules. "It may be so for other music," replied Shuja-ud-daula, "but mine is the gift of the Emperor of Hindostan and not of your Majesty, nor am I your subject but only your well-wisher." This bold answer had its effect; the King consented, and it became a custom for Shuja-ud-daula's music to strike up as soon as that of the King had done playing[3].'

Various accounts are given of the conduct of Shuja-ud-daula in the battle of Panipat; some authorities say that he took no active part in it, but according to Francklin, it was mainly owing to his skill and courage that the victory was gained; Ahmad Shah is said to have embraced him

[1] 'Shah Alam,' p. 66.

[2] Dow's 'History of Hindostan,' vol. ii. p. 357.

[3] Sair-ul-Mutakherin, section 2, p. 181.

when all was over, to have called him his son, and ordered the victory to be proclaimed in his name. Sir Henry Lawrence's estimate of the character of Shuja-ud-daula is probably as correct as any other that could now be made:—'He was an able, energetic, and intelligent Prince, and he possessed at least the ordinary virtues of Eastern rulers[1].' I do not doubt that he also possessed their ordinary vices. Middleton, the British Resident at his Court, said that 'in most of his transactions with him he had experienced much duplicity, evasion, and deceit.' The justice of the view taken by Sir Henry Lawrence is, however, supported on the whole by all that we know of his relations with the English Government during the administration of Clive and Hastings. This at least is certain, that he was not the contemptible coward and villain of Burke and Mill and Macaulay.

In 1764, events which have no direct connection with the present narrative brought Shuja-ud-daula into conflict with the English, and his power was completely broken by the decisive battle of Buxar. He sent his family into Rohilkhand, and he himself followed, and applied to Hafiz Rahmat and Dundi Khan for assistance. His reception was hospitable, but the Rohilla chiefs were little disposed to interfere in his behalf. When, however, in the following year he attempted to renew the war with the English, a small force was sent to join him under the command of a son of Hafiz Rahmat; whether it took part in the short contest that followed is a matter on which the authorities differ. In May 1765, the Vizier, who had obtained the services of a body of Marathas, was defeated by General Carnac at Kora, and he resolved to throw himself on the generosity of the English. He was honourably received, but final arrangements were delayed pending the arrival of Clive who had returned to India a short time before. In August 1765, he met Shuja-ud-daula and the Emperor at Benares and Allahabad.

There was, in Clive's opinion, one line of policy which it

[1] Essays, p. 97.

was above all things necessary to follow for ensuring the safety of our possessions in Bengal. That policy was the maintenance, at all times, of a strong and friendly state on the borders of our own provinces. There was, he held, no other means of keeping them apart from the contests that were going on without intermission in Northern India, and of preserving an effectual barrier against the destructive inroads of the Marathas. This policy was in complete accordance with the views of the Court of Directors. They looked with extreme alarm on the prospect of a Maratha war, and on the results that would follow the ruin of the Vizier. They anticipated the necessity of having to maintain a war 600 miles beyond the boundaries of our own territories, from the success of which no advantage could be derived, and in which defeat might be fatal[1]. For these reasons Clive resolved to restore to Shuja-ud-daula the whole of his former dominions, excepting the provinces of Kora and Allahabad[2]. These he gave to the Emperor 'as a royal demesne for the support of his dignity and expenses.' Although at this time almost nothing remained of the power of the Moghal Sovereigns, the remembrance of past greatness and the conflicting jealousies of those into whose hands the fragments of the empire had fallen, still gave to the Emperor a position of considerable importance[3]. On the 12th of

[1] Letter to President and Council, Feb. 19, 1766. See also letter from Court of Directors, November 11, 1768, par. 32, Fifth Report, App. No. 12.

[2] The town of Kora, now much decayed, is about 100 miles to the north-west of Allahabad. It was a place of importance, and the capital of a province of the Moghal empire. The provinces given to the Emperor by Clive were often called Kora and Karra, the latter being the name of a considerable town about 40 miles to the north-west of Allahabad.

[3] 'The small remains of that puissance and splendour, which had dignified and decorated the throne of the Moguls, was now daily consuming away under the feeble government of their successor Shah Alam. The great dependencies and revenues of the empire had been squandered and torn from it to become the prey of the servants and supporters of the Crown. The independent greatness of its former vassals now hardly allowed the mere name of subordination; and the King was apparently suffered to retain possession of the scanty relics of dominion, because internal jealousy alone prevented the extinction or usurpation of his titular sovereignty; which, besides, was made use of as a political pageant to attract some small popu-

August, 1765, the famous arrangement known as the grant of the Diwáni was made, under which the Emperor formally assigned to the Company the right of collecting the revenues of Bengal, Behar, and Orissa, and the Company on its part agreed to pay to him annually twenty-six lakhs of rupees. A few days later a treaty of strict alliance was concluded with the Vizier, under which, if he were attacked, we were bound to assist him to the utmost of our ability, and in consideration of the restoration of his territories he agreed to pay £500,000 to the English Government. These arrangements were accepted by the Vizier with much gratitude, for he had expected no such favourable terms. Although suspicions were sometimes felt regarding his intentions, the alliance remained unbroken throughout the life of Shuja-ud-daula, and the close connection between him and the English had an important bearing on the subsequent history of the Rohillas, because it brought about, before many years had passed, the interference of the English in the affairs of Rohilkhand. For, as we shall see, Hastings followed steadily the policy of Clive, and treated the support of the Vizier and the protection of his dominions against the Marathas as conditions absolutely essential to the security of our own possessions[1].

larity to the party which carried it with them.' Fifth Report from the Committee of Secrecy, 1782.

[1] Among the British Museum MSS. there is an interesting letter written by Warren Hastings, in December 1812, to the Marquis of Hastings, then Earl of Moira, who was about to leave England to assume charge of the office of Governor-General. After saying that 'our foreign dependencies and political alliances appear to be too much extended' he makes the following reference to Oudh:—'I except from the application of the preceding observations the dominions of the Nabob of Oudh, which from their contiguity and his absolute dependence on the Company, approach almost to an integral part of our own; and any calamity befalling them would affect our own interests as much or rather much more than if it befel our own, as in that case we should be charged with the necessity of repelling it by extraneous force without command of its constitutional authorities.' Hastings goes on to say that 'it needs not the spirit of divination to foretell that the whole of that country, comprising with our own all the territory bounded by the north of the Ganges, will in process of time become the avowed property of the British nation.' MSS. 29,233, and 29,234; the former contains the original draft of the letter written by Hastings himself.

A few months later an attack by the Marathas on the districts assigned to the Emperor by the English was believed to be imminent, and Clive invited the Vizier and the Emperor's representative to meet him at Chapra to discuss measures of mutual defence. He thought at one time that it might be desirable to obtain the adhesion of the chiefs of the Rohillas and Jats to a league with the English and the Vizier for this purpose; but 'from consideration of the little advantage the Company would deduce from such distant allies in case of an invasion, he chose to leave this matter unfinished, and to entrust Shuja-ud-daula with the management of such treaties as he might think convenient for his own and the Company's welfare.' The Vizier, however, promised to enter into no agreement of the kind without the previous approval of the English Government [1].

Although the Emperor had gladly agreed to Clive's arrangements, he had not abandoned the hope of returning to Delhi. In several of his letters to the Court of Directors, Clive stated that the Emperor had been in communication with the Marathas with the object of inducing them to help him to carry out this project. On the 8th of September, 1766, he wrote as follows:—'From the deputies at Chapra of the Maratha chiefs, and also from the letters they brought, it evidently appears the Maratha forces are assembled at the King's requisition, and upon the positive assurances he gave that an English army would join them to escort him to his capital. His Majesty has indeed laboured hard by every artifice of persuasion, intrigue, and negotiation, to succeed in his favourite scheme, which we are convinced would terminate in his own ruin, and destroying the peace of the whole empire.' Again, on the 9th of December, 1766, Clive wrote that 'the King had plied every engine of state artifice and deceit to disturb the repose of the empire by arming, for the purposes of his wild ambition, a power who in a short

[1] Letter from Clive, Carnac, and Verelst to Court of Directors, September 8, 1766.

time would shake the foundation of his throne, and deprive him of that independent and comfortable revenue which he now possesses for the support of his dignity[1].'

Early in 1767 Clive left India, making over the Government to Verelst. In 1768 doubts were felt in regard to the designs of Shuja-ud-daula, and a fresh treaty was made with him, renewing and confirming the stipulations of the treaty of 1765, with additional conditions restricting the strength of his army to 35,000 men, none of whom were to be drilled or equipped like English troops. This treaty was soon allowed to become a dead letter, for when Hastings succeeded to the government he considered it to have been not only uncalled for, but to have been opposed to the fundamental principles by which our relations with the Vizier ought to be guided.

During the next three years the power and insolence of the Marathas went on increasing. They made no actual attacks on the Vizier or on the English, but they sent, on several occasions, demands couched in imperative terms for the payment of *chauth* or tribute from our provinces of Bengal and Behar. Even the Court of Directors, who always desired that the efforts of their servants in India should be confined to the defence of their existing territories and those of the Vizier, were so much alarmed by the progress of the Marathas, and at the 'terror and despondency spread by them in the minds of those powers which were the remote barrier of our possessions,' that they admitted that they might have to consider 'how far we may be disposed to carry our arms beyond the bounds of our provinces, or the territories of our allies, and become the parties in an offensive war[2].'

The Emperor continued to live at Allahabad, maintaining his nominal dignity by means of the revenues of the provinces assigned to him by Clive, and by the subsidies from Bengal, but when, in 1771, the Marathas occupied Delhi, he fancied that this afforded a good opportunity

[1] Verelst, App. 4 and 5.
[2] General letter to Bengal, August 28, 1771; Fifth Report, App. No. 7.

for reviving the projects which he had long cherished. It served the purpose of the Marathas to promise to restore him to greater dignity and power, and in spite of the strong objections of the English, whose approval he had asked, he left Allahabad in May 1771, with a force of 16,000 men, which with the help of the Vizier and the nobles of the Court, he had managed to collect. The English Government, although they refused to give their sanction to his departure, desired to remain on good terms with him, and they allowed him, first, however, withdrawing their own officers, to retain in his service some battalions of sepoys who had been trained in the European fashion. The English Commander-in-Chief and the Vizier accompanied him to the frontiers of the Kora province, where, says Francklin, 'having again renewed their solicitations to detain him, but without effect, they took their leave[1].'

During the rainy season the Emperor remained near Farukhabad, and the death of Ahmad Khan Bangash, the chief of the province, gave the opportunity of obtaining a considerable sum of money from his successor. After accepting all the demands and conditions of the Marathas, the Emperor entered Delhi on the 25th December, 1771.

[1] 'Shah Alam.'

CHAPTER V.

A. D. 1772. MARATHA INVASION OF ROHILKHAND.—ACTION TAKEN BY THE VIZIER AND THE ENGLISH.—TREATY OF ALLIANCE BETWEEN THE ROHILLAS AND VIZIER.

The Marathas invade and overrun Rohilkhand.—Flight of Rohilla chiefs.—Alarm of the Vizier.—Appeals for help to the English.—Sir Robert Barker meets the Vizier.—The Vizier's proposals.—He marches with Sir Robert Barker to the Rohilla frontiers.—Negotiations between the Vizier and the Rohillas.—Defeat of the Rohillas by the Marathas.—An English Brigade ordered to march into Oudh.—Further negotiations and intrigues between the Vizier, the Rohillas, and the Marathas.—An English officer sent to Hafiz Rahmat.—Treaty of alliance between the Vizier and Rohillas.—The Marathas leave Rohilkland.

THE Marathas had not forgotten the active part that the Rohillas and the Vizier had taken against them at Panipat, and that a heavy debt of vengeance remained to be repaid. They had for some time been threatening to renew their invasion of Rohilkhand, and there were special reasons which made the Emperor encourage the design. Zabita Khan was anxious to recover the position which his father had held as First Minister of the empire, but he was looked on with jealousy and apprehension by the Emperor. His territories were chosen as the first object of attack, and immediately after the arrival of the Emperor at Delhi, the Marathas marched against him. The Emperor in person accompanied them, his troops being under the command of the Persian Najf Khan, a man of ability and courage. The Marathas and Najf Khan marched to the fords across the Ganges near Shukartar, a strong fort belonging to Zabita Khan near the Rohilla border, on the right bank of the river. The Rohillas disputed the passage, but three of their chief officers having been killed, they were soon defeated. 'And here,' says the Sair-ul-Mutakherin, 'it must be recollected that the Rohillas are a race exceeding covetous, little susceptible of control, and of such a temper as to prove ungovernable on the sight of ever so little plunder. The moment they saw their three commanders slain, they commenced plundering each other; and a scene of confusion, and wounding and slaughtering taking place, they rushed furiously against each other, and thought only of plunder and booty[1].'

Successful resistance to the invasion was impossible, and the Marathas marched through Rohilkhand, plundering and devastating the country. Zabita Khan's family fell into their hands, and this was afterwards remembered for other reasons. 'Among the children of Zabita,' writes Mr. Keene, 'was his eldest son, a beautiful youth named Gholam Kadir Khan, whom the Emperor is said by tradition to have transmuted into a harem page, and who lived to exact a fearful vengeance for any illtreatment that he may have received[2].'

All pretence of respect for the Emperor was now thrown aside by the Marathas.

'Their insolence,' the Bengal Government wrote to the Court of Directors some months afterwards, 'was now immoderate. Their success had been equal to their most sanguine expectations, and seemed to pave the way for further depredations to the southward; they were in possession of the person of the King, whose authority they contemned, and whose name and mandates they regarded solely as the instruments of their own aggrandizement; and so far were they from re-establishing him in his government, that they positively refused to perform their engagements of sharing with him the spoils of the vanquished, and he was left almost destitute, in the midst of a rich and plentiful camp, of the common necessaries required to support at least an appearance of dignity[3].'

[1] Vol. iii. p. 250.

[2] Keene's 'Moghul Empire,' p. 95. In the same work, pp. 175–185, will be found an account of the cruelties committed in 1788 by Gholam Kadir Khan on the miserable Emperor and his family, and of his own horrible fate.

[3] Letter from Bengal, November 10, 1772. Fifth Report, App. No. 11.

From the time in which the Marathas began their attack on Rohilkhand it became clear that the English might be forced to undertake military operations beyond the Vizier's frontiers, as the only means of protection to Oudh and to their own territories.

Between Oudh and Rohilkhand there is, as I have already shown, no natural boundary, the two provinces forming one continuous plain between the Himalaya and the Ganges. The greater part of the water of the river in the upper portion of its course has now been diverted into canals which have changed the whole face of the country, but in the last century it was only in Northern Rohilkhand that the Ganges during the winter months was fordable. It was consequently only through Rohilkhand that the Marathas could find easy access into Oudh. That province, Hamilton wrote,

> 'is invulnerable to those marauders, excepting through the former country, as their numerous bodies of horse have no sure means of advance and retreat but by the shallows of the Ganges during the dry season; their desultory method of carrying on war not suiting with the construction of bridges, and other tedious and expensive military works, such as might give them a command of the passage of unfordable rivers, nor their mode of fighting calculated for the defence of them.'

Nothing could exceed at this time the alarm of the Rohilla chiefs, for they were too weak to oppose the Marathas with any hope of success. They retreated to the forests below the mountains on the Kumáon borders, and intrenched themselves in strong positions, while bands of Maratha horse spread themselves over the country, plundering and burning and destroying in their usual fashion. The only chance of escape seemed to the Rohillas to lie in a renewal of their alliance with the Vizier who, under somewhat similar circumstances, had expelled the Marathas from Rohilkhand twelve years before. Hafiz Rahmat and the other chiefs wrote letters urgently begging for his assistance, and Zabita Khan sent to him a blank treaty which might be filled up as he chose.

The alarm of Shuja-ud-daula was hardly less than that of

the Rohillas. The Marathas now seemed to have become as formidable as before the disaster of Panipat. They made no secret of their intention, when they had finished the occupation of Rohilkhand, to carry their operations into Oudh, where they would find not only full satisfaction for their lust of plunder, but ample opportunity of retaliation on the Vizier for past injuries. It was, at the same time, commonly reported that they had resolved to carry their conquests beyond the limits of Oudh into the rich possessions of the English in Behar and in Bengal.

In January 1772, the Vizier wrote to the Calcutta Government, of which Cartier was then President, insisting in the strongest terms on the peril to which he and the English were exposed, and he asked that the Commander-in-Chief, Sir Robert Barker, might meet him at Faizabad, with the object of coming to some arrangement for defence against the common danger. The Calcutta authorities were disinclined to commit themselves to any active policy which might involve them in war. They were anxious that other powers should resist the Marathas, but were afraid of giving their own co-operation.

'The means,' they wrote to the Madras Government on the 3rd February, 1772, 'of those princes whose extent of territory or consequence in the empire should lead them to combine their strength to stem the torrent and prove a counterbalance to the Maratha power, are not inadequate, if they could be brought to act on one general plan for the security of the whole, but, as it is, they are divided, irresolute, and incapable of taking any effectual measure to arrest the pending danger. It is to no purpose that we have stimulated the Vizier to undertake, in conjunction with the Rohillas, something of sufficient importance to convince them that a vigorous opposition will follow any further advances they may make to the eastward; he will do nothing without the aid of a body of our troops, which however at this particular juncture we do not deem it prudent to grant him[1].'

On the 20th January, 1772, Sir Robert Barker met the Vizier, and on the following day he sent to Calcutta a

[1] Fifth Report, App. No. 21.

report of the communications that had passed between them.

'The Vizier,' he wrote, 'informed me with much concern and anxiety his present situation was become so critical, that measures were necessary to be taken without loss of time for preventing what inevitably threatened his reputation and possessions. To obey his Majesty's directions under the present circumstances, he was resolved not to do, for the Maratha chiefs had gained too great an ascendancy over his Majesty for him to support the dignity of his station, by which he might be necessitated to concur in measures opposite to his inclination and interest, or otherwise leaving the King under worse pretences than not joining him at all. To remain inactive and see the Rohillas reduced was as bad or worse, for he very justly observed that the Rohillas would, to prevent a total extirpation, undoubtedly give up a part of their country, and would of consequence be necessitated to join their arms with the Marathas. Such a general confederacy would inevitably fall on him, as their next object in view, and he further observes that in this case he must claim the performance of our treaty for the defence of his possessions. Or, on the other hand, should the Marathas not receive any conditions of peace from the Rohillas, and the King determine on their overthrow, such an acquisition of country and riches would strengthen that power (of the Marathas), already arrived at too great a height, to a very dangerous degree, particularly as by establishing themselves so immediately adjoining to his dominions they would be ever ready to fall on him when opportunity offered. Under this dilemma he has only two plans to adopt; the one will require a show of support and approbation of the English Government; the other to remain in his present situation waiting the event of consequences, and relying on the support of his friends and allies. To prevent, however, his own reputation from suffering, and the trouble and expense which must necessarily and will most certainly attend his friends the English by their assistance, he could wish they would adopt his first plan, and proposes the march of his whole force to that frontier of his dominions contiguous to the possessions of the Rohillas. He has already received letters from Hafiz Rahmat Khan, the son of Dundi Khan, and Zabita Khan, requesting his assistance to save them from the impending blow. A coulnama or treaty has been sent him from the latter, with blanks for filling up such terms as may be most agreeable to him. And he is assured that on his appearance at the frontiers with the approbation of the English Government, which he observes can no way appear or be credited but by my being with him, he can effect a compromise between the Rohillas, the Marathas, and the King, so that by giving up a part of their (the Rohillas') country for his Majesty's support, they shall remain in possession of such parts as will be a barrier to his own dominions; for he observes that the King is uneasy in his present situation, and would most heartily join in any accommodation to render himself more independent of that aspiring power. The Marathas, from such appearances, would not refuse a compromise for a sum of money, since by advices from the Deccan it is not improbable that they may be wanted for the defence of their own possessions.... In this case His Excellency observes he can with propriety take upon him the office of Vizier, and much greater confidence will be placed in his proposals, from the knowledge of the concern the English have in these negotiations, by the presence of their chief officers; but without the appearance of such a support he will not undertake it.... He has requested a battalion of sepoys might be ordered from the garrison of Allahabad to the lines of Cawnpore, which I have taken upon me to direct. Should the Nabob's proposal meet with the concurrence of the Board and his negotiations prove successful, I shall deem it one of the luckiest events that could have happened for the interest of the Company; for the knowledge of such an accommodation, affected by the mediation of the English, will strengthen their reputation, and will be the only means of preventing the almost certainty of an attack on the Vizier's or Company's possessions, sooner or later [1].'

In a subsequent letter, written on the 28th January, 1772, Sir Robert Barker reported that the Vizier had told him that he had at one time been himself desirous of obtaining possession of Rohilkhand, and that the Rohillas, knowing this, would certainly be suspicious of his intentions unless he were supported by the English.

'His Excellency,' Sir Robert Barker wrote, 'observed to me that

[1] Fifth Report, App. No. 21. I have quoted Sir Robert Barker's report almost *in extenso*, because Mill's version of it is inaccurate. It would be supposed from his account that the Vizier proposed to make over to the Emperor a portion of the Rohilla territories in Rohilkhand. No such proposal was made. It is clear from Sir Robert Barker's report, and from subsequent papers, that the Vizier's suggestion was that the Rohillas should transfer to the Emperor the districts in the Doáb which had been given to them by Ahmad Shah Abdali, but of which they had seldom held actual possession, and which were now occupied by the Marathas. The whole of Rohilkhand, which served as 'a barrier to his own dominions' would, according to the Vizier's proposal, have been left to the Rohillas. He was right in his anticipation that the Rohillas would agree to such an arrangement, although they objected to his subsequent proposal that he should retain a portion of their districts in the Doáb for himself. Another account of the interview with the Vizier, very similar to that which I have quoted, is given in a letter from Sir Robert Barker, dated May 15, 1772, printed in Forrest's Selections, vol. i. p. 9.

I was no stranger to the terms he was on with the Rohillas, and he openly confessed his inclination and wish at one time to reduce those powers. Since the death of Dundi Khan, for whom he had an utter aversion, he has been more reconciled, and he now discovers it is highly necessary for political reasons to protect them in their present establishment; that this difference between them has occasioned a diffidence on their side, and that he shall not be credited unless the English appear to adopt the system, and his pride would be hurt was he to attempt it and be refused. The letters from the Rohilla chiefs are wrote to him in a style as if he was one and the same as the English, and he doubts that without such a concurrence they mean to do nothing with him alone[1].'

The difficulties anticipated by the Vizier were doubtless well founded. There had never been any real friendship between him and the Rohillas; the contests that had taken place in the time of his father had not been forgotten; he was always afraid that the Rohillas would be compelled or persuaded to come to terms with the Marathas and give them a passage into Oudh; the Rohillas, on their part, were always suspicious of the Vizier's intentions. There was another reason, perhaps more important than any other, which rendered the establishment of good relations between the two parties difficult. Shuja-ud-daula and his followers were Shiahs, while the Rohillas were Sunnis, and the animosity between the two Mohammedan sects was so great that it was really easier for the Rohillas to join the Marathas than to enter into an alliance with the Vizier.

Acceptance of the Vizier's proposals committed the Bengal Government to very little, and on the 3rd February, 1772, they were approved. Sir Robert Barker was ordered to accompany the Vizier on his expedition, and 'to act on the part of the Honorable Company in the negotiations that may occur on this subject,' and the Vizier then marched with his troops towards the frontiers of Rohilkhand.

It soon became clear that the difficulty of making any arrangement was great. The Vizier, the Rohillas, and the

[1] Fifth Report, App. No. 21.

Marathas were all utterly unscrupulous, and each knew that no trust could be placed in either of the others. If exceptions had to be made to this rule in favour of the Vizier, they were solely the result of the fact that he could not act independently of the English.

When Shuja-ud-daula reached the frontier of Rohilkhand with Sir Robert Barker, he proposed to Hafiz Rahmat that active operations should be taken by their united forces against the Marathas. His overtures were received with much suspicion. Hafiz Rahmat, however, stated in general terms his desire to co-operate for mutual defence, and he suggested that the Vizier should march to the assistance of Zabita Khan. The Vizier refused to venture on any such operation without the support of an English force, and proposed that Hafiz Rahmat should join Zabita Khan, while he would himself cross the Ganges, and recover from the Marathas the districts in the Doáb which had formerly been given by Ahmad Shah Abdali to Hafiz Rahmat and Dundi Khan. This, Shuja-ud-daula urged, would tend to divert the attention of the Marathas from the invasion of Rohilkhand. According to Sir Robert Barker the Rohillas were willing to give up such portion of these districts 'as might be judged necessary for the support of the Royal House,' but they refused to agree to a further proposal by the Vizier that, in consideration of the charges that he would have to incur in driving out the Marathas, he should himself retain as large a share of these districts as that given to the Emperor[1].

This plan was therefore abandoned, but, on receiving from Sir Robert Barker an assurance of the good faith of the Vizier, Hafiz Rahmat agreed to march to Zabita Khan's assistance, while the Vizier's army was to remain in position within the borders of Oudh on the frontier of Rohilkhand. Before, however, any further action could be taken, another large force of Marathas crossed the

[1] Letter from Sir R. Barker to Select Committee, Feb. 25, 1772. Fifth Report, App. No. 21.

E

Ganges and completely defeated the Rohillas. The Emperor's troops co-operated with the Marathas. 'The panic' (Sir Robert Barker wrote to his Government) 'which now ran through the whole Rohilla tribe was inconceivable; each chief considered nothing but the safety of himself and family, and having left their towns and villages to the plunder of their own rabble they most shamefully fled to the jungles, leaving the whole country open to the enemy.'

Fearing that the Marathas would follow up their successes by an immediate attack upon himself, the Vizier entreated Sir Robert Barker to issue orders for the march of a Brigade of English troops to his assistance, in anticipation of the sanction of the Calcutta Government. Seeing the danger to be real, Sir Robert Barker sent orders to Colonel Champion, who commanded the 1st Brigade at Dinapore, to march into Oudh, so that in case of necessity the means of supporting the Vizier might be at hand. He afterwards stated his belief that this movement had stopped the advance of the Marathas and caused them to 'lose the season to conclude their operations,' and that if it had not been ordered the alarm of the Vizier would have become so great that he would have entered into some arrangement with the Marathas.

The Marathas were now very desirous of breaking up the alliance between the Vizier and the Rohillas. With this object they entered into communication with both parties, holding out in each case such inducements as they thought likely to be successful. The details of their offers to Hafiz Rahmat are not known, but on the 25th February, 1772, Sir Robert Barker wrote that his great object was to prevent a compromise between the Rohillas and Marathas. He was endeavouring (he said) to encourage the Rohillas, and to persuade them that although the Marathas might gain some temporary advantage, the rainy season, which was not far off, would give them an opportunity of recovering their losses[1]. Shortly afterwards he feared that

[1] Fifth Report, App. No. 21.

the Vizier might make terms with the Marathas, who had sent an envoy to his camp with tempting offers. They proposed to make over to him a part or even the whole of Rohilkhand, on condition that they retained for themselves all the Rohilla territories on the other side of the Ganges, and that an agreement for the payment of *chauth* were entered into. 'It was a matter,' the Select Committee of the Government in Calcutta wrote to the Court of Directors, 'of very little concern to the Marathas who held possession of Rohilkhand provided their own emolument was primarily and principally considered[1].' The Vizier, seeing that the power of the Rohillas seemed irretrievably broken, appeared strongly inclined to accept the offers of the Marathas. On the 9th March, Sir Robert Barker wrote to the Governor that it was with great difficulty that he

'could prevent the Vizier entering into schemes that are improper both to his own interest and to the Company. At one time he is for taking advantage of the dismayed Rohillas, and seizing the country of Hafiz Rahmat; at another time he is desirous of treating with the Marathas in hopes of possessing himself of the Rohilla country. In short not a day passes over his head but he has some new scheme which it is with trouble I can overset. But I am convinced he will undertake nothing without our approbation.'

On the following day Sir Robert Barker wrote again to the same effect, that

'the Vizier, although sensible of the danger of arrangements with the Marathas, can scarcely withstand the bait they hold out to him. I shall, however, amuse His Excellency from these flighty projects[2].'

These negotiations were soon interrupted. In the middle of March the Vizier broke off communications with the Marathas, and ordered their envoy to leave his camp, in consequence of intelligence that greatly incensed him and all Mohammedans, that the Marathas had dug up and burned with many indignities the body of Najib-ud-daula.

[1] Letter to Court of Directors, November 10, 1772, MS. Records, India Office.

[2] British Museum MSS., No. 29, 198, Private letters to the Governor, Hon. John Cartier.

Sir Robert Barker had always maintained that the only wise policy for the Vizier was to form a strict alliance with the Rohillas, and to attack the Marathas with their united forces. But Shuja-ud-daula was afraid to adopt any active measures without the assistance of English troops, for he distrusted his own strength, and the defeat of the Rohillas had been so serious that little dependence could be placed upon them. Sir Robert Barker had no authority to give promises of armed support, for the Bengal Government was above all things anxious to avoid war with the Marathas. Under these circumstances, the Vizier at last declared to Sir Robert Barker that he had no choice left to him. It was certain, he said, that when the Marathas had completed the conquest of Rohilkhand they would attack him; he must therefore enter into some arrangement by which they could be induced to retire.

On the 9th April, Sir Robert Barker reported the arrival of another Maratha envoy, and that the Vizier had sent an agent of his own to the Marathas, thinking that they would agree to evacuate Rohilkhand if a large sum of money were paid to them. He suggested that if the Rohillas would provide a crore of rupees, a portion of that amount might be given to the Marathas, while he himself would retain 'a sufficient sum to defray the expenses which he had been at for the march of his troops, and the extra expenses of the English forces, with an overplus to reward him for the undertaking [1].'

Sir Robert Barker strongly opposed these communications with the Marathas who, he was convinced, could not be trusted, and the Vizier promised to conclude no engagement without his approval. Hoping to bring about some arrangement with the Rohillas, Sir Robert Barker, early in April, sent one of his officers, Captain Harper,

[1] Letter from Sir R. Barker, British Museum MSS. No. 29,198. According to a letter from the Select Committee to the Court of Directors dated March 10, 1772, the Vizier hoped to keep the lion's share of the 100 lakhs, and to pay thirty or forty lakhs to the Marathas. The Rohillas were said to be willing to give altogether sixty lakhs.

to confer with Hafiz Rahmat, and he was accompanied by an envoy from the Vizier [1].

The negotiations between Shuja-ud-daula and the Marathas led to no result, and on the 10th May Sir Robert Barker reported that they were entirely broken off. Captain Harper had returned with assurances from Hafiz Rahmat which seemed satisfactory, and Sir Robert Barker renewed his advice that an alliance should be at once concluded with the Rohillas. The Vizier himself now became anxious to adopt this policy, fearing that the Marathas might otherwise offer to the Rohillas terms which would induce them to join in an attack upon himself. The breach between the Vizier and the Marathas was complete, and he never again attempted to enter into any arrangement with them.

Captain Harper was now again sent to Hafiz Rahmat to invite him to come in person to the camp at Shahabad and settle the terms of an agreement.

'The Rohillas,' Sir Robert Barker wrote on the 15th May, 'who are preserved from extirpation, have expressed their acknowledgment in several letters from their chiefs to me, particularly Hafiz Rahmat's letter, wherein he says:—"At this juncture you and the Vizier with a view to the interest of the Rohilla chiefs have proceeded as far as Shahabad. It has been productive of the greatest advantages; but for this the Marathas even now had entered this country. We owe this benefit to the Almighty, and the friendship of you and the Vizier [2]."'

After some hesitation on the part of Hafiz Rahmat, who was suspicious of the Vizier's good faith, he consented to meet him; on the 25th May he arrived at Shahabad and was received with much honour by the Vizier and Sir Robert Barker. Zabita Khan and the other principal chiefs came also to the camp.

Negotiations continued until the 17th June, when a treaty of alliance, offensive and defensive, was concluded

[1] Letters from Sir R. Barker to the Select Committee, April 9 and May 20, 1772, Fifth Report, App. No. 21.

[2] Forrest's Selections, vol. i. p. 12.

between the Rohillas and the Vizier. The treaty was in two parts; the first was of a general character, and was to the following effect:—

'Treaty entered into between the Vizier of the empire, Shuja-ud-daula, and the Rohilla Sirdars reciprocally interchanged.

First, friendship is established between us; and we, Hafiz Rahmat Khan, and Zabita Khan, and all the other Rohilla Sirdars, great and small, have agreed and determined with the Vizier of the empire, Shuja-ud-daula, that we adhere to the substance of this writing, and never deviate from this agreement; that we esteem his friends as our friends and his enemies as our enemies; and that we and our heirs, during our lives, shall adhere firmly to this our oath and agreement; that we shall be united and joined together for the protection of the country of the Vizier, of the empire, and of our own country; and if any enemy, which God forbid, should make an attempt against us and the Vizier, we the Rohilla Sirdars and the Vizier of the empire shall use our joint endeavours to oppose him. We, all the Rohilla Sirdars, shall also join and unite in any measure that may be determined by the Vizier of the empire for the benefit of the Nawab Mohammad Zabita Khan. We, both parties, swear by the Almighty, his Prophet, and the sacred Koran, that we will firmly adhere to this solemn agreement, nor ever deviate from this our treaty. This treaty, confirmed by oath, and sealed in the presence of General Sir Robert Barker, written on the 11th of the month Rabi-ul-awal, 1186 Hegira.'

The second part of the treaty was as follows:—

'Agreement on the part of the Rohilla Sirdars with the Vizier.

The Vizier of the empire, Shuja-ud-daula, shall establish the Rohilla Sirdars in their different possessions, obliging the Marathas to retire either by peace or war; this to depend on the pleasure of the Vizier. If at this time, without either war or peace, the Marathas, on account of the rains, shall cross and retire, and after the expiration of the rainy season they should again enter the country of the Rohillas, their expulsion is the business of the Vizier. The Rohilla Sirdars, in consequence of the above, agree to pay forty lakhs of rupees[1] to the Vizier in the following manner:—As the Marathas are now in the country of the Rohilla Sirdars, the Vizier of the empire shall march from Shahabad, as far as may be necessary, to enable the families of the Rohillas to leave the jungle, and return to their habitations:—Ten laks of rupees in specie, in part of the above sum, shall then be paid; and the remaining thirty lakhs in three years, from the beginning of the year 1180 Fasli.

This agreement sealed in the presence of General Sir Robert Barker[2].'

[1] Equal to about £500,000. A lakh was about £12,500.

[2] The date of the treaty is given in Aitchison's Treaties, vol. ii. p. 5, as

The signature of this treaty proved a most important event in the history of the Rohillas, for the non-fulfilment of its conditions led ultimately to their ruin. Without the active intervention and persuasion of Sir Robert Barker no such arrangement between the Rohillas and the Vizier would have been made, and both parties looked on the attestation by the English General as a guarantee on behalf of the English Government. This was the view taken by Hastings:—'Both deeds,' he wrote, 'were executed in the presence of General Sir Robert Barker, and his signature affixed to both as a witness to them. But the same act made him the guarantee of both, and virtually, by his representation, extended the same obligation to the Company; for it has been shown that he was the instrument of the negotiation, and that the Rohillas themselves had refused to treat with the Nabob alone, that is, without the junction of the English name and faith with his[1].'

When the treaty had been signed, Hafiz Rahmat, Zabita Khan, and the other chiefs left the Vizier's camp, both parties giving strong assurances of cordial friendship for the future.

The Marathas would probably under no circumstances have remained in Rohilkhand during the rainy season, for they would not have ventured to leave the Ganges, at that time of the year an impassable obstacle, between them and the main body of their army, and their knowledge of the treaty concluded between the Rohillas and the Vizier with the approval of the English General made this the more

June 13, 1772, but Sir Robert Barker, in his official letter of the 17th June, says that 'the treaty of alliance was finally concluded in my presence this morning.' I have quoted the translation of the treaty sent by him with that letter. The translation of the first part corresponds almost exactly with that in Aitchison's Treaties. The translation of the second part given by Sir Charles Aitchison is worded differently from that originally sent by Sir Robert Barker, but is the same as that quoted by Hastings in his report to the Council dated October 4, 1773. The purport of the two versions is, however, identical. The treaty is printed in Appendix 21 to the Fifth Report from the Committee of Secrecy.

[1] Defence before the House of Commons, 1786.

certain. Before the treaty was actually signed they had made evident preparations for departure; immediately afterwards the rainy season began, and before any further action could be taken by the Vizier they crossed the river and evacuated Rohilkhand. They had been in possession of nearly the whole country for several months, and their devastations had been frightful. The people of Rohilkhand, however, during such calamities as this, had, as I have already explained, one advantage over those on the other side of the Ganges. They were within easy reach of the swamps of the Tarái and of the tract of forest below the Himalaya. By flying to those places of refuge they could usually save their lives and some of their property, and when the invasion was over they returned to their fields and rebuilt their villages.

On the departure of the Marathas the Rohillas re-occupied the country without opposition. The wife and son of Zabita Khan, several ladies of Najib-ud-daula's family, and a daughter of Ali Mohammad, had been carried off by the Marathas, and these, on representations made by Shuja-ud-daula's agent at Delhi, were sent back. The Marathas also released, through his intercession, four hundred women who had been taken away from Rohilkhand. The Vizier and Sir Robert Barker returned to Faizabad in Oudh[1].

[1] For an account of the misrepresentations of Mill in regard to the treaty between the Rohillas and the Vizier, see Appendix C.

CHAPTER VI.

A.D. 1772. HASTINGS GOVERNOR OF BENGAL.—HIS POLICY.—EVENTS IN ROHILKHAND.

Hastings becomes Governor of Bengal.—Constitution of the Government.—The Select Committee.—Views of Hastings regarding the relations between the English, the Vizier, the Marathas, and Rohillas.—Dissensions in Rohilkhand.—Rebellion of Hafiz Rahmat's son.—Zabita Khan joins the Marathas.—Alarm of the Vizier.—Demands of the Marathas on the Vizier.—He applies for aid to the English.—Reply of Hastings.

ON the 13th April, 1772, while the events narrated in the last chapter were in progress, Warren Hastings took his seat as Governor of Bengal.

At this time no definite system had been laid down for the conduct of the Government. It was entrusted to the Governor and a Council consisting of nine members, but their respective powers were undefined. On the 11th November, 1773, Hastings, in a letter to the Court of Directors, giving his opinion on the necessity for a better organisation of the Government, wrote as follows :—

'Our constitution is nowhere to be traced but in ancient charters, which were framed for the jurisdiction of your leading settlements, the sales of your exports, and the provision of your annual investment. I need not observe how incompetent these must prove for the government of a great kingdom, and for the preservation of its riches from private violence and embezzlement. The powers of the Governor, although supposed to be great, are in reality little more than those of any individual in his Council. Their compliance, his own abilities, or a superior share of attention, and the opinion that he possesses extraordinary powers, may give him the effect of them, and an ascendant over his associates in the administration; but a moment's consideration is sufficient to discover the nakedness of his authority, and to level him with the rest.'

He went on to say that personally he had no reason to complain :—

'Happily I find myself sufficiently secured against such effects.

The notice with which you have distinguished my services, the injunctions which you have laid on the other Members of the Board to afford me their support, and the degree of responsibility which you have been pleased to attribute to my particular conduct, have contributed to strengthen my hands against any improper opposition. At the same time, I must do the gentlemen of the Board the justice to declare, that I have found in them so candid a disposition to co-operate with me in every measure for the public good, that I feel no want of extraordinary powers for myself, nor under such favourable circumstances is it my wish to possess them. I mention this want only as a defect in the service which is rendered still more important by the false opinion that the principal authority rests constitutionally in the hands of the President, when in effect it is merely accidental[1].'

The business connected with the relations of the Government with Foreign States was transacted by a Select Committee consisting of the Governor and two members of the Council. All reports were addressed to them, and orders were issued by them. Matters of special importance were laid by them before the whole Council. It is clear that from the time in which Hastings became Governor until the change of Government in October 1774, the whole power, in respect of the transactions with which we are now concerned, was practically in his hands[2].

Hastings arrived in Calcutta from Madras in February 1772, and before he took charge of the office of Governor, two months later, he had formed decided opinions on the position of affairs in Northern India, and on the relations between the English, the Vizier, the Emperor, the Marathas, and the Rohillas. Among the Hastings manuscripts in the British Museum there are some valuable private letters, relating to matters of public interest then pending, sent

[1] Fifth Report, App. No. 5.

[2] The following quotation is taken from a private letter from Hastings to Sulivan, dated November 11, 1772: 'In assemblies which are formed for making new laws, or for extraordinary business, opposition and hesitation are of great utility and even of necessity. In an executive body they are dangerous and may prove fatal. Current business always requires decision. The business of this government is all of that kind. We have no time to talk. The whole day is too little to act, and it is infinitely better to proceed even to error than to procrastinate in the pursuit of sure and proper measures.' British Museum MSS. 29,127.

by him from Calcutta to his friends in England. In one of these, written on the 26th March, 1772, to Sir George Colebrooke, we can trace the main features of the policy which he afterwards consistently carried out in regard to Oudh, the Doáb, and Rohilkhand. I shall quote a portion of this letter because it throws light on the motives by which his subsequent action was guided:—

'In the King we have another idol of our own creation to whom we have bound ourselves to pay an annual tribute, and most punctually have we paid it even when he was in arms against us, for such I consider the cause he is now engaged in. His title, dignity, state, and the territory which he possesses, he holds by our bounty; and what has he given us in return? A piece of paper which acknowledges our right to the dewannee of Bengal, a right which we can have no pretence to hold from him, because we denied his right to possess a single acre in either of the provinces. We hold the sovereignty of them by the best of all titles, power. He could not transfer what he never had to give; and twenty-six lakhs of rupees, £325,000 sterling, are rather too much to give away annually for the purchase of a very flimsy argument, not intrinsically worth three halfpence. You have been deceived, if you were told that the Powers of India set any value on the King's grants. They laugh at them. Not a state of India ever paid him a rupee, not one of his natural subjects offered any kind of submission to his authority, when we first fell down and worshipped it. Yet for this idle pageant we have drained the country, which has a right to our protection, of its current specie, which is its blood; for him we continued to exhaust it of its wealth, while we wanted means to furnish the necessary expenses of the Company, while we draw on them for crores and run them crores in debt, and to this wretched King of shreds and patches are we almost to this day sending supplies of treasure to enable the only enemies we have in India to prosecute their designs of universal conquest, which if successful must end in our destruction; for the Marathas are not his protectors on the principles which we observe. We have been his tools, the instruments of his grandeur. He is theirs, and his name, authority, wealth, and all he possesses is theirs with his person. The moment I came I remonstrated with Mr. Cartier against this man's being allowed any further payments; for his bills were still received and discharged from the treasury at Murshedabad; but on his assurance that an order had been sent forbidding the payment of any sums at the city but by express order from the Presidency, I have remained hitherto silent on the subject, determined to refuse consent to the sacrifice of a single rupee to the King or any of his adherents, whether he continue in the hands of the Marathas, or throw himself again a shackle upon ours, until the commands of my superiors shall authorise it. On this you may depend, and I think I speak the sentiments of the other Members of the Board, or of most of them. I forgot to add to the list of our benefactions the adverse and impolitic part which we have always acted against our useful ally, Shuja Daula. From our earliest connection with this Prince we have always entertained a jealousy of his power, and a suspicion of his designs upon these Provinces. Such of the measures with which I have been acquainted as respect him have been all formed on these prepossessions. I know not how well they may be grounded, but this I know that the sure way to make a man your enemy, whether in public or in private life, is to believe him one; and I know too that Shuja Daula is so little able to contend with the Company that he is unable to stand without them. What then have we to fear from him, that we should take every occasion to reduce his strength, and peck at his authority? I think among other curious instances of this kind it was gravely proposed to him, and insisted on, that he should keep only a limited number of sepoys; an impotent and wanton exercise of power which he could not fail to resent, which he might safely yield to, and yet maintain ten times the stipulated number without a possibility of its being proved against him. The consequences of this policy, however, are such as were intended. He is now so weak, or so he is represented, that on every little alarm our army must run to his assistance, or he is in danger of being destroyed, and he is at the absolute disposal of the Commander-in-Chief, whose only duty appears to be to attend and direct him. Of this we have a recent instance in the following detail of our late political operations.

'The Marathas have been making great strides towards the conquest of all India. They have been some time masters of the country of the Jats, and they have possessed themselves of all the Rohilla and Pathan dominions on the West of the Ganges. The only part of the Rohilla territory which remained, was a large tract of land lying to the north of the province of Oudh, and shut in on the West and North by the Ganges, and the woods and mountains of Tartary among which the Ganges loses itself. Sekkertaul, the capital of this country, stands on the bank of the river[1].

'The Marathas have lately crossed the river, attacked and utterly routed the Rohilla army which lay there for the guard of the fort, and taken possession of Sekkertaul. The Rohilla chiefs—planet-struck—have run off to their strongholds, and are running off to the hills, so that the whole country lies at their mercy. They have not, however, made great progress in it, and I think they will not, because the river will be impassable in the month of June, which will make it difficult, if not impracticable, for them to get back again. Should this happen they will be at our mercy, for as their horse cannot act in the rains,

[1] More correctly Shukartár, a strong fort on the right bank of the Ganges, occupied by Najib-ud-daula, and after him by Zabita Khan.

and our infantry can, if we should be tempted to take the advantage of so favourable a situation, and march a force against them, which in such a case I think we ought, they cannot avoid us, and unless our military spirit and skill have entirely left us, they must be destroyed. I do not pretend to much military knowledge, but I think I am safe in this conclusion.

'I have told you what may happen. I will now inform you what has passed. General Barker, alarmed at the success of the Marathas, instantly sent orders to Colonel Champion who commands the first brigade quartered at Patna, to march into the province of Oudh, and informed the Select Committee what he had done, representing the Vizier as frightened out of his wits. It is remarkable that he had recommended it to the Board to station that brigade near the Currumnassa some time before. It was in readiness to march some time before their orders could reach it, and the first news which we received of its having marched were sent down in private letters. The Committee disapproved of this act of self-authority, for which they saw no necessity. There was no present danger, nor any likely to come on this season. The Vizier had not made any requisition to the President for our aid, nor did any of Sir Robert Barker's letters intimate that he had made any application of the kind to him. They therefore sent orders to the brigade to halt wherever those orders should reach it. In the meantime we wait for fresh intelligence to enable us to judge whether it shall proceed or return. In its present position it can be of no use. The premature appearance of hostility may draw hostilities on ourselves, or it may put our enemies on their guard. It can be of no present service, and therefore I should have been better pleased that the brigade had been recalled to our own borders. Much space would not have been lost in the way; the Marathas would have been less alarmed at our moving, and the authority of the Government would have been maintained, a trivial object indeed on the present occasion, because the like may easily be prevented from happening again. It is most probable that I shall be in the chair by the time that a formal requisition may come from the Vizier for aid. I do not think he wants it, but I shall wish before it is granted that a provision be made for the charge of it. It is indeed stipulated by treaty that all extra charges are to be borne by the Vizier, but this is very insufficient. The pay and common batta of such a force are enormous. These charges are the Company's, and their provinces are drained to defray them, while the country which we protect is enriched with so much additional circulation. The whole expense ought to be borne by the Vizier. At the same time our alliance with him might be easily placed, as it ought to be, on a footing of more credit and satisfaction to him, and of more utility to ourselves. We should leave him the uncontrolled master of his own dominions. We should assist in making him such, and enabling him to be an useful ally instead of a burden to us. He should have the most convincing assurances given him that we had no other object in our mutual alliance than mutual security. If he would keep up a body of good cavalry which we shall always want, and turn off all his rabble of infantry which he never can depend upon, he may then be of service to us, and not a mere suspected dependent. How these points are to be effected I yet know not, as I much doubt whether they will be consonant to the sentiments of those gentlemen who are with him. I shall endeavour to accomplish them and I am greatly deceived if you will not approve of my plan.

'The last letter from the General informs us that the Vizier instead of providing for his defence is planning schemes for joining to worry the Rohillas, and in his last he alludes to an offer of the Marathas to cede to him all the Rohilla countries on that side of the river, with the view of purchasing his acquiescence in their attempts to possess themselves of the territory which lies on the other side. Such a compromise is not likely to take place. I wish it could, and beg leave to refer you to the map for my reasons [1].'

In other letters written about the same time Hastings expressed his fear that we were on the eve of war with the Marathas, a calamity which he was most anxious to avoid, and to guard against which, it was, in his opinion, essential that we should strengthen and defend the Vizier. Referring, in a letter to Du Pré, to the reports that the Marathas had offered to give up to him the whole of Rohilkhand, on condition that he would not interfere with them in the Doáb, Hastings repeated his regret that no such compromise seemed possible, 'for (he said) I see less danger from it than from running headlong into war with the Marathas [2].'

The cessation of the Maratha invasion brought no peace to Rohilkhand. General co-operation and unity of purpose could alone have given to the Rohillas a chance of safety, but fatal dissensions now broke out. One of the most worthy of their chiefs, Sirdar Khan Bakshi, died.

[1] Private letter to Sir George Colebrooke, 26th March, 1772, British Museum MSS. 29,127. In this allusion to the map, Hastings evidently refers to the point on which he frequently insisted, that there could be no real security for the Vizier against the Marathas while the road into Oudh was open to them through Rohilkhand, and that danger to the Vizier meant danger to our own provinces. The schemes of the Vizier to which Hastings refers were those mentioned in Sir R. Barker's letter of 9th March, 1772. See *sup.* p. 51.

[2] British Museum MSS. 29,126.

'For ninety years,' writes the native historian, 'he had lived in this vale of wretchedness and sorrow; he was a holy and religious person; from the day of mature discernment to the last respiration of mortal existence he was daily seen in the congregations of the mosques, and in the assemblies of the pious; he was a man just in his sentiments and upright in his dealings; he was not, like others of his tribe, a violator of the ties of friendship, or an oppressor of the helpless; and excepting the due returns of the revenue he took not from the indigent labourer or the useful tiller of the soil a single exaction; previous to the final departure of that immortal spark which connects the human with the divine existence, whilst his reason was yet alive to the concerns of this transitory state, he made an equitable distribution of the blessings he enjoyed from Providence among his heirs [1].'

His sons quarrelled over their inheritance, and sanguinary conflicts followed.

A more serious event was the open rebellion of Hafiz Rahmat's son, Inayat Khan. He defeated the troops sent against him by his father, and Hafiz Rahmat being much alarmed, had recourse, writes Hamilton, 'to a stratagem perfectly consistent with the duplicity of his character; he caused a grant to be drawn out in the name of Inayat Khan, of the district of Salimpur, which he sent to him with a letter, assuring him of his forgiveness, taking blame to himself for a deficiency of parental indulgence, and desiring him to go and take possession of the lands of Salimpur, which he hoped would be considered by him a sufficient present provision, and promising to reward his obedience in the amplest manner.' The artifice succeeded; Inayat Khan accepted the proposal, and was then seized by his father's orders. Hafiz Rahmat at first declared his intention of putting his son to death, but was persuaded to spare his life. Not long afterwards Inayat Khan died in extreme misery. 'Thus,' says the native historian, 'was the parental imprecation amply fulfilled on him, Hafiz Rahmat three different times during his rebellion having gone to the mosque, and prayed aloud, saying, "Cause the cup of his life, O God! to overflow while yet in his youth, so that no fruit may ever spring from that inauspicious branch,

[1] Quoted by Hamilton, p. 178.

and never let me be exposed to the shame of again beholding his face[1].'"

Shaikh Kabír, the best soldier of the Rohillas, died about the same time, and they were further weakened by the incompetency of Muzaffar Jang, the Afghan chief who had succeeded his father in the frontier province of Farukhabad.

The most serious misfortune of all, and one for which there could be no remedy, was the defection of Zabita Khan from the alliance with his Afghan countrymen. According to one account, the Marathas, when they released his family, had done so on condition that he should join them. He had taken an active part in the negotiations which led to the treaty with the Vizier, and his fidelity to the Rohillas was of the utmost importance to them. In July 1772, he openly joined the Marathas, and made a separate peace, on the understanding that all his possessions should be restored to him, and that he should be re-instated in the office of First Minister, which had formerly been held by his father and by himself at the Emperor's Court.

Shuja-ud-daula was much alarmed at Zabita Khan's proceedings, for he believed that they would be immediately followed by serious attempts on the part of the Marathas to induce Hafiz Rahmat and the other Rohilla chiefs to adopt a similar course, and that after the rainy season was over a combined attack would be made on his own dominions. The Marathas, indeed, did not disguise their intentions. Learning that a treaty of alliance against themselves had been entered into between the Rohillas and the Vizier, they now, as the Select Committee wrote to the Court of Directors, 'made a show of revenging themselves upon the latter, and demanded of him, if he would ensure his own tranquillity at the conclusion of the rains, to cede to them the provinces of Kora, Allahabad, and Benares, to deliver into their hands the settlement he had made with the Rohillas, to discharge all sums for which the king now

[1] Quoted by Hamilton, p. 183.

stood indebted to them, and to unite with them against every opponent [1].'

On receiving this summons, the Vizier immediately wrote to Hastings, urging in strong terms the extreme danger to which he was exposed. He said that an attack was imminent after the rainy season, and he called on Hastings to be ready to send a large force to his assistance at the beginning of the winter. 'My enemy speaks plainly, and demands my country [2].'

In reply to this letter, Hastings, on the 23rd July, assured the Vizier that the English would join, to the utmost of their power, in the defence of his territory, and that immediate preparations should be made in case their troops were required. He said that assistance, however, could only be given for the defence of the Vizier's own dominions, and that without authority from the Company he could not allow the English troops to go beyond the Vizier's frontiers, or to engage in an offensive war against the Marathas. He at the same time wrote to the Maratha chiefs in Northern India, 'acquainting them of our extreme dissatisfaction at the hostile appearance which they had for some time carried towards the Nabob Shuja-ud-daula, and that however we might on our own part be pacifically inclined, we considered ourselves as firmly bound by treaty to defend his territories against every invader [3].'

[1] Letter to Court of Directors, dated November 10, 1772. MS. Records, India Office.

[2] British Museum, MSS. 29,198. Letter from the Vizier not dated, but received by Hastings on July 17, 1772.

[3] Letter to Court of Directors, November 10, 1772, MS. Records, India Office.

CHAPTER VII.

A.D. 1773. CESSION OF KORA AND ALLAHABAD TO THE MARATHAS.—THE MARATHAS INVADE ROHILKHAND AND ARE EXPELLED BY THE ENGLISH AND THE VIZIER.

The Marathas occupy Delhi.—They force the Emperor to grant to them Kora and Allahabad.—Alarm of the Vizier and English.—Fears of alliance between the Marathas and Rohillas.—The Marathas again invade Rohilkhand. —An English Brigade ordered to assist the Vizier.—Instructions to Sir Robert Barker.—The English and the Vizier's troops enter Rohilkhand.—Doubtful attitude of the Rohillas.—Negotiations between Hafiz Rahmat and the Marathas.—Reports by Sir Robert Barker.—Perfidy of the Rohillas.—The Vizier suggests their expulsion from Rohilkhand.—Hafiz Rahmat agrees to carry out the conditions of his former treaty.—The English attack the Marathas, who retreat.—Conference between Sir Robert Barker, Hafiz Rahmat, and the Vizier.—Hafiz Rahmat promises to fulfil his engagements.—Proposals of the Vizier in case of default by the Rohillas.—Answer of the Bengal Government. —The English march against the Marathas who evacuate Rohilkhand.—Letter of Sir Robert Barker to the Marathas.—The Marathas return to the Deccan. —Hafiz Rahmat evades payment of the sums due to the Vizier.—The Vizier and the English troops return to Oudh.

THE Emperor, who before this time had discovered his mistake in trusting the Marathas, was most unwilling to receive Zabita Khan as his Minister. The Marathas insisted that he should do so, and on this and other pretexts they marched towards the end of 1772 to Delhi. Najf Khan and his troops made a respectable defence, but on the 22nd December they were forced to surrender. The Marathas no longer maintained towards the Emperor even an outward show of respect. Zabita Khan was restored to office, and the Marathas compelled the Emperor to give to them a grant of the provinces of Kora and Allahabad which had been assigned to him by the English.

When the news of these proceedings reached the Vizier his alarm was extreme, and he wrote to the English Government begging in urgent terms that Sir Robert Barker, the Commander-in-Chief, might immediately be sent to him, to concert measures of military co-operatoin and defence [1]. The Vizier's apprehensions were well founded. The Marathas openly declared their intention of taking possession of Kora and Allahabad, and if they could have effected this extension of their power and have occupied Rohilkhand, it would, without doubt, have been fatal to the Vizier unless the English had actively and constantly interfered in his defence. 'Had the Marathas been allowed,' Hastings afterwards wrote, 'to subdue the Kora district and the country of the Rohillas, the Vizier's territory would have been open to their incursions; their numerous horse might have plundered it in spite of the efforts of our infantry, and their continued ravages might have obliged him to come to an accommodation with them, as was once apprehended, on terms which would have afforded them an easy entrance into our own possessions [2].'

Much doubt was felt by Hastings in regard to the real intention of the Marathas, but it was resolved that

[1] See letters from the Vizier, Fifth Report, App. No. 18:—'My mind is in anxiety and uneasiness, for if the Marathas become victorious, and they bring his Majesty to another condition, you must then reflect in what situation are you and I, my friend, and that there is room for perplexity and distress to every one. You, my friend, will not now remain negligent to this quarter, and in forming your plans accordingly. Affairs now carry with them a different aspect, and you must consider this with much attention and circumspection, and that whenever the enemies of his Majesty have conquered him, you must then certainly understand that they will entertain an intention in this quarter. My country is in reality the door of Bengal, and I am what you may call the barrier to that country; it is therefore absolutely necessary that you remain careful and attentive to yourself, and in forming your plans for this quarter, and the sending General Barker is in the highest degree proper and advisable.'

[2] Defence before the House of Commons.

F 2

measures should immediately be taken for the defence of the districts abandoned by the Emperor, and that the fortress of Allahabad should be occupied by English troops.

It seemed at first probable that the Marathas would move southward through the Doáb towards Kora before renewing the invasion of Rohilkhand, and this opinion was strengthened by the knowledge that Zabita Khan and his Rohilla followers were acting in concert with the Marathas, and that efforts were being made to induce Hafiz Rahmat to join them. It was feared that the Rohillas generally would follow Zabita Khan's example, and that the result might be a joint invasion of the Vizier's dominions, the Rohillas advancing from the north-west, while the Marathas marched towards Kora and Allahabad. Hastings, some time before this, believed that the alliance between the Marathas and Rohillas had already been agreed upon, for in November 1772, he wrote, in a private letter to Sir George Colebrooke in England, 'The Rohillas, whom the Vizier had engaged by treaty to protect him against the Marathas, and who had sworn to be his allies to the Day of Judgment, and to pay him forty lakhs of rupees for his friendship, have deserted him and gone over to the Marathas [1].'

It was resolved that until the plans of the Marathas were better known it was desirable to keep the troops in readiness, but not to make any actual advance. All doubts were soon removed. The Marathas came to the conclusion that the most effectual way of inducing Hafiz Rahmat to join them was to invade Rohilkhand. Avoiding Zabita Khan's territories, they consequently, early in 1773, marched in force to Ramghat, where the Ganges was fordable, and they sent letters to Hafiz Rahmat and to the other Rohilla chiefs, demanding payment of the bonds for fifty lakhs of rupees given to them through Safdar Jang twenty years before. The Rohillas made no serious

[1] British Museum MSS. 29,127.

attempt to dispute the passage of the river, and the Marathas entered Rohilkhand. Sir Robert Barker subsequently stated that their army consisted of not less than 50,000 men, almost entirely cavalry.

The case had now occurred which had been provided for in the treaty of the previous year, under which Shuja-ud-daula was bound to expel the Marathas from Rohilkhand, but it had become very doubtful whether the Rohillas now desired his help, or whether, on the other hand, they did not intend to join the Marathas against the Vizier.

Although it was known that Hafiz Rahmat was negotiating with the Marathas, this, so long as the Rohillas were left to their own resources, proved nothing in regard to their real intentions. It was impossible for them to resist single-handed the Maratha invasion, and it was no matter for surprise that they should endeavour to gain time by making concessions which they could afterwards repudiate. In their Consultations of the 7th January, 1773, the Bengal Government referred in the following terms to the existing situation :—

> 'We will suppose, which indeed is most likely, that the Marathas will immediately possess or attempt to possess themselves of the province of Kora and the other lands ceded to them by the King, and that they may be tempted likewise to invade the Vizier's territory. In such case, it is probable that their new ally Zabita Khan will be immediately despatched to his own dominions to unite himself with Hafiz Rahmat and the other Rohillas, and with them, and from that quarter, make their incursions, while the Marathas enter it to the southward. It is, however, still more probable that the Rohilla chiefs, who have sought their present safety in a treacherous alliance, to which necessity compelled them, with the Marathas, will from the same principle abandon their cause, or employ the confidence reposed in them to re-establish their own independence rather than contribute to the aggrandizement of a power which in the end must overwhelm them[1].'

Hastings soon came to the conclusion that whatever action might ultimately be taken by the Rohillas, the danger of their joining the Marathas would be much in-

[1] Fifth Report, App. No. 18.

creased if they saw that the Vizier and the English were disinclined to protect them. It was therefore decided that a brigade of English troops should immediately be sent to assist the Vizier in carrying out the stipulations of his treaty of the previous year, and in expelling the Marathas from Rohilkhand.

Instructions were issued to Sir Robert Barker, on the 18th February, 1773. He was told that 'the situation of affairs on the frontiers of our possessions and in the countries of Kora and Oudh requiring the appearance of the Company's forces to encourage their allies and check the hostile designs of the Marathas,' he was to assume command of the troops that were to be employed, and discuss personally with the Vizier 'the best plan of operations for fulfilling the objects of his commission, the defence and security of his country and of the provinces of Kora and Allahabad.' Rohilkhand was to be included in 'the line of defence,' and Sir Robert Barker was 'authorised to enter into a treaty with Hafiz Rahmat for the defence and protection of his dominions on such conditions as shall fully indemnify the Company for the additional charge and hazard which may be incurred by such an engagement.' 'Should,' it was added, 'Hafiz Rahmat Khan either fall into the hands of the Marathas, or from any other similar circumstances be rendered incapable of entering into such an engagement, you are still to consider his dominions as an object of your operations, and if the Vizier require you to undertake their defence, and engage to perform the conditions which we have desired you to claim from Hafiz Rahmat Khan, you will not hesitate to comply, but adopt the measure heartily, and pursue it as included in the instructions for the immediate defence of the Vizier's dominions.' Sir Robert Barker was strictly to confine his operations to the country east of the Ganges, 'to expel all hostile invaders,' but on no account to cross the river, and 'studiously to avoid engaging the Company in an offensive war with the Marathas.' One exception was allowed in the execution of these orders.

Sir Robert Barker might cross the Ganges for the protection of the Kora province, if it should become, in his opinion, dangerous to allow the Marathas 'to be unmolested near its borders,' or, if it became necessary, 'to pursue a signal success.' He was to take possession of Kora, 'as in alliance with the King'; the civil administration was to remain in the hands of the King's officer, who, however, was to be under Sir Robert Barker's control and be accountable to the Company for the revenues 'till such time as it shall be finally settled in what manner they are hereafter to be disposed.' It was estimated that the monthly charge thrown upon the Company by the defence of Kora would be about one lakh of rupees, and this sum was to be paid from the revenues of the province. If the strength of the force at Sir Robert Barker's disposal appeared to him insufficient to cope with the Marathas he was authorised to order up a part or the whole of the 2nd Brigade of the troops stationed at Patna, keeping in this case 'the most watchful eye on the motions of the Marathas,' lest they should seize the opportunity of invading the Company's provinces when comparatively denuded of troops. In regard to the charges incurred for the protection of the Vizier's dominions the following instructions were given:—

'It is further the determination of the Board, of which you will take particular notice, that no operation for the Vizier's defence shall be carried into execution without a previous stipulation on his part for the extraordinary charge attending the succours we afford him. We have estimated this at Rs. 115,000 per month, and have required an assignment on his revenue for the amount. You will therefore, as a preliminary, demand and receive the assignment required by us; and in case an additional force should be hereafter called for on his requisition you are, previous to their march, to require also and receive a proportionable assignment for the extra expenses on that account. If, in either case, the Vizier should refuse complying with these requisitions in their fullest extent, and shall persist in the refusal, it is our positive command that you immediately abandon him and withdraw your whole force from his territory, either employing it, if needful, in the Kora province agreeable to the instructions hereafter given, or remanding to Behar such part of it as shall exceed the exigencies of that service. But in such an event you are not to fail giving us the most speedy advice that we may resolve on what future measures are to be pursued. The recovery of the arrears due from the Vizier for the expenses of the last campaign is also to be a particular object of your attention. You are to endeavour immediately to get these discharged, or a proper security given for the payment on a future day [1].'

On the 1st March, 1773, the Bengal Government sent a report of all their proceedings to the Court of Directors. In it the objects were explained for undertaking the proposed operations in Rohilkhand.

'Our reasons,' it was said, 'are obvious. By allowing the Marathas to get a footing there, the frontier of the Vizier's dominions on that side having no natural boundary or defence would be continually exposed to their incursions, as by excluding them from that space we form a complete field of operations, with the river for a barrier, difficult at all times for an enemy to pass, and dangerous to them in their retreat. To have remained idle spectators while the Marathas were invading the dominions of the powers with whom we were most intimately connected, would have made them look upon us as weak and inactive, and consequently a fit subject of their attempts, but to show ourselves active and steady in support of our friends must impress them with an idea of our strength and vigour, and destroy any hopes they might entertain of prevailing against us in our own territories. We look, therefore, on our present measures as the best means to prevent a general rupture with them; at all events as we can never be absolutely assured against the enterprises of so capricious a people, if we have a war with them it is better to meet them beyond the line of your own frontiers, supporting the Vizier, our best barrier, our expenses paid, and in a manner defending ourselves, rather than to confine ourselves to our own possessions and our own resources [2].'

It was explained soon afterwards to the Court of Directors that there was no apprehension that the Vizier would object to the charges which it had been proposed that he should bear, and, it was added:—

'We hope you will approve the vigour which we have observed on this occasion. We are sorry to say that although we have been compelled by indispensable measures to become parties in these political contests, we scarce see a possible advantage which can compensate the hazard and expense which you must incur by them. The sum stipulated by the Vizier, for the monthly payments of the extra charges of the brigade, although much exceeding what was formerly allowed

[1] Fifth Report, App. No. 18; Forrest's Selections, vol. i. p. 34.
[2] Fifth Report, App. No. 17.

for the like service, is both inadequate to its importance, and their pay still continues a drain on your own provinces. Added to these considerations, the stipulated payments, scanty as they are, have been so tardily made, that we have been always compelled to make remittances for them, and have been subjected to other obvious inconveniences on this account. It is therefore to put an end to this practice, and to establish a rule of punctuality in the future payments to be made for the assistance afforded by our army, that we have been thus peremptory [1].'

Shuja-ud-daula made no objection to the conditions proposed to him, and Sir Robert Barker, with a brigade consisting of two battalions of European Infantry, six battalions of sepoys, and a company of Artillery, marched to join the Vizier's army. Shuja-ud-daula wrote to assure Hafiz Rahmat that he and the English would soon arrive to assist the Rohillas against the Marathas, in fulfilment of the treaty of the preceding year, and invited him to be ready to co-operate actively in the common cause. The combined forces advanced rapidly through Oudh, and early in March 1773, they entered Rohilkhand, and moved towards Ramghat, where the main body of the Marathas, which had not advanced far beyond the Ganges, was still encamped.

The attitude of Hafiz Rahmat and the Rohillas remained in the highest degree doubtful, and it is clear that they were strongly inclined to follow the advice of Zabita Khan and abandon the alliance with the Vizier. The following account is given by Hamilton of their proceedings at this time:—

'Hafiz Rahmat unwilling, however able he might be, to take upon himself the entire fulfilment of the engagement which he had entered into with Shuja-ud-daula the preceding year, was desirous, if he could not altogether evade it, at all events to bear as little as possible of the burden; and he had already applied to the other chiefs, endeavouring to convince them of the necessity of their assisting him in the discharge of the obligation which had been agreed to by him for their common benefit. His remonstrances, however, were attended with no effect. Some declared that he had no right to bind them to such

[1] Letter to Court of Directors, March 31, 1773, MS. Records, India Office.

a condition, whilst the majority ridiculed the idea of any treaty whatever being held obligatory upon the contracting parties, where it could either be infringed with benefit, or broken without danger. Many indeed were not without a suspicion that if Hafiz Rahmat should obtain their subsidies in this behalf, he would convert the money to his own use, and still endeavour to break his contract with the Vizier, so that they would remain as liable to be involved in a quarrel with that power on this account as ever; and they unanimously advised Hafiz Rahmat, in case he should be again pressed by the Vizier, on various pretences to amuse him with delusive hopes, and to trust to future events to extricate him, without expense, from his obligation. Hafiz did, in effect, adopt this last plan, which was much more consonant to his own ideas of political management than any other, and determined, in case the Marathas should attempt a second irruption into Rohilkhand, to avoid soliciting the aid of his former protectors, an interview with whom would inevitably lead to demands which he was now resolved not to comply with [1].'

According to Hamilton, Hafiz Rahmat had at one time thought that the Rohillas might themselves be able to defend the fords on the Ganges, and thus avoid the necessity of requiring help from the Vizier; but when this hope had to be abandoned in consequence of the passage of the river by the Marathas at Ramghat, he resolved to enter into an alliance with them. 'All these schemes were frustrated by the rapid and unwished for advance of the allied army, and Hafiz Rahmat found himself, by his own crooked and temporizing policy, entangled in a labyrinth of perplexity and distress [2].'

Little is known regarding the negotiations between Hafiz Rahmat and the Marathas, but Sir Robert Barker believed that an actual treaty had been entered into, under which in return for an engagement on the part of the Marathas that they would protect the Rohilla territories, Hafiz Rahmat agreed to pay to them a sum of money and allow them to pass through Rohilkhand into Oudh. 'It is certain,' Sir Robert Barker wrote, in a private letter to Hastings, 'that the Rohillas have engaged in a double agreement, promising to the Marathas by a treaty written on the Koran to pay them forty-five lakhs

[1] Hamilton, p. 190. [2] Hamilton, p. 193.

of rupees, and have actually advanced five lakhs in part payment [1].'

The Vizier afterwards referred to the same subject in a paper which he gave to Hastings:—'Hafiz Rahmat Khan sent the holy Koran, which contains the religion of the Mussulmans, to the Marathas, as a token of his friendship. He also gave them five lakhs of rupees, and established a friendship and good understanding with them. The whole world are well acquainted that envoys of Hafiz Rahmat were with the Marathas, and treated with them in the above manner [2].'

The fact of his negotiations was indeed so notorious that Hafiz Rahmat himself did not deny it, although he excused himself on the plea that he acted under compulsion.

'The Marathas requested,' he said in a letter to Hastings, 'with many inducements that I would let them pass through my territories, assuring me that they would commit no depredation or ravages on the ryots, and they would pass through with expedition to the Soubah of Oudh, or withersoever they thought proper; they also agreed to remit to me a large sum on account of the stipulation, and to do whatever was agreeable and would give satisfaction to the Rohilla Sirdars [3].'

The position of affairs was described by Sir Robert Barker, on the 6th March, in a letter to the Bengal Government. The Marathas, he said, remained inactive at Ramghat; they had sent Zabita Khan to Hafiz Rahmat with hopes of persuading him to join them; they were threatening the Afghan chief of Farukhabad; they had sent an envoy informing the Vizier of their intention of taking possession of Kora and Allahabad, and desiring him to remove any troops that he might have in those

[1] Letter dated May 10, 1773, British Museum MSS. 29,1339. In an official letter, written on the same day, Sir R. Barker said that the sum to be paid by the Rohillas was thirty-five lakhs. In the private letter above quoted he says that this was a mistake, and that the sum was forty-five lakhs.

[2] App. to Fifth Report, No. 19; Forrest's Selections, vol. i. p. 61.

[3] App. to Fifth Report, No. 19; Forrest's Selections, vol. i. p. 60. The letter of Hafiz Rahmat, and the Vizier's narrative, written in reply, are given *in extenso* in Appendix C.

districts. A few days later, on the 10th March, Sir Robert Barker, in a private letter to Hastings, wrote as follows:—

'The Marathas are at Ramghat, where they are threatening Hafiz Rahmat with fire and sword if he does not immediately join them with money and troops. Zabita Khan has been deputed to Bareilly to induce Hafiz to cross the river; in consequence of this, Hafiz has actually marched to Aonla, the place of rendezvous for the Rohilla forces, yet it is supposed he is only making these appearances to assure the Marathas, and means not to declare either for them or the Vizier, but play the same game over again as he did last year, that is, treat with both parties and adhere to neither. Affairs are in a state of very great suspense. The Marathas, from the motions we have made, will not venture to cross the river, Hafiz will continue his double dealings, and here we shall remain at a very heavy expense watching each other's motions until the rains set in[1].'

In this last remark Sir Robert Barker was referring to the instructions by which he was prohibited from crossing the Ganges to attack the Marathas, and which, in his opinion, prevented him from inflicting on the enemy a defeat that would have been fatal to all their chances of success. He added, in the same letter, that he was satisfied that but for the presence of his troops 'the Marathas would undoubtedly have crossed the Ganges, joined the Rohillas, and ravaged the Vizier's dominions[1].'

As the Vizier and the English advanced, no communications were received from Hafiz Rahmat. On the 14th March the English troops were about thirty-five miles from Ramghat, while the Rohillas were marching towards the Ganges, with the apparent intention of joining the Marathas before the Vizier and the English arrived. On the 16th March Sir Robert Barker believed that this intention would be carried out, and in a private letter to Hastings he wrote that the Vizier, enraged at the perfidy

[1] Brit. Museum MSS. 29,133. See also Letter to Court of Directors, March 31, 1773, Fifth Report, App. No. 18, par. 6:—'In the General's subsequent advices he gives us information that the good effects of the step he has taken were already apparent, as it had prevented the Marathas crossing the river, forming a junction with the Rohillas, and laying waste the Vizier's country.'

of the Rohillas, had reverted to the opinion that they ought to be expelled from Rohilkhand and the country be united to his own dominions. The Vizier desired him to inform Hastings that if the English would enable him to execute this project, he would pay to the Company fifty lakhs of rupees; that he would give his assistance in making over to the Emperor the districts of the Doáb, then in possession of the Marathas; that he would induce the Emperor to resign his claim to the tribute paid from the revenues of Bengal, Behar, and Orissa, and acknowledge those provinces to be the property of the Company; and that if the districts of Kora and Allahabad were transferred to him, he would give to the English in exchange all his own territory lying to the south of the Ganges, excepting Benares.

> 'These, sir' [Sir Robert Barker wrote], 'are proposals of the highest importance, but a matter which I could not introduce in a public letter. I shall, however, address to you a public letter which you may either produce before the Board or not, and His Excellency will also write, since the opportunity is critical and short, the season far advanced, and the return of letters tedious. The Nabob wishes also that in case any of these proposals take place, since they in some measure occasion a revolution, to have the ratification performed in your presence at Benares, which may be done in the rains when the operations of the campaign are over. Excuse my writing in a hurry and the roughness of the sketch, since it is only the outline of a plan that will admit of much contemplation [1].'

This was the first serious suggestion by the Vizier of the annexation of Rohilkhand to his own territories. Hastings sent no immediate answer to Sir Robert Barker's letter, which reached him about the 1st April. Probably he did not think it desirable to discuss the proposal until further information had been received, but on the 3rd April he referred to the subject in a private letter to Sir George Colebrooke in England. 'The Vizier,' he wrote, 'has fixed his ambition on the Rohilla country which adjoins his, and is included by the Ganges and the

[1] Private letter from Sir R. Barker, 16 March, 1773, British Museum MSS. 29,133.

mountains of Tartary, and has made tempting offers for our assistance in conquering it for him. It would be a complete addition to his dominions, and the hostile part which the Rohillas have taken against him would justify the measure. It is but newly suggested, and I can say no more upon the expediency or probability of its taking place[1].'

On the 20th March the English troops were close to Ramghat. The main body of the Marathas was on the opposite bank of the Ganges, but a considerable force had suddenly crossed the river and marched towards the camp of Hafiz Rahmat, which was only a few miles distant. He, Sir Robert Barker wrote, 'had been carrying on the same double dealings as heretofore practised by that treacherous sect,' and the Marathas, in the hope of forcing him to come to an immediate decision, resolved to surprise him, if possible, by a sudden attack. To carry out their project it was first necessary to make themselves masters of a small fort occupied by the Rohillas. This was attacked by the Marathas, and the Rohillas, having expended their ammunition, surrendered. By this time, however, the English troops were so near that the Marathas did not venture to continue their expedition, and they retreated rapidly to the Ganges. The Maratha forces were now posted on both sides of the river, which was easily fordable. Sir Robert Barker hoped to bring on an engagement, but the Marathas contented themselves with cannonading the English camp from the high ground on the opposite bank of the Ganges, and Sir Robert Barker, not being allowed to cross the river, could find no opportunity of attacking them.

It now became clear that the Marathas had no inclination of risking an encounter with the English, and on the 21st March Hafiz Rahmat, seeing that further hesitation was impossible, declared to the Vizier that he was ready to carry out his former engagements. It was then deter-

[1] British Museum MSS. 29,127. This letter is printed in Gleig's 'Warren Hastings,' vol. i. p. 310.

mined to make an immediate attack on the Marathas with the whole of the allied forces. The Vizier and the Rohillas were to operate on the left bank of the Ganges, while Sir Robert Barker, who had resolved to disregard the orders that he had received, was to cross the river and attack the enemy on the other side. The English at once proceeded to carry out their part of the plan, and on the 22nd March they crossed the Ganges without opposition, and, as the depth of water nowhere exceeded three and a half feet, without difficulty. The Marathas immediately broke up their encampment, retreated rapidly, and did not halt until they had put a distance of more than twenty miles between themselves and the English. Their forces consisting almost entirely of cavalry, and ours of infantry, no pursuit was possible, and on the 23rd March Sir Robert Barker recrossed the river into Rohilkhand. The combined movement that was to have been made by the Vizier and the Rohillas had not taken place, for the Vizier continued to be suspicious of treachery on the part of Hafiz Rahmat, and he did not venture to attack the Marathas while he believed that at any moment the Rohillas might go over to the enemy.

On the return of Sir Robert Barker, the Vizier and Hafiz Rahmat went to his camp, and a conference was held, at which the English General did everything in his power to bring about a satisfactory agreement. Hafiz Rahmat promised to lose no time in paying the instalments due under the treaty of the preceding year, and the Vizier, who, in Sir Robert Barker's words, was 'a good deal assuaged by the coming in of Hafiz,' agreed to renew the alliance on the former conditions. He at the same time told Sir Robert Barker that when he had received the stipulated payment of forty lakhs of rupees, he would pay one half of the amount to the Company. This promise seems to have been made without any demand on the part of the English, but the Vizier probably anticipated that some such question would be raised, because it was well known that the payments made by him towards the expenses of the English troops had fallen far short of the actual charge. He was doubtless at the same time anxious to produce, by this show of liberality, a favourable impression on the English authorities when they had to consider the proposals which he intended immediately to make, to meet the case of a failure on the part of the Rohillas to carry out their engagements. This was a contingency which, after all that had occurred, could not be left out of consideration.

On the 24th March Sir Robert Barker referred to this subject for the first time in his official correspondence. 'In default,' he wrote, 'of the fulfilling of this agreement by the Rohillas, His Excellency agrees to pay the sum of fifty lakhs of rupees to the Company, for their aid in putting him in possession of the Rohilla districts, commonly known as the territories of Hafiz Rahmat[1].' On the same day the Vizier himself wrote to Hastings:—

'I have promised the General that whenever we shall drive the Marathas out of the Rohilla country, and Hafiz Rahmat Khan shall fulfil his agreement by the payment of forty lakhs of rupees, I will give half that sum to the English Sirdars. Should the Rohilla Sirdars be guilty of a breach of their agreement, and the English gentlemen will thoroughly exterminate them and settle me in their country, I will in that case pay them fifty lakhs of rupees in ready money, and besides exempt them from paying any tribute to the King out of the Bengal revenues[2].'

An answer was sent to Sir Robert Barker's letter by the Bengal Government on the 15th April. He was censured for having disobeyed the orders under which he had been forbidden to cross the Ganges, and was again told that the main object of his operations was the defence of the Vizier's dominions, which were exposed to the danger of invasion if the Marathas were allowed to occupy Rohilkhand; the measures taken by him for the protection of Rohilkhand, and the Vizier's proposal to pay to the Company one-half of the sum due to him by the Rohillas were approved, but the Government declined to

[1] Fifth Report, App. No. 18.

[2] Fifth Report, App. No. 21.

commit itself to any opinion in regard to the course to be followed in the event of Hafiz Rahmat refusing to carry out his engagements. It was admitted that the plan suggested by the Vizier would be highly advantageous to him, by extending his dominions, making them more easily defensible against the Marathas, and freeing him from troublesome neighbours, but even, it was said, if we should become justified by the treachery of the Rohillas in assisting the Vizier to carry such a plan into effect, 'we can never consent to engage in it without such previous conditions as shall secure to the Company an equivalent for so important a service rendered to our ally. And here we cannot avoid expressing our regret that in the whole course of our alliance and operations with the Vizier, this necessary and equitable precaution has never yet been sufficiently attended to, but every measure we have adopted in conjunction with him appears to have been calculated for his particular advantage.' In the case therefore of the Rohillas failing to observe the conditions of the treaty, Sir Robert Barker was forbidden to undertake any hostile operations against them without further instructions[1].

A reply was sent by Hastings to the Vizier's letter on the 22nd April. It led to important consequences, but it will be convenient to refer to it separately, instead of interrupting the narrative of the events in progress in Rohilkhand.

At the interview between Sir Robert Barker, the Vizier, and Hafiz Rahmat, it was agreed that an immediate

[1] Fifth Report, App. No. 18. In a private letter to Sir Robert Barker, dated April 20, Hastings referred to the Vizier's proposal. He said that according to the latest information which he had received, an arrangement had been entered into between Hafiz Rahmat and the Vizier, and that 'this seemed to overset the principle on which the plan was grounded. Nevertheless it is worth consideration, and I shall be glad if it can be carried into execution on grounds of public justice, and on conditions which will make the Company amends and satisfy them for the employment of their army at so great a distance from their own possessions. The present time is not, I conceive, necessary for the execution of such an enterprise.' British Museum MSS. 29,117.

advance should be made by their combined forces against the Marathas who had still a large force on the banks of the Ganges. They were in possession of Sambhal and other places near the river, and they had constructed a bridge of boats at Púth, in the Moradabad district. Hoping to seize the families of Hafiz Rahmat and other chiefs, the Marathas resolved to make a sudden raid upon Bisauli, a place about thirty miles distant from their camp. Sir Robert Barker hearing of this intention, marched hastily to intercept them; they abandoned their design, levying a contribution from the town of Moradabad as they passed. They were rapidly followed by the English, and on the 28th March the whole of the Maratha forces precipitately retreated across the Ganges, destroying the bridge, and leaving behind them much of their baggage. Rohilkhand was now entirely freed from the invaders, and Sir Robert Barker reported to Hastings his belief that there was no probability of their return. This anticipation was fulfilled more completely than the English General anticipated, for neither in that nor in any future year did the Marathas renew their attacks on Rohilkhand [1].

During the following month the Marathas made, from time to time, threatening movements as if they again proposed to cross the Ganges. They still declared their intention of taking possession of Kora and Allahabad, and forced Najf Khan to write to Sir Robert Barker, summoning the English, in the name of the Emperor, to surrender those provinces, and informing him that peace depended on obedience to these orders. Sir Robert Barker's reply was very plain-spoken:—

'The intentions and sentiments of the Marathas,' he wrote, 'are clearly comprehended. You will now openly declare to the Maratha chiefs that the English Sirdars formerly made a present of these provinces to the King for his expenses only, and consequently will not on any account whatever give up their pretensions to them. It is therefore necessary that the Maratha Sirdars, if they are desirous

[1] British Museum MSS., Private letter from Sir R. Barker to Hastings; and Fifth Report, App. Nos. 18 and 21.

of peace, desist from their demands for Kora and Karra, and also leave the regulation of the empire to the King and to the Vizier, being a matter with which the Maratha Sirdars have no kind of concern and that they themselves return to the Deccan. The English Sirdars are not desirous of molesting any without cause, but if this should not be agreeable to the Maratha Sirdars, with the assistance of the Almighty it is certain that they shall not carry back with them that power, wealth, honour, or the name which they have acquired[1].'

This letter, Sir Robert Barker afterwards heard, 'had astonished the Maratha Sirdars a good deal.'

After the retreat of the Marathas, Hafiz Rahmat remained in the neighbourhood of Púth, guarding the fords across the Ganges, and acting under the advice of Sir Robert Barker, the Vizier did not press the Rohillas for the payment of their debt. It was feared that any such immediate demand might have the effect of making them again think of joining the Marathas. Sir Robert Barker was extremely angry that he was still forbidden to cross the Ganges, and attack the Marathas in the rear. The time, however, at which such an operation might have been desirable from a military point of view, soon, in Sir Robert Barker's own opinion, passed away, for towards the end of April the Ganges had become unfordable owing to the melting of the snow in the mountains. The same cause put an end to all immediate danger of the return of the Marathas. They withdrew from the right bank of the river, and marched towards the Jumna. In May internal revolutions and contests of the Maratha chiefs in the Deccan led to the recall of their armies from Northern India, and they went home, leaving small garrisons at Etawa, and at some other places in the Doáb. These dissensions were fortunate for the English and for the Vizier. The Maratha power which had boasted a revenue of £10,000,000 sterling, and an army of which the cavalry alone exceeded 100,000 men, was divided among contending chiefs.

On the final departure of the Marathas the Vizier, whose expenses had been great, began to demand payment of the sums due by the Rohillas. Sir Robert Barker urged

[1] British Museum MSS. 29,134.

upon Hafiz Rahmat the necessity of fulfilling his engagements, seeing that the conditions of the treaty had been, with the help of the English, carried out by the Vizier. Not only had the Marathas been expelled from Rohilkhand, but, excepting to a small extent near the Ganges, the country had been protected from devastation. Hafiz Rahmat admitted the liability, but nothing could be got from him except general professions and excuses for delay. Sir Robert Barker believed that the Rohillas had satisfied themselves that the Vizier and the English considered the maintenance of their power necessary to the security of Oudh, and that it was improbable that hostile measures would be taken against them. In his opinion there was only one means by which they could be induced to carry out their engagements:—it was to inform them that in the event of their failure to discharge their obligations to the Vizier, the English would assist him in expelling them from Rohilkhand. But the orders that he had received made this impossible. They 'deprived him,' he wrote, 'of the only means of enforcing payment, namely, that of frightening the Rohillas to performance of their treaty; it is well known that neither promises nor oaths have been able to bind this treacherous sect of people to their engagements; their own interests or their own fears are the only springs by which they can be moved [1].'

On the 12th May, as there was no reason for remaining longer in Rohilkhand, the Viziers' army began its march towards Oudh. On the following day Sir Robert Barker reported that 'Hafiz Rahmat declines answering the payment of the treaty until he can consult the other Rohilla Sirdars who are to bear a proportion of it, but it appears more to delay time, that he may discover how the affairs of this quarter are likely to turn out. . . I beg leave to send you the copy of the Rohilla treaty, by which you will perceive how literally it has been executed and per-

[1] Letter from Sir R. Barker, May 6, 1773, Fifth Report, App. No. 18.

formed, notwithstanding the evasion of their chiefs[1].' A week later Sir Robert Barker wrote again that all attempts to obtain a satisfactory reply from Hafiz Rahmat having failed, the Vizier had started for Lucknow, and that he was following with the English brigade.

[1] Fifth Report, App. No. 21.

CHAPTER VIII.

A. D. 1773. THE CONFERENCE AT BENARES BETWEEN HASTINGS AND THE VIZIER.—THE TREATY OF BENARES.

Views of Hastings regarding protection of Oudh against the Marathas.—His letter to the Vizier proposing conference.—Failure of Hafiz Rahmat to carry out his engagements.—Hastings goes to Benares.—Urgent questions to be settled.—Instructions from the Council.—Payment for troops employed in the Vizier's service.—Cession of Kora and Allahabad to the Vizier.—Treaty with the Vizier.—Letter from the Emperor.—Reply of Hastings.—The charge against Hastings of despoiling the Emperor.—Mill on the treaty with the Vizier.—Reasons given by Hastings.—The propriety of his action.—Macaulay's description.

SIR Robert Barker, during the two campaigns in Rohilkhand, had steadily adhered to the policy of maintaining, if it were possible, the power of the Rohillas, and Hastings had supported his efforts in that direction. But Hastings never doubted that the only effectual means by which complete security against the Marathas could be obtained for Oudh and for the British provinces, was by giving to the dominions of the Vizier their natural boundaries, and including within one ring-fence the whole of Rohilkhand and Oudh. It has been shown that he held this opinion before he became Governor, and everything that had since happened had tended to confirm it. He thoroughly understood the position of the Rohillas; he knew how the power of these foreign soldiers had been, not many years before, established in Rohilkhand, and how it had been maintained, and that, apart from questions of political expediency, it deserved no consideration. He knew also that the notorious perfidy of the Rohillas made it dangerous to allow any important interests to depend upon them. When he received the Vizier's letter, to which reference was made in the last chapter, it had already become probable that the Rohillas would fail to carry out the conditions of the treaty, and in that case it was certain that the question of the necessity of annexing Rohilkhand to the Vizier's dominions would have to be seriously considered. Hastings was not prepared, however, to discuss this subject until all doubt regarding the action which the Rohillas intended to take had been removed. The questions connected with the provinces of Kora and Allahabad, which had been given by the Emperor to the Marathas, were more immediately pressing, and there were other matters regarding which Hastings had long been anxious.

The letter written by him in the preceding year to Sir George Colebrooke, which has already been quoted [1], shows how strongly he held the opinion that the terms of the alliance with Shuja-ud-daula had been extremely onerous to the English, and involved financial burdens which it was neither expedient nor just that they should bear. No opportunity could be more favourable than the present for re-opening this question, and on the 22nd April, 1773, the following letter was sent by Hastings to the Vizier:—

'I have received your Excellency's letter, mentioning the particulars of your operations against the Marathas, your promise to the General that "whenever the Marathas shall be driven out of the Rohilla country, and Hafiz Rahmat Khan shall fulfil his agreements by the payment of the forty lakhs of rupees, you will give half that sum to the Company, and that should the Rohilla chiefs be guilty of a breach of their agreement, we will thoroughly exterminate them and settle your Excellency in the country; you will in that case pay them fifty lakhs of rupees, ready money, and exempt the Company from the King's tribute." Upon the same subject the General has also written to me very fully. Every circumstance you have written to me I consider as a proof of the cordial attachment which subsists between us, and of the confidence and reliance which you place in the friendship of the English Company, but the points which you have proposed require much consideration, and the previous ratification of a formal agreement before I can consent to them; otherwise I may incur the displeasure of my employers. It is true that I have long thought the junction of the Rohilla country with yours, either by a sure and permanent obligation of friendship, or

[1] See p. 61.

by reducing them to obedience if they should render such an attempt justifiable by any act of enmity or treachery, would be an advisable point for you to attain, because by that means the defensive line of your dominions would be completed by including within it all the land lying on that side the river Ganges, and you will be in no danger from an attack on that quarter, whenever the Marathas shall commit disturbances in another. But it appears to me that this is an object not to be attained by an occasional visit of that country; and its distance from the province of Bengal will not admit of the continuance of the English forces longer than the period which remains of the dry weather. You will please to remember they were sent for your assistance, and to defend the province of Kora against the Marathas; thus far only I am authorised by the commands of my superiors to employ them beyond the limits of their own possessions, and even this is the cause of a heavy loss and risk to their affairs, especially in the expenses of their troops and stores, and in the absence of so great a part of their force, which was originally destined for the sole defence of the countries dependant on Bengal. You have frequently repeated in your letters the remark, that to wait till the enemy was at your door, and then to write for the assistance of our forces would answer no good purpose, but that every year the same cause would require their return to the same service, and pass without effecting any purpose to real advantage. My friend, all this is true; but it proceeds from the want of proper measures having been taken, and from the imperfect footing on which affairs between us have been established. The concern which the Company take in your safety, and the duties of friendship which their commands and our own inclinations equally enjoin us to observe inviolably to their allies, and especially to one so closely united to them by an approved attachment, would not suffer us to withhold our aid when your affairs required it; but it has always been with reluctance that we have suffered the army to pass the frontiers of our own country, because the loss and inconvenience attending it was certain; and although, joined with your forces, there is no cause to fear the most powerful efforts of our enemies, yet the events of war are at the disposal of the Almighty, and the only fruits which the most splendid successes can afford us, are the reputation of having maintained the faith of our alliance in opposition to every incentive of self-interest and self-defence; thus circumstanced, we are precluded from deriving any benefit from your support, and ours can only afford you a relief from present danger without any provision for future security. For these reasons I have often wished for a personal interview with you, for the purpose of removing difficulties and of perpetuating the alliance with your Excellency on terms more suitable to our mutual interests. Your Excellency hath also repeatedly expressed the same inclination. I therefore write, that if your affairs will at this season admit of your giving me a meeting, I will hasten to obtain it as soon as I am able after the receipt of your letter in reply to this; if otherwise, I must wait for it at some more distant period, as the affairs of this Government will indispensably require my presence at this place after three or four months, and it is uncertain when I shall again have an interval of leisure for such a journey. In the meantime as your Excellency and the General are at a great distance from the province of Kora, and the affairs of that province require the presence of a person on behalf of the Company, to regulate and take charge of it, until it shall be determined in what manner it shall after be disposed of, I have judged it advisable to depute Mr. James Lawrell, a gentleman of the Council of Calcutta, on this service, and he will set out accordingly in a few days; which I hope you will approve [1].'

All attempts to induce Hafiz Rahmat to carry out his engagements having failed, the Vizier, after his return to Oudh in May 1773, replied to the letter which he had received from Hastings, and expressed in strong terms his anxiety that the proposed interview should take place as soon as possible [2]. Towards the end of June the necessary arrangements were made; in July Hastings left Calcutta, and on the 19th August he met the Vizier at Benares. He was accompanied by Vansittart and Lambert, two members of the Council; Sir Robert Barker, the Commander-in-Chief, was also at Benares during the conference.

It was now certain that the Rohillas had no intention of carrying out the conditions of the treaty. Before, however, describing the negotiations that took place in regard to

[1] Fifth Report, App. No. 21.

[2] 'Hafiz Rahmat, having for some time acted a very double part, at last joined the army and continued his promises of fulfilling the treaty, but protracted the time until the Marathas had retired, and the troops were in consequence recalled. Being then relieved from the apprehension of present danger, he declined paying up the stipulated sum, on pretexts of inability, and that it was necessary first to consult the other Rohilla chiefs. The Vizier, highly exasperated at this conduct of the Rohilla, proposed immediately to compel him into a compliance with his engagements by marching into his country, or in case of his refusal, to reduce it and unite it to his own. For this purpose he applied to your Administration for their aid and concurrence. . . . While these important matters were under consideration, the Vizier frequently expressed an earnest desire of a personal interview with our President, and this measure appearing the most effectual means of bringing them to a conclusion and of strengthening that friendship in which the Company are united with the Vizier, we recommended it to the Council and it was carried into execution.' Letter from Select Committee to Court of Directors, October 11, 1774. India Office Records.

Rohilkhand, it will be convenient to refer to the questions relating to the provinces of Kora and Allahabad, and to the settlement of the terms on which military assistance would in future be given to the Vizier.

Nearly one-third of the whole military expenditure in Bengal was at this time incurred for troops maintained for the purpose of strengthening the Vizier rather than for service in our own provinces. The Vizier had agreed to pay on this account 115,000 rupees a month, but it was an admitted fact, and a cause of constant complaint, that this sum was altogether insufficient to meet the actual charges. In March 1773, the Bengal Government wrote to the Court of Directors that

> 'The sum stipulated by the Vizier for the monthly payment of the extra charges of the brigade, although much exceeding what was formerly allowed for the like service, is both inadequate to its importance, and their pay still continues a drain to your own provinces. Added to these considerations, the stipulated payments, scanty as they are, have been so tardily made, that we have been always compelled to make remittances for them, and we have been subjected to other obvious inconveniences on this account.'

In a subsequent letter the Government wrote to the same effect:—

> 'The alarm of an invasion of the Marathas had for three successive seasons occasioned the march of one of the brigades, at the requisition and for the assistance of the Vizier, but the sum stipulated as an indemnification for this extraordinary expense, being not only greatly inadequate to the actual amount, but often irregularly paid, the Company was subjected to a heavy charge, their military strength greatly weakened, and the wealth of the country was exported in the pay of the troops. Under such circumstances, the friendship of Shuja-ud-dowla grew to be a burden to the Company, and it was evident that an union subsisting on terms so unequal could neither be cordial nor lasting. It became therefore necessary to provide some remedy for this defect in our alliance [1].'

There can be no doubt that all this was true. It was politically important to the English that the power of the Vizier should be supported, but to him their support

[1] Letter to Court of Directors, October 11, 1774. India Office Records.

was more important still, and it was not reasonable that serious burdens should be placed on our own people for a purpose from which he derived the chief benefit. Referring to this subject, and to his visit to Benares, Hastings wrote afterwards to the Court of Directors, 'The Board judged with me that it might afford a fair occasion to urge the improvement of our alliance, by obtaining the Vizier's consent to a more equitable compensation for the expense attending the aid which he occasionally received from our forces.' He was the more anxious to arrive at a satisfactory arrangement because the Company was at this time, both in India and in England, in a condition not far removed from bankruptcy. When he left Calcutta there were less than fifty thousand rupees in the treasury, a debt of a million and a half sterling had been incurred, the Government had vainly attempted to borrow more, and the Directors at home were urgent in their demands for remittances.

Before starting for Benares, Hastings had received from the Council full authority to enter into any arrangements which he thought desirable, and written instructions, no doubt drafted by himself, were given to him, describing in general terms the objects of his mission. It was said that the treaties subsisting between the Company and the Vizier had been 'settled upon an unequal footing. We are called on every occasion to his assistance, without any immediate advantage to our employers, or even any regular or adequate adjustment of the stipulation in the treaty for the payment of our expenses. . . . It is therefore advisable to effect an alliance with him on grounds of reciprocal advantage and support.' It was thought reasonable that when our troops were employed, as had often been the case, for the benefit of the Vizier beyond the limits of our territories, the whole expenses should be borne by him, but this, it was added, 'can only be effected by your address and judicious management, as the engagements now subsisting between us, from which we mean not to depart, do not entitle us to claim it as a right.' The manner in which the questions relating to Kora and Allahabad were to be settled was left to Hastings to decide. If the Emperor should desire to renew his former connection with the Company, these provinces might be restored to him on condition of his renouncing all claim to the future payment of tribute from Bengal; in this case it was suggested that he might entrust the administration of his affairs to the Vizier, and live at Allahabad or elsewhere within the Vizier's territories, 'in a state more suited to the moderate compass of his genius, and the reduced influence of his family.' If, however, no such arrangement could be made with the Emperor, it would be held that Kora and Allahabad had reverted to the Company as the original proprietors. As it would be unwise to retain in our own hands the administration of provinces entirely separated from the rest of our territories, the best course, if the Vizier were willing to agree to it, would be to make over Kora and Allahabad to him, receiving in exchange the districts of Chunar and Ghazipur situated on our existing frontier. 'A free intercourse of commerce' between the Company's and the Vizier's dominions ought, it was said, to be provided for, and reference was made to some other matters of minor importance. With regard to Rohilkhand, the instructions were as follows:—'We have found it necessary this season, for the more effectual protection of the Vizier's dominions, to extend our operations to the country of the Rohillas, on the north of the Ganges. We approve of your concerting with the Vizier any plan which may be necessary for his future security on that side, consistently with the spirit of the Company's orders[1].'

When Hastings reached Benares he at once commenced his negociations with the Vizier. They were conducted by Hastings personally; his knowledge of the native language was so good that the assistance of an interpreter was not wanted, and no one was present at the

[1] Instructions to the Governor, June 23, 1773, Fifth Report, App. No. 13.

conferences except Hastings, the Vizier and his Minister; consequently everything that is known regarding them is derived from the accounts given by Hastings himself[1].

Sir Robert Barker was asked to supply an estimate of the actual cost of a brigade of troops when employed in the service of the Vizier beyond our own frontiers. He estimated it at 210,000 rupees a month, and the Vizier agreed to the proposal that the charge should be fixed at this amount, instead of 115,000 rupees which he had hitherto been paying.

As there was little doubt that the brigade would usually be quartered in the Vizier's territories, it was considered that the practical result of this agreement would be that the Company would be relieved from the charge of its maintenance. As a fact, however, even this increased sum proved insufficient to cover the actual expenses incurred.

When these conditions had been accepted by the Vizier, Hastings was ready to discuss other questions.

It has been related that, in February 1773, temporary arrangements had been made for the charge of the provinces of Kora and Allahabad, and, towards the end of April, a member of the Council, James Lawrell, was deputed 'to take possession of them on behalf of the Company, both for securing the Company's rights, and as a preparatory step to any exchange of those districts, or other mode of cession which may be resolved on;' he was to receive charge from Sir Robert Barker, and he was invested with full powers of control over their administration[2].

Although, as Hastings said, these provinces had been resumed 'not from the King, whose property and right were annulled by his own alienation of them, but from the Marathas their new proprietors,' he thought it proper to

[1] 'Fortunately the habit which I had acquired of speaking the Hindustani language, though imperfect, yet aided on the part of the Vizier by a very clear and easy elocution and an uncommonly quick apprehension, greatly facilitated this mode of communication, and not only forwarded the conclusion of our debates, but, I am persuaded, left him much better pleased with what had passed than if it had been conveyed to him through the doubtful channel of an interpreter.' Minute by Hastings, October 12, 1773.

[2] App. Fifth Report, No. 18.

invite the Emperor to send an envoy to Benares, vested with powers to treat upon the subject. The Emperor at first consented, but afterwards refused to take part in the conference. He referred Hastings to the Vizier, to whom he sent no instructions except that he was to demand payment of the arrears of the Bengal tribute, the regular payment of it in future, and the restitution of Kora and Allahabad.

The invitation to the Emperor was repeated, but no answer was received, and Hastings proceeded to treat with the Vizier.

The suggestion that the Company should receive the districts of Chunar and Ghazipur in exchange for Kora and Allahabad proved so distasteful to the Vizier that it was at once dropped, and Hastings, when he returned to Calcutta, said that he had not pressed it because he had no wish to obtain more territory, and that he thought it much wiser to obtain 'the means of relieving the distresses of the Company by an acquisition of ready money, rather than of embarrassing them by an extension of possession.' The Vizier was anxious to obtain Kora and Allahabad, not only on account of their actual value, but in order, as he said, 'that he might have the credit of re-possessing all the territory which he before enjoyed, and had inherited from his father.' There was in fact, in the opinion of Hastings, no other way of disposing of these districts even if we received nothing in return.

Subject to the stipulation to which I have already referred, that the terms on which the Vizier had hitherto received military assistance from the English should be revised, Hastings offered to cede to him Kora and Allahabad, on condition that he should pay forty-five lakhs of rupees in three instalments to the Company.

After much discussion, and many attempts to induce Hastings to accept a smaller sum, the Vizier agreed to the proposal, which was undoubtedly very advantageous to him[1]. The gross annual collections of revenue from the

[1] There is a full account of this discussion in the Diary noticed below.

two provinces were estimated at nearly thirty-five lakhs of rupees, which, when the Emperor was in possession, had been reduced by grants of jagirs and other alienations to twenty-eight and a half lakhs. According to Lawrell's estimate, the net annual receipts, after deducting all charges for protection and administration, exceeded twenty-two lakhs of rupees.

Before the treaty was executed, it was determined, as I shall presently explain, to postpone all hostile measures against the Rohillas, and, as this decision diminished the financial responsibilities of the Vizier, he agreed to pay fifty instead of forty-five lakhs of rupees on account of Kora and Allahabad.

A treaty was finally concluded on the 7th September, 1773, in the following terms:—

'The Vizier of the Empire, Asiph Jah Shuja-ul-Mulk, the Nabob Sujah-ul-Dowla, Aboo-ul-Munsoor Cawn Bahadur, Sifdar Jung Sippah Salah, on the one part, and Warren Hastings, Esq., President of the Council, Governor of Fort William, and Commander-in-Chief of the forces of the English Company, in the Provinces of Bengal, Behar, and Orissa, for and in the name of the English Company on the other part, do agree in the following articles:—

(1) Whereas in the treaty concluded at Allahabad, the 16th of August, 1765, between the Vizier and the Company, it is expressed that the districts of Kora and Allahabad were given to His Majesty for his expenses, and whereas His Majesty has abandoned the possession of the aforesaid districts, and even given a sunnud for Kora and Karra to the Marathas to the great prejudice of the interests both of the Vizier and the English Company, and contrary to the meaning of the said treaty, and hath thereby forfeited his right to the said district, which has reverted to the Company from whom he received it, it is therefore agreed that the aforesaid district shall be put into the possession of the Vizier on the following conditions; and that in the same manner as the province of Oudh and the other dominions of the Vizier are possessed by him, so shall he possess Kora and Karra and Allahabad for ever. He shall by no means and under no pretence be liable to any obstructions in the aforesaid countries from the Company and English chiefs, and exclusive of the money now stipulated, no mention or requisition shall by any means be made to him for anything else on this account. This agreement shall be observed by all the English chiefs, Gentlemen of the Council, and by the Company, nor shall it ever be broken or deviated from.

CONDITIONS.

He shall pay to the Company fifty lakhs (50,00,000) of sicca rupees according to the currency of the province of Oudh as follows, viz :—

		Rs.
In ready money		20,00,000
In two years after the date hereof, viz :—		
The first year	15,00,000	
The second year	15,00,000	
		30,00,000
Sicca Rupees		50,00,000

(2) To prevent any disputes arising concerning the payments which shall be made by the Vizier for the expenses of the Company's troops that may march to his assistance; it is agreed that the expenses of a brigade shall be computed at two lakhs ten thousand (2,10,000) sicca rupees per month, according to the currency of the province of Oudh. By a brigade is meant as follows, viz :—

Two battalions of Europeans,
Six battalions of Sepoys,
One company of Artillery.

The expenses of the said troops shall be defrayed by the Vizier from the time that they shall have passed the borders of his dominions till they return within the borders of the province of Behar, and exclusive of the above-mentioned sum no more shall on any account be demanded from him. Should the Company and the English chiefs have occasion to send for the troops of the Vizier, the Company and the English chiefs shall also pay their expenses in the like manner.

Signed, sealed, and solemnly sworn to by the contracting parties at Benares, this 7th day of September, in the year of our Lord 1773. In the presence of us—

JOHN STEWART.
WILLIAM REDFEARN.'

A statement was attached to the treaty showing the manner in which the monthly expenses of a brigade had been calculated, and giving in detail the charges for pay, batta, victualling, carriage and camp equipage, hospitals, and contingencies [1].

After this agreement with the Vizier had been concluded, a letter arrived from the Emperor. It invited Hastings to 'remit our tribute from Bengal, and give up Kora and Allahabad, which will give the utmost satisfaction to our sacred person.' The Emperor added a postscript in his

[1] Fifth Report, App. No. 19; Forrest's Selections, vol. i. p. 54.

tribute to His Majesty Shah Alum, we must declare that his own conduct has rendered that measure not only expedient but absolutely necessary. The junction of His Majesty with the Marathas, the defeat of his army by their troops, and the cession of the provinces assigned for his support, were circumstances so alarming that it became the indispensable duty of our President and Council to seize the opportunity which then offered for preventing those provinces from falling into the hands of the Marathas, who were not only become formidable to our ally, Shuja-ud-Dowla, but were evidently aspiring to universal conquest. Although the provinces of Kora and Allahabad were reserved to the King by the treaty of 1765, we can by no means allow that His Majesty acquired by this treaty a right to resign them into the hands of our enemies. As the Vizier of the Empire is the first officer under His Majesty, and as the territories in question were formerly held by the Vizier, we cannot but be of opinion that our servants acted with great propriety in committing them again to his management when it became absolutely impossible for His Majesty to hold them in his own immediate possession. And as the King had not only withdrawn himself from our protection and abandoned the countries assigned to him, but also continued, by his presence, to countenance the depredations of the Marathas, we fully approve the resolution of our President and Council under these circumstances, to suspend payment of the tribute to His Majesty; as we think the general principles of self-preservation warranted them to withhold resources which, if sent, they knew must fall into the hands of the Marathas, and which they had every reason to believe would be appropriated to the use of their army, and contribute towards enabling them to commit hostilities on our own provinces, or on those of our allies. For the above reasons, we, upon the maturest deliberation, confirm the treaty of Benares; and we also hereby direct that no further remittances be made to the King, without our express permission first obtained for the purpose."'

It is not necessary to say more upon this subject. It is clear that the whole arrangement regarding Kora and Allahabad was just and proper, and one which, under similar circumstances, the most scrupulous European Government would not, even at the present day, hesitate to adopt. Before leaving this subject, I will, however, refer briefly to Macaulay's description of these transactions.

'The Company had bound itself to pay near three hundred thousand pounds a year to the Great Mogul, as a mark of homage for the provinces which he had entrusted to their care; and they had ceded to him the districts of Kora and Allahabad. On the plea that the Mogul was not really independent, but merely a tool in the hands of others, Hastings determined to retract these concessions. He accordingly declared that the English would pay no more tribute, and sent troops to occupy Allahabad and Kora. The situation of these places was such, that there would be little advantage and great expense in retaining them. Hastings, who wanted money, and not territory, determined to sell them. A purchaser was not wanting . . . Shuja Dowla, then Nabob Vizier, was on excellent terms with the English. He had a large treasure. Allahabad and Kora were so situated that they might be of use to him and could be of none to the Company. The buyer and seller soon came to an understanding; and the provinces which had been torn from the Mogul were made over to the government of Oudh for about half a million sterling [1].'

Thus, according to Macaulay, whose account is obviously taken from Burke and Mill, the whole transaction was one of simple and unprovoked spoliation, undertaken by Hastings for the sole purpose of obtaining money. That the Emperor had deliberately, and in spite of our remonstrances, thrown himself into the hands of the Marathas; that he first abandoned and then ceded to the most dangerous of our enemies the provinces which we had given to him; that to have allowed those provinces to fall into the hands of the Marathas would have exposed the Vizier and ourselves to imminent peril; that to go on paying tribute to the Emperor would have been to pay it to the Marathas, and that he himself would not have received a farthing,—these, and indeed all the facts of the case are unnoticed. There is a fine ring in Macaulay's sentences, but they are not history.

[1] Macaulay's Essays: Warren Hastings.

CHAPTER IX.

A.D. 1773. THE CONFERENCE AT BENARES (*continued*). —NEGOTIATIONS REGARDING THE EXPULSION OF THE ROHILLAS FROM ROHILKHAND.

Draft of treaty for expulsion of the Rohillas.—The Vizier desires to postpone the expedition.—Hastings' private diary.—Reasons for postponing operations. —Hastings returns to Calcutta.—His report to the Council.—The Marathas in the Doáb.—The Vizier renews proposal for expulsion of the Rohillas.— Discussions in Council and reply to the Vizier.—Report to Court of Directors. —The Vizier declines the assistance of the English troops.

I PROPOSE to reserve for a later part of this work a more complete examination of the reasons which led Hastings to the conclusion that the expulsion of the Rohillas from Rohilkhand was necessary for the security of Oudh and of our own provinces. I shall now describe the negotiations which took place upon this subject between him and the Vizier. The conferences regarding Rohilkhand were carried on simultaneously with those described in the last chapter. The departure of the Marathas from Northern India, in consequence of the serious revolutions that had occurred in the Deccan, had rendered it certain that they could not renew their attacks, at the very earliest, before the close of the rainy season at the end of 1774. The settlement of the Rohilla question seemed, therefore, to Hastings less immediately pressing than it had been before, and as we shall see, there were other serious reasons which made him wish for delay. The Vizier, on the other hand, urged with undeniable truth that the success of the enterprise which he had proposed would be more easy and more certain if it were at once undertaken than if it were postponed. There could now, he said, be no interference on the part of the Marathas, who if they had been present in force might probably have re-entered Rohilkhand, knowing that the Rohillas would readily join them and accept any terms that might be offered. On the other hand, there were rumours that a fresh invasion of India from Afghanistan was impending, and the Vizier was doubtful whether this might not be a reason for delay. The result of the discussion was that Hastings, while he agreed with the Vizier that nothing short of the annexation of Rohilkhand to Oudh would afford permanent security against the Marathas, said that he would himself express no final opinion in regard to the measures to be immediately adopted, and that he was content to leave it to the Vizier to determine whether a joint expedition against the Rohillas should at once be undertaken, or whether it should be postponed. He was even ready, he said, to give up the project altogether if the Vizier should so desire[1]. The Vizier gave as his opinion that the expedition should take place, and Hastings accepted his decision.

It has been mentioned that, while the campaign of 1773 was in progress, Shuja-ud-Dowla had proposed, in the event of the failure of the Rohillas to carry out their engagements, to pay fifty lakhs of rupees in consideration of receiving the assistance of the Company's troops in obtaining possession of Rohilkhand. Having now consented to meet the whole of the actual expenses of the Brigade employed in his service, he offered to pay forty lakhs if the expedition were successfully carried out. This was agreed to, and the following draft of a treaty was accepted by both parties:—

(1) 'Whereas the Rohilla chiefs, in the month of June 1772, entered into a treaty with the Vizier, in the presence and with the concurrence of General Sir Robert Barker, by which they engaged to pay him forty lakhs of rupees for his assistance against the Marathas, and which treaty they have treacherously broken; it is therefore agreed that a Brigade of the Company's forces shall join the Vizier, and assist to punish them, and that he shall pay the whole of its expense.

[1] MS. Diary referred to below.

By a Brigade is meant: two battalions of Europeans, one company of Artillery, and six battalions of Sepoys, and the expense is settled at Sonaut Rupees 210,000 per month. The Company's troops shall not cross the Ganges, nor march beyond the foot of the hills. The Vizier shall retain as his own that part of the Rohilla country which lies on the north-east side of the Ganges, but in consideration of the Company's relinquishing all claim to share in the said country, although it is to be conquered by their joint forces, the Vizier engages to make them an acknowledgment of forty lakhs of rupees, and in future to defray the whole expense of the Company's troops, agreeable to the data above-mentioned, whenever he has occasion for their assistance, notwithstanding it is stipulated in the second article of the treaty of Allahabad, concluded by the Vizier and the Company on the 16th August, 1765, that he shall pay only their extraordinary charges.

(2) The Vizier may retain the Brigade aforesaid, on the above-mentioned terms, as long as he shall require it, unless it shall be necessary to recall it for the defence of the Company's own territories, and he may employ them for the protection of any part of his country; but they shall be kept together in one body, and not dispersed on different commands, except such detachments as the commanding officer shall judge necessary in the time of actual service. He may return the whole or part of the said Brigade whenever he has no further occasion for their services, and he shall cease to defray their expenses as soon as they shall enter the province of Behar. But as the Company cannot risk the credit of their arms by allowing a smaller force to remain with the Vizier than half a Brigade, it is provided that he shall either retain one half of the Brigade or return the whole. Upon their dismission they shall depart with all convenient expedition, and to prevent any future disputes from arising on this subject, the time of their march to the borders of his own province shall be computed at the rate of five coss per day from the place where they commenced their march.

(3) The Vizier engages to pay the forty lakhs of rupees, stipulated in the First Article, by monthly payments of four lakhs, to commence from the 10th June, 1774, but should any accident (which God forbid) oblige our forces to retire from the Rohilla country, and prevent the Vizier from obtaining possession of it, the said forty lakhs shall not be demanded[1].'

When everything seemed to have been settled, the Vizier suddenly began to express doubts whether he was not undertaking greater pecuniary responsibilities than he could fulfil.

Among the unpublished manuscripts in the British Museum there is an interesting paper, written by Hastings

[1] Fifth Report, App. No. 45; Forrest's Selections, vol. i. p. 150.

for his own use, containing his diary of proceedings at Benares[1], and I make from it the following quotations:—

'The Vizier said he saw no other means of removing the present difficulty but by concluding the Kora business and postponing the Rohilla expedition to another year. This I told him I had no objection to. It was his business, not mine, though it did not appear to me how it would mend the matter, since he would be equally unable to provide the ready money payment, with which the Rohilla expedition had no connection. He said it was true, but it would save him the expense which preparations for the campaign would put him to, and the money which he had destined for that purpose might be applied to the immediate payment of the Kora payment. I acquiesced in his reasons and expressed my approbation of his opinion, repeating that when I agreed to engage in the Rohilla scheme I took a great risk upon myself, and that I believed the Company would be better pleased if their troops were withdrawn to their own territories than employed in distant wars, although the event might be a means of future security to him and to themselves' ... 'I dread [the Vizier said] whatever may interfere to disturb our union and disappoint my hopes. There is such a delicacy in the strictest friendship that affairs of accounts and money may destroy it, for if a man would sow dissension between two of his most intimate friends his surest way to do it would be to persuade one to borrow money of the other. This is my case. I want not money, I desire not to enlarge my territory, I am content with what I possess, and should have sat down in quiet and in peace with all mankind if others would have let me. The designs of the Marathas against me and the necessity of obviating them have forced me often to go to war. How could I avoid it? Whenever I have taken the field it has been for my own safety, not from enmity to others. This being the case, I wish to postpone the Rohilla plan, and to confine my present views to the possession of Kora and Allahabad, if it be agreeable to you, because I foresee that if I undertake both they may

[1] MSS. 29,212. The greater part of this diary is in the handwriting of Hastings. A portion of it has been misplaced and bound up with other papers in collection 29,233. There is another complete copy in MSS. 29,234. In a letter from Hastings to Sulivan, dated March 22, 1773, also in the British Museum, he refers to the diary, a copy of which was sent with his letter:—'The conferences held with the Vizier are faithfully and exactly related, for it was a part of my daily occupation to write down, the instant we parted, everything that had passed between us, and as my whole attention, I may say my whole heart, was fixed on the success of my commission, I scarce could have forgot a word of business that occurred on these occasions. I have left the whole uncorrected in its original dress, with all my own defects, as well as his Excellency's, undisguised in it.'

exceed my ability; and if I should fail in my engagements God knows what would be the consequence. I can attend to the business of Kora and Allahabad, if I have no other business to divert my attention, in such a manner as effectually to ensure the possession of it, and I have no fears about the payments which I have agreed to, but if I am engaged with the Rohillas, with the monthly charge of the army, the forty lakhs to pay for possession of that country, and forty-five for Kora and Allahabad, I fear the engagement is too weighty and I may fail in it. I wish to agree with you for Kora and Allahabad only. I will go to Fyzabad and, instead of ten lakhs ready money, five in three months, and five in four months, I will give twenty lakhs at once in ready money, which I can do when I am free from other calls. I replied that I was much better pleased to engage with him for this article alone than for that regarding the Rohillas to which I had always felt a repugnance, both on account of its distance, the uncertainty whether such a plan would be approved by the Company, and the uncertain duration of it. On all accounts it were much better set aside.'

The reasons which led Hastings to accept so readily the Vizier's proposal to postpone operations against the Rohillas were afterwards more fully explained by him. Although he was as much convinced as ever that the policy of uniting Rohilkhand to the Vizier's territories was wise, he had begun to entertain grave doubts whether it was expedient to undertake the expedition under the circumstances that then existed. It could not be denied that it was contrary to the orders of the Court of Directors to embark in any fresh schemes of conquest. 'The Company at home (Hastings said) was exposed to popular clamour, all its measures liable to be canvassed in Parliament, their Charter drawing to a close, and His Majesty's Ministers unquestionably ready to take advantage of every unfavourable circumstance in the negotiations for its renewal[1].'

There were also considerations of a personal nature, affecting himself and his colleagues in the Council, which it was difficult to disregard.

'I owed,' he said, 'my appointment in the government to motives which, though highly honourable to those who had nominated me to it, were but a limited and transitory dependence. I had no natural

[1] Consultations, November 26, 1773; Fifth Report, App. No. 23.

interest at home, no personal connections, nor any other means of support than such as I might gradually and eventually acquire by my reputation in office. In the meantime, all my actions were to be viewed through a very remote medium, with a thousand refractions of private interest, secret misrepresentation, general prejudice, and the precipitation of unformed judgment ; and above all the situation of my employers not allowing them the free exercise of theirs. The measure itself derived its propriety from circumstances of nice relation and various detail, which few could understand without some previous knowledge or study of antecedent events and local situation, and which were easily liable to misconstruction. It was repugnant to the general policy of the Company, and depended for its sanction on constructive orders, of which the Court of Directors, who framed them, had a claim at least to the sole right of interpretation. These considerations, with others of a similar nature, pressed with a more sensible weight upon my mind at this time, by the means of recent advices privately received from England, which reached me while I was within a few days of my arrival at Benares, and by which I learnt that a new Commission had been appointed from home, to make enquiry into the state of the Company's affairs in Bengal, and to supersede the powers of its actual administration. . . . I well knew what my duty required of me, and that I was determined on performing, in despite of every inferior concern, yet when I was relieved from the obligation by the Nabob's renunciation of his design, which could be prosecuted only at his requisition, and therefore no duty of my own opposed the forbearance of it, I might then both naturally and allowably yield some indulgence to my private feelings. I certainly was glad to be freed from the embarrassments which I had apprehended in the prosecution of the plan, though I should have paid no regard to them had I been still required to proceed in it [1].'

Hastings wrote to the same effect in a private letter to Lawrence Sulivan, on the 12th October, 1773 :—

'The Rohilla chiefs, when attacked by the Marathas, made an offer of forty lakhs of rupees to the Vizier, of which he promised to give half to the Company, for his assistance, and engaged themselves to pay it by a solemn treaty. We have delivered them from the Marathas, and the Rohillas have paid nothing. . . . The Rohilla country lies open on the south. It is bounded on the west by the Ganges, and on the north and east by the mountains of Tartary. It is to the province of Oudh, in respect both to its geographical and political relations, exactly what Scotland was to England before the reign of Queen Elizabeth. The reduction of this territory would have completed the defensive line of the Vizier's dominions, and of course left

[1] Defence before House of Commons, 1786.

us less to defend, as he relies on our strength entirely. It would have added much to his income, in which we should have had our share... I was glad to be freed from the Rohilla expedition, because I was doubtful of the judgment which would have been passed upon it at home, where I see too much stress laid upon general maxims, and too little attention given to the circumstances which require an exception to be made for them. Besides this, an opinion still prevails of the Vizier's great power, and his treacherous designs against us, and I cannot expect that my word shall be taken as a proof of their non-existence.... On the other hand, the absence of the Marathas, and the weak state of the Rohillas, promised an easy conquest of them, and I own that such was my idea of the Company's distress at home, added to my knowledge of their wants abroad, that I should have been glad of any occasion to employ their forces, which saves so much of their pay and expenses [1].'

The result of these discussions was an agreement to postpone the expedition against the Rohillas, but there was no real change of policy, and Hastings 'gave the Vizier every reason to expect that whenever it could be with prudence resumed, and he desired it, it should be undertaken [2].'

When this had been settled, the Vizier wished to know the opinion of Hastings on some other points. I give the following extract from his diary; it illustrates the character of Shuja-ud-daula's policy, and the somewhat cynical views which Hastings took of the situation.

'The Vizier asked my advice whether he should persuade the Rohillas to attack the Marathas in those places which they have lately conquered between the rivers [3], which would bring on a new war with them, and enable him to take his advantage of both when they should have weakened each other by mutual hostilities. I commended the project, but expressed my apprehension of the consequences which might prove equally pernicious to him whether the Marathas returned on such provocation or not; by drawing their hostilities upon himself in the first instance, as there is no doubt they would come, if at all, with a force capable to defeat the Rohillas; or by strengthening the hands of the Rohillas if they should succeed in their attempts and the

[1] British Museum MSS. 29,127; Gleig, vol. i. p. 357. A part of this letter was quoted by Hastings in his Appeal to the Court of Directors, December 3, 1774; Fifth Report, App. No. 45; Forrest's Selections, vol. i. p. 41.

[2] Consultations, November 26, 1773; Fifth Report, App. No. 23.

[3] i.e. in the Doáb between the Ganges and Jumna.

Marathas not return. He admitted the conclusion, and said he would not think of it. But, added he, suppose the Rohillas should attempt anything against the Marathas; shall I in that case attack them and engage a body of the Maratha horse to ravage their country? I replied, by no means. The force which they could bring him would be so inconsiderable that they would do him no service, and if it consisted of only ten men it would give them a plea to claim a share in the conquests which he should make; in a word, that any union between him and the Marathas would be hurtful both to his interests and his friendships. He asked if he should compromise for the forty lakhs due by the Rohillas by treaty. I advised him to take what he could but not give up a rupee. Whatever deficiency there should be in their payments would serve as a fair pretence for any future designs he might form against them[1].'

As no final conclusion had been arrived at, it was necessary to keep the negotiations with the Vizier in regard to the Rohilla expedition as secret as possible, but Hastings had communicated every day confidentially to the three Members of the Council who were present with him at Benares all that had occurred. In the official account of his proceedings, written on his return to Calcutta, he referred to the subject in the following general terms only:—

'The Vizier was at first very desirous of the assistance of an English force to put him in possession of the Rohilla country lying north of his dominions and east of the Ganges. This had long been a favourite object of his wishes, and you will recollect that the first occasion of my last visit was furnished by a proposal of this kind. He had certainly just grounds of resentment against the chiefs of this nation, who had not only failed in their engagement to pay him forty lakhs of rupees for his protection against the Marathas, but had actually supplied them with money when they appeared in arms against him. He offered to make the Company a consideration for this service of forty lakhs of rupees, besides the stipulated sum for the expense of the troops, but he afterwards laid aside this design, fearing that it would disable him from fulfilling his engagement for Kora and Allahabad.

[1] This word 'pretence' has evidently the meaning often given to it by old writers, and signifies 'ground or reason assigned.' Thus Milton: 'Spirits on our just pretences armed Fell with us.' The word is used in the same sense in the Fifth Report of the Committee of Secrecy, in a passage referring to the Rohilla war: 'The Vizier who seems to have been attentive by every means to secure the conquests he had made, wished to have an interview with the King under that pretence.'

The measures to be pursued for his security on that quarter must therefore be determined by future occurrences. I was pleased that he urged the scheme of this expedition no further, as it would have led our troops to a distance from our own borders, which I would ever wish to avoid, although there are powerful arguments to recommend it[1].'

When Hastings returned to Calcutta, he resolved, with the approval of the Council, to appoint a permanent Resident at the Court of the Vizier, and Nathaniel Middleton was chosen for the post.

Hastings reached Calcutta in the first week of October 1773. His visit to Benares had been, he considered, altogether successful. He had repelled the insolent pretensions of the Marathas to appropriate the provinces which had been given to them by the Emperor, and which, by better right than any others could assert, had reverted to our Government; by ceding those provinces to the Vizier he had strengthened our ally, and had avoided the serious embarrassments which our own possession of them or the adoption of any other plan would have entailed; although nothing had been finally settled regarding Rohilkhand, the negotiations with the Vizier had established a clear basis on which the question could be again taken up and disposed of. The financial arrangements had been fair and advantageous to both parties, and when they were afterwards called in question, there was hardly any part of his

[1] Report to the Council, October 4, 1773; Fifth Report, App. No. 19; Forrest's Selections, vol. i. p. 51. Mill, without any foundation of fact, has insinuated that Hastings gave a false account of the reasons for postponing the Rohilla expedition. 'If (he says) we may believe the representations of the President, whose representations, however, upon this subject, are so full of management and ambiguity that they are all to be received with caution, the Nabob represented himself unable to meet the pecuniary obligations under which the acquisition of both territories would lay him to the English Company, and desired for that reason to suspend his attack upon the Rohillas.' Mill's next sentence is as follows: 'It was agreed, however, between him and the President, that whenever the time convenient for the extirpation of that people should arrive, the assistance of the English should not be wanting.' This is an example of Mill's unfounded statements. No one, as I shall show, ever had any idea of 'extirpating' the Rohillas in the sense here implied.

administration on which Hastings dwelt with greater satisfaction [1].

As already related, when the Marathas retreated to the Deccan before the rainy season of that year, they had left garrisons in the Doáb, and they still occupied Etawa and the districts formerly granted by Ahmad Shah Abdali to Hafiz Rahmat and Dundi Khan. The dissensions among the Marathas at home had become more virulent than ever, their forces in Northern India were small, and serious resistance being improbable, the Vizier, although Hastings had dissuaded him from the project, saw that there was a good opportunity of seizing a territory which had now become especially valuable to him because it adjoined his new provinces of Kora and Allahabad. On the 23rd October, Hastings received a letter from him saying that he had heard of the murder of the Maratha Chief Narayan Ráo; he expressed his intention of taking possession of Etawa and the neighbouring districts, and enquired whether the English would assist him in his proposed operations if he had occasion to ask for their help.

No immediate answer appears to have been sent to this letter, but on the 18th of November another letter arrived from the Vizier. In it he said that he

[1] Referring to this subject in a private letter thirteen years afterwards, Hastings gave the following account of his proceedings: 'He left Calcutta with less than 50,000 rupees in the treasury, and after means unsuccessfully tried to borrow money. He returned with twenty lakhs in specie, and with thirty more in actual receipt, with an annual fund established of twenty-five lakhs more in the establishment of the army subsidy. This sum he settled for the army, whenever it should be wanted, for the support of our ally the Nabob of Oudh; and by making the terms fixed, and the employment and dismission of the troops optional to the Nabob, he most effectually rendered their appropriation, and the subsidy with it, perpetual. He established the alliance between the two states on conditions of such equal advantage that the representatives of both parted equally satisfied, and had the succeeding governments pursued the same line, and the Nabob Shuja-ud-dowla lived, Oudh would have been a shield of defence and a source of wealth to Bengal, while it derived reciprocal support and the means of wealth from Bengal.' Letter to Mr. Anderson, September 13, 1786; Gleig, vol. iii. p. 302. The original draft of this letter in Hastings' handwriting is in the British Museum MSS. 29,170.

had learned that Hafiz Rahmat, and other Rohilla chiefs had

'intentions of taking possession of Etawa and the rest of the country belonging to the Marathas. I therefore write to inform you that if such is their intention I will not put up with it, but shall undoubtedly undertake an expedition against them; for, in the first place, they have not made good a single daum[1] of the forty lakhs of rupees according to their agreement, and, in the next, they are now going to take possession of another country. This I will never submit to, and am therefore determined to punish them. During our interview at Benares we had some conversation on this subject, and it was then agreed on that I should pay to the Company the sum of forty lakhs of rupees after the expulsion of the Rohillas, and two lakhs ten thousand rupees monthly, on account of the English Brigade, during my operations in the Rohilla country; and that I should, with the assistance of the English forces, endeavour to punish and exterminate the Rohillas out of their country. If therefore these terms are agreeable to you, I desire to know whether you will assist me with the English forces, or you will not.'

The Vizier then repeated the conditions formerly accepted, but which had been given up at his own request, and on a separate paper accompanying the letter he gave the following summary of his proposals:—

'On condition of the entire expulsion of the Rohillas I will pay to the Company the sum of forty lakhs of rupees in ready money whenever I shall discharge the English troops, and until the expulsion of the Rohillas shall be effected I will pay the expenses of the English troops,—that is to say I will pay the sum of Rs. 210,000 monthly[2].'

On the day after this letter was received, Hastings and the Select Committee of the Council recorded the following Resolution:—

'That should the Vizier persist in his intentions with respect to the Rohilla country, and determine to prosecute the enterprise with steadiness to a conclusion, this Government, considering the strict alliance and engagements which subsist between the Company and Shuja-uddowla, and particularly what passed between the Vizier and the President at the conference at Benares, cannot on this occasion refuse him support and assistance; that the terms proposed by the Vizier

[1] *Dám*, a small copper coin, the fortieth part of a rupee.

[2] Fifth Report, App. No. 22; Forrest's Selections, vol. i. p. 76.

appear highly advantageous to the Company, not only on account of the sum which is ultimately stipulated as a consideration of this service, but by immediately relieving them from the heavy expense of a large part of their army. Provided, therefore, full assurance and security can be obtained of the Vizier's intention and ability to make good the many payments which will in this event be due to the Company, Resolved, that the 2nd Brigade now quartered at Dinapore be ordered to march on the Vizier's requisition, . . . and that every preparation be made for putting the 2nd Brigade in readiness to take the field on the shortest notice.'

It was at the same time decided that Hastings should prepare an answer to the Vizier's letters, and write to the Emperor and to the Rohilla chiefs, 'requiring from them an explanation of their intentions with regard to the Doáb.'

On the 22nd November, Hastings laid before the Committee the following draft of a letter to the Vizier :—

'Some days ago I received your letter, containing the intelligence of the death of Narayan Ráo, the late Sirdar of the Deccan, and the succession of Raghunath Ráo to the government at the same time; intimating your resolution to take possession of the country in the Doáb, which formerly belonged to the Rohillas and is now possessed by the Marathas; and desiring to know whether I will send the English forces in case you should have occasion to call for their assistance. I am since honoured with another letter from you to the following purport, viz.: "That you have learnt that Hafiz Rahmat Khan and other Sirdars have intentions of taking possession of Etawa and the rest of the country of the Doáb belonging to the Marathas; and that in such case you are resolved to carry into execution the plan which was concerted between us at Benares, for their expulsion from the country lying to the north of yours; and desiring to know whether I will assist in the execution of this design;" repeating the conditions formerly proposed, with other particulars of importance which I clearly understand. As the objects of both the above letters are intimately connected, and admit of only one and the same determination, I shall reply particularly to both in this address.

'With respect to the Doáb, you are the master to act in whatever manner you shall deem most fitting for the advancement and security of your own affairs. You know that you may always command the forces of the Company for the defence of your own dominions. If you should engage in a war beyond their borders, and should stand in need of assistance, I certainly cannot sit still and see your danger without endeavouring to relieve you; and for that reason I hope you will avoid an enterprise at this distance, which you cannot be well assured of performing with your own strength, as the commands of my superiors are, as I have repeatedly informed you, peremptory, that I shall not suffer their arms to be carried beyond the line of their own boundaries, and those of your Excellency their ally, although in one instance I have ventured to go beyond them.

'Concerning the country of the Rohillas, whatever was formerly proposed at Benares, that I am now equally ready to agree to; that is, the Brigade which is now at Dinapore shall march whenever you require it to join you, and proceed with you into the country of the Rohillas, which lies north of your dominions, to assist you in the entire reduction of it; and your Excellency on your part will supply them monthly with the stipulated sum of 210,000 rupees for their expenses; and whenever the country shall be so far conquered, that you shall remain in possession of it, although the enemy may lurk in the hills and jungles, or a few refractory zemindars, as is usual, may withhold their allegiance, and your Excellency shall dismiss the Brigade, you will on its departure pay forty lakhs of rupees to the Company as a consideration for that service. To prevent future misunderstandings, I have been thus explicit. I must beg leave further to add that if the expedition shall be once undertaken, it will be absolutely necessary to persevere in it until it shall be accomplished. You will therefore reflect whether it will be in your power to make the above payments punctually with others which are already due; and whether you can resolve on going through with the undertaking. If you are not certain of accomplishing these necessary points, I must request that you will suspend the execution of your undertaking till a more favourable time, as I cannot hazard or answer for the effects of the displeasure of the Company, my masters, if they shall find themselves involved in a fruitless war, or in an expense for the prosecution of it. But if you are satisfied of punctuality to perform these conditions, and will engage to perform them, the Brigade which is at Dinapore shall attend you on your requisition; and that there may be no delay, if you will signify your orders for the march of the Brigade to Mr. Lane, the chief at Patna, and will send a letter from him to me, containing your acquiescence in these conditions in the form enclosed, he will cause the Brigade to proceed to you immediately, being furnished with the proper orders from me to the Commander of the forces for that purpose. On the receipt of your first letter, I ordered all the detachments of the Brigade at Dinapore to be assembled, and every preparation to be made to enable it to take the field, and I hope it will be in readiness for that purpose whenever you may require. Although, in the enclosed form, I have mentioned nothing of the mode in which the money for the expenses of the army is to be defrayed, I think it proper to observe that it would be highly expedient that a sure and effectual mode be previously formed for the regular payment of the army. This will prevent difficulties, and will be the subject of much ease both to you and myself, as the charges of the army must be regularly paid, or the most fatal consequences may attend the neglect of it, and I have not money to send with it[1].'

The correspondence with the Vizier was ordinarily conducted by the Select Committee consisting of Hastings and two members of the Council, but, when the draft letter which Hastings had prepared was laid before the Committee, doubts arose as to the propriety of issuing orders of such extreme importance on the Committee's authority alone, and it was resolved that the whole of the proceedings should be considered by the Council at large. They were laid before it accordingly, with a Minute in which Hastings explained his own views on the questions to be decided.

'The President thinks it requisite to accompany this reference with a brief explanation of the nature of the measure proposed, and of the motives which determined his opinion in the Resolution of the Select Committee now before the Board, in the following Minute:—

'I have long considered the power of the Rohillas as dangerous to the Vizier, the only useful ally of the Company, and as such have wished to see it annihilated. We have till lately had a very imperfect knowledge of the Rohilla States, and consequently the advices transmitted to our Honourable Masters on that subject must have been too defective for them to form an accurate judgment upon them. It is our duty to correct our information to them as we receive more light, and I am inclined to believe that such information would induce them to adopt the system with regard to those powers which are now proposed. I must therefore declare that although the Honourable Court of Directors have been pleased to rank the Rohillas among the powers capable of opposing the Marathas, I cannot regard them in that light. Their country is too remote from that of the Marathas, and too much out of the line of the incursions of those people for them either to be able to oppose them with effect or to have much to apprehend from them. The Marathas may occasionally attack them from the allurements of plunder only, but they can never form a systematic scheme of conquest over a country so distant and so difficult to hold. On the other hand, the Subahdar of Oudh must always be an object of jealousy and enmity to the Rohillas. His power is to be dreaded by them, and the situation of their country contiguous to his, and in a manner enclosed within the same natural

[1] Fifth Report, App. No. 22; Forrest's Selections, vol. i. p. 78.

boundaries, must make the possession of it always a desirable object with him both for security and advantage. These are sources of enmity between them which from the nature of things cannot fail of producing suitable effects, and it is more probable that we should soon see the Marathas and Rohillas join in hostilities against the Vizier than that they should continue in war with one another. But let us next view the advantages which would result to the Vizier, the ally of the Company, and to the Company itself, from his possession of that part of the Rohilla country which is the object of the expedition now proposed. Our ally would obtain by this acquisition a complete state shut in effectually from foreign invasions by the Ganges, all the way from the frontiers of Behar to the mountains of Thibet, while he would remain equally accessible to our forces from the above provinces either for hostilities or protection. It would give him wealth of which we should partake, and give him security without any dangerous increase of power; and would undoubtedly by bringing his frontier nearer to the Marathas, to whom singly he would be no match, render him more dependent on us and cement the union more firmly between us. I must further declare that I regard as none of the most inconsiderable benefits to the Company of this measure, besides the forty lakhs held out to us, the easing them immediately of the burden of one third of their whole army, while at the same time it is employed usefully for their interests, and conveniently for keeping up its own discipline and practice in war.

'With these reasons for the prosperity of the expedition, on general principles I must confess I entertain doubts as to its expediency at this time, arising from the circumstances of the Company at home exposed to popular clamour, all its measures liable to be canvassed in Parliament, their Charter drawing to a close, and His Majesty's Ministers unquestionably ready to take advantage of every unfavourable circumstance in the negotiation for its renewal. In this situation there appears an unusual degree of responsibility annexed to such an undertaking. I would therefore recommend it to serious consideration, and at the same time I think it my duty to declare that I find myself embarrassed in a peculiar manner in my decision, from the circumstance of what passed between the Vizier and myself at Benares. The Board will recollect that this very country was included in the line of defensive operations which they thought fit to adopt last year in support of the Vizier; and it is now necessary to acquaint them more fully that the Vizier at the interview did propose this expedition to me and earnestly solicited my assistance; that I regarded this request as a lucky circumstance in the negotiation, and availing myself of it, as the means of purchasing the Vizier's compliance in the other measure, which was the principal object of my mission, I consented to it, engaging to assist him in the enterprise on the conditions with which the Board are already acquainted. Afterwards, from a suspicion of his own ability to make good so many pecuniary engagements at once as those he had come under, he himself made the proposal for suspending the Rohilla expedition; but the condition which took its rise from it, viz. that the future payments of the extra charges of the army sent at any time to his assistance should be fixed at 210,000 rupees per month for a Brigade, was still allowed to be made an Article of the new treaty. And it was further agreed that the stipulation for Kora, which I had before with difficulty raised to forty-five lakhs of rupees, should now be made fifty, in consideration of his being exempted from the additional burden of the projected campaign, and better enabled to fulfil his other payments. It is unnecessary to explain the motives which urged the Vizier to make concessions for the liberty of relinquishing a point which he had apparently so much at heart, and which I was not solicitous to pursue; the detail would be tedious. The gentlemen who were with me, and to whom I made daily communication of the progress of the negotiations, will remember that such was the issue of this part of them. The expedition remained only suspended; and I gave him every reason to expect that whenever it could again be with prudence resumed, and he desired it, it should be undertaken. This is the predicament in which I now stand with the Vizier; and although, from a fear of his not being able to fulfil his part of the agreement, I wish to avoid in engaging in the project at present, yet it appears to me that a direct refusal, after what passed, would have an unfriendly aspect, and might admit of the construction of artifice and insincerity in our dealings with him. Moved by the doubts which I have expressed to the Board, and thus hampered by my situation with the Vizier, no better method occurred to me for freeing us from this dilemma than the letter which is now in reference before the Board. I have there expressed my consent to the expedition on terms which, if he agrees to them, are most likely to secure the advantages hoped from it, but which are more likely to make him relinquish the design. I trust the Board will find it so guarded, both in the substance and expression, that the Vizier must necessarily feel himself engaged to perform every condition required of him with the most rigid punctuality, at the hazard of forfeiting the Company's friendship, or revolt against the terms imposed upon him, and drop all thoughts of prosecuting the design; and that, I verily believe will be the issue of this correspondence.'

The questions thus laid before the Council, in which nine members were present, were debated for three successive days; no two members agreed exactly in their opinions, and it was difficult to reconcile them. At last they all agreed to leave it to Hastings to draw up a resolution expressing, as well as he was able, the general view. On the 26th November, he accordingly drafted a resolution in the following form, and this was accepted by the whole Council:—

'The Board, after due consideration of the matter in reference from the Select Committee, and of the President's representation, concur heartily in wishing to avoid the expedition proposed, without entering into the discussion of the propriety of such an enterprize on general principles. The Board see in their full force all the circumstances of doubt as to its present expediency which the President has so clearly set forth, and they are also sensible of the embarrassment he is under, from what passed on the subject between him and the Vizier at Benares. They are equally solicitous to save the honour of the Company and watch over its interests, and for that reason they approve of the letter now before them which seems equally calculated to save both. The conditions, if accepted, would undoubtedly secure the greatest possible advantage from such an enterprize, but they appear to them more calculated to drive the Vizier into a refusal, which is what they trust in as its most probable and almost infallible consequence, and which they wish for as the proper result of this proposition and the present circumstances of affairs. Agreed, That the President be requested to forward the letter, as prepared by him, to the Vizier; and that the order of the 19th instant, to the Chief at Patna, and to the Commanding Officer at Dinapore, be forthwith issued [1].'

Sir Robert Barker, while he approved the letter to the Vizier, recorded a separate Minute. He was of opinion that it would have been good policy on the part of the Company to assist the Vizier in the conquest of Rohilkhand if Kora and Allahabad had not been already given to him, but that under existing circumstances this would make him dangerously powerful, unless, indeed, he would agree to cede to us the zemindari of Chait Singh of Benares.

'If,' Sir Robert Barker wrote, 'the Vizier has the Rohilla country added to those of Oudh and the provinces of Kora and Allahabad, he will be in possession of a revenue of nearly two crores and a half per annum, a sum that in some future day might render an enterprising genius a very troublesome neighbour on the north-west frontiers of the Company's dominions. And although we have no present occasion to suspect the sincerity of Shuja-ud-dowla's attachment to our interest, yet

[1] Fifth Report, App. No. 23; Forrest's Selections, vol. i. p. 81. For an account of the three days' discussion see Hastings' Appeal to the Court of Directors, December 3, 1774, Fifth Report, App. No. 45; Forrest's Selections, vol. i. p. 148.

it must not be forgotten that he is an Hindostaner, or that a successor might enter the government with very different ideas and disposition. The General agrees with the President that the Vizier's dominions would become compact, and not subject to invasion, but the General supposes it will become too compact, and not sufficiently open to invasion. It is the apprehension of invasion that cements the Vizier's friendship with the English, and makes him that staunch ally we find him[1].'

The reasons which had led Hastings at Benares to acquiesce in the wish of the Vizier that the expedition against the Rohillas should be postponed weighed heavily ont he minds of the Council.

'The Board,' Hastings afterwards wrote, 'rested their wish to avoid the expedition solely upon their doubts of the consequences which might personally affect us, at the same time that they were sensible of the advantages it would secure to the Company. . . . My sentiments on the propriety of the expedition had undergone no change, but I will not deny that I felt myself influenced by the same fears which operated on the other Members of the Council, that the propriety of the measure might not be seen in the same light by our constituents, which we knew, from the temper of the times, might not only draw upon us their severe resentment, but aggravate the load of popular odium which has of late fallen on their servants[2].'

[1] Fifth Report, App. No. 23; Forrest's Selections, vol. i. p. 81. Sir Robert Barker at no time objected to the Rohilla expedition on the ground that it was unjust, nor did he ever doubt that the Rohillas deserved punishment for their perfidy. Mill's reference to this Minute is misleading, and it is for this reason that I now notice it. When Sir Robert Barker was with Hastings at Benares, he expressed doubts regarding the expediency of the expedition on account of 'the interruption which it would probably receive from the King and the Marathas, and the unsteadiness of the Vizier's disposition.' This is stated in the Diary of Hastings, quoted above. Sir Robert Barker also disapproved the cession of Kora and Allahabad to the Vizier, partly because it set aside the treaty entered into in 1765 with the Emperor, but also because he thought the terms granted to the Vizier much too favourable. He said that considering the heavy expenses of the Company, these provinces ought not to have been given up for so small a sum as two years' revenue. See minutes by Sir Robert Barker, Fifth Report, App. Nos. 13, 19, and 33; and Minute by Hastings, App. No. 12. Sir Robert Barker was much displeased because he had not been invited to take part in the conferences with the Vizier. Hastings appears, however, to have treated him otherwise with great consideration. He was anxious that Sir Robert Barker should have commanded the British troops in the final campaign against the Rohillas, but this was not possible in consequence of his resignation of the service. He was evidently a far superior officer to Colonel Champion, who took his place.

[2] Appeal to the Court of Directors, Fifth Report, App. No. 45; Forrest's Selections, vol. i. p. 41.

On the 10th of January, 1774, an answer was received from the Vizier, declining to undertake the expedition against the Rohillas under the conditions that had been offered. The letter was as follows :—

'I have received your friendly letter, informing me that the English Brigade is at my service, either for the protection of my own dominions, or to assist me in my operations against the Rohillas. It is known that the firmest union subsists between us, and I am certain that you will suffer the English forces to join me for the protection of my own dominions; but as the distance between us is now so great, that much time will be taken up in writing to you and receiving your answer, for precaution sake I request you will send a positive order to the Commander-in-Chief of the forces at Patna to march them to the frontiers of Oudh or Kora (both which countries now belong to me), whenever I shall require them. At present I have no occasion for them, and should I chance to call for them, I will not require their proceeding further than the frontiers of Kora and Karra. I make this request by way of precaution only, and to guard against future events. Whenever I shall write to the Commander-in-Chief for the troops, let them immediately be sent, and it is becoming our union that you give orders accordingly, which will give me great satisfaction. My friend, I request this of you that I may be at ease with respect to my own dominions, as well as to prevent future delays, otherwise I have at present no occasion for the troops[1].'

On the 17th January, 1774, the Bengal Government sent the following report to the Court of Directors :—

'It was with pleasure we found the plan we had adopted answer so completely to our intention. The Vizier, on receipt of the President's letter written agreeably to the Resolution of the Board, returned an immediate answer, declining our assistance in his distant expedition on the conditions we required, but at the same time desiring the Brigade might be held in readiness to march whenever he shall find it necessary to call on it for the defence of his own dominions. The affair being happily terminated in the manner we wished, we shall now remain spectators only of the operations of the different powers in those distant parts, preserving, however, a watchful eye over the course of events, that we may be prepared to interpose whenever the interests of the Honourable Company are likely to be affected by them. In this view we shall, in compliance with the Vizier's request, hold one Brigade in readiness to march to his assistance within his own

[1] Fifth Report, App. No. 25; Forrest's Selections, vol. i. p. 91.

territories, including the provinces of Kora and Allahabad, and we acknowledge we shall not be sorry to find that he calls for them on this footing, as we shall then be eased of so considerable a part of the military expense, and have the discipline of our troops preserved in an actual service at so little distance from our frontiers[1].'

[1] Fifth Report, App. No. 25.

CHAPTER X.

A. D. 1774. THE VIZIER AND HASTINGS RESOLVE TO INVADE ROHILKHAND.

The Vizier expels the Marathas from the Doáb.—He forms alliances with Zabita Khan and other Rohilla chiefs.—He enters into a secret agreement with the Emperor.—He again resolves to invade Rohilkhand and asks for the assistance of English troops.—Hastings complies with his request.—Colonel Champion appointed to command the troops.—His instructions.—His dissatisfaction.—Strength of the British and the Vizier's army.—Disturbed condition of Rohilkhand.—Dissensions between the Rohilla chiefs.—Advance of the allied forces.—Envoy sent to Hafiz Rahmat.—State of affairs in Rohilkhand.

ALTHOUGH the Vizier had declined the assistance of the English he had by no means abandoned the project of invading Rohilkhand, but he thought it prudent, in the first instance, to obtain possession of Etawa and the neighbouring districts of the Doáb, in which small Maratha garrisons still remained. Hastings, although he had refused the co-operation of British troops in carrying out this plan, subsequently agreed to the Vizier's request for the loan of a few pieces of heavy artillery, and these were sent to him in charge of an English officer[1]. In November 1773, the Vizier marched upon Etawa. The Marathas offered no opposition and withdrew their garrisons across the Jumna. There were other measures which Shuja-ud-dowla thought expedient. He went to Farukhabad, and induced the Rohilla chief Muzaffar Jang to enter into engagements which severed his connection with his countrymen in Rohilkhand, and made him virtually dependent on the Vizier. Zabita

[1] See Vizier's letter received December 17, 1773, and Minute by Hastings, September 15, 1776. Forrest's Selections, vol. ii. p. 554.

Khan who, in consequence of the departure of the Marathas, had shown an inclination again to join Hafiz Rahmat, was persuaded by Shuja-ud-dowla to abandon all such ideas, and to promise his help when the time came for carrying out the attack upon Rohilkhand. The Vizier also thought it desirable to obtain the Emperor's approval of his projected expedition. With this view he entered into communication with the Minister, Najf Khan, and assisted him in recovering Agra which had fallen into the hands of the Jats. The result was a secret agreement, carefully concealed from the English Government, under which the Vizier promised to give to the Emperor one half of 'such new territories as he might wrest from the possession of usurpers,' and the Emperor engaged to bestow the other half on the Vizier [1].

These arrangements were settled in December to Shuja-ud-dowla's satisfaction, and within less than a month from the time in which he had stated that he had no present occasion for military assistance he again wrote to Hastings and declared his intention of immediately attacking the Rohillas; he agreed to all the conditions on which the co-operation of a British force had previously been offered to him, and he asked that a brigade might be at once ordered to join him and take part in the proposed expedition. His letter reached Calcutta on the 3rd February, 1774 [2].

This rapid change in the plans of the Vizier was attributed by Hastings to the success with which his operations in the Doáb had been attended, and to his conviction that there was now no danger of interference by the Marathas.

It was impossible for the Bengal Government, after what had passed, to refuse consent, and orders were issued for complying with the Vizier's requisition. Colonel Champion had been appointed provisional Commander-in-Chief in succession to Sir Robert Barker, who had resigned the service, and on the 14th February, 1774, instructions were sent to him. He was desired to assume the command

[1] Fifth Report, App. No. 27. [2] Fifth Report, App. No. 26.

of the troops which were already marching towards the Vizier's territory; he was informed that the object of the expedition was 'the reduction of the Rohilla country lying between the Ganges and the mountains;' papers were sent to show the conditions agreed upon between the Government and the Vizier; operations were to be strictly confined within the limits of Oudh and of Rohilkhand; the troops were on no account to be permitted to cross the Ganges; the military conduct of the expedition was left entirely to the Commander-in-Chief; stringent orders were given to ensure the punctual payment of the troops; in the event of the Vizier failing to furnish the stipulated monthly subsidy, he was to be informed that this was considered equivalent to an expression of his wish to receive no longer the co-operation of the English troops, and Colonel Champion was in that case to suspend operations, return to Benares, and await further orders. When the Vizier ceased to require the services of the Brigade it was to return to our own provinces. Further details were to be settled personally by Colonel Champion with Shuja-ud-dowla, but on this point a special warning was given. If it became necessary to meet the Vizier at any place within the territories lately held by the Marathas in the Doáb, Colonel Champion was to take with him no military force except a personal guard, so that the interview might not be construed as an act of hostility on the part of the English Government towards the Marathas. Finally, it was said, 'we recommend in the strongest manner that you cultivate a good understanding with the Vizier, and that you pay the strictest attention to the behaviour and discipline of the troops, that no subject of complaint may arise on that head, either from himself or from any people of the countries with whom we are not in a state of hostilities[1].'

Colonel Champion's powers were strictly confined to the military conduct of the expedition. He was instructed that 'in all points but such as immediately respect the

[1] Fifth Report, App. No. 26; Forrest's Selections, vol. i. p. 92.

K

operations in the field, the Vizier is solely empowered to prescribe.' Hastings preferred to entrust to Middleton, the Resident, the management of all political relations, and he remained with the Vizier throughout the campaign. This was very distasteful to Colonel Champion, who saw that less confidence was placed in his judgment than that which had been given to Sir Robert Barker, his predecessor in the command of the army. He was also much dissatisfied with his military position, and with his rank, which was that of Colonel only. He wished to receive the rank of Brigadier-General, but the Government held that they were prevented by the orders of the Court of Directors from complying with his request[1]. He assumed the command with feelings far from cordial towards Hastings, towards the Vizier, or towards Middleton.

The British force consisted of one Company of Artillery, the 2nd European Regiment, the Select Picket, composed of about 100 cadets waiting for their commissions, and the 2nd Brigade composed of six battalions of Native Infantry under the command of Colonel Galliez. The Vizier's army is said to have numbered 100,000 men, but nothing certain is known of its strength or composition.

During the time that had elapsed since the Marathas had been compelled by the English and the Vizier to abandon their attacks upon Rohilkhand, the condition of affairs in that province had become more disturbed than ever. Further spoliations of the family of Ali Mohammad had occurred, and fresh dissensions and conflicts had arisen among the chiefs.

'Notwithstanding,' says Hamilton, 'the very advanced age of Hafiz Rahmat, he still perhaps possessed spirit and abilities sufficient to have enabled him to bear with success the great weight thrown upon his shoulders, had any tolerable degree of harmony subsisted among the then leading members of the community, but that unanimity which alone could render them formidable now no longer prevailed among them; the authority of Hafiz, as Chief Guardian of the State, was slighted by some and openly renounced by others; they regarded the

[1] Consultations, February 21, 1774, India Office Records; Forrest's Selections, vol. i. p. 94.

superiority he assumed with envy; and the manner of his obtaining that pre-eminence had rendered him particularly obnoxious to the sons of Ali Mohammad and their party; so that he found himself tottering on the pinnacle of an usurped authority, without the support of a single friend in whom he could venture to confide. In addition to a total defect in mutual alliance and general co-operation, many other circumstances concurred to weaken the power of the Afghan independencies in the Northern provinces at this period. Zabita Khan had been drawn off from their interest, as already related; and the death of Ahmad Khan Bangash left the principality of Farukhabad in the hands of Muzzafar Jang, a weak and ignorant young man, who so far from being able to add force or stability to any union which might have been entered into by them for their general defence, had it not in his power to support himself, and was constrained, the year before, to have recourse to Shuja-ud-dowla to protect his city from the attempts of a petty detachment of Marathas. Add to this that in Rohilkhand the seeds of contention which had been sown in the original formation of the government, had long since sprung up; a mutual jealousy and avowed animosity which had effectually restrained the different leaders from each other, induced every man, in the present unsettled state of affairs, to aspire at a separate independence utterly inconsistent with their political consequence as a collective body; and the total relaxation or suspension of the general laws, attendant upon such a state of anarchy, could not fail of producing the most mischievous effects among a people naturally of a fierce and untoward temper, and possessed of a disposition so addicted to violence and rapine, as would at any time have required the sternest exertions of justice to restrain it within bounds. The Hindu farmers, and other original inhabitants of the country, groaned under the worst species of military vassalage, whilst the upstart Mussulman despots who held them in subjection, were, by their perpetual feuds, disabled, as we have seen, from affording them the smallest protection against armies of barbarous marauders, who every year spread their devastations among them, almost without resistance. The haughty and turbulent spirit of the Afghans could not long submit to that strict control which was necessary to procure any tolerable degree of regularity or subordination in a government composed of so many independent members. Consequently, orders were no longer heard or obeyed; the administration of justice, the collection of revenue, and the intercourse of commerce, were all at a stand; the roads were infested with bands of armed ruffians, and every enormity had grown to such a height as was not likely to yield to any remedy which in the present state of things could possibly be supplied. Such was the state of the Afghan powers in these countries a few months before the commencement of the celebrated Rohilla war[1].'

[1] Hamilton, p. 209.

In the beginning of April 1774, the English troops were not far from the Rohilla frontier, and the Vizier, crossing the Ganges by a bridge of boats, returned from the Doab into Oudh with his army, and joined Colonel Champion near Shahabad. He then sent an envoy to Hafiz Rahmat, with a copy of the treaty of 1772, and made a formal demand of immediate payment of the sums due to him, on pain of the consequences.

'Hafiz Rahmat,' Hamilton tells us, 'answered the Vakil with hopes of success in his deputation, and in the meantime applied to the several chiefs, desiring them either to enable him forthwith to discharge this demand, or to join him in the field; they had already resolved on the latter alternative. The Vakil, after some delay, was sent back to his master with an evasive answer, and Hafiz Rahmat proceeded from Pilibhit to Aonla, where he set up his standard and sent notices through the country, requiring the Rohillas to repair thither. Here he was joined by Faizullah Khan and others, and as no remedy now appeared except open resistance, Hafiz attempted to inspire into the several leaders a resolution to act with unanimity and firmness in support of the common cause; but all his efforts were rendered void by the spirit of jealousy and faction already mentioned, which contributed to destroy them much more effectually than the sword of the enemy. . . . He offered (to two of the principal chiefs) bonds of indemnification, engaging either to hold himself personally responsible, or to give assignments upon his country for such sums as they might advance from their own finances for the public service. Notwithstanding these assurances they did not entertain such an opinion of Hafiz as would induce them to place any dependence upon his promise, and having previously entered into a private league to support each other, absolutely refused to advance any money, declaring they would oppose by force whoever should offer to compel them. . . . Several other chiefs threw small sums into the grand treasury, but this mode of supply was not generally adopted, and after all the sum collected was very insufficient to defray the necessary charges. In fact, so low were their finances reduced by their dominions for the two preceding years having been the seat of war, that few of the Rohilla chiefs had it in their power to contribute largely. . . . Shuja-ud-dowla, well aware of their present temper, employed a multitude of emissaries among them, who by working upon the hopes of some and the fears of others, increased their mutual jealousy and distrust. Neither the Bakshi nor the Khansamah joined the Rohilla army till some time after its formation, the Vizier having entered into a negotiation with them, and partly by threats, partly by promises, prevailed on them, whatever appearance prudence might render necessary, to remain essentially neuter in the ensuing dispute; and they were themselves sufficiently disposed, in the present state of things, rather to forsake than to assist their countrymen, as they knew that if the Afghans should make an effectual resistance and repel the invaders, Hafiz would amply revenge himself upon them for their late opposition to him. Mahbullah Khan and Fattehullah Khan, the sons of Dundi Khan, neglected to appear in the field, or to assist in any measures of general co-operation until several days after the enemy had entered into the country, as they had also privately received a message from Shuja-ud-dowla, who sent them a Koran, a sacred pledge of mutual faith among Mussulmans, with assurances of his protection, provided they should not join Hafiz Rahmat on the present occasion; and to this they returned a favourable reply; but with a fraudulent inconsistency, perfectly in character, they proceeded to Aonla at the head of a considerable force within four days after. Perhaps, indeed, these intrigues of Shuja-ud-dowla, whose character was well known, would have assisted but little in shaking the fidelity of any of the chiefs, had not they been strengthened in their operation by the general dread of Hafiz Rahmat. . . . From the time that the death of his colleagues had thrown the principal power into his own hands, Hafiz Rahmat had so often made an intemperate use of the ostensible authority with which, as "Chief Guardian of the State," he was vested, and which he had been able to support only by superiority of military force and territorial resources, that however respected for his abilities and bravery, and revered for the apparent sanctity of his manners, he was almost universally dreaded and disliked, and as he was aware of this disposition in his countrymen, the intrigues he continually kept on foot to support his influence had considerably widened the breaches before existing among the members of a naturally turbulent and distracted State. . . . "To sum up all," says the Rohilla narrator, "a surprising degree of animosity and discord had long since arisen in Rohilkhand, and each person was employed in, nay, was earnestly bent upon, the eradication of his neighbour; and in order to effect the destruction and overthrow of his own immediate kindred and connections was ready to enter into league with foreigners and strangers; the event was what might be expected,—what indeed soon appeared in the course of the succeeding occurrences." In such circumstances it is not surprising that even at this awful moment, when a foreign enemy was about to overwhelm them, the chiefs were so dubious of each other that no general system of defence was adopted, nor any orders executed with the promptitude and alacrity necessary in so critical a juncture[1].'

Other contemporary English authorities give no information regarding the condition of affairs in Rohilkhand, but the Sair-ul-Mutakherin contains a description which agrees substantially with that of Hamilton. I quote it

[1] Hamilton, pp. 220–229.

because it shows the belief of the most intelligent of the native historians of that time, and it is a characteristic specimen of a curious and interesting work.

'With a view to put an end to his disputes with the Rohillas, or to demonstrate to the world the natural perverseness of their temper, the Vizier sent word to Hafiz Rahmat the principal ruler among them, desiring him to remember how he had come in time to the assistance of his nation against the Marathas, and how he had rescued it effectually from the destruction intended them, by paying in their stead a mighty sum of money, which had saved their country from devastation and ruin; he added that all the return made him for his effectual interposition was only a variety of tergiversations and delay in the repayment of a sum due to him, and which they had not yet thought of providing for; so that matters standing as they were, the Rohillas must prepare themselves for war, or pay without delay the sum advanced for their sakes. This message did not fail to make great impression on Hafiz Rahmat, who was a man of great sense and much foresight. He sent word to Fatehullah Khan, and to the other children of Dundi Khan, as well as to Faizullah Khan, son to Ali Mohammad Rohilla, and even to all the principal men of the Rohilla nation, and informed them that he wished to see them assembled at a certain place, as he had something of importance to impart. When they were assembled, he sent them the following message: "Shuja-ud-dowla, who has disciplined his troops, and mounted his artillery in the Frenghi (European) manner, and who besides is supported by the English power, intends to attack you, and to make a conquest of your country, as well as of mine. My opinion is that we shall never be able to stand before people that pour a shower of fire in the ranks of their enemies. Is it not better then to avert so great an evil by repaying him without delay the money promised and which after all is nothing but his due? For I inform you that we shall never be able to resist his attack." Whilst the Rohilla princes were assembling, Shuja-ud-dowla had sent secret assurances to the sons of Dundi Khan, that he had no business with either their family or their dominions, which were on the other side of the Ganges, but that it was only on condition that they would remain quiet, without interfering by their assistance to others; else they might reckon upon their falling in the same fire that would be kindled to consume the others. But this message made as little impression upon them, and those senseless men instead of listening to Hafiz Rahmat's advice, and paying their share of the money he had so long stipulated for them, were on the contrary averse to any accommodation, and preferring their money to any other consideration, they were exciting others to a war; and this was the general opinion of the Rohilla princes, who being in general young, ignorant, and proud of their bodily strength and valour, preferred war to a payment, and even exhorted the others to reject all thoughts of an accommodation, pretexting their inability to pay, and describing the ruinous state of their country. It was in vain that Hafiz Rahmat was preaching that they would never be able to stand before the fire of the Frenghees; that it would produce clouds of smoke out of their breasts and that of their families, and that they would be obliged to run away from the field of battle, and to lose their characters as soldiers. All that produced no conviction; doubtless it was because the Rohillas having been guilty of an infinity of cruelties and extortions towards the inhabitants of Hindostan, it was high time that they should in their turn experience to the full all the violences which they had hitherto committed upon others. The time appointed by the Omnipotent Avenger was come, nor was it in their power to retard it by a single moment. Blinded by their own ignorance and prejudices, those senseless men thought only of taking the field and coming to a battle [1].'

[1] Sair-ul-Mutakherin, vol. iii. p. 260.

CHAPTER XI.

A.D. 1774. THE CONQUEST OF ROHILKHAND AND EXPULSION OF THE ROHILLAS.

Correspondence between Colonel Champion and Hafiz Rahmat.—Battle and defeat of the Rohillas.—Death of Hafiz Rahmat.—Honourable conduct of the Vizier.—Character of Hafiz Rahmat.—Faizullah Khan becomes head of the Rohillas.—He retreats to the foot of the hills.—Collapse of the Rohilla power.—Question of payments due to the English.—Negotiations with Faizullah Khan.—His proposals rejected.—Treaty between Faizullah Khan and the Vizier.—Treatment of the Rohillas.—Secret treaty between the Emperor and Vizier.—Hastings refuses to interfere.

ON the 12th April, when Colonel Champion had almost reached the frontier of Oudh with his Brigade, he received a letter from Hafiz Rahmat [1].

'Last year,' he wrote, 'when the Marathas advanced to the bank of the Ganges, the Nawab Vizier, General Barker, and you came here. I declined all alliance with the Marathas, and regarding my former connections with the said Nawabs, I concluded firm friendships with them, as is clearly known to you. Tuckoo, a Maratha chief, having crossed the Ganges and penetrated into this country, the Nawab Vizier and General advised that I should advance to oppose him, in which the Nawab's army was to assist me. It, however, joined me not. I opposed the enemy with all possible expedition, and obliged them to recross the river with shame and ignominy. After this the Nawab and General invited me to them. I joined them, and the Nawabs having proposed to cross the Ganges, and intimated so to me, I was ready to accompany them across. Thank Heaven, in the particulars of amity and fidelity I have never been deficient, which you are perfectly sensible of. When I obtained an

[1] This correspondence between Hafiz Rahmat and Colonel Champion has not hitherto been printed. For some unexplained reason it was not sent to the Government until the 2nd January, 1775, after the close of the war when Colonel Champion had returned to Calcutta. It is recorded in the Secret Consultations of that date; India Office Records.

interview with the Nawab Vizier at Shahabad, and concluded a friendly alliance with him, the General observed, "Performance of this treaty will be regarded by us both." In this space, nothing has proceeded from me contrary to those friendly agreements, yet has the Nawab Vizier imbibed enmity. As you have come in lieu of the General, Sir, I am extremely happy, and write to tell you so. I hope to be favoured with your agreeable letters the conferers of pleasure.'

On the 13th April Colonel Champion replied that the only advice that he could give was that Hafiz Rahmat should in all respects conform to the wishes of the Vizier. On the 17th April the allied forces entered Rohilkhand, and on the following day a second letter arrived from Hafiz Rahmat. He said that he had always acted in accordance with the Vizier's pleasure, and asked for explicit information regarding his present wishes.

On the 19th April Colonel Champion answered as follows :—

'The Nawab's pleasure is this, that for having afforded the Rohilla tribe aid and assistance for three years, the sum of two crores of rupees has been expended. You also know what the Nawab's expenses have been, and his pleasure I have now written. If you think proper, write to me distinctly what your ability is, but it is most desirable that you comply with the Nawab's demand. In this matter whatever you think proper to do distinctly inform me of, and I shall impatiently expect your reply. If I receive not your answer to-day I shall advance towards you with the army to-morrow.'

An official report was sent to Hastings by Colonel Champion on the same day, in the following terms :—

'Hafiz Rahmat has by letter expressed earnest inclinations to come to an accommodation with the Vizier, which has been the cause of my halting here to-day. The Nabob claims no less than two crores of rupees, and unless he greatly abates his demands it is not likely that an amicable decision can take place.'

An answer was at once sent by Hafiz Rahmat to this letter, and it reached Colonel Champion on the 19th April.

'You intimate,' he wrote, 'that the Nawab's pleasure is this, that for aid and succour afforded the Afghan tribe for three years, heavy sums have been expended; that I should write what my ability is, and act conformably to the Nawab's pleasure. Sir, in the particulars of aid and expenses what the Nawab has said that is true. From the decease of the Nawab Safdar Jang, the Nawab's friendship and favour has always been apparent, notwithstanding you were not then in these parts; and it is universally known too that from the first there has been no neglect on our part in the dues of good wishes and amity; and Heaven knows that regarding our engagements I have defeated the designs of his enemies to the extent of my power. Accordingly, in the preceding year, when the Marathas wanted to invade Kora and the countries eastward, and advanced to the banks of the Ganges, they sent messengers requesting a passage through my territories, refraining to demand a supply, and entering into other agreements of which you are well acquainted. I, regarding the firm connection which has subsisted for fifty or sixty years between the Nawab and me, avoided all alliance with them, and explicitly wrote so to him and General Barker. The particulars also which have occurred are well known to you. My motive for this was that whenever the Nawab Vizier, the illustrious English, and we acted in concert, our affairs would proceed well. From the beginning to this day I have always wished for the Nawab's friendship and good wishes, and never failed in the particulars of sincerity and attachment to him. Why then is this enmity and hatred from him? It is not unknown that we Afghans, with the young Nawab Zabita Khan, have a lakh of people on these two the smallest districts of Delhi, and with difficulty subsist ourselves, and in all respects are obedient to the Nawab's pleasure. Now also will we not depart from it at any time, our country, our effects, all we have is of the Nawab. As you enjoined me to write a reply speedily, and your messengers conformably to your orders are impatient, and the tents of the other chiefs are distant, I therefore send a confused reply. The chiefs will meet this afternoon; to-morrow an explicit answer shall be written and sent. You, Sir, who are compassionate, will surely exert the efforts of friendship.'

On the 22nd April another letter, to which the seals of Hafiz Rahmat and three other chiefs were attached, reached Colonel Champion, who, with the Vizier, had continued to advance. It contained assurances, couched in submissive terms, of a desire to comply with the Vizier's wishes. It urged the poverty of the chiefs, and suggested that

'a trusty accountant be sent on the part of the Vizier, who informing himself of our incomes and our expenses for troops, servants, families, and travellers it would then appear whether after all necessary expenses sufficient remained to fulfil the Nawab's demands. In this particular we will use no deceit, but when subsistence is acquired by agriculture with a thousand difficulties whence is power and ability to come? The soldiers who have removed hence, and are in the Nawab's and other service, are a clear proof of our poverty. Moreover, from our proximity and ancient friendship the state and strength of every chief is not concealed from the Vizier, nor with how severe misfortunes our lives pass away. I am hopeful that this matter, being inquired of the Nawab, justice will be required. By the favour of God, the Nawab is replete in implements of war and in fortune, but from collecting particles the treasuries of grandeur are not increased. Apparatus of war and multitudes of troops are purely for reserve and the well government of the country; it is befitting that he show favour to me and turn to the adjusting his country, and I hope that being forgiven the demand by the Nawab's great clemency, whenever the Marathas approach this part to be freed from their demands. God willing, I will duly perform my services and duty, nor fail in the smallest particular. His fame and generosity will be illustrious far and near, and hope of his favour and benefit will cause all to flock to him. His compassion to Mussulmen will be cause of pleasure to God and his Prophet, and my fault has not been of such degree as to require severe chastisement. In all respects we conform implicitly to the Nawab's pleasure, and whatever I have is his gift. You, Sir, are wise and powerful, and a doer of justice. What I have truly written without any deception, that weigh well in the scales of justice, and laying it before the Nawab represent to him that I throw myself on his mercy for forgiveness and therefore am hopeful of pardon; and notwithstanding he has much displeasures with me, yet as I am acquainted with your noble and forgiving disposition, surely you will regard me as yourself, and show favour and compassion.'

On the copy of this letter the following memorandum is recorded:—

'The Colonel and Vizier esteeming Hafiz's letter to be intended merely to gain time, as he expected to be joined with other troops, and having determined to fight the Rohillas in the morning, the following note was returned by his cossids to Hafiz Rahmat: "22nd April, 1874; The Nabob has not given any reply that I can write to you. Consequent to this, should he do so, it shall be written to you in a day or two, and I hope it will be such as will prove satisfactory to you."'

Although full of the common-places of oriental flattery, it is clear that the letters from Hafiz Rahmat would have offered no basis for negotiation even if there had been a desire on the part of the Vizier for an amicable arrangement. But no such desire existed. The time for negotiation had passed[1].

[1] It will be observed that Colonel Champion, in his letter of April 19 to the Bengal Government, said that the Vizier claimed no less than two

According to the Gulistan-i-Rahmat, one more attempt to preserve peace was made by Pahar Sing, the Diwan of Hafiz Rahmat. He strongly advised his master not to risk a battle, and offered to find the means of paying thirty-five lakhs of rupees to the Vizier, if he were allowed to visit Colonel Champion, and ask his mediation in obtaining a reasonable period of grace. 'But Hafiz said that as he had not the money, and as none of the Sirdars were willing to contribute towards the payment, he would not borrow, and was prepared to die in defence of his country. Pahar Sing again offered to procure the money from some merchants, but Hafiz would not consent, observing that, as he must die some time, he could not fall in a better cause[1].'

The rest of the story is soon told. The two armies met on the 23rd of April, 1774[2], at Miranpur Katra, in the district of Shahjehanpur. The Rohillas were reported by Colonel Champion to be 40,000 strong, but their numbers are stated by Hamilton, with greater probability, to have been 28,000, with 60 guns. We have few details of the battle except those furnished by Colonel Champion, and, as I shall have to show, his animosity against the Vizier was so great that implicit confidence cannot always be placed in his statements. After a gallant resistance the Rohillas were defeated with a loss said to amount to more than 2,000 men, and Hafiz Rahmat was killed. 'It is impossible,' Colonel Champion wrote, 'to describe a more

crores of rupees. Colonel Champion is not likely to have been mistaken, but his statement does not appear to be supported by his letter of the 19th April to Hafiz Rahmat, nor do the letters of Hafiz Rahmat show that a demand for any definite sum had been made by the Vizier. The translation of the correspondence with Hafiz Rahmat is obviously very imperfect.

[1] In the Gul-i-Rahmat, the grandson of Hafiz Rahmat says that Colonel Champion endeavoured at the last moment to stop the war, by writing to Hafiz Rahmat and promising that, if the money due to the Vizier were paid, he would effect a peace. 'But death had deprived him of all his friends and supporters; he had therefore withdrawn his heart from the world, and was desirous of martyrdom.' It is certain that no such communication was made by Colonel Champion.

[2] Colonel Champion called the battle the 'Battle of St. George,' the 23rd April being St. George's Day.

obstinate firmness of resolution than the enemy displayed; numerous were the gallant men who advanced, and often pitched their colours between both armies, in order to encourage their men to follow them.' According to Hafiz Rahmat's son and grandson, the defeat of the Rohillas was in a great measure due to the treachery of several of their own chiefs who joined Shuja-ud-dowla while the action was going on[1].

The brunt of the battle fell, as has always happened in our Indian wars, on the British troops. Colonel Champion complained bitterly that the Vizier himself, with nearly the whole of his cavalry and a large number of guns, remained inactive on the ground that the English army had left in the morning. After describing the flight of the Rohillas, Colonel Champion's despatch thus continues:—

'And now came on the after-game of the few horse the Nabob sent to the field. No sooner was the enemy irrecoverably broken than they pushed after them, and got much plunder in money, elephants and camels, &c., &c., &c. Their camp equipage, which was all standing, and proves we came on them by surprise, with whatever effects they could not carry off, fell a sacrifice to the ravages of the Nabob's people, whilst the Company's troops, in regular order in their ranks, most justly observed, "We have the honour of the day and these banditti the profit." I wish I could pay the Vizier any compliment on this occasion, or that I were not under the indispensable necessity of expressing my highest indignation at his shameful pusillanimity; indispensable, I say, because it is necessary that the Administration should clearly know how little to be depended on is this their ally.'

We need not believe in the 'shameful pusillanimity' of the Vizier. 'Shuja-ud-daula,' as Sir Henry Lawrence writes, 'whatever were his faults was never before accused of cowardice.' The official returns of killed and wounded seem to make it probable that the Vizier's infantry took a larger share in the action than might be supposed from Colonel Champion's despatch, for while the loss of the Company's English and Native troops was 132, that of the

[1] Gulistan-i-Rahmat, p. 116; Gul-i-Rahmat, Elliot, vol. viii. p. 312.

troops of the Vizier, not including his cavalry for which there is no return, was 254. Two English officers were wounded, but none were killed [1].

The following description of the death of Hafiz Rahmat, is given by his grandson :—

'He went to the tent of Faizullah Khan, and said, "My end is near at hand. So long as I remain alive, do not turn away from the field; but when I fall, beware, do not press the battle, but leave the field directly, and flee with my children and dependants to the hills. This is the best course for you to take, and if you act upon my advice, it will be the better for you." After giving these directions, he mounted his horse, and marched against the enemy with ten thousand horse and foot. He had proceeded only a short distance, when the advanced force of the enemy came in sight, and fire was opened from cannons and muskets. Ahmad Khan, son of the Bakhshi, who had made a secret engagement with Shuja-ud-daula, now fell back, and set the example of flight, which many others followed. Hafiz Rahmat had only about fifty supporters left when he drew near to the Telingas and English. He was recognised by his umbrella of which spies had given a description, and a cannon was levelled against him. He advanced in front of all his companions using his utmost efforts. The cannon balls fell all round, and at length one struck him on the breast. He was lifted off his horse, and after taking a sip or two of water, he drank the cup of martyrdom [2].'

Whatever degree of blame may be justly due to Shuja-

[1] Colonel Champion's despatch will be found in Appendix No. 26, Fifth Report, and in Forrest's Selections, vol. i. p. 96. See also his letter, in which reference is made to the Vizier's conduct, dated March 2, 1775, Forrest's Selections, vol. ii. p. 332. Accounts of the battle are given by Hamilton, and in the Sair-ul-Mutakherin, vol. iii. p. 261. Macaulay's version of the story is worth quoting as an illustration of his love of rhetorical embellishment: 'The dastardly sovereign of Oude fled from the field. The English were left unsupported, but their fire and their charge were irresistible. It was not, however, till the most distinguished chiefs had fallen, fighting bravely at the head of their troops, that the Rohilla ranks gave way. Then the Nabob Vizier and his rabble made their appearance and hastened to plunder the camp of the valiant enemies, whom they had never dared to look in the face.' The statement that Shuja-ud-daula 'fled from the field' is a mere flight of imagination; neither Colonel Champion nor any other authority asserted or suggested anything of the kind. The same may be said of the distinguished chiefs who fell fighting bravely; with the exception of Hafiz Rahmat himself no Rohilla chief of importance was killed. Colonel Champion reported in his despatch that a son of Hafiz Rahmat had been killed, but this was a mistake.

[2] Gul-i-Rahmat; Elliot, vol. viii. p. 312.

ud-dowla for his conduct during and after the action, his behaviour on the death of Hafiz Rahmat was honourable. On the day on which the battle was fought, Middleton, the English Resident, who was present at the time, sent news to Hastings of the victory, and informed him that the Vizier had ordered the body of Hafiz Rahmat 'to be interred with every honour due to his rank and distinction [1].' The son of Hafiz Rahmat himself has confirmed this statement. 'A Sawar,' he writes, 'named Sultan Khan, severed the head of Hafiz Rahmat from the body and carried it in triumph to Shuja-ud-daula, who placed it and the body in a palanquin, covered it with shawls, and sent it to Bareilly. The principal inhabitants of the town went out to meet the body, and after the proper forms had been observed, it was interred [2].' Soon after the death of Hafiz Rahmat, a mausoleum, still to be seen at Bareilly, was erected to his memory by his relations. Thus ended the Rohilla dominion. Counting from the time when Ali Mohammad's power was first established to the death of Hafiz Rahmat, who during nearly the whole period was the chief personage in the State, it lasted less than thirty-five years.

I quote the description which Hamilton has given of the character of Hafiz Rahmat :—

'Whether we consider him as a soldier or a statesman, he was certainly entitled to some degree of respect. As the director of a factious and disturbed government, he by the superiority of his talents and address kept together its several parts much longer than could have been expected, considering the nature of the people with whom he had to deal, and the unfortunate events under which they laboured.

[1] Letter from Middleton, British Museum MSS. No. 29,134. Colonel Champion did not deny this, which he certainly would have done if it had not been true, but he more than once referred to the subject after the war was over. In his letter to the Government dated Jan. 30, 1775, he speaks of the Vizier 'exulting over the pale head of Hafiz,' and in his letter dated March 2, 1775 (printed in Forrest's Selections, vol. ii. p. 335), he enclosed, but without comment, an extract from his Persian Interpreter's Journal of April 23, 1774, which says; 'After the action the Vizier, who had remained on the bank of the nullah that we marched from until the success of the day was known, came to the Colonel's tent, bringing with him the head of Hafiz, which he expressed a good deal of pleasure having in his possession.'

[2] Gulistan-i-Rahmat, p. 117.

His personal bravery and firmness in the hour of danger would have enabled the Rohillas to support themselves with success against all foreign enemies, and to have protected their dominion from the many calamities in which it had been involved for some years past, had he been properly supported by his colleagues, and it was this spirit that determined him, on the failure of every other resource, to prefer an honourable death to an inglorious submission. But, however praiseworthy his conduct in these situations may appear, the circumstances of his rise to power, as well as the use he often made of that power when acquired, must detract greatly from his merit; and it remains to be regretted that such happy endowments should have been blended with the most mischievous of all vices, and that a grasping and unprincipled ambition should have induced him to betray the trust of his friend, and usurp the inheritance of his wards, in a manner which tarnishes all his great qualities and throws a perpetual slur on his memory[1].'

Reference has already been made to the condition of Rohilkhand under the government of the Rohillas, and to some of the personal qualifications of Hafiz Rahmat. It is probable that he deserved a better character than that which Hamilton has given to him. It must be remembered that the work on which Hamilton's history is based, and from which much of it is translated, was written by a servant of Faizullah Khan, and that it avowedly expressed the opinions of his master. It was not to be expected that the son of Ali Mohammad would be disposed to take a favourable view of the character of the man by whom the members of his own family had been treated with scant justice, and had been deprived of the greater part of the possessions left to them by their father.

The histories of the life of Hafiz Rahmat, written by his son and grandson[2], throw little light on his character as a ruler. I have already quoted from the Gulistan-i-Rahmat a passage regarding his abolition of taxes upon trade; the same work extols his liberality towards the widows and sons of his soldiers who fell in battle, and towards learned and pious men, but the qualities which are chiefly dwelt upon are the strictness of his religious observances, his fasts and prayers and sacrifices. 'It is not surprising,'

[1] Hamilton, p. 237.

[2] See Preface.

writes his son, 'that a ruler who studied so little his own ease, whose whole life was spent in performing his duty to his God and to his fellow-creatures, should have been beloved in life, and regretted in death; indeed his fall caused a general mourning throughout Kather[1].' Mr. Elliott, writing at Bareilly in 1814, after 'a residence of many years in Rohilkhand,' tells us, in the preface to his translation of the Gulistan-i-Rahmat, that 'the memory of Hafiz Rahmat was held in the highest veneration.' Although I cannot doubt that these recollections of the Rohilla Chief and of his times were coloured by the abominable misgovernment of the Oudh rulers after Shuja-ud-daula's death, they have nevertheless some value. On the whole I cannot pass upon Hafiz Rahmat so harsh a judgment as that of Mr. Whiteway, who sums up our knowledge of his character in the opinion that, although he was a fairly successful ruler, his leading qualities were avarice and insincerity[2].

On the death of Hafiz Rahmat, Faizullah Khan, the eldest surviving son of Ali Mohammad, a man of capacity and courage, became the acknowledged head of the Rohillas. He fled, with the remains of the army, to Rampur, and thence, taking with him his family and his treasure, he retired northwards, through the Terái and forest in the Bijnor district, to Laldhang, a strongly situated post at the foot of the Garhwal mountains, beyond the boundaries of the Rohilla territories. Here he was joined by large numbers of his countrymen, and he was soon in command of a considerable force. No resistance was attempted in the plains of Rohilkhand. The power of the Rohillas, having been merely that of an army of foreigners holding in subjection a numerous people of another and a hostile faith, necessarily collapsed with military defeat.

'Nothing,' writes Hamilton, 'could exceed the terror and confusion of the Afghans throughout Rohilkhand, on learning the disastrous issue of a battle which at once annihilated their power and decided the fate of their dominion. Neither were their fears confined to the

[1] Gulistan-i-Rahmat, p. 117. [2] Calcutta Review, 1875, p. 223.

L

progress of the victorious army. Wherever the defeat of the Rohillas became known, the Hindu zemindars, each of whom is possessed of a stronghold attaching to the chief village of his district, shut their forts, and refusing their late masters succour or protection, plundered without distinction all whom they found flying towards the hills, so that numbers of the Afghans, who would otherwise have joined their countrymen at Laldhang, returned to their homes, and there quietly awaited the event... Many more were encouraged to this by the generous and temperate conduct of the British troops, whose characteristic virtues were not more displayed by their gallantry in the late engagement, than by their humanity after it. In the close of the action, whilst yet flushed with recent victory, they advanced by divisions and marched through the Rohilla camp with all the disciplined coolness and regularity of a review: not a man offering to leave his post, or to seize on any part of the spoil which was scattered over the plain around them; and on the same evening all the wounded Rohillas who appeared to be in a curable state were taken into the English hospital, and attended with the same care as their own people; and these circumstances undoubtedly contributed not only to the reputation of the conquerors, but to the facility of their subsequent success[1].'

Early in May Colonel Champion reported to the Government that the whole of the Rohilla country was in the Vizier's possession, and the Resident was consequently instructed to demand an acknowledgment that the forty lakhs of rupees which the Vizier had agreed to pay had now become due. It was said, however, that it was not intended to insist on immediate satisfaction of the claim, and that the Government wished the time and conditions of payment to be arranged between the Resident and Vizier. When this demand was made the Vizier not unreasonably expressed surprise; he said that although the country was in his possession, the Rohillas had not been finally expelled from it, since Faizullah Khan's army still remained on its borders, and that, under the engagement into which he had entered, payment of the forty lakhs was not due until he declared that he no longer required the services of the English brigade. The Vizier's contention was obviously true; the demand was not pressed, and no payment was made until the troops had been withdrawn, after the change in the Government when power had passed

[1] Hamilton, p. 243.

from the hands of Hastings into those of the majority of the Council [1].

Faizullah Khan lost no time in endeavouring to open negotiations with the commander of the English forces and the Vizier, and towards the end of May he sent an envoy to Colonel Champion with definite proposals. He offered, if he were placed in possession of the whole of Rohilkhand, to pay to the Company eighty lakhs of rupees in three years, or, if it were preferred, to pay that sum to the Vizier, under a guarantee from the English of the Vizier's good faith, and to place his son in the hands of the English as a hostage until the money was paid. As an alternative arrangement, he offered to pay thirty lakhs of rupees annually to the Vizier and to 'give the Company twenty-five lakhs if they will influence the Nabob to put him in possession of the country and guarantee the treaty.' He also offered to have 15,000 men ready to join the English and Vizier on all occasions. Colonel Champion thought that it would be wise to accept these proposals, and he seems to have believed that Faizullah Khan could have carried out the engagements into which he was ready to enter, but he reported to Hastings on the 28th May that the Vizier 'had rejected them all with the greatest disdain.' Hastings would not listen for a moment to Faizullah Khan's offers, and he desired that the Vizier should be in every way discouraged from accepting them. His letter, sent to Colonel Champion on the 17th June, 1774, is interesting, because it repeats very clearly the reasons which had led him to take part in the war :—

'I have one general objection to the whole of these propositions, which is, that they are diametrically opposite to the principle on which

[1] Fifth Report, App. No. 27. See also note by Colonel Champion's Persian interpreter, dated June 12, 1774, describing an interview between Colonel Champion and the Vizier. App. No. 23 to Colonel Champion's letter dated January 30, 1775; Consultations of February 14, 1775, India Office Records. In reporting the matter to the Court of Directors, the Government gave a somewhat different account, thinking it, I suppose, inexpedient to tell the Court that they had made a demand which was not justified. See Letter to Colonel Champion, May 23, 1774, and Letter to the Court of Directors, dated October 19, 1774.

the Rohilla expedition was on our part undertaken, which was not merely on account of the pecuniary acquisition of forty lakhs of rupees to the Company, for although this might have been an accessory argument, it was by no means the chief object of the undertaking. We engaged to assist the Vizier in reducing the Rohilla country under his dominion, that the boundary of his possessions might be completed by the Ganges forming a barrier to cover them from the attack and insults to which they were exposed, by his enemies either possessing or having access to the Rohilla country. This our alliance with him, and the necessity of maintaining this alliance so long as he and his successors shall deserve our protection, rendered advantageous to the Company's interest, because security of his possessions from invasions in that quarter is in fact the security of ours. But if the Rohilla country is delivered to Faizullah Khan, the advantages proposed from this measure will be totally defeated. The same objections from the Vizier will take place against him as against Hafiz Rahmat; he will be actuated by the same principles of self-defence, and the same impressions of fear, to seek the protection of other powers against the Vizier, and of course will create the same jealousies and suspicions in the mind of the Vizier, with the additional and strong incentive to a mutual animosity, of an enormous debt, which probably Faizullah Khan will find no other means to get clear of, but by engaging in hostilities against the Vizier. The Board undertook the Rohilla expedition on a firm conviction that the Vizier would be able to maintain his conquest of it, and that it would make his other dominions more defensible. For the reasons before assigned, and with respect to myself, I declare that if I had not been morally certain of the justness of this reasoning, I would not have consented to enter upon the enterprise at all[1].'

This refusal of Hastings to listen to the proposals of Faizullah Khan was included in the Articles of Charge against Hastings brought forward by Burke in 1786, in the House of Commons, but it was afterwards abandoned. It is remarkable that Burke, who was indignant at the receipt by the English of forty lakhs of rupees from Shuja-ud-daula, should have declared these offers of Faizullah Khan to be 'strictly consonant to the demands of justice.' Mill says nothing about their rejection. It would have been inconvenient to call attention to the reasons given by Hastings for refusing to listen to them, because in his letter to Colonel Champion he had repeated

[1] Fifth Report, App. No. 27.

his explanation of the real objects with which the war had been undertaken, an explanation which Mill has always studiously suppressed. In fact, as Hastings observed in his answer before the House of Commons to the Twenty-second Charge, it was impossible that Faizullah Khan could have carried out his proposals. 'No consequence,' he said, 'can be more remote from the premises than that the performance of so extravagant an offer would have followed the acceptance of it. . . . The extravagance of the offer was a clear proof of the insincerity of the man who made it, and so I treated it[1].'

While these negotiations were going on, the Vizier endeavoured, with considerable success, to conciliate the Rohilla chiefs who had not joined Faizullah Khan. Letters were sent to them desiring them to remain quietly at their homes, and assuring them of protection. The Hindu population had no inclination to encourage resistance on the part of its late masters, and nearly the whole of Rohilkhand was soon in the Vizier's possession, and in a state of tolerable tranquillity. When, however, the rainy season had set in, military operations against Faizullah Khan became extremely difficult, and at the same time it was clear that delay in bringing the war to an end might be dangerous. In July, alarming reports of the probable return of the Marathas were received; it was believed that the Emperor was intriguing with them, and that he was advising Faizullah Khan, who would have been ready to pay largely for help, to continue his resistance. It was urged strongly by the Vizier that the attack on Faizullah Khan could not safely be postponed, but Colonel Champion was averse to undertaking operations during the rainy season in a most difficult and most unhealthy country. Hastings became anxious that there should be no avoidable delay, and sent orders to that effect. The English troops with those of the Vizier accordingly marched towards the foot of the hills, and at the end of August they were

[1] Articles of Charge, No. 22, presented to the House of Commons, May 5, 1786; and Answer by Warren Hastings.

not far from the strongly fortified positions of the Rohillas. These were outside the recognised limits of Rohilkhand, to which Colonel Champion had been ordered to confine his operations, and he hesitated to advance beyond them. Authority was, however, sent to him to attack the Rohilla army wherever it might be found, and he was strongly urged by Hastings to pursue the most vigorous measures for terminating the war. Negotiations were again opened, but it was not until the 2nd October, when the advanced posts of the English were within a mile of those of the Rohillas, that a decisive step was taken by Faizullah Khan. On that day he came into Colonel Champion's camp, and appealed to him to effect an honourable arrangement with the Vizier. Hastings had insisted on the importance of bringing the war to an end as soon as the objects with which it was undertaken had been sufficiently secured, and he wrote to Colonel Champion that he hoped that the Vizier would 'conciliate the affections of the Rohillas to his Government by acceding to lenient terms[1].'

On the 7th October, 1774, a treaty was concluded between the Vizier and Faizullah Khan, and it was attested by Colonel Champion. It provided that Faizullah Khan should retain possession of the territory formerly allotted to him in Rohilkhand by his father Ali Mohammad, with the city and district of Rampur. Its nominal revenue was nearly fifteen lakhs of rupees, but this was said to be less than the actual amount. It was stipulated that Faizullah Khan should retain in his service a force of not more than 5,000 men, that he should, if called on to do so, render certain military services to the Vizier, and enter into no correspondence with any powers excepting the Vizier and the English. Faizullah Khan, it was further provided, 'shall send the remainder of the Rohillas to the other side of the river.' He agreed 'that whatever the Nabob Vizier directs, I will execute, and I will at all times and on all

[1] Letter from Select Committee to Colonel Champion, September 8, 1774.

occasions, both in adversity and prosperity, continue his firm associate [1].'

On the day after the treaty was executed, Colonel Champion reported to Hastings that 'as Faizullah Khan is restricted to a small body of men, such of the troops disbanded by him as the Vizier does not choose to entertain, are to cross the Ganges without delay.' He said in the same letter, that Faizullah Khan had agreed to give up to the Vizier one half of the treasure in his possession, but it was subsequently settled, with the consent of both parties, that in lieu of this, Faizullah Khan should pay fifteen lakhs of rupees. This agreement was carried out, but no reference was made to it in the treaty. The Vizier also wrote to Colonel Champion that he was willing to take into his own service 10,000 or 15,000 of Faizullah Khan's soldiers [2].

Immediately after the signature of the treaty, the Vizier and the English withdrew their forces; Faizulluh Khan went with his 5,000 men to Rampur, and assumed quiet possession of the country assigned to him; the rest of the Rohilla troops marched, under the command of some of their chiefs, across the Ganges into the districts of Zabita Khan, their countryman. The number of Rohillas who thus left Rohilkhand is said by Hamilton to have been 17,000 or 18,000. According to Colonel Champion it was about 20,000, including camp followers [3]. Many of the Rohilla soldiers entered the service of Zabita Khan, and many soon returned to Rohilkhand, and obtained employment with Faizullah Khan or in the army of the Vizier. No Rohillas except those under arms with Faizullah Khan were compelled to cross the Ganges; the rest were unmolested, and either remained in their former homes or settled in the Rampur State. Whatever may have been the misgovernment or absence of government in Rohilkhand after the fall of the

[1] Fifth Report, App. No. 44.

[2] Fifth Report, App. Nos. 44 and 45; Consultations, February 14, 1775, India Office Records.

[3] Evidence before Committee of House of Commons, May 3, 1786.

Rohilla dominion, there is no reason to suppose that either at this or at any subsequent time the Rohillas suffered any special persecution or oppression from the Oudh authorities.

Several months before the conclusion of the arrangement with Faizullah Khan, there were rumours of the existence of the treaty which the Vizier had entered into with the Emperor, without the knowledge of the English Government, for the partition of Rohilkhand. On the 5th May, 1774, Colonel Champion stated that he had heard reports to this effect, and asked for instructions in case they should prove true. There was a difference of opinion in the Council as to the answer that should be given, but on the 23rd May orders were sent in accordance with the views of Hastings and the majority:—

'As we have no knowledge of any treaty of partition between the King and the Vizier, we can take no cognizance of the breach of it. Our engagements with the latter are to aid him in the conquest of the Rohilla country, and if he is opposed by Najf Khan, or the King himself should personally interfere, you are to pay no regard to either, but steadily and invariably prosecute the tenor of your original instructions against all opponents of whatever power or character they may be. We cannot entertain so bad an opinion of the Vizier as to suppose him capable of acting in avowed breach of a treaty, but if any plea of that kind should be made for contesting our right to occupy any part of the Rohilla country yet unconquered, it will be proper to put the question to him, whether such treaty does exist or not? If he should acknowledge such a treaty you must undoubtedly abstain from further hostilities in abetment of his breach of faith; but we repeat that though in reply to a question proposed by you to us for your instruction, we have thus given you our opinion, yet we do not apprehend the possibility of such a case occurring, and if the Vizier should deny having engaged in such a treaty we can neither authorize you to examine the identity of it, nor do we see by what means you could investigate the truth[1].'

On the 16th May, Colonel Champion sent a further report on the same subject. Najf Khan had arrived at his

[1] Fifth Report, App. No. 27.

camp with a considerable force, and informed him that before the war began the Vizier

'prevailed with him to go to Delhi, in order to influence his Majesty to take the field and countenance the conquest of the Rohillas, on the express condition that half of the country should go to his Majesty. That he, Najf Khan, accordingly induced the King to leave Delhi and display the royal standard; that his Majesty having, however, been taken ill was obliged to relinquish his intentions of continuing in the field in person, but commissioned Najf Khan to represent him, and act in his name as if he were present; that accordingly Najf Khan with his army were in full march to join the Vizier when he received the news of the defeat of the Rohillas; that his business here was to demand the performance of the condition on which the King's troops took the field; that he had sent for a copy of the agreement, and would not declare his business to the Vizier until it came[1].'

Najf Khan left the English camp without producing the treaty, but on the 17th June Colonel Champion received a copy of it with a letter from the Emperor, inviting him to remind the Vizier of his promise, and to 'send to the Presence the proportion stipulated to us.' This was shown by Colonel Champion to the Vizier, who acknowledged the authenticity of the treaty; he produced the counterpart agreement under the Emperor's seal, but said that the Emperor, not having come in person according to his engagement, had forfeited any benefits which he might have claimed. Neither in the treaty or in the counterpart agreement was there any condition to the effect that the Emperor was to take the field in person, but the Vizier's statement on this point was in accordance with that made to Colonel Champion by Najf Khan, and as the authority of the Emperor himself was little more than nominal, and actual power was in the hands of Najf Khan, it was in fact with him rather than with the Emperor that the agreement had been made. It may be assumed that both parties were equally insincere, and while there can be little doubt that the Vizier never had any intention of fulfilling his promises, if it should afterwards seem more profitable to break them, Najf Khan and the Emperor gave to him, by

[1] Fifth Report, App. No. 27; Forrest's Selections, vol. i. p. 106.

their failure to carry out their part of the engagement, an ostensible reason for his own disregard of his obligations. In reply to Colonel Champion's request for instructions in regard to these proceedings, the following orders were sent to him on the 14th July:—

'With respect to the treaties mutually interchanged between the King and the Vizier, as the latter insists on secret conditions which invalidate the King's apparent right; as the treaties were formed without the knowledge or participation of this Government, which could have no right or plea to interfere but that of being guarantee to them; and as an interposition would be productive of much inconvenience and embarrassment, without the possibility of deriving either credit or advantage from it, we again recur to the answer which you received from the Board on this very subject in their letter of the 23rd May, declaring we will have no concern in these engagements, the execution of which we leave entirely to the parties themselves. It is our intention to persevere in pursuit of the object which originally engaged us in the present enterprise, and to adhere strictly to our engagements with the Vizier, without suffering our attention to be diverted by foreign incidents or occurrences[1].'

The decision of Hastings to refuse all interference was, under the circumstances, the only one that could be adopted, and if there had been any inclination to further the aims of the Emperor it would have been effectually dispelled by the reports repeatedly sent by Colonel Champion of intrigues hostile to the interests of the English and of the Vizier in which the Emperor was engaged. His proceedings were referred to on the 24th August, 1774, in a letter from the Bengal Government to the Court of Directors:—

'The King has lately taken into his service Sumroo, the notorious assassin of the unfortunate prisoners at Patna; it is also said that he has invited Ghazi-ud-din and Mir Kasim to his court and that he has written letters to the Abdali and to the Maratha chiefs, soliciting their return to that quarter, and to Faizullah Khan, encouraging him to persevere and flattering him with hopes of success. These indications of his Majesty's indisposition towards us, for which many obvious causes may be assigned, are not likely to affect your interest, at least not materially, since his solicitations will have little weight with the powers to whom they are made, and who know that he has neither wealth, territory, nor personal command, to give them credit[2].'

[1] Fifth Report, App. No. 27.

[2] This account of the treaty between the Emperor and the Vizier is taken from the official correspond-

ence between Colonel Champion and the Government, printed in Appendix No. 27 to the Fifth Report of the Committee of Secrecy, and from India Office Records. An account of the transactions connected with the treaty will also be found in the letter to the Government written by Colonel Champion on the 30th January, 1775 (see Fifth Report, App. No. 45, and Forrest's Selections, vol. i. p. 218); it dwells on everything unfavourable to the Vizier, and is in some essential respects inconsistent with the statements made in his own official letters while the campaign was going on. The question of this treaty has no important bearing on the history of the war, and my only reason for referring to it in detail is that Mill, who, as usual, has suppressed all that it would have been inconvenient to quote, has found in it an opportunity for attacking Hastings and his Government. See his History, book v. chap. vi.

CHAPTER XII.

DISCONTENT OF THE ENGLISH TROOPS.

Refusal of Hastings to allow the troops a share of plunder.—Discontent of Colonel Champion and his officers.—Reports sent to Hastings by Colonel Champion, Middleton, and the Vizier.—Alarm of the Bengal Government.—Special meeting of the Council.—The claim of the troops to share of plunder refused.—Discontent of the troops and anxiety of Hastings.—Proposed grant of donation to the army by the Vizier.—Hastings refuses sanction.—Alarming reports from Middleton.—Colonel Macleane sent by Hastings on a secret mission to the camp.—His reports.—Discontent of the officers of the army towards Colonel Champion.—Address of the officers to Hastings.—Colonel Champion returns to Calcutta and renews complaint regarding refusal of share of plunder.—Amount of plunder obtained by the Vizier.

I HAVE hitherto made no reference to the atrocities said by Burke, and Mill, and Macaulay to have been perpetrated during the Rohilla war, because it seemed desirable to treat separately this part of the commonly received story. To enable it to be properly understood there is, however, another subject to which it is necessary to refer.

In Colonel Champion's official despatch of the 24th April, reporting the defeat of the Rohillas, nothing was said of any atrocities, but in a passage already quoted, he charged the Vizier with 'shameful pusillanimity,' and referred to the plunder of the enemy's camp. 'The Company's troops,' he wrote, 'in regular order in their ranks, most justly observed—we have the honour of the day and these banditti the profit.'

These remarks of Colonel Champion were not dictated by motives of humanity or regard for discipline. They were the first sign of the fact that he and his officers were extremely dissatisfied because they had obtained no share of the plunder, and their discontent soon assumed alarming

not already, in consequence of my letter to the Governor of the 28th ultimo, you will now be pleased to interest yourselves on their behalf, for it must be extremely discouraging to your troops, if they are not attended to on this occasion. By their gallantry they have reduced this country, and of course gained to the Company half a million of money; they have moreover been the enrichers of Shuja-ud-daula to an immense amount; before their faces he has seized these riches, and he has not even thanked them for their services. These matters, Gentlemen, are, in my opinion, of the utmost importance, and deserve your most serious consideration. The good temper and forbearance of your army under such temptation is matter of the greatest admiration, and a source of much satisfaction to me, but I must confess that I am afraid if some mark of favour and gratification for their services is not manifested, it may be dangerous ever to try an experiment of this kind again, or to put the temper and patience of any part of your troops so much to the proof. Situated as I am, it falls only to my province to submit these matters to your wisdom and deliberation, and I have only at present to add that, upon my honour, self-interest has not dictated a line of this address, to which I have been prompted by a just sense of the Vizier's conduct, and a warm regard for troops who have rendered themselves very dear to me and whose interest I shall ever seek to promote [1].'

When these demands, couched in language that was almost menacing, reached Calcutta, they were declared by Hastings to be 'of the greatest importance and of the most alarming tendency,' and they were rendered more serious by the letters of the Vizier and of Middleton which showed how strongly Colonel Champion's proceedings had been resented. On the 22nd May, in a private letter to Middleton, Hastings expressed his 'alarm at the repeated complaints with which the letters of Colonel Champion are filled against the Vizier,' and said that while he implicitly accepted the Commander-in-Chief's statements so far as they dealt with facts, he feared that he might be induced by his prejudices against the Vizier to place upon the facts a wrong construction.

On the 2nd June a special meeting of the Council was called, and the papers were laid before it by Hastings with a note in which he stated his hope that the judgment of the Government on Colonel Champion's demands 'would

[1] Fifth Report, App. No. 27; Forrest's Selections, vol. i. p. 106.

be decisive, and their orders peremptory.' He had himself already sent two letters to Colonel Champion on the subject.

'The very idea of prize money,' he said, 'suggests to my remembrance the former disorders which arose in our army from this source, and had almost proved fatal to it. Of this circumstance you must be sufficiently apprized, and of the necessity for discouraging every expectation of the kind among the troops. It is to be avoided like poison.' . . . 'The only instance wherein our troops in the present service could have any pretensions to it, by the customs of war, would be in the actual assault of a place by storm; in every other case it is clear that the capture becomes the sole property of the power carrying on the war. In the instance of Pilibhit, which made no sort of defence whatever, but fell with the whole Rohilla country into the hands of the Nabob, in consequence of the victory, we had no more right to search or interfere at all in the riches it contained than we had to ransack every defenceless village or house in the open country for plunder[1].'

On the 3rd June, official orders were sent to Colonel Champion. The Government refused to admit the claim of the army to share in any plunder which might be acquired by the Vizier.

'You will take,' they wrote, 'the proper method to convey a positive and firm declaration to the troops, that they are not to expect any share of the riches acquired by the Vizier in their conquest. Indeed, the consequences which you signify to us are to be apprehended from our refusing this gratification are sufficiently alarming; but at the same time, were there no other reason, the very appearance of so dangerous a spirit in the troops would determine us to oppose it in the beginning; and we rely on your conduct and firmness and that subordination which experience has taught us it has been always your pride to maintain, for enforcing, with the support of your second in command and the other field-officers, these orders, and procuring a complete acquiescence in them from all the officers and soldiers of the army. Indeed we are persuaded that the general disposition is to obedience, however a few unruly spirits or unthinking men may have expressed different sentiments. We conclude in recommending, in the warmest manner, that you exert yourself in bringing the troops to a proper disposition on the subject in question; that you discourage in future those occasional reports of riches and treasure found by the Vizier, which are generally founded on idle rumour and the cupidity of self-interest of individuals, and which can only tend to mislead the soldier into hopes which can never be realised, and instil notions into him very incompatible with his duty and profession[2].'

[1] British Museum MSS.; Gleig, vol. i. p. 421 and 427.

[2] Fifth Report, App. No. 27.

The anxiety of Hastings was soon increased, for, on the 2nd June, Middleton sent to him privately a letter reporting the 'alarming situation of affairs,' and the 'unhappy misunderstanding which had for a considerable time subsisted between the Vizier and the Commander-in-Chief,' and which had commenced in the earlier part of the campaign.

'During the general confusion,' he wrote, 'which succeeded the defeat of the Rohillas, it unfortunately happened that some of the Nabob's officers or dependents, as they themselves asserted, were plundered by the English sepoys, and on a complaint to His Excellency a representation was made to the Commander-in-Chief, who caused a strict inquiry and search to be made through the different corps in the brigade, but without being able to fix on the persons who had committed the outrage or discover the unlawful plunder [1].'

The next cause of discontent, Middleton said, was the action taken by Colonel Champion at Pilibhit, 'since which period a want of cordiality and mutual confidence has become daily more observable. Every day produces the warmest remonstrances from the Nabob on subjects which, but for the unhappy misunderstanding which has occurred, could never have claimed a moment's reflection.' A few days later Middleton returned to the same subject, and said that the Vizier complained of the conduct of the English sepoys towards the people of the villages [1].

On the 3rd July, Colonel Champion reported that he had carried out the orders sent to him on the 3rd June.

'I assembled,' he wrote, 'the second in command, and all the other field officers yesterday morning, and communicated to them the orders of the Administration regarding the claim of this division of the army to a share of the riches acquired by the Vizier in consequence of the battle of St. George. The gentlemen unanimously requested of me to assure Government that they will ever prove obedient soldiers, and of course continue to impress the officers and soldiers under their command with a due sense of good order and subordination, but they also desired it might be respectfully intimated that they hope to be excused if they cannot acquiesce in the opinion which has been delivered regarding the rights and customs of war [2].'

[1] Private letters, British Museum MSS. 29,134.

[2] Fifth Report, App. No. 27. This despatch from Colonel Champion is a characteristic example of his style. It begins as follows: 'I have to tes-

Colonel Champion did not again urge officially these claims to a share of plunder, but the discontent of the troops continued, and became a cause of increasing anxiety to Hastings. On the 4th August he wrote to Middleton in the following terms:—

'I have received very alarming reports of the disposition of the troops in the field. Though they have not come to me from authority, yet the nature of the intelligence, and the manner in which it has been communicated to me, compel me to pay attention to it. A spirit of sedition must be visible to every eye, and therefore I desire you will inform me, if you have reason to believe that such a spirit does prevail, as the measures which may be taken after the conclusion of the rains ought to be formed accordingly. I am told that the whole army are disappointed, and loudly complain that they are denied a share in the plunder of the country, that they are discontented with the service and violently disaffected towards the Vizier. Inform me of such particulars as have come to your knowledge, or which you can obtain upon this subject. Write to me fully, plainly, and without reserve. I write this in confidence, and desire that you will not communicate the contents of it to any one. You need not be apprehensive about what you may write to me in reply; the subject is too delicate on my side, and too dangerous on yours, to be communicated without the last necessity[1].'

Shuja-ud-daula's alarm at the dissatisfaction of the English troops was as great as that of Hastings, and in the hope of appeasing it he determined to give to them a large donation of money. On the 7th August, Middleton sent to Hastings the following report:—

'I fear he considers an immediate declaration of his intentions the surest and probably the only expedient left him to regain the attach-

tify real concern that any part of my letter appeared to carry so great a degree of warmth; and it gives me still more pain that it should be considered to convey a reflection, and even to impart an impeachment of administration. When gentlemen practised in thinking are assembled to deliberate, the order, the unreserve of one or more, if such there should happen to be among them, will be tempered by the equanimity, the circumspection, and political knowledge and experience of their colleagues. An individual cannot have these advantages; therefore I must think for myself, must write for myself; this I can say, however, that if there has been warmth, it has not been of argument; excuse me, then, gentlemen, to the Board, if I, who am myself a soldier, in endeavouring to express my ideas of the merits and eminent services of my followers, have not been able to divest my language of the glow natural to the perception of the mind on such occasions.'

[1] Private letter, British Museum MSS. 29,117.

ment and good will of our troops, for the vein of dissatisfaction and disgust which in general runs through the brigade is too perceptible to have escaped his notice, and I doubt many have been imprudent enough to declare with too much freedom sentiments which, at least, ought to have been concealed from him. I acquainted the Nabob I should without delay address you on this subject, and hoped he would take no further steps until I could be furnished with your instructions. If, however, as I own I am too much inclined to suspect, this act of generosity proceeds more from the dictates of prudence and Hindostan policy than a real sense of gratitude, I am apprehensive my advice will have little weight. Nevertheless, I consider it my duty to oppose the measure until it has received the sanction of your authority[1].'

On the following day, the 8th August[2], Colonel Champion reported to Hastings that he had received a letter from the Vizier stating his intention of giving a gratuity of seven lakhs of rupees to the troops, and on their behalf he asked permission to accept it. The Vizier afterwards proposed to present three lakhs of rupees to Colonel Champion and 50,000 rupees to the officers, but of this Colonel Champion said nothing until the following December, when he returned to Calcutta, after the new Government had come into power. He then stated that he had refused to take the money

'because, when the note was sent to me, I had in my own mind determined to add it to the general fund; it was my resolution to convince my followers and companions in the field that I only desired to share with them in the advantages as I had done in the honours of the war, and I can with great truth assure you, gentlemen, that I perceive much more pleasure and self-approbation in throwing these three lakhs into the common fund, and taking my chance of drawing a proportion, than I should have had in receiving ten times the sum in any other manner[3].'

[1] Private letter, British Museum MSS. 29,135.

[2] Fifth Report, App. No. 27; Forrest's Selections, vol. i. p. 111.

[3] Letter dated 13th December, 1774, Forrest's Selections, vol. i. p. 158. See also Minute by Clavering, Monson, and Francis, 11th January, 1775, para. 65, Fifth Report, App. No. 45; and Colonel Champion's evidence, 28th December, 1774, India Office Records; Forrest's Selections, vol. i. p. 175. No explanation of Colonel Champion's long silence regarding the Vizier's present to himself and the officers appears to have been given; but I do not suggest that he had any unworthy motives. He was privately accused by Francis of having been induced, by a large bribe from Faizullah Khan, to protect the Rohillas, and of having taken an immense fortune to England; but unsupported statements of this kind

Colonel Champion's letter announcing the Vizier's donation to the troops reached Hastings at the end of August and increased his anxiety. On the 27th of August he wrote personally to the Vizier, and begged him to postpone his gift at least until the war was over. 'Although,' he said, 'I am well persuaded that your Excellency has been impelled by motives of pure generosity and a just sense of merit, it will not have that appearance with the world, but it will be believed that it was the effect of an unbecoming requisition on the part of the army, and given to appease their discontent[1].' On the same day he wrote to Middleton. He said that if the claim of the troops had not been made in so clamorous a manner and urged as a right, he would have been ready, after the conclusion of the war, to suggest to the Vizier the propriety of giving them a donation for their services; but that after what had occurred, and while the campaign was still in progress, he could not sanction the proposal that had been made.

'To do so,' he said, 'would have the appearance of reproach, and imply that their duty required a mercenary incitement, and that the Vizier's bounty could only be extorted from him by intimidation. I cannot, therefore, give my consent to the proposed donation, whatever the Vizier's motive may be, and I desire that you will in my name dissuade him from it, and even insist on his postponing his intention till it can be executed at such a time and under such circumstances as may admit of its taking place with credit to the army, and appear with a good grace in him. While the troops are in action or while they manifest in any manner their discontent with the service or dissatisfaction to him, it will be indignity in him to offer so unseasonable a gift, and it will afford a precedent of the most dangerous kind for enacting similar largesses hereafter by the like violent means[2].'

Before the wishes of Hastings were made known to the Vizier, he had already given to Colonel Champion an obli-

made by Francis deserve no credence. In his letter of the 13th December, Colonel Champion wrote as follows: 'It is certain that in offering that money the Vizier had in view the satisfying the Company's troops for their share of plunder, as well as the gratifying them for the hardships they had undergone in the course of the war.' Forrest's Selections, vol. i. p. 158.

[1] Letter to the Vizier, British Museum MSS. 29,135.

[2] Private letter, British Museum MSS. 29,117.

gation for the payment of the money in six months. The Government refused to discuss the subject further, and informed Colonel Champion that they were precluded from doing so by the prohibition of Parliament, contained in the Regulating Act 13 (Geo. III.), under which no servants of the Company, civil or military, were allowed to receive any presents upon any pretence whatever[1].

About the 22nd September, Hastings received from Middleton a letter containing still more alarming accounts.

'I have,' he wrote, 'in my former addresses intimated to you in general terms the disposition of this brigade towards the Vizier, so far as it became my duty from His Excellency's repeated instances, but the subject was too delicate for me to enlarge upon unless enjoined by your commands. Believe me, sir, I now enter upon the task with the utmost diffidence, but your orders are peremptory, and my obedience shall be implicit. I find myself under the disagreeable necessity of confirming by my concurrent report the alarming reports which have been conveyed to you regarding the troops in the field. A general dissatisfaction does most certainly prevail, and has been carried great lengths in public discourse. It seems to have commenced soon after our engagement with the Rohillas, when the troops found themselves deprived of a share of the plunder taken in the enemy's camp, and without any hopes of an equivalent from the Nabob. Murmurs and complaints were heard in different quarters of the camp, but were less violent and unrestrained than they have since broke out; for while the result of the public representation from the Commander-in-Chief on behalf of the army remained in suspense, the troops were buoyed up with expectation of a favourable decision upon their claim, and their discontent was manifested only in exclamation and severe reflections upon the Nabob; but a more general and alarming spirit of disaffection visibly succeeded the publication of the honourable Board's sentiments upon the appeal made to them. It has been confidently affirmed that the judgment of the Council in this instance is erroneous, that no authority whatever can withhold from the troops privileges and prerogatives which the customs and usage of war have established, and which are invariably observed in His Majesty's service, and that the laws of England would decree to the troops a proportion of the advantages, whatever they may be, which the Company may derive from their services in the present expedition. An appeal from the decision of the Board is, I believe, actually resolved upon, and an address to the Supreme Council, intended to be

[1] Fifth Report, App. No. 27.

subscribed by the superior officers of the brigade, has, I am informed, been handed about for approbation. What has been the reception it has met with, or who is the author, I cannot take upon me to determine, but that such letter has been circulated to the commanding officers of the different corps seems not to admit of a doubt. The plunder of Faizullah Khan's camp has been the topic of public discussion in the lines ever since our march from Bisauli, and the officers as well as men have made no secret of their determination to avail themselves of any temptations which may fall in their way, without submitting their right to the decision of a future decree. In justice, however, to many gentlemen, who, I am convinced, are better disposed, it is incumbent upon me to assure you this licentious spirit does not prevail without exception, but I have too much reason to believe the majority of the brigade have imbibed it, and should an action at last decide the contest with Faizullah Khan, I fear the event will prove a full confirmation of what I have asserted. The Nabob seems aware of the consequences to be apprehended. Colonel Champion has indeed intimated them to him, and this possibly may be one cause of that strong inclination which His Excellency has latterly shown to compromise matters with Faizullah Khan. Should an accommodation take place, and the gratuity which the troops have been acquainted they are to receive from the Nabob be regularly paid, I apprehend it will go far towards removing the present discontent, but if any circumstances occur to render the latter doubtful, which, from the situation of His Excellency's affairs and his disposition, seems an event within the bounds of probability, it is the opinion of everyone I have ever conversed with on the subject, as well as my own, that the most serious consequences may be expected to ensue. The above, sir, may I think be depended upon as a faithful and impartial representation of the disposition of the army, to which I shall only add that the Nabob, fully apprized of the disaffection of the troops towards him, has frequently intimated to me his earnest wishes that this brigade might as soon as possible be relieved, and has urged me in the strongest terms to address you on the subject. If I have paid too little regard to these entreaties, I flatter myself, sir, you will attribute it to a diffidence, arising from the nature of the subject, not irreconcilable with the delicacy of my situation. In obedience to your commands, I shall in future make the occurrences of the army an object of my notice, and shall not fail to communicate to you every particular coming within my knowledge which may in any degree affect the service [1].'

When he received this letter, Hastings resolved to send to the camp in Rohilkhand an officer whom he could trust, with instructions to ascertain everything of import-

[1] Private letter, dated 3rd September, 1774, British Museum MSS. 29,135.

ance, and endeavour to reconcile the dissensions between the English army and the Vizier. Colonel Macleane, the Commissary-General, was chosen for this duty. He was sent under the personal orders of Hastings; no information regarding his mission was communicated to the Council, and the matter was one that required such delicate handling that every precaution was taken to secure absolute secrecy. It was given out that it was necessary for the Commissary-General to make personal inquiries in regard to the supplies that would be required for the army in case the war should be prolonged. No notice of the real objects of Colonel Macleane's deputation is to be found in any official papers, and the only person whom Hastings took into his confidence appears to have been Middleton, who was privately told by him, on the 27th September, that he would learn from Colonel Macleane 'his private sentiments on some points of very great consequence.' On the same day he wrote to Colonel Macleane, who had already left Calcutta, and enclosed a letter addressed to Colonel Champion explaining the duty with which Colonel Macleane had been entrusted. 'From the disposition,' he wrote, 'which you perceive him to bear towards me or towards yourself, I leave it to your discretion to deliver or suppress my letter [1].'

Colonel Macleane travelled with the greatest possible speed, but he did not reach the camp in Rohlkhhand until the 12th October. The treaty of peace had been signed a few days before, and the state of affairs was far from satisfactory. When the attack on Faizullah Khan's position was believed to be imminent, Colonel Champion had thought it necessary, in spite of the orders that he had received, to pacify the troops by holding out hopes that

[1] Private letters, British Museum MSS. 29,117. It is clear from some remarks contained in Colonel Champion's 'Refutation of the Vizier's Charges,' sent by him to the Government in January 1775, when Hastings was contending with the hostile majority in the Council, that Colonel Macleane did not think it expedient to deliver the letter, for Colonel Champion was evidently, when he wrote, in complete ignorance of the objects for which Col. Macleane had been sent.

they would be allowed compensation for the share of plunder to which they considered themselves entitled. The following account of their behaviour on the 28th September, and of his own proceedings, was given by Colonel Champion himself after the war was over:—

'Well assured of the great advantage the enemy had in the strength of their situation, sensible that nothing but the strictest observance of good order could ensure our success, and having reason to be suspicious lest the troops, mindful of past neglects, should suffer their discontent to get the better of their moderation, and impel them to disperse in search of plunder, I assembled the field officers at head quarters. Some proposed to stipulate with His Excellency for twenty, some for fifteen, and the most moderate for ten lakhs, in lieu of plunder, and that the troops should be acquainted of it before the attack. I told the gentlemen, that if His Excellency should offer five lakhs, I thought it would be advisable to accept of them, both on account of the imminent danger which would ensue from any disorder of the troops, and the small probability of discovering the riches of a people accustomed to bury their treasure, declaring, however, my wishes that the Vizier might offer a larger sum. The gentlemen, satisfied of my good inclination, said no more on the subject. . . . Mention being made to His Excellency of the plunder, he observed that he had certain intelligence where the riches of the enemy lay buried, that he knew the English could never discover the treasure, and therefore he would not give them one cowrie; a circumstance which I thought it prudent to conceal carefully from the knowledge of the troops[1].'

On the 12th October, Colonel Macleane reported to Hastings that he had arrived just in time to prevent 'a deputation of the captains to Colonel Champion to demand whether any notice has been taken of the army in the treaty with Faizullah Khan, as they were ready to storm the place before the treaty took place.' On the 16th October he wrote again at greater length. He said that although the state of affairs was very unsatisfactory there was no danger of anything like actual mutiny.

'When,' he wrote, 'matters ran highest, there were not three men of any consideration who would not have shuddered at the very thought of mutiny. Indecent clamour, I am sorry to say, not only prevailed but was encouraged, but the more clamorous the authors of it were,

[1] Fifth Report, App. No. 45; Forrest's Selections, vol. i. p. 232.

the more necessary they found it, in points of service, to behave well and obediently. I flatter myself that I am in the right track to succeed in that part of my commission which relates to the army. I do not mean, however, that matters can possibly be now brought to the very point you could wish, but I have reason to believe they will be so moderated as to give you very little uneasiness. In my letter of the 12th instant I mentioned that a remonstrance of a disagreeable nature would, I was apprehensive, be signed by all the captains relative to the late treaty with Faizullah Khan. The ferment ran very high, particularly against the Commander-in-Chief, who has lost all credit and weight with the army, and I was for two days very uneasy lest some unruly spirit should prevail over the more moderate. It was very necessary for me to act vigorously and without delay, but it was also very necessary to conceal that I had any particular inducement to do so, and to make it appear that the business of my department only had drawn me to camp. The first step I took was to see Mr. Middleton, to whom I opened myself confidentially, though he had not yet received any letter relative to me from you. I gave him the first intimation of what was going on, and we took our measures in concert. The thing we desired was to bring the army back to that point from which they ought never to have departed, an appeal to you, and a reliance on your justice in every circumstance of their real or supposed grievances, and our endeavours, I may venture to say, will be crowned with success [1].'

On the 26th October, Colonel Macleane sent another report to Hastings. He had taken into his confidence three of the superior officers who were his personal friends and whom he could trust, and with their help he appears to have been able to bring influence to bear upon the troops. He informed Hastings that several modes of proceeding had been advocated in the camp, but that at last it had been agreed that an address should be sent to Hastings himself, 'submitting respectfully to his determination and craving protection and good offices for the army,' and this was to be signed by the field officers only, 'not in the tumultuous way of all the captains as they had intended.' This address was taken by the officers to Colonel Champion, who at first approved it and said that he would gladly send it to Hastings, but he afterwards objected to the form in which it was written and wished it to be altered. This

[1] Private letter, British Museum MSS. 29,135.

proposal of the Commander-in-Chief was met by the officers 'with an absolute refusal,' 'a proof,' Colonel Macleane said, 'of the very little weight which he now has with the army, as he had not a friend to acquaint him previously of a thing known to every captain and subaltern almost under his command.' Two private letters from officers of the army illustrate the feeling towards Colonel Champion, which at this time prevailed. 'The man,' one of them wrote to Colonel Macleane, 'has now discovered himself, and must be execrated by us; but I entreat your kind interposition to ward off any sinister scheme he may practice against us, as I am now confident he can be guilty of any meanness.' As the officers would not consent to alter the address, they sent it to Middleton with a request that he would forward it. It was sent to Hastings on the 28th October with a letter under the joint signatures of Middleton and Macleane[1]. It did not reach him until after the arrival in Calcutta of Clavering, Monson, and Francis. He then laid it before the Council, with a recommendation that the matter should be referred to the Court of Directors for orders, and that meanwhile the money offered by the Vizier should be placed in deposit. This course was adopted[2].

When Colonel Champion returned to Calcutta on the termination of the war, he renewed his complaint of the refusal to allow the troops a share of the booty acquired by Shuja-ud-daula.

'This remarkable complaisance to the Vizier was,' he said, 'inexplicable.' 'As we are now on the subject of plunder, permit me to offer my attachment to the army in apology for begging of you to attend to it a little farther. According to the letter and to the meaning of my instructions, I had authority to proceed to the conquest of the Rohilla country, if the Vizier required it, with the Company's troops only. Supposing then, gentlemen, that the Nabob had found himself sufficiently engaged in the Doáb, and that I had effected the Rohilla conquest, can it be alleged that the Company's troops would have

[1] Private letters, British Museum MSS. 29,135.

[2] Consultations, 19th December, 1774, India Office Records; and letter to Court of Directors 4th January, 1775, Fifth Report, App. No. 45.

taken charge of the riches found in the forts and cities merely on account of the Vizier, and that they must afterwards have delivered them over to His Excellency? Impossible! And it follows, of course, that his being present could only entitle him to a proportion. I submit, therefore, whether the giving up of the rights of the army was not in effect sacrificing the interest of the nation, inasmuch as the riches of the individuals contribute to the support of the state[1].'

It is not possible to give any opinion regarding the value of the treasure and property of Hafiz Rahmat and other chiefs which fell into the possession of the Vizier, or regarding the amount which he obtained from the plunder of the country. Colonel Champion supposed that he had gained altogether as much as a crore and a half of rupees. Middleton thought that the sum might, perhaps, be about half that amount, and in a private letter to Hastings, he wrote as follows:—'His Excellency has been apprized of the immense plunder which the public have accorded to his conquest, and has repeatedly observed to me in the course of conversation that he is willing to relinquish the whole for an acquittance of the stipulation [of forty lakhs] which he is bound to pay the Honourable Company on the dismission of the brigade. . . . If to the immense charge of supporting this, the Vizier's army, we add the expense

[1] 'Refutation of the Vizier's Charges,' Fifth Report, App. No. 45; Forrest's Selections, vol. i. p. 219. I believe that this account of the discontent in the army and of the anxiety of Hastings is the first that has been published, and the wish of Hastings, that the reasons for Colonel Macleane's mission might remain unknown, would have been fulfilled, but for the existence in the British Museum of the secret correspondence on the subject. Mr. F. C. Danvers has been good enough to trace for me in the India Office Records the subsequent history of the Vizier's gift. On the 15th December, 1775, the Court of Directors wrote that the existing Act of Parliament rendered the acceptance of the money impossible, but that they would consider the propriety of applying for a special Act to authorise it. On the 25th March, 1777, the Bengal Government reported to the Court that they had received another address from the army, and asked for orders. Correspondence between England and India continued, and at last, on the 14th March, 1786, the Court authorized the payment of the money 'to the several claimants or their legal representatives.' Unclaimed shares, it was said, might be given to the Orphan Military Funds, 'if it may be done with propriety.' It was not until August 1787, nearly thirteen years after the conclusion of the war, that the claims appear to have been finally settled.

of his civil establishment and the subsidy to our troops, it will appear evident that the wealth he has accumulated, although it should exceed my estimate, has not been equivalent to his disbursements in the field [1].'

[1] Private letter, 11th July, 1774, British Museum MSS. 29,135.

CHAPTER XIII.

THE 'EXTERMINATION' OF THE ROHILLAS.

The atrocities said to have been committed in the Rohilla war.—The charges of Burke.—Macaulay's version of the story.—Mill on the extermination of the Rohillas.—Mr. John Morley.—Mill's statements altogether false.—Origin of the charge.—The Persian correspondence between the Vizier and Hastings.—Explanations given by Hastings in refutation of the charge.—British Museum MSS.—Paper by the Persian Interpreter.—The charge absolutely unfounded.—The evidence of Colonel Champion, Middleton, and other officers.—No Rohillas killed except in battle. Honourable termination of the war.—Treatment of the Rohilla soldiers.

IN order that nothing may be wanting in my description of the indictment brought against Hastings on account of the atrocities said to have been committed in the Rohilla war, I shall make some quotations from the charges of his chief accusers. The first is taken from the speech delivered by Burke on Fox's East India Bill :—

'The next sale was that of the whole nation of the Rohillas, which the great salesman, without a pretence of quarrel, and contrary to his own declared sense of duty and rectitude, sold to the same Shuja-ud-daula. He sold the people to utter extirpation for £400,000. Faithfully was the bargain performed on our side. Hafiz Rahmat, the most eminent of their chiefs, one of the bravest men of his time, and as famous throughout the East for the elegance of his poetical compositions (by which he supported the name of Hafiz), as for his courage, was invaded with an army of an hundred thousand men and an English brigade. This man at the head of inferior forces was slain valiantly fighting for his country. His head was cut off and delivered for money to a barbarian. His wife and children, persons of that rank, were seen begging a handful of rice through the English camp. The whole nation, with inconsiderable exceptions, was slaughtered or banished. The country was laid waste with fire and sword, and that land, distinguished above most others by the cheerful face of paternal government and protected labour, the chosen seat of cultivation and plenty, is now almost throughout a dreary desert, covered with rushes and briars and jungles full of wild beasts. The British officer who commanded in the delivery of the people thus sold felt some compunction at his employment. He represented the enormous excesses to the President of Bengal, for which he received a severe reprimand from the civil governor, and I much doubt whether the breach caused by the conflict between the compassion of the military and the firmness of the civil governor be closed at this hour[1].'

My next quotations are made from the First Article of Charge presented by Burke to the House of Commons on the 4th April, 1786:—

'That the said Warren Hastings . . . did, in September 1773, enter into a private engagement with the said Nabob of Oudh . . . to furnish him for a stipulated sum of money, to be paid to the East India Company, with a body of troops, for the declared purpose of thoroughly extirpating the nation of the Rohillas. . . . That the said Nabob of Oudh did, in consequence of the said agreement, and with the assistance of British troops, which were ordered to march, and subjected to his disposal by the said Warren Hastings and the Council, unjustly enter into and invade the country of the Rohillas, and did there make war in a barbarous and inhuman manner, by an abuse of victory; by the unnecessary destruction of the country; by a wanton display of violence and oppression, of inhumanity, and cruelty; and by the sudden expulsion and casting down of a whole race of people, to whom the slightest benevolence was denied. When prayer was made not to dishonour the Begum (a princess of great rank whose husband had been killed in battle) and other women, by dragging them about the country, to be loaded with the scoffs of the Nabob's rabble, and otherwise still worse used, the Nabob refused to listen to the entreaties of a British Commander-in-Chief in their favour, and the said women of high rank were exposed not only to the vilest personal indignities, but even to absolute want; and these transactions being by Colonel Champion communicated to the said Warren Hastings, instead of commendations for his intelligence, and orders to redress the said evils, and to prevent the like in future, by means which were suggested, and which appear to have been proper and feasible, he received a reprimand from the said Warren Hastings, who declared that we had no authority to control the conduct of the Vizier in the treatment of his subjects: And that Colonel Champion desisted from making further representations on the subject to the said Warren Hastings, being apprehensive of having already run some risk of displeasing, by perhaps a too free communication of sentiments.—That in consequence of the said proceedings, not only the eminent families of the chiefs of

[1] Speech, December 1st, 1783.

the Rohilla nation were either cut off or banished, and their wives and offspring reduced to utter ruin, but the country itself, heretofore distinguished above all others for the extent of its cultivation as a garden, not having one spot in it of uncultivated ground, and from being in the most flourishing state that a country could be, was, by the inhuman mode of carrying on the war, and the ill government during the consequent usurpation, reduced to a state of great decay and depopulation, in which it still remains [1].'

The contrast is curious between this clumsy invective and Macaulay's version of the story:

'Then the horrors of Indian war were let loose on the fair valleys and cities of Rohilcund. The whole country was in a blaze. More than a hundred thousand people fled from their homes to pestilential jungles, preferring famine, and fever, and the haunts of tigers, to the tyranny of him, to whom an English and a Christian government had, for shameful lucre, sold their substance, and their blood, and the honour of their wives and daughters. Colonel Champion remonstrated with the Nabob Vizier, and sent strong representations to Fort William; but the Governor had made no conditions as to the mode in which the war was to be carried on. He had troubled himself about nothing but his forty lacs; and although he might disapprove of Sujah-Dowla's wanton barbarity, he did not think himself entitled to interfere except by offering advice. This delicacy excites the admiration of the biographer. "Mr. Hastings," he says, "could not himself dictate to the Nabob, nor permit the commander of the Company's troops to dictate how the war was to be carried on." No, to be sure. Mr. Hastings had only to put down by main force the brave struggles of innocent men fighting for their liberty. Their military resistance crushed, his duties ended; and he had then only to fold his arms and look on while their villages were burned, their children butchered, and their women violated [2].'

[1] After these quotations from Burke it is needless to give others from the speeches of less famous men, or from the numerous pamphlets of that time. Many of the latter were, as Hastings said in his Defence before the House of Commons, 'filled with the most scandalous and libellous abuse to influence the prejudices of the public.' The following is a specimen of some of the accounts of the Rohilla war: 'The fatal battle was fought which iniquitously decided the melancholy fate of the brave, industrious, populous, and inoffensive Rohilla nation. It is conjectured that above 500,000 industrious husbandmen and artists, who were also, for the most part, able warriors, together with their families, were deliberately driven openly across the Jumna to receive an asylum from their late enemies and plunderers, the Marathas. The Rohilla provinces are now a barren waste, almost totally deserted by their remaining inhabitants.' Tract No. 132, India Office Library.

[2] It seems to me probable that Macaulay, although he placed the name of 'Gleig's Memoirs of the Life of

I have quoted this passage from Macaulay's essay, because many thousands of Englishmen have long believed that it describes faithfully one of the most abominable crimes recorded in the history of their country. Although I know that it contains hardly a line that is true, I do not propose to criticize it. I yield to no one in respect for Macaulay or in recognition of his services to India, and I feel that while he was misled, it is not Macaulay that we should chiefly blame. I do not doubt that he accepted the statements of Burke and Mill without independent enquiry, that he assumed, as a matter of course, that they were true, and that no suspicion crossed his mind that the testimony which he trusted was worthless.

Leaving the domain of invective and rhetoric, I come now to the sober facts of history. Mill has professed to give them, and to give also the authorities by which they are supported [1].

'Though Faizullah Khan,' he tells us, 'with his treasures and the remains of the army, had made good his flight toward the mountains, the whole country lay at the mercy of the Vizier, and never probably were the rights of conquest more savagely abused. Not only was the ferocity of Indian depredation let loose upon the wretched inhabitants, but as the intention of the Vizier, according to what he had previously and repeatedly declared to the English government, was to exterminate the Rohillas, every one who bore the name of Rohilla was either butchered, or found his safety in flight and exile.'

A note is appended by Mill to this passage :—

'"The inhumanity and dishonour," says Colonel Champion, in his letter of June 12th, 1774, "with which the late proprietors of this country and their families have been used, is known all over these parts; a relation of them would swell this letter to an immense size. I could not help compassionating such unparalleled misery; and my

Warren Hastings' at the head of his essay, had never read the book, for if he had done so he would hardly have written this. Gleig had printed some of the letters of Hastings, which showed how entirely false these charges were, but it is difficult to blame any one who finds it impossible to wade through that most tedious and confused and unsatisfactory of biographies.

[1] It is not worth while to give extracts from the Minutes and letters in which Hastings and the Vizier were denounced in unmeasured language by Francis and his colleagues after the new government had been established in Calcutta. The bitter hatred of Francis afterwards found full expression in the speeches and charges of Burke.

requests to the Vizier to show lenity were frequent, but as fruitless as were those advices which I almost hourly gave him regarding the destruction of the villages, with respect to which I am now constrained to declare that although he always promised as fairly as I could wish, yet he did not observe one of his promises, nor cease to overspread the country with flames, till three days after the fate of Hafiz Rahmat was decided." In another letter he says, "Above a lakh of people have deserted their abodes in consequence of the defeat of Hafiz." Fifth Report, App. No. 27. In another, "The whole army were witnesses of scenes that cannot be described." That the President was perfectly aware of the designs of the Vizier, before his engagement to assist in them, sufficiently appears from his own letter to that chief, dated the 22nd of April, 1773:—"I have received," says he, "your Excellency's letter, mentioning . . . that, should the Rohillas be guilty of a breach of their agreement [viz.: about the forty lakhs], we will *thoroughly exterminate* them, and settle your Excellency in the country; you will in that case pay the Company fifty lakhs of rupees, and exempt them from the King's tribute." Ibid. App. No. 21. In the Nabob's own letter to the President, of the 18th November, 1773, he says, "During an interview at Benares, it was agreed that I should pay, &c. . . . and that I should, with the assistance of the English forces, endeavour to punish and *exterminate the Rohillas out of their country*." Ibid. App. No. 22. Mr. Hastings only admits the atrocities in part, and then defends them in a curious manner; that is to say, not only by the example of Indian barbarity in general, but by the example of British barbarity on the subjects of the Vizier. "I believe it to be a truth," says he, "that he [the Vizier] began by sending detachments to plunder. This I pronounce to have been both barbarous and impolitic. But too much justified by the practice of war established among all nations of the East; and I am sorry to add by our own; in an instance (which the Vizier has a right to quote in vindication of the charges against him) of a detachment employed in the war in which we were engaged with him in the year 1764, to burn and ravage his country." He then quotes a letter from Major Champion, who commanded the detachment, which says, "Two separate parties have been sent into the enemy's country, the one of which was as high up as Buxar, and (according to the directions given me) there are destroyed upwards of a thousand villages. Had not the rains, &c., prevented, we should have done very considerable more damage." Minute of the Governor-General dated 10th January, 1775, in the Fifth Report *ut supra*, App. No. 45 [1].'

If this be true, I hope we shall all agree with Mr. John Morley when he asks—

'Can any Englishman who loves his country, read of this execrable

[1] Mill, Book v. chap. 1. The italics are those of Mill.

crime, even at this distance, without feeling his ears tingle with shame? . . . When these atrocities were represented to Hastings, he replied, with incomparable self-possession, that they were usual in Eastern warfare, and what was more, that the English, when at war with this very Nabob of Oude, ten years before, had burnt and ravaged his country in the same way in which he was burning and ravaging the country of the Rohillas. War cannot be made with rose-water, but it will scarcely be pretended that a governor lending his troops for a sum of money to another ruler, who with their indirect aid overruns a whole district with fire and sword, deserves credit for protecting a suffering people against rapacious sovereigns.'

Mr. Morley adds a note expressing astonishment at the assurance with which, in his edition of Mill's History, Wilson, 'with Colonel Champion's own words before him on the page,' has called in question the accuracy of Mill's statements[1].

Mr. Morley was justified in assuming that Mill had quoted correctly the words of Colonel Champion and of Hastings, but they have in both cases been garbled rather than quoted, nor did Hastings ever make any reply to the representations of Colonel Champion at all resembling that which Mr. Morley supposes. Mill has deliberately suppressed and perverted the facts.

Two questions have to be investigated. What was the nature of the atrocities actually committed during the war, and what was the conduct of Hastings in regard to them?

It will be seen, from the extract that has been given from Mill's History, that he has asserted, on the authority of Hastings himself, not only that the extermination of the Rohillas was part of the original design of Shuja-ud-daula, but that their extermination was agreed to by Hastings when he consented to give the assistance of British troops. Mill has not said a word to show that any different interpretation of the intention of Hastings and the Vizier had ever been or could be suggested, or that Hastings himself had repeatedly repudiated the charge, and had declared it to be absolutely without foundation.

The correspondence between Hastings and the Vizier

[1] Edmund Burke, p. 203.

was carried on in Persian. The original letters have perished or cannot now be discovered, and the words 'exterminate' and 'extirpate,' on which the charge was based, are those of the official Interpreter who translated the Persian letters into English. In the translations of the Vizier's letter of the 24th March, 1773, and of the letter received from him on the 18th November, 1773, the word used is 'exterminate[1].' The word 'extirpate,' more commonly employed in the Charges of Burke and by others, is found in the translation of a letter from the Vizier to Hastings, received on the 28th November, 1774:—

> 'Ambassadors came on the part of Faizullah Khan to Colonel Champion, to confer with him concerning an accommodation which the Colonel proposed to me. As I was determined to extirpate the Rohillas, I would not listen to any proposals of peace. Consider, my friend, that it was my absolute determination to extirpate the Rohillas, and that I requested the assistance of the English troops for that purpose.'

This passage was quoted by Colonel Champion, on the 30th January, 1775, in his reply to the charges of the Vizier, to which I shall again refer, and it was repeated by Clavering, Monson, and Francis, in a Minute written on the 11th January, 1775:—

> 'In our opinion,' they said, 'it is needless to look for farther evidence of the nature of the Vizier's designs or of the approbation it received from Mr. Hastings. It cannot now be a question, whether from the first he meant to extirpate the Rohillas or not, or whether Mr. Hastings was originally apprized of that design in its full extent[2].'

To these remarks by the hostile Majority in the Council, Hastings made the following reply:—

> 'I am charged with a concealed design, formed in concert with the Vizier, to "extirpate" the Rohillas, and much use is made of this discovery, both by the Majority in the letter before me, and by Colonel Champion in his Vindication. The word, in the original language of the letter, which is here translated "extirpate," means to "expel or remove." In another passage of the letter it is joined with a word which does literally mean to "extirpate or root out"; and both

[1] See pp. 80 and 117.

[2] Fifth Report, App. No. 45; Forrest's Selections, vol. i. p. 192.

passages mean no more than that it was the intention of the Vizier to expel or remove the Rohillas from the country which they occupied, without suffering the smallest vestige of their power to remain in it. In this sense, I most certainly did agree to assist the Vizier, and so did the late President and Council, nor can I conceive how the war could have been undertaken with any other object. The Majority know as well as myself that the Rohillas are not the people of the country, but a military tribe who conquered it, and quartered themselves upon the people without following any profession but that of arms, or mixing in any relation with the native inhabitants. I have already described the nature of this tribe in the ninth paragraph of my observations on the first letter of the Majority, and the same account of them has been given by Colonel Leslie and Major Hannay, and, if I mistake not, by Colonel Champion himself, in their examination before the Board on the 19th and 28th of December. Major Hannay's words are remarkable; I beg leave to quote them. "I have learned from many people that it is only within fifty years that the Rohillas are become masters of the country to the north of the Ganges. That they were originally Afghans, come into Hindostan under a Sirdar named Daud Khan, and that they conquered that country from the Hindus, and that since that time they have followed no profession than that of arms, and the ancient Hindus have cultivated the country. The Rohillas are Mussulmen, of the sect of Omar, and the cultivators of the country are Hindus. I suppose the proportion to be about nine Hindus to one Mussulman[1].""

Hastings wrote again in his Defence before the House of Commons, on the 2nd May, 1876:—

'The "extirpation" consisted in nothing more than in removing from their offices the Rohillas who had the official management of the country, and from the country the soldiers who had opposed us in the conquest of it. Nor was the process a sanguinary or hard one, as they had only to pass the Ganges to their countrymen on the other side of it. In a word, we conquered the country from the conquerors of it, and substituted another rule in the place of theirs, upon the same principle of right and usage (the right of the war being pre-supposed), as a British Commander in Europe would expel the soldiers of a conquered town, and garrison it with his own, which by the same mode of speech, and with equal propriety, might be called an "extirpation."'

I have found among the British Museum Manuscripts some interesting evidence in confirmation of the statement thus made by Warren Hastings. The most important part of this evidence is a paper by the Persian Interpreter, who

[1] Letter to the Court of Directors, 22nd February, 1775, India Office Records. 5th Report, App. No. 45; Forrest's Selections, vol. ii. p. 268.

made the original translations of the Vizier's letters. The following is an extract :—

'Another material obstacle has been the great stress laid by those who accused Mr. Hastings before the House of Commons upon certain words and expressions made use of in the written documents (I allude particularly to translated papers) which they produced in support of their charges, when perhaps they bore a very different sense in the original papers. Any one who has been accustomed to translate from one language to another must know how difficult it often is to find words which shall exactly express the meaning of the original. Few, therefore, confine themselves to a literal translation, but endeavour to render it in terms as near their conception of its sense as possible, and I believe it rarely happens that two people would give the interpretations precisely in the same words. If this is true of European languages, where the idioms and modes of expression bear so great an affinity, how much more must it be with respect to an European and Asiatic language, than which no two things can be more dissimilar. On this point I can speak to a certainty, having so often experienced it during the time I held the office of Persian Interpreter in Calcutta. One particular instance has been the subject of much declamation and drawn much undeserved censure on Mr. Hastings. It is the expression made use of by the Nabob Shuja-ud-daula in his correspondence respecting the Rohilla war, which is rendered by the word to "exterminate" or "extirpate." It is the more incumbent on me to explain this, because I am apt to believe that I was the person who first so translated it. I conceive that the Persian word, which is "*istesaul*," never conveyed the meaning which has been affixed to it in this country, of massacring the whole body of the Rohillas, but merely that of destroying the power of those conquerors or expelling them as a body from the country ; and so it certainly appears to have been understood, for when they were totally reduced by the joint arms of the Vizier and the English, one of the chiefs of that nation, Faizullah Khan, was suffered to remain in possession of a considerable tract of country and keep on foot a large body of troops, whilst the remainder were removed to the other side of the river to their countrymen under the dominion of one of their chiefs named Zabita Khan. The words of the grant dated 7th October, 1774, from the Vizier to Faizullah Khan are : "He shall send the remainder of the Rohillas on the other side of the river." I certainly never understood the Persian word in the sense which has been affixed to it in the Charge, and with regard to the English word into which I rendered it, I might have been justified by the authority of Dr. Johnson, who explains it in one sense "to remove." At any rate I certainly understood the word in this sense, and so applied it, viz. : the total abolition of the power of the Rohillas, and their expulsion from the borders of the country—*extra terminos*. Hard indeed would be the situation of a person in high office, whose fortune, fame, and even possibly life itself, were made to depend on the interpretation given to an expression in a foreign language by an interpreter who perhaps in the hurry of business adopted the first word which presented itself to him as similar to his original. I am sure, if this is the case, every Governor ought to be his own translator, and not to trust everything clear to him in the power of another who may either from ignorance, carelessness, or enmity, easily bring down ruin on his head[1].'

I have quoted the letter of Hastings, dated the 22nd February, 1775, in which he says that the correct meaning of one of the two words in the Vizier's letter which had been translated by the English term 'extirpate' was 'expel or remove.' The original manuscript draft of this letter is in the British Museum[2]. It was corrected by Hastings, and parts of it are in his own handwriting. Opposite the words 'expel or remove,' the word '*ikhráj*' is written in the margin, in Persian characters, with the obvious intention of showing that this was the expression used by the Vizier. This marginal note has every appearance of having been written at the same time with the letter itself.

One more piece of evidence bearing on this subject may be noticed. In his 'History of the Rohilla Afghans,' Hamilton, describing the attack made in 1745 on Ali Mohammad, says that 'the Emperor resolved, if possible, to root out the Afghan freebooters and expel them entirely from Katehr,' and he adds, referring to the Persian manu-

[1] British Museum MSS. No. 29,225. This paper has no signature or date, but its author was, I suppose, William Redfearn, who was Persian Interpreter in 1773. He says: 'Two years have elapsed since Mr. Hastings was brought to the Bar in Westminster Hall.' The paper must therefore have been written in 1789. It gives other illustrations of mistakes caused by errors of translation. Thus a petty and dependant Raja became a 'King,' and the Begums of Oudh were all called 'Princesses.' With regard to the latter, the Interpreter says: 'Everyone must remember the cruelties which were said to have been inflicted on the 'Princesses' in the Khord Mahal, or Little Seraglio, and which, if they were ever exercised at all, were no more to be imputed to Mr. Hastings than to the government of this country.' Many of these so-called 'Princesses' were, he says, women of the lowest classes, picked up by Shuja-ud-daula on his marches, with whom no women of rank would hold communication.

[2] MSS. No. 29,136, vol. v.

script on which his work is founded, 'The term in the original is *istisál*, the casual interpretation of which, upon another occasion, into "extirpate" has given rise to great and unfounded clamour; the true meaning is here exhibited, both in the translation of it, and in the circumstance to which it applies[1].'

The facts that have now been stated appear to me to show that one of the expressions translated by 'extirpate' or 'exterminate' was certainly '*istisál*,' and that it is highly probable that the other expression which received the same translation was '*ikhráj*.'

'*Istisál*,' although often used in Persian, is an Arabic word, and Lane, than whom there is no greater authority on Arabic, gives as its signification—uproot, eradicate, extirpate, pull up from its roots or foundation. He gives examples showing that the word is used in two senses, either to remove from its place or to destroy altogether. Wishing to obtain the further judgment of one who could speak on such a subject with indisputable authority, I submitted the statements of Hastings and the Persian Interpreter to Dr. C. Rieu, Keeper of the Oriental Manuscripts in the British Museum, with the following inquiry:—Assuming that in the Persian correspondence between the Vizier and Hastings the word '*istisál*' was applied to the Rohillas in the manner that has been stated, does that word necessarily convey the idea ordinarily implied by the English words 'exterminate' or 'extirpate,' that is, that the whole body of the Rohillas was to be destroyed and utterly swept away; or, on the other hand, is the explanation of the word '*istisál*' given by Hastings and the Interpreter admissible; that the intention was merely (in the words of the former) 'to expel or remove the Rohillas from the country which they occupied, without suffering the smallest vestige of their power to remain in it.' Dr. Rieu informed me, in reply, that it is certain that the word '*istisál*' by no means necessarily implies any

[1] Hamilton, p. 60.

barbarous intention of 'extermination' or 'extirpation.' The word, he said, strictly signifies 'uproot,' and it appeared to him that the sense in which it was used by the Vizier and Hastings can now best be interpreted by the manner in which the 'uprooting' of the Rohillas was actually carried out. If it be true that, in the words of Mill, 'every one who bore the name of Rohilla was either butchered, or found his safety in flight,' then we may infer that this was the sort of 'uprooting' that was contemplated. If, on the other hand, it be true, as stated by Hastings, that the 'uprooting' actually 'consisted in removing from their offices the Rohillas who had the official management of the country, and from the country the soldiers who had opposed us in the field,' and that 'the process was not a sanguinary or hard one, as they had only to pass the Ganges to their countrymen on the other side of it,' then we may infer that the word '*istisál*' was used in the sense which Hastings and the Interpreter declared that it was intended to bear.

With regard to the term '*ikhráj*,' it would, Dr. Rieu informs me, be correctly rendered by the words of Hastings, 'expel or remove[1].'

So much for the use of the words 'exterminate' and 'extirpate.' The question remains whether the Rohillas

[1] Dr. Rieu has been good enough to allow me to quote him as my authority, and he has thus enabled me to say that no question remains regarding the proper interpretation of these Persian expressions. In referring to the translation of the Vizier's letter received on the 18th November, 1773, in which the word 'exterminate' is used, it may be noticed that the term 'expulsion of the Rohillas' is three times employed; and it is clear that this was intended to have the same meaning as 'extermination.' The following passage from Milton gives a good illustration of the sense in which, according to Hastings, the word *istisál* was used:

> 'Yet half his strength he put not forth, but checked
> His thunder in mid-volley; for he meant
> Not to destroy, but root them out of heaven.'

It may be added, that the meaning which the Persian Interpreter says that he attached to the word 'exterminate,' is even now by no means obsolete. Thus, the Century Dictionary gives, as its first meaning, 'to drive out or away, to banish,' and quotes the following illustration: 'How far in any particular district the vanquished were slain, how far they were simply driven out, we never can tell. It is enough that they were exterminated, got rid of in one way or another within what now became the English border.' E. A. Freeman, Amer. Lects. p. 133.

were in fact exterminated or extirpated in the sense in which Mill has used the former term. He has made it appear that his statement is supported by the authority of Colonel Champion. I assert, on the other hand, that no single authority, whether of Colonel Champion or of any other person, can be quoted in its support, and that it is disproved by the evidence of Colonel Champion himself.

Colonel Champion was examined before the House of Commons on the 3rd of May, 1786. I take from his evidence the following questions and answers bearing on this particular point:—

'Were the military part of the nation, excepting those who fell in battle, put to death, or only required to cross the Ganges?

'To the best of my remembrance, they were only required to cross the Ganges.

'You have said a considerable number remained in the Rohilla country under Faizullah Khan. Can you inform the House about what number remained?

'I can only answer to the best of my recollection that there might be, including followers, about 45,000 men.

'Do not you mean of the whole nation settled in the Rohilla country?

'Those men that were under arms.

'Can you inform the Committee about what number of the Rohillas were required to pass the Ganges?

'It is impossible for me to ascertain the number, but I suppose about 20,000, followers included.

'Do you think there were as many fell in battle and slaughtered as passed the Ganges?

'What fell in battle might be about one-eleventh part of what passed the Ganges; I know nothing of any being slaughtered.

'Whether any of the Rohillas were permitted to remain in the Rohilla country, except those who remained under the government of Faizullah Khan?

'I do not recollect there were.

'Do you understand then that the whole Rohilla nation amounted only to those who remained under Faizullah Khan, those who fell in battle, and the 20,000 who crossed the Ganges?

'By no means.

'What then became of the residue?

'If it is meant of the inhabitants of the country, many and many thousands remained. I thought the question related only to those in arms.

'Whether any persons were driven across the Ganges except people in arms and the followers of the camp and their families?

'I do not believe there was a man[1].'

On the 11th May, 1786, Major Balfour, who served under Colonel Champion during the campaign, was examined before the House of Commons. He said that he supposed that 20,000 Rohillas in arms had crossed the Ganges after the treaty with Faizullah Khan, and that the number of followers, women, and children, who went with them might have amounted to as many more; that they immediately solicited protection from their countryman Zabita Khan, into whose country they had gone, and that many of them afterwards returned to Rohilkhand and lived there unmolested. He supposed that between two and three thousand Rohillas had been killed in battle, and on being asked the question—'Do you believe that any Rohillas were put to death except those who fell in battle?' he answered,—'I never heard of one; I believe there were none.'

Middleton, the English Resident with the Vizier during the campaign, was examined before the House of Commons on the 22nd May, 1786. He said that 'he knew of no instance of cruelty, in the course of the war upon the Rohillas, either by Shuja-ud-daula or by his orders;' that he understood the article in the treaty with Faizullah Khan, requiring the Rohillas to leave the country to apply only to the troops under arms and their chiefs; that they crossed the Ganges into the territory of their countryman, Zabita Khan; that many of them, although not publicly permitted, returned to Rohilkhand and either went to Faizullah Khan or enlisted in the Vizier's army. He was asked whether 'after the Rohilla chiefs had been deprived of the

[1] It is difficult to suppose that Colonel Champion's evidence was always correctly reported. For instance, he was asked 'whether the Rohilla nation consists of Mahometans or Hindoos?' and he replied, 'I believe they are Hindoos.' Other answers are hardly intelligible. This may perhaps be to some extent explained by the fact that he was in bad health when he was examined, with, in his own words, 'his memory much weakened.'

sovereignty of the country, could any expedient have been thought of for disposing of the Rohilla soldiers, equally safe for the peace of the country and more favourable to them than that of compelling them to cross the Ganges,' and he answered—'I cannot suggest any.' In reply to the question, 'Have you ever heard whether the Rohilla soldiers were averse to that article of the treaty which compelled them to cross the Ganges,' he said, 'If they had been averse to it, I conceive they had the power of preventing Faizullah Khan from acceding to it.'

Enough has been said regarding the general charge that the Rohillas were exterminated, and that 'every one who bore the name of Rohilla was either butchered, or found his safety in flight and in exile.' The whole story is fictitious. There is not a particle of evidence to show that any Rohillas were killed except those who fell in battle. The war ended with a treaty honourable to both parties, under which a considerable part of Rohilkhand was restored to Rohilla dominion, and the Rohilla state thus founded has remained from that day to this in the possession of the Rohilla descendants of Faizullah Khan. The stipulation of the treaty, that men actually under arms should leave Rohilkhand, was perfectly reasonable. It was necessary for the peace of the country, and it involved little hardship, for all that happened to the Rohilla soldiers whom it affected was that after a march of a few miles they crossed the Ganges into the territory of Zabita Khan, their own countryman. The facts cannot be summed up more accurately than in the words of Hastings, that have been already quoted:—'We conquered the country from the conquerors of it, and substituted another rule in the place of theirs, upon the same principle of right and usage (the right of the war being pre-supposed), as a British Commander in Europe would expel the soldiers of a conquered town, and garrison it with his own, which by the same figure of speech, and with equal propriety, might be called an 'extirpation.'

CHAPTER XIV.

THE CHARGE THAT ATROCITIES WERE COMMITTED AND DEFENDED BY HASTINGS.

Colonel Champion's first report of excesses by the Vizier's troops.—The replies of Hastings and of the Government.—Colonel Champion's first report of maltreatment of the families of Rohilla chiefs.—The reply of the Government.—Further reports from Colonel Champion and letter from Hastings.—Orders sent to Middleton regarding alleged cruelties of Vizier.—Colonel Champion sends further accounts of maltreatment of Hafiz Rahmat's family.—Orders of the Government.—Failure to obtain from Colonel Champion the information called for.—Hastings again writes to Middleton on the subject.

I COME now to the charge that atrocious cruelties were committed, and that they were, at least in part, admitted and defended by Hastings. It is of course possible that this charge might be well founded, although the charge of exterminating the Rohillas might be false. Among all the accusations brought against Hastings, and usually believed on the authority of Burke, and Mill, and Macaulay to be true, no accusation has thrown such odium on his character as that which describes the manner in which he received Colonel Champion's reports of the cruelties committed in the war, and in which he excused and defended them.

The first reference to any excesses of the troops of the Vizier is contained in a private letter from Hastings, sent in reply to one written by Colonel Champion when the army entered Rohilkhand, and before the defeat of the Rohillas. Colonel Champion's letter is not forthcoming, but it is clear from the reply of Hastings, from the instructions of the Government, and from other papers, that the Vizier had given orders for the devastation of the country, but that the English Commander protested against them and succeeded, after a short time, in stopping their execution. Hastings, in his letter, wrote as follows:—

'On this occasion I cannot omit to take notice of the sensible and humane counsel which you gave to the Vizier on the orders issued by him for laying waste the Rohilla country, a measure which would have reflected equal dishonour on our arms and reproach on his authority had it been continued. You wisely judged that to effect the conquest of the country it was almost as necessary to conciliate the minds of the people as to defeat the actual rulers [1].'

Colonel Champion's despatch announcing the defeat of the Rohillas reached Calcutta on the 9th May; it said nothing of any atrocities, but Hastings, in the answer of the Government, written on the same day, took the opportunity of referring to the correspondence which had passed between himself and Colonel Champion, and of repeating officially the commendation which he had already given privately to Colonel Champion.

'We are exceedingly happy,' it was said, 'to learn from the communications which the President has made to us, that you have in the course of the campaign been so attentive to maintain the strictest order and discipline among the troops, and that you from the beginning opposed, and at last obtained a stop to be put to the devastation of the Rohilla country by the army of the Vizier; a mistaken policy altogether incompatible with the design of the war, and repugnant to humanity, and we have a sensible pleasure in testifying our entire approbation of your conduct in this respect [2].'

The first reference made by Colonel Champion, after the defeat of the Rohillas, to any maltreatment of the people of the country generally, or of individuals, is found in a letter to the Select Committee, from the camp near Bareilly, dated the 4th May, 1774. The greater part of the letter,

[1] This letter is printed by Gleig, vol. i. p. 420, and there is a MS. copy of it in the British Museum. The date, 16th May, is evidently a mistake for 6th May. The letter begins by saying that Hastings had, on the morning on which he wrote, received from the Vizier the news of the defeat of the Rohillas, and that he would not wait for Colonel Champion's confirmation of the news before congratulating him on the victory. The letter from the Vizier arrived on the 6th May.

[2] Letter to Colonel Champion, dated 9th May, 1774, MS. Records, India Office; Forrest's Selections, vol. i. p. 101.

which is a long one, dealt with other matters, but it contained the following sentences:—

'It is said that Ahmad Khan has given his country, which lies between Dundi Khan's and Zabita Khan's, to the King, and indeed the treatment of the family of Hafiz will perfectly justify the other chiefs in every step they can take to avoid coming under the power of Shuja-ud-daula. This much I am under the necessity of declaring, that I am greatly afraid the Vizier's behaviour to the family of the Nabob Hafiz Rahmat Khan, and to the inhabitants of his country, will render our connection with him reproachful to us, and tend to lessen that reputation of our justice which had heretofore prevailed in these countries[1].'

An official reply to this letter was sent by Hastings on the 23rd May. I may here observe that the average length of time in which letters from the camp in Rohilkhand reached Calcutta, a distance of nearly a thousand miles, was about seventeen days, and in the rainy season it was more. Answers to letters were seldom received in much less than six weeks. So far as postal communication was concerned, Rohilkhand was then about as far from Calcutta as it is now from London, and this must be remembered in considering the means actually possessed by Hastings of controlling proceedings at the seat of war.

'In two paragraphs of your letter before us,' he wrote to Colonel Champion, 'you barely mention the Vizier's treatment of the family of Hafiz Rahmat; but in the last place where you notice it you draw an inference that "it will render our connection with the Vizier reproachful to us, and tend to lessen that reputation of our justice which had heretofore prevailed in these countries." Where so serious a conclusion was to be deduced, we cannot but lament that being withheld from a knowledge of the premises on which it is grounded, should disqualify us from passing a judgment. It has been an invariable maxim in the policy of the Company's government, in the execution of any enterprises which they have undertaken in behalf of their allies, to interpose their protection in favour of the conquered princes, for the security of their lives and honour; and it will unquestionably be the care and attention of this Administration to adhere to this maxim, which has greatly contributed to the reputation of the British name, and to perform what may be incumbent on them on the present occasion. We desire, therefore, to be immediately advised of the particulars of the treatment which you allude to, that we may judge of

[1] Fifth Report, App. No. 27; Forrest's Selections, vol. i. p. 103.

the measures proper to be adopted. In the interim, we recommend to you to urge, in your own behalf, and in the name of the Board, such remonstrances to the Vizier, against any rigorous treatment of the Rohilla chiefs and their families as you may think the occasion to require. From the readiness which the Vizier testified in a former instance, to be influenced by your advice and persuasion, we flatter ourselves we may expect the same good fruits from your interposition now[1].'

A few days after these orders had been despatched, Hastings received a private letter from Colonel Champion, dated the 10th May, enclosing an official request that he might be allowed to return to Calcutta.

'Not only do I wish,' he wrote, 'to get down as soon as possible to put my little affairs in the best order for my return to Europe, but I must be candid enough to unbosom myself to you freely, and confess that the nature of the service, and the terms on which I have been employed, this campaign have been inexpressibly disagreeable. The authority given to the Vizier over your army has totally absorbed that degree of consequence due to my station. My hands have been tied up from giving protection or asylum to the miserable. I have been obliged to give a deaf ear to the lamentable cries of the widow and fatherless, and to shut my eyes against a wanton display of violence and oppression, of inhumanity and cruelty. The Company's interest constrained me in public to stifle the workings of my feelings, but I must give them vent in private. Though we had no active part in his base proceedings, yet it is well known that the success of our arms gave him the power of perpetrating these enormities; and I much fear, that our being even silent spectators of such deeds will redound to the dishonour of our nation, and impress all Hindostan with the most unfavourable opinion of our Government. As matters now are, I know of no remedy that would so effectually re-establish our character for justice and clemency as your taking the family of Hafiz under the wings of your mercy and protection, and influencing the Nabob to make provision for them in some degree suitable to their birth. It would affect your sensibility too much were I to descend to particulars; let it suffice, that the Nabob Mohabbat Khan, the eldest son, and the rest of the family of Hafiz, who are under close confinement (the Begums and other women included), have been driven to the necessity of making private supplications for a little rice and water. I wish, my friend, to leave scenes which none but the merciless Shuja can bear without heart-bleeding pain. Relieve me, therefore, as soon as possible and oblige, yours, &c.[2].'

[1] Fifth Report, App. No. 27.

[2] Fifth Report, App. No. 45; Forrest's Selections, vol. ii. p. 286. In his official letter, dated 10th May, Colonel Champion wrote as follows: 'There is not a single enemy

A reply to this letter was immediately sent by Hastings. On the 27th May, he wrote to Colonel Champion in the following terms:—

'I am extremely sorry that the line which was drawn to separate your authority from the Vizier's has been productive of such grievous consequences as you mention. It never could have been suspected by the Board that their orders to you would have tied up your hands from protecting the miserable, stopped your ears to the cries of the widows and fatherless, or shut your eyes against the wanton display of oppression and cruelty. I am totally at a loss to distinguish wherein their orders have laid you under any greater restraint than your predecessors. No authority which the Board could have given you could be capable of preventing the effects you mention, since they could give you no control over the actions of the Vizier further than the weight and influence of your counsel and advice. The orders under which you at present act leave to the Vizier the power of directing the services to be performed, but leave you master of the means of performing them. This clear distinction of your respective powers was formed to prevent all disputes, by removing every subject of doubt. If, in the exercise of his authority, the Vizier is guilty of oppression and other excesses, he alone, as the agent, is culpable of it. You have a right, and it is your duty, to remonstrate against any part of his conduct, which may either dishonour the service or prove prejudical to the common interest, but I protest I do not know what you could do more, or what the whole Board, personally present and invested

in arms throughout all these countries, so that the service of the campaign is effectually over. After the rivers shall have swelled, the army will not be able to act in the field till the beginning of December; and as the situation of my affairs very pressingly urges the necessity of my presence at Calcutta, I am to request you will favour me with your permission to return to the Presidency, and to commit the charge of the army to Colonel Galliez in my absence.' He was told in reply, on the 3rd June, that he was permitted to return to Calcutta 'whenever he thought the circumstances of the campaign, as well as his own convenience, would allow. Fifth Report, App. No. 27. In his letter written after his return to Calcutta, on the 30th January, 1775, he gave another and in the opinion of Hastings the true reason for his wish to leave the command of the army:—'I had very early signified to the Governor how exceedingly disagreeable I found my situation. The unhandsome manner in which, I must be pardoned to say, I thought myself treated, on account of the impropriety that had appeared to me in reposing a greater trust in the Vizier than in the Company's Commander-in-Chief, had determined me to return to the Presidency, as soon as the rivers should have swelled, either to have matters put upon a more becoming footing or to have taken my leave for England, which in case of failure in this particular I had resolved to do even if no successor should arrive.' 5th Report, App. No. 45; Forrest's Selections, vol. 1. p. 225. The dissatisfaction of Colonel Champion with the position assigned to him has been already noticed. See p. 130.

with their full authority, could do more. They could exercise no coercive power over the Vizier without committing a violence equal to any of these we should complain of. The picture you have given of the Vizier's conduct, though general and allusive only, is shocking to humanity; but surely your advice and strenuous remonstrance against acts of oppression and wanton cruelty ought to prove some restraint, and, if not, would be a justification of your conduct. You have afforded the instance, at the commencement of your present operations, when the Vizier put a stop to the ravages of the country at your intercession. I have addressed the Vizier in the strongest terms on the subject of his general conduct, alluded to in your letters. If you will point out any other more effectual remedy to such proceedings, or any addition which could be given to your authority, not liable to the objection of establishing a divided power or an unjust usurpation of his authority, I will gladly agree to it; but to take the family of Hafiz Rahmat immediately under our protection would furnish him with a just plea to refuse his compliance with the stipulation made for the present service, as it would be in effect to conquer the country for the Company, and not for him. The Vizier would have cause to suspect, and the world would adopt the same belief, that with the person of the hereditary claimant of the country we meant to reserve a right, at some convenient period, to take possession from him; and while such an opinion prevailed, neither could he establish government in it, nor remain steady in his confidence and fidelity towards us. On better recollection, I have declined writing to the Vizier myself on this subject, as intimated in the beginning of this paragraph, lest the solicitude I might express on account of the family of Hafiz Rahmat should increase their misfortunes, but I have instructed Mr. Middleton to make the strongest representation on this subject, which will perhaps have a better effect than anything I could say from myself[1].'

On the same day on which this letter was written, Hastings wrote to Middleton, the Resident with the Vizier.

'Colonel Champion,' he said, 'complains of the conduct of the Vizier in suffering, and even ordering his troops to ravage the country, and in his cruel treatment of the family of Hafiz Rahmat. This is a subject on which I cannot write to the Vizier. It might widen the breach between him and the Commander-in-Chief, and probably influence the Nabob to some private revenge on the unhappy remains of Hafiz Rahmat's family. I desire, therefore, that you will take an immediate occasion to remonstrate with him against every act of cruelty or wanton violence. The country is his, and the people his subjects. They claim by that relation his tenderest regard and unremitted protection. The family of Hafiz Rahmat have never injured him, but have a claim to his protection in default of that of which he has

[1] Private letter, British Museum MSS. 29,117; Gleig, vol. i. p. 425.

deprived them. Tell him that the English manners are abhorrent of every species of inhumanity and oppression, and enjoin the gentlest treatment of a vanquished enemy. Require and entreat his observance of this principle towards the family of Hafiz. Tell him my instructions to you; generally, but urgently, enforce the same maxims; and that no part of his conduct will operate so powerfully in winning the affections of the English as instances of benevolence and feeling for others. If these arguments do not prevail, you may inform him directly that you have my orders to insist upon a proper treatment of the family of Hafiz Rahmat, since in our alliance with him our national character is involved in every act which subjects his own to reproach; that I shall publicly exculpate this Government from the imputation of assenting to such a procedure, and shall reserve it as an objection to any future engagements with him when the present service shall have been accomplished[1].'

I shall show further on how the instructions of Hastings were carried out, and shall give Middleton's account of the representations made by him to the Vizier.

On the 18th May, Colonel Champion, in a letter that has already been quoted, referred in angry terms to the plunder of the country, but these statements must be received with caution, because, as I have shown, they were not made on account of the Vizier's inhumanity, but on the ground that no share of the plunder had been given to the British troops.

On the 28th May, when Colonel Champion reported to Hastings the proposals made by Faizullah Khan with the object of terminating the war, he wrote as follows:—

'Above a lakh of people have deserted their abodes in consequence of the defeat of Hafiz; they will ever seek an opportunity of returning; sixty or seventy thousand of them, though few in arms, are with Faizullah Khan, in a place surrounded by a jungle and almost inaccessible[2].'

[1] Fifth Report, App. No. 27; Gleig, vol. i. p. 438.

[2] Fifth Report, App. No. 27. It is interesting to trace the processes of famous artists. These words of Colonel Champion were the basis, and there is certainly no other, for the following high sounding sentence of Macaulay: 'More than a hundred thousand people fled from their homes to pestilential jungles, preferring famine, and fever, and the haunts of tigers, to the tyranny of him to whom an English and a Christian Government had, for shameful lucre, sold their substance, and their blood, and the honour of their wives and daughters.'

It is very probable that this was substantially true, but Mill was altogether wrong when he quoted the statement as a proof of the Vizier's cruelty towards the Rohillas. It obviously referred to the Hindu inhabitants of the country, and not to the Rohillas, and, even with respect to the former, Colonel Champion had no intention of making any charge against the Vizier. He mentioned the fact incidentally as an illustration of the difficulties with which the Vizier had to deal. I have already explained that it was the established custom in Rohilkhand for the people, when danger threatened, to go off with their families and their cattle and their valuables, and take refuge in the comparatively safe country within easy reach in the Tarái and forest below the hills. It was the more certain that they would do so in the earlier parts of this campaign, in April and May, because at that season there are no important crops on the ground, and almost all agricultural operations are suspended.

On the 12th June, Colonel Champion sent his reply to the letter of the 23rd May, in which he had been ordered by Hastings to furnish full particulars of the maltreatment to which Hafiz Rahmat's family had been subjected. He began by stating that one of his objects had been 'to be invested with full authority to effectually prevent the Vizier from perpetrating any enormity, under the shield of our force, that could in any degree redound to the discredit of our reputation.'

'In compliance,' he went on to say, 'with the Board's desire, I am now to mention a very unpleasing subject. The Vizier's treatment of the family of Hafiz Rahmat, &c., the inhumanity and dishonour with which they, Mahibullah Khan, his brother Fatehullah Khan, late proprietors of this city and country, and their families have been used is well known over all these parts; a relation of them would swell this letter to an immense size, and withal prove very disagreeable reading. I send you translations of two letters and copy of the third, which affecting as they are, will convey but a faint idea of the treatment these unhappy people have met with. I could not help compassionating such unparalleled misery, and my requests to the Vizier to show lenity were frequent, but as fruitless as were those advices which I almost hourly gave him regarding the destruction of the villages, with respect to which

O 2

I am now constrained to declare, that though he always promised as fairly as I could wish, yet he did not observe one of them, nor cease to overspread the country with flames till three days after the fate of Hafiz Rahmat was decided; but, gentlemen, "as in all points excepting such as immediately respect the operations in the field, he is solely empowered to prescribe," the reputation of the British name is in his hands, and the line which has been laid down for me is very clear. The above families have been despatched to Faizabad, that their maltreatment might not be so generally known to us. I have, however, frequent accounts of them, and it will give me the most sensible pleasure that you stretch forth the hand of benevolence effectually to relieve them from so indescribable a misery; and that you may the better devise the means of so doing, without subjecting them to greater misfortunes, I am to inform you that every application of mine in their favour, though professedly taken in good part by the Vizier, yet only served to procure them more rigorous treatment [1].'

The letters referred to by Colonel Champion were from the sons of Dundi Khan and from the wife of Hafiz Rahmat; the latter I give in extenso:—

'The English gentlemen, renowned through Hindostan for justice, equity, and compassionating the miserable. Hafiz Rahmat Khan for forty years governed this country, and the very beasts of the forest trembled at his bravery. The will of God is resistless. He is slain, and to his children not an atom remains, but they are cast from their habitations, naked, exposed to the winds, the heats, and the burning sand, and perishing from want of even rice and water. How shall I either write or speak my condition? My sighs dry my ink and scorch my paper. 'Tis evident as the sun, the English are brave and merciful, and whosoever they subdue, their children they preserve, who forget their sorrows by the kind treatment they receive; nor draw they the sword in an unjust cause. Yesterday I was mistress of an hundred thousand people. To-day I am in want even of a cup of water, and where I commanded I am a prisoner. Fortune is fickle; she raises the humble and lowers the exalted; but I am innocent, and if any one is guilty it is Hafiz. But why should the children be punished for the errors of their father? I am taken like a beast in a snare, without resting place by night, or shade by day. From you, sir, I hope justice and compassion, for I am as a bird confined in a cage; 'tis better to give up life by the dagger than famish thus by hunger and thirst. You, I hope, sir, will reflect on my state, or my misfortunes will be doubled. I have nothing left. Pardon this paper [2].'

[1] Fifth Report, App. No. 27.

[2] These two letters will be found in Appendix No. 27, Fifth Report. The extract which I have given from

In another private letter to Hastings, dated the 15th June, 1774, Colonel Champion wrote as follows:—

'I am most heartily disposed to believe that the Board did not suspect their orders could have such consequences as have fallen out; they could not have foreseen so sudden and so total an expulsion and downfall of a whole race of people; they could not have supposed that a man, exalted and supported by British arms, could pay so very little deference to the advices and counsel of a British Commander; nor was it possible to conceive that a man, who had himself tested the gall of misfortune, should be so totally unmindful of the unbounded and unparalleled grace shown to him, as to delight in denying a single ray of benevolence to others. Such, however, has been the case, and in due intimation of it I have discharged that which was incumbent upon me. I too can say that the Nabob, as the agent of oppression, is alone culpable. But, whilst all Asia knows that the English gave him the rod, and whilst they in vain look up to them as those who ought, if not direct the application, at least to prevent an ill use being made of that rod, will they not reasonably conclude that the scourges which the agent gives are connived at? Will they not say that every English chief is another Sujah? It is not to me what restraints were laid on my predecessors; none of them were ever in similar circum-

Colonel Champion's letter of the 12th June, 1774, should be compared with the quotations from it which Mill has professed to make. [See p. 176.] Colonel Champion charged the Vizier with ill-treatment of the family of Hafiz Rahmat Khan and of the two sons of Dundi Khan and their families; he said nothing of cruelty to the Rohillas generally. Mill desired to quote authority for the statement that, in accordance with the declared intention of the Vizier and Hastings to exterminate the Rohillas, they had been treated with atrocious cruelty. Colonel Champion, neither in this letter nor in any other, had made any such general charge; but there was one way by which Mill's object could be gained. Those parts of Colonel Champion's letter were suppressed which showed that he was referring solely to the treatment of particular individuals. It was thus made to appear that the terms 'inhumanity and dishonour,' and 'unparalleled misery,' had been applied by Colonel Champion to the Rohillas generally, 'the late proprietors of the country,' whereas they were only applied in fact to the treatment of the two sons of Dundi Khan and their families, and to the family of Hafiz Rahmat. Having put Colonel Champion's words into a shape in which they suited his purpose, Mill quotes them in support of the statement that 'every one who bore the name of Rohilla was either butchered, or found his safety in flight or exile.' Colonel Champion on one occasion only charged the Vizier with any sort of cruelty towards the Rohillas generally, and even this charge referred only to their soldiers after the defeat of Hafiz Rahmat. In his letter dated 30th January, 1775, written after his return to Calcutta, he said that the Vizier had refused to give assistance in transporting their wounded to the English hospitals or in burying their dead. Fifth Report, App. No. 45; Forrest's Selections, vol. i. p. 242. See *inf.* p. 205.

stances, nor do the grievances which I have represented against from public views (for I could for a time sacrifice, or at least conceal, my own private feelings) appear to me to have at all been without a preventative, nay an easy and effectual one, and that too without coercive means, or being liable to the objection of any usurpation of the Vizier's authority, which I am as far from desiring as yourself. . . . I am glad you did not address the Vizier concerning the family of Hafiz; your good sense figured circumstances as they really were. I did not mean or say that Hafiz's family should be rendered independent of Sujah Dowlah. I wrote to Mr. Hastings requesting that he would take them under his protection, by influencing the Nabob "to make provision for them in some degree suitable to their birth." They themselves proposed that any or as many of the sons as the Nabob pleased should remain in his hands, but prayed him not to dishonour the Begum and other women, by dragging them about the country to be loaded with the scoffs of his rabble and otherwise still worse used; but he was deaf, maugre all my entreaties, which you will find, by my letter of the 12th, were also ineffectual with regard to the destruction of the villages; a circumstance with respect to which I am now sorry I did not undeceive you sooner, but it proceeded from a real disinclination to enlarge upon his excesses, which has also prevented me from descending to the particulars of his conduct [1].'

Colonel Champion's letter of the 12th June was laid before the Select Commitee by Hastings on the 1st July, with the following memorandum :—

'The President informs the Committee that on the first mention made by Colonel Champion of the cruelties exercised by the Vizier upon the family of Hafiz Rahmat, he sent instructions to the Resident, of which he begs leave to record the following copy, which he flatters himself the Committee will judge to have been the most likely to prove effectual for the relief of their distress, and the only means which on such occasion he could have taken to have influenced the Vizier to a more generous conduct [2].'

Hastings was much dissatisfied with Colonel Champion's answer, and it seemed to him that the cruelties imputed to the Vizier were being used as a means of compelling the

[1] Papers on the Rohilla war, India Office Library. A part of this letter was quoted by Clavering, Monson, and Francis, in their letter to the Court of Directors, dated 30th November, 1774. See *inf.* p. 227. It was originally a private letter, but was brought on official record by Hastings. Fifth Report, App. No. 45.

[2] Fifth Report, App. No. 27. The letter to Middleton, to which Hastings here refers, has been given on p. 193.

Government to give to Colonel Champion the increased powers which he had long been anxious to obtain, and the refusal of which had from the first been strongly resented by him. Hastings had resolved to listen to no such demands, and the correspondence going on regarding the claims of the army to a share of the plunder of the conquered country made him the less disposed to place confidence in Colonel Champion's impartiality or discretion. A reply was sent on the 1st July to his letter. The Government refused to give him any additional authority. He was told that the Government itself possessed no such power of absolute control over the actions of the Vizier as he appeared to wish to exercise, and that much less could such power be delegated to the Commander of the army; that if it were otherwise, we should become the masters instead of the allies of the Vizier, and

'the Commander-in-Chief would become the arbiter of peace and war. . . . At present we stand thus with the Vizier: we have engaged to support and assist him in a specific service, and stipulated for a certain compensation to the Company; when that service shall be performed, the conquered country, its riches, its inhabitants, and all other acquisitions must be at his disposal, nor have we a right by our agreement to interfere. If indeed it should happen that elevated by successes, and secure under our protection, he should in the exercise of his authority commit such enormities as we should deem unworthy of the character of our ally, we would not fail in that case to remonstrate against them, and take such other steps as should appear best adapted for bringing him to a more just sense of propriety in his conduct, but we should not esteem ourselves either obliged or entitled to interfere with authority, or to put power into the hands of our Commander-in-Chief effectually to prevent any measure in the management of his own affairs, which he should think fit to pursue. . . . The intemperate and tyrannical conduct of the Vizier after his conquest, as you have represented, cannot fail to prove highly dissatisfactory to us, and although we do not regard ourselves either as answerable for his actions, or obliged absolutely to interfere for restraining them, yet we should have been glad to have been furnished with such materials as would enable us, upon good grounds, to expostulate with him on the injustice and impropriety of such a conduct. It was in this view that we requested you to acquaint us with the instances of his cruelties, but we confess ourselves exceedingly disappointed in receiving, instead of a precise account of facts, only three letters of loose declamation, which however pathetically written, contain not one single instance of the Vizier's particular cruelty towards the family of Hafiz, and indeed express only such sentiments as we can easily conceive to exist in the breasts of that unfortunate family, from reflecting on the sad reverse of their fortune alone, without suffering any peculiar hardship in their case, or uncommon act of oppression in the Vizier. For this reason, we repeat our desire to be furnished with a particular account of the treatment which the family of Hafiz has received, and we shall then take such steps for their relief as the circumstances shall require. In the meantime, we hope that the remonstrances which the President informs us he has directed the Resident to make to the Vizier on this subject, will be sufficient to render any more direct interposition needless. We conclude with taking notice of an expression in your letter which, in our judgment, conveys a reflection equally improper and unjust. It is that in which you say "the reputation of the British name is in the hands of the Vizier." If this were the case, we who put it into his hands would undoubtedly stand responsible to our country and employers for the wanton prostitution of so precious a trust. But we do not agree that we have in any shape left the national honour at his disposal, or that the British name can be affected by any of his actions, independent of us. Our engagements with the Vizier are clearly defined, and such as we can justify on principles of sound policy and attention to the Company's interest. We afford him our assistance; our honour we commit into no hands but yours, where we trust it is perfectly safe, and that by your conduct in the field, and by maintaining discipline among the troops, the British name will acquire new lustre, and the campaign be the means of spreading more wide our national reputation, unconnected with that of the Vizier[1].'

Although Colonel Champion remained in Rohilkhand for several months after he received these orders, he never sent the 'particular account of the treatment which the family of Hafiz had received,' and which the Government had called upon him to furnish. When, on the 3rd of May, 1786, he was examined before the House of Commons, he was asked whether this was true, and he replied:—

'In answer to that question, I must observe that repeatedly, before the date of that letter and afterwards, I thought the remonstrances I made were sufficient, and therefore did not comply with the orders I received.'

He sent no reply at all until the 3rd September, when he referred to the subject in the following terms:—

'It is true, gentlemen, that declamation is usual in representing distress; and therefore I should not have been surprised that the letters

[1] Fifth Report, App. No. 27.

which I transmitted to you had but little effect on your perceptions, if I had not at the same time attested the truth of the complaints, which I will venture to say bear more than one or two instances of cruelty; I might add others, such as these unhappy captives being driven to the necessity of supplicating and receiving alms from myself and gentlemen of my family to purchase sustenance; their even begging for water to drink, their struggling who should first be served with it, &c. In short, the gross maltreatment of these families amounts to an axiom in the minds of the English army, and even in the Vizier's own troops [1].'

When this letter from Colonel Champion arrived, Hastings, hopeless apparently of getting from Colonel Champion the distinct statement of facts which he had demanded, again wrote to the Resident.

'I enclose,' he said, 'an extract from a letter of Colonel Champion to the Select Committee, on the subject of which I am earnestly solicitous to have the fullest and most certain information. The enormities he insists upon are of a nature that I think could not have escaped your observation. The Colonel must receive every information of this kind at second hand, and he may be deceived or circumstances may be much exaggerated; but his representation is peremptory and positive, and the Vizier must appear in the darkest colours on our records if what the Colonel affirms stands uncontroverted. I wish the truth to appear, neither glossed by favour nor blackened by prejudice; let me therefore beg of you to furnish me with the fullest information you can obtain of the Vizier's treatment of the family of Hafiz, &c., and to support your accounts with the strongest proofs that can be produced. Hitherto the circumstances of that kind which you have had to mention have been satisfactory [2].'

[1] Fifth Report, App. No. 28.

[2] Letter dated 24th September, 1774, British Museum MSS. 29,135. This letter has been printed by Gleig, not quite accurately, vol. i. p. 441.

CHAPTER XV.

THE CHARGE THAT ATROCITIES WERE COMMITTED AND DEFENDED BY HASTINGS (*continued*).

Falsehood of the charges against Hastings.—Complaints of Colonel Champion against the Vizier after the close of the war.—Other evidence regarding the cruelties said to have been committed.—The reports of Middleton in reply to the orders of Hastings.—Evidence of Colonel Champion and other officers taken before the Council.—Hamilton's History.—Statements by the Vizier.—Accounts by the son of Hafiz Rahmat.—The Sair-ul-Mutakherin.—Mill's calumnies against Hastings.—The truth regarding the conduct of the war.—The war conducted with unusual humanity.

I HAVE quoted every report made by Colonel Champion from the beginning to the end of the war, respecting atrocities committed by the Vizier, and I have shown the manner in which every report was treated by Hastings. The falsehood of the charge that these atrocities were defended by him has, I think, been made clear.

I shall now show what further evidence respecting the conduct of the war is on record, and I shall first refer to statements made by Colonel Champion himself after the war was over.

In November 1774, Shuja-ud-daula sent to Hastings a letter filled with complaints against the English Commander-in-Chief and his troops. The new Government had then come into power, and a copy of the Vizier's letter was given to Colonel Champion. On the 30th January, 1775, he sent to the Council a long letter, full of violent invective against the Vizier, refuting the charges brought by him and explaining his own proceedings in great detail, but in most confused and rambling style. I shall quote everything in his letter which bears upon the subject of the Vizier's cruelties:—

'The war was over early in October. There remained no more towns to plunder, no new discovered hoards of treasure to dig up, no unhappy man to rob of his wealth, no miserable woman of her raiment. . . . I submit whether the giving up the rights of the army [to a share of plunder] was not in effect sacrificing the interest of our nation, inasmuch as the riches of the individuals contribute to the support of the State. But passing over this remarkable complaisance to the Vizier as inexplicable, we shall march from Pilibhit and accompany His Excellency towards Bisauli, dragging in triumph the disconsolate Begum and children of the brave but unfortunate Hafiz, the widow of his eldest son Inayat Khan, the wife of his eldest surviving son, Mohabbat Khan, and some hundreds of miserable captive women on carts. Leaving Bareilly and Aonla behind us, and trusty slaves of His Excellency to see the inhabitants indiscriminately plundered for the behoof of their master, we arrived at Bisauli, when the whole army were witnesses of scenes that cannot be described. . . . The propositions [of Faizullah Khan] were not, it's true, agreeable to the Vizier; they were not favourable to his ambitious designs, nor to his inhuman plan of extirpation. I informed the Governor of Sujah having received them with disdain, and when I candidly told His Excellency that I should act in the matter agreeably to the orders of Government, he anticipated the answer which I received by saying that "Mr. Hastings will tell you as I do." But though His Excellency gave himself the liberty of divining this, how was it possible that I should believe that we were to consult the Vizier's interest and aggrandizement only? I could not, as a Company's servant, give place to such an idea. I know that Sujah's acquisitions in plunder have exceeded the expenses of the campaign, even including the forty lakhs which he had promised to pay to the Company. I had with regret observed that the part the English took in the war brought their national character into the highest disrepute. I had remarked, and all the officers of the army had remarked, that His Excellency's haughtiness increased with the power which we put into his hands. . . . I have already fully confuted the Vizier's calumnies, but I shall nevertheless glance over His Excellency's letter once more and take notice of such parts as may have hitherto escaped me. "Consider, my friend," says His Excellency repeatedly to Mr. Hastings, "that it was my absolute determination to extirpate the Rohillas, and that I requested the assistance of the English for that purpose." However well it is known that His Excellency is equal to the barbarous design for which he thus publicly and daringly avows he solicited the aid of the English, is it possible we can believe that the respectable gentleman here traduced could have been privy to so horrid a purpose? Could he have so entirely overcome the feelings of humanity? Could he have been so lost to every sense of honour as to prostitute the English troops and to stain the glory of the British name by subscribing to a preconcerted massacre? What is not His Excellency capable of advancing?... It may not be improper to observe that on our way from Shahabad to Pilibhit, it was usual to send safeguards to the villages contiguous to head-quarters to preserve them from destruction; but the moment the sepoys were withdrawn to proceed on their march, the villages were set in flames by way of bonfire for His Excellency. Afterwards, when we were cantoned at Bisauli, many jemadars who resided at the distance of ten, twenty, and thirty miles, very frequently sent to entreat for even one sepoy to protect them; and though they could not always be supplied, it is sufficient to show the opinion which the natives entertained of our troops. Besides my Aide-de-camps, who had the charge of detaching these sepoys, several other officers in town are perfectly acquainted with these circumstances. . . . His Excellency is very unreasonable in his railing against the unfortunate family of Hafiz; and there is a palpable impertinence towards me in his manner of expression; although he could not command the winds, he had in his power to have treated the captives with tenderness; he could have ordered it so that these illustrious prisoners should not have been distressed for food or raiment; yet the truth is that they were covered with vermin, were reduced to the severe necessity of making supplications for private charities, and actually received alms from several gentlemen. But the Minutes which my Aide-de-camp took down from reports of trusty harcarrahs stationed for the purpose of bringing faithful intelligence regarding the prisoners, will speak more plainly their miserable situation, and at the same time prove how moderate I was when under examination on these subjects, and how reluctant I have hitherto been to enlarge on the excess of the Nabob[1]. His behaviour to the families of Mohibullah Khan and his

[1] These 'Minutes' have never, I believe, been printed, but they are to be found in the India Office Records among the Appendices to Colonel Champion's letter. There is nothing to show whether they were written at the time or compiled afterwards. They are called 'Intelligence relative to His Excellency the Vizier's treatment of the families of the late Nabobs Hafiz Rahmat and Dundi Khan in their confinement, taken down from the accounts of trusty hircarras stationed with those families, by order of the Commander-in-Chief.' These notes describe the gross neglect of the prisoners; state that they were crowded together in tents and suffered extreme discomfort; that the women were stripped of their jewels; that the food supplied was insufficient; that the guards were insolent, &c. It is evident from the questions afterwards sent by Hastings to Captain Macpherson, by whom these notes were written, that Hastings doubted their accuracy and believed that they had been compiled to support Colonel Champion's statements. He called for information regarding the hircarras from whom the reports were said to have been received, why they had been stationed with the prisoners, and to whom they sent their intelligence, and (he asked)

brother, Fattehullah Khan, who possessed a country of about twenty lakhs of rupees per annum, was yet more criminal. Before the commencement of the war he corresponded with them; and upon his assurances of protection and friendship, they remained at peace in Bisauli, the capital of their district. . . . [Three letters are then quoted by Colonel Champion, assuring these chiefs and their mother of protection. A note is added: 'Such was the Vizier's regard for the Rohillas, and such his regard for humanity, that he refused to give any assistance either in transporting their wounded to our hospitals, or burying their dead.] Upon the faith of these letters the deluded chiefs remained in their habitations, in full confidence of being treated

'are these Minutes to which you have attached your signature exact copies of those taken at the time, or have they been since revised and methodised by you or any other person?' The answers to these questions are not forthcoming. [See Appendix D.] When Colonel Champion was examined before the House of Commons, on the 3rd May, 1786, an attempt was again made to obtain some definite information regarding the authority on which his statements had been made; but it failed to elicit anything of value. The following is extracted from his evidence: 'Whether you had any other proof of the rigorous treatment of the Rohilla prisoners than their own representations?—The proof I had was chiefly from spies placed in a situation to receive that intelligence. —Whether the spies you mentioned acquainted you with particular instances of cruelty, or only gave you general information? Did they name particular persons on whom the cruelty was committed, and the particular species of cruelty?—I believe that in the correspondence, the manner in which I received the intelligence is particularly pointed out and the hardships that were inflicted.—Then you was not acquainted with any particular instances, except what are stated in the correspondence with the Governor and the Council?—Everything is at large in the correspondence.—Whether, after you received the directions of the Governor and Select Committee to state particular instances, you applied either to the same spies, or to any others, or to any other persons, to furnish you with any other particulars than what you had before that time stated?—I before observed, I cannot carry my remembrance to every particular occurrence. The correspondence will explain the whole.—Who employed the spies?—By my orders.—Whether you employed a confidential Aide-de-camp, or other officer under your command, to ascertain the truth of the cruelties and barbarities that were represented to you by the Rohilla prisoners, and the intelligence given by the spies?—The duty was allotted to one man for that purpose.—Who was that man?—Colonel Macpherson. —What was the intelligence he gave you on that subject?—It is mentioned in the correspondence.—What was the duty of Colonel Macpherson?—He had the charge of all the spies.—Was it anything more than to receive the intelligence brought by those spies and to make his report of it to you? —I said before I received all the intelligence from him.—Do you mean the intelligence only from the spies, or any other intelligence?—There is a kind of intelligence that comes by letter. I had no other intelligence than what came by him.—Did you employ Colonel Macpherson for the purpose of obtaining a knowledge of any supposed cruelties exercised against the Rohillas?—I answered that before.'

as friends by the Nabob, and being left undisturbed in their possessions. The moment he arrived at Bisauli, however, they were put into rigorous confinement, denied access to their families, robbed of their property, and themselves and their women treated not only with dishonour and indignity, but even with cruelty. The unhappy chiefs preferred frequent complaints to me in the most moving terms, and sent the Nabob's original letters to prove how much he had deceived them:—"He has deprived us of our country, of our riches, and even of our honour, and not satisfied with that he is going to send us prisoners to Faizabad. We desire no country, no riches, no houses, but at Bisauli are the tombs of our noble ancestors; near them, under some shade, we beg permission to spend the remainder of our days as faqueers. Relying on the Vizier's promises, we remained in this country, otherwise we should have fled as the other chiefs did, and have preserved our character and honours; these he has taken away with our effects, and how has he dishonoured us is known to all." It was this deceitful conduct, this inhuman treatment that filled the minds of all the fugitive chiefs with such a distrust and detestation of the Nabob. And although my representations of the distresses of the family of Hafiz were ungraciously received, and I am sorry to say gave me but little encouragement to plead the cause of the unhappy, yet I regret exceedingly that I have so long suppressed my inclinations of endeavouring to alleviate the misfortunes of the much injured chiefs to whom these letters were addressed, and who as well as the family of Hafiz I have good reason to believe are even now stinted of the necessaries of life, and when I was on the way down I received the affecting accounts of the death of twenty-five of these ill-fated prisoners since their arrival at Allahabad for want of sustenance.—"Whoever has lost a father and brother in war, has fallen from the dignity of a throne, and, become a prisoner, will undoubtedly suffer much misery." The analogy between the style of this paragraph and a letter which I received some time ago from another quarter on the same subject is worthy of observation. We grant that the fall of a father, and of a brother, and the loss of a throne, were sufficient causes for impressing the souls of the family of Hafiz with sorrow, but what shall we think of that unfeeling man who added cruelty to the burthen of their afflictions? What shall we say of him who in violation of all faith, in breach of every sacred tie under the artful mask of dissembled friendships, not only robbed the family of Dundi Khan of their throne, but even despoiled them of their honour, and not contented with depriving them of their liberty, has embittered the draught of their misfortunes by unexampled severity in their bondage. You find these unhappy people in the utmost dread, lest the Nabob should hear of their complaint, let me, therefore, hope and entreat, gentlemen, that whatever it may be your pleasure to do in their favour may be so ordered and concerted as that they may not be exposed to the implacable resentment of Shujah. . . . What would have been the consequence if the army had been repulsed or greatly thinned, which must have been the case even on the most favourable supposition [if the Rohillas had persisted in declining the Vizier's offers]. . . . Such would very naturally be the language of the gentlemen in the direction, had their army been repelled, or had they even been victorious at the expense of a great number of lives unneccessarily thrown away, and I must confess that I think their highest indignation would be most justly excited. Supposing, however, our success out of question, and that the Rohillas had all been cut off, what benefit would have derived, what profit to the Company? The administration had declared the forty lakhs due in May, and they were not to reap any further advantage, but admitting for a moment that the gentlemen in Leadenhall Street were of so forgiving a disposition as to overlook the neglect of the Company's interest, would they not be incensed at the wanton sacrifice of above one hundred thousand lives? The language of the British Senate on such an occasion would be very serious, "We condescended to admit of your keeping a military force for the preservation of your factories and the protection of your trade; you have abused our indulgencies, have entered into an unprovoked war, have hired out His Majesty's subjects for your private emolument, and to crown all have brought an indelible stain on your country by the massacre of an innocent people." The Company would throw the blame upon their Administration, and these gentlemen would endeavour to transfer it to the Commander-in-Chief. I thank God that it is out of their power. I have often successfully fought the battles of the Company, and have acquired them riches and to myself renown. I have been the assertor of their neglected rights. I have been mercifully disposed towards a persecuted people, and I have endeavoured to alleviate the affliction of the miserable and unhappy. I have stood forth for the honour of humanity, and for the glory of my King and of my country. . . . It is an easy matter to accuse, but allegations unsupported as the Vizier's fall of themselves. Conscious that no man was ever more injuriously aspersed than I have been, and sensible of the disrepute into which His Excellency has irrecoverably plunged himself, it might perhaps be enough for me to have said, I defy the slander, and it is not incumbent on me to prove a negative. It too frequently happens that the most irreproachable are thus maliciously accused; and though they cannot be formally condemned, yet I am afraid the generality of mankind are so prone to think ungenerously of their fellows that innocent men often lay under the most unjust imputations. Happy he who in such a situation can put his hand on his breast, and say all is quiet, all is serenity within. Fortunately for me, however, gentlemen, on this occasion, I have been able to stand forth; I have bearded the calumniator, and have brought such a load of truth upon his back as shall make the burthen irksome[1].'

[1] Fifth Report, App. No. 45; Forrest's Selections, vol. i. pp. 218–249.

I have already mentioned that Colonel Champion was examined before the House of Commons on the 3rd May, 1786[1]. Several extracts have been given from his evidence, and further quotations would serve no useful purpose. He stated in general terms that to the best of his recollection the Vizier had carried on the war with unnecessary cruelty, but he gave no new facts, and apologized to the Committee for his inability to do so.

'I beg to observe,' he said, 'that near twelve years have elapsed since that period, in the course of which time not one year has passed in which I have not been confined to my bed eight months; in consequence of which I find my memory much weakened, and I have it not in my power to answer to facts. I therefore desire the indulgence of the Committee to refer to the correspondence which passed between the Board, Mr. Hastings, and myself, for such circumstances as I cannot immediately recollect.'

Everything written or said by Colonel Champion, from first to last, regarding the cruelties committed by the Vizier has now been noticed. Mill has quoted no other authority. I shall next show what other evidence is forthcoming.

The action taken by Hastings on the reports of Colonel Champion was described in the last Chapter, and the letters were quoted which he sent to Middleton on the subject, when he had failed to obtain from Colonel Champion himself the information that he desired. I shall now give everything of importance in the letters received from Middleton in reply. The first was written on the 17th June, 1774:—

'Although I cannot by any means acquit the Nabob of the charge which the Commander-in-Chief alleges against the Vizier on the score of his treatment of Hafiz Rahmat's family, and his wanton ravages of the country, I can almost venture to affirm that his conduct in these particulars would appear on a scrutiny to have been less culpable than Colonel Champion has been taught to believe. To you, honourable sir, who are not unacquainted with the pride and haughtiness of the Nabob's demeanour, it will not appear extraordinary that he should have more enemies than most other men. Even his own servants are very frequently the first to asperse his character and to accuse him of actions which, with all his vices and imperfections, I am persuaded he is incapable of committing. The universal prejudice and dissatisfaction which his denying the army a gratuity they had built with

[1] See p. 185.

'Notwithstanding,' he said, 'the Vizier's repeated assurances to me, I had still reason to believe from the reports which were daily propagated and obtained universal credit, that his treatment of these unhappy people was such as I could not, consistent with the terms of your instructions, pass unnoticed. I accordingly remonstrated against it, and pointed out to His Excellency wherein his conduct, if faithfully represented, appeared to merit censure. I again warmly urged the prudent and conciliatory measures recommended in your instructions to me of the 27th May, and fully explained to him how intimately the reputation of our national character was connected with every act of his present administration. Thus far premised, I intimated to him, in plain terms, that I had received your peremptory orders to insist upon a proper treatment of the family of Hafiz Rahmat, in default of which he would most assuredly incur your displeasure, and forfeit every claim to that support and protection which the English have on all occasions manifested such readiness to yield him. His Excellency seemed less surprised than hurt at the style of this address, and asked with an appearance of concern, "Whence arose the necessity of prescribing to him a conduct which a due regard to his own reputation, in preference to every other tie, would actually suggest." He observed that he had many enemies, and that the influence of prejudice had drawn a reproach upon his character, which as he now considers he did not merit, it behoved him by every means in his power to remove. He positively denied everything I had taxed him with on the score of his treatment of Hafiz Rahmat's family, offering to stake his innocence on whatever test I chose to propose, and further, as he was convinced, not only from my remonstrances but the concurring circumstances that his conduct in general, but particularly with respect to his treatment of his captives, had been represented to you in a partial and unfavourable light, he hoped you would be pleased to indulge him with the particulars of the charges which may have been alleged against him, and at the same time point out his accusers, that he may attempt that justification which your satisfaction and his own reputation render so essentially necessary. In reply to these reflections, I observed that the knowledge of matters so publicly talked of could not possibly be confined to the immediate scene of action, that various channels must have conveyed it to the Presidency, and the union of so many opinions would naturally give it credit, although unsupported by the direct evidence of facts. Colonel Champion has informed me that he has a multitude of letters from the family of Hafiz Rahmat, pointing out, in the most pathetic terms, the distress and misery they are exposed to. These would be the surest criterion to judge the Nabob's conduct by, but while these unhappy people were so immediately in his power, and no effectual checks upon him, it would be dangerous to produce such vouchers [1].'

[1] Private letter, British Museum MSS. 29,155. This letter was printed with Middleton's evidence before the House of Commons, 24th May, 1786.

On the 22nd and 24th May 1786, Middleton was examined before the House of Commons. Some extracts from his evidence have already been given, and I have quoted his statement that he knew 'of no instance of cruelty, exercised in the course of the war upon the Rohillas, either by Shuja-ud-daula, or by his orders[1].' He said that after he sent his letter of the 5th July to Hastings 'he had reason to think more favourably of the character of the Vizier,' and that he 'found that many of the reports that had been propagated to his prejudice, from the best information he could obtain, were without foundation.'

Shortly after the close of the campaign, the hostile Majority of the new Government began to inquire into the transactions connected with the war. Their Minutes contained several references to passages in Colonel Champion's letters in which he had mentioned the cruel conduct of the Vizier, and, in December 1774, Hastings proposed that as Colonel Champion and two officers who had held important commands in the army, Colonel Leslie and Major Hannay, had arrived in Calcutta, they should be called before the Council and be personally examined with the special object of ascertaining the truth. After some objections on the part of Francis this was agreed to, and the three officers were examined by the Council on the 19th and 28th December[2].

Colonel Champion seems to have been little inclined to give any evidence; his answers were meagre and evasive, couched in such general terms, and so extremely short, that they add little to our knowledge.

The following are the only parts of his evidence which bear upon this subject:—

(1) 'Was the Vizier guilty of oppression over the inhabitants of the new conquered country?

[1] See p. 186.

[2] The evidence of these officers was not printed with the papers contained in the Appendix to the Fifth Report of the Committee of Secrecy, but is recorded in the MS. copies of the Consultations of the Calcutta Government preserved in the India Office. The answers of the officers, but not all the questions, have been printed in Forrest's Selections, vol. i. pp. 5[illegible]-66.

'It appeared so to me.

(2) 'Did the Vizier send out parties to burn and ravage the country of the Rohillas on the commencement of the war, or was Hafiz Rahmat Khân the aggressor in this instance?

'The Vizier.

(3) 'Are the Rohillas the native inhabitants and cultivators of the country, or were they only in possession as conquerors, &c.?

'The Rohillas are in possession of it as conquerors only; the native inhabitants are not of the same sect or religion.

(4) 'Have the native inhabitants deserted the country since the conquest of it, and in what state is it at present?

'The native inhabitants are still remaining, and the country is in a flourishing state.'

On the 2nd January, 1775, Colonel Champion wrote to the Government that he wished to correct 'some mistakes and inaccuracies' in his evidence, and to this answer he added that the country was 'in a flourishing state, considering it so immediately after the war.'

(5) 'Was the Vizier guilty of cruelties to the families of the Rohilla chiefs, and in what instances?

'It appeared to me that he was guilty of cruelties to the families of the Rohilla chiefs, but as to the instances I must refer to my Minute.

(6) 'Did you hear of a report of any attempt made by the Vizier to violate the chastity of the wives and daughters of Rohilla chiefs, &c., and do you believe there were grounds for the report?

'I did hear such a report, but as to the grounds I have none sufficient to prove the accusation, but the report was made to me.'

Questions by General Clavering:—

'When the Vizier began plundering and burning the country, did you make any representation to him upon it?

'I did.

'Did you represent to the Vizier your opinion of the ill treatment of the prisoners?

'I did.

'Were not some of the families of the chiefs left destitute of necessaries for their subsistence?

To this question his answer was 'No,' but on the 2nd January, he corrected this, and answered the question in the affirmative, and added, 'It was reported to me that they were in want of everything that could make their situation tolerably comfortable.'

'In what way were they ill treated?

'It was reported to me that they were in want.

'Did you inform the Governor, Mr. Hastings, of the Vizier's conduct towards the country and the prisoners?

'I did.

'How did the Governor take your representations?

'To the best of my recollection, he wrote to the Vizier to be more moderate in his behaviour.

'Did the Governor seem to be pleased at your making this representation to him?

'I refer to the Governor's letter, written in answer.

'When you expostulated with the Governor on the disgrace and dishonour which this war brought on the British arms, what answer did he make to these expostulations?

'I cannot charge my memory, but beg leave to refer to the correspondence.'

I will now notice the evidence given by Colonel Leslie. The first questions were the same as those put to Colonel Champion.

To the question [1][1] whether the Vizier had been guilty of oppression to the people of the country, Colonel Leslie made the following answer:—

'I would beg leave to distinguish between the real inhabitants and the acquired ones. By the acquired ones I mean the Rohillas or Afghans who conquered the country and became the masters of it. I believe the Gentoo inhabitants were not oppressed; the ryots have been as much cherished by him as they ever were under any former government, except at the time of the march of the army through their country, but they returned to their ploughs immediately and seemed to be as happy as ever.'

Referring to this answer, General Clavering said:—

'I observe that you mentioned that the Vizier behaved well to the ancient inhabitants, and I now desire to know how he behaved to the Rohillas.'

To this question Colonel Leslie replied:—

'The prisoners who fell into the hands of the Vizier, which I believe to be very few, are now entertained in his service; there are some of the sons of Hafiz Rahmat, two particularly whom I know and have often seen riding in his suite. He generally took one of these out with him all the time he was at Bisauli; their appearance was good, and

[1] This and the following numbers within brackets refer to the questions given on pp. 212, 213.

I think the same as the rest of his cavalry, and they appeared contented, but no doubt he kept a watchful eye upon them.'

The following extracts give all that is important in the rest of Colonel Leslie's evidence regarding the conduct of the Vizier:

(2) 'The day before our march from Shahabad the country upon the opposite side of the river Garrah was in flames, and upon my inquiring into the matter I learned it was by order of the Vizier, that he had sent several detachments of his light cavalry for that purpose, but I believe the inhabitants of those villages had withdrawn themselves from them and taken sanctuary in Shahjehanpur.

(4) 'The native inhabitants after I left Bisauli, between that and Sambhal, were all at their habitations, and had returned to their cultivation of the country. When I went down towards the banks of the Ganges it was highly cultivated, but about Pathargarh, which was the place of arms and retreat of the Rohillas, before they retired to Laldhang as their last resource, there was no cultivation but sugar.

(5) 'I protest I have heard a great deal of severity exercised on the families of the chiefs of the Rohillas, but I cannot speak positively to any of them but from hearsay. I am afraid there was too much reason to give the world a liberty to say that they were ill treated. There was one instance in which I thought it was necessary that I should interfere. I had been sent into Pilibhit, where the wife and family of Hafiz Rahmat were, and after a series of conversations with his sons, at which Major Hannay and Mr. Murray were present, I had a message from the Begum to request that I would speak to her. I returned for answer that I was sorry it was out of my power, as my conduct was prescribed to me, but that I would receive any message she would send to me. She sent her son, in return, to acquaint me that the business she wanted to speak to me on was to beg that I would intercede with Colonel Champion to protect her from any insult which might be offered her by the Vizier. In consequence of her request, I went to Colonel Champion and begged that he would give every sanction in his power and address the Vizier upon the occasion, which the Colonel promised to do. This is the only occasion I had to apply to Colonel Champion on the subject; I hear that many others did exist. I have heard a great deal of it, and had reason to disbelieve a great deal; as the reports were so improbable, I did not give ear to them. The messages of the Begum mentioned no instance of severity or ill treatment to her; at that time nothing could have happened, as it was the very day we marched to Pilibhit.

(6) 'Those are the vague reports which I wished in general to inform you of, but indeed there were particular ones which were attended with such circumstances that I could scarce give any credit to from the situation of the parties. There was a particular one at

Bisauli, one of the daughters of the Rohilla chiefs of that place, whom they said he had committed violence upon, and that she in consequence poisoned herself; and knowing the situation of the Vizier at that time I thought it almost impracticable, which made me to give very little credit to the stories which I heard at the time of such a nature.'

Questions by Francis :—

'When you were sent into Pilibhit, did the Begum send the trinkets and ornaments of the women to you desiring your acceptance of them, and what answer did you send her?

'The Begum did send her trinkets and ornaments. When Major Hannay and Mr. Murray and I were sent to Pilibhit, we went as three commissioners in conjunction with three of the Vizier's to examine the treasury and search for military chests of the beaten army. We searched the treasury and every other part but the zenanas, which we were forbid to enter. The women of the zenana sent their trinkets from a supposition that they were a part of the treasure, which we returned to them, acquainting them that we did not come in search of their trinkets but for the treasure deposited there.

'Did the Vizier afterwards take away more trinkets and ornaments from the women?

'I believe he did; I am pretty sure he did take them away the next day.

'Was it the enormity of the reports circulated concerning the Vizier's conduct to the families of the Rohilla chiefs which made you think them improbable?

'No, it was not; they were the circumstances of the reports.

'Do you believe the Vizier ever entered the zenanas of any of the Rohilla chiefs?

'I don't know; I believe he did.

'Is not the family of a noble Moor dishonoured by a man's forcibly entering the zenana and seeing the women?

'Yes, I believe it is.'

Major Hannay was examined on the same day. I make the following extracts from his evidence :—

(1) 'To the best of my knowledge I saw no signs of oppression to the inhabitants of the new conquered country, but from particular inquiries which I had an opportunity of making of the country people they said they had met with no treatment that they could complain of; that from the treatment they had met with they had no reason to fear greater severity from the Vizier than their former masters.

(2) 'I believe both the Vizier and the Rohillas were concerned in burning the villages. I was informed that some days before our

arrival at Shahabad the Rohillas had burned some villages towards Mamdi, in the Vizier's ancient dominions.

(4) 'Several of the native inhabitants of course had followed the Rohillas to Pathargarh and Laldhang, but the proportion of them was very small, and several of them to my knowledge returned, before the war was finished, to their former habitations. At the time that I went upon an expedition from Bisauli to Sambhal, Moradabad, and Rampur, the country appeared to be in good cultivation, the inhabitants were employed in tilling it. It is in general one of the best cultivated countries I have seen in Hindostan, and very well inhabited, and the people appeared to be as busy at that time as if there had been a profound peace, and under no kind of apprehension from the conquerors. At, or some time after the battle of St. George, Eugee Khan was returning from Delhi to rejoin his master the Vizier, and had taken possession of all the country from Anupshahar and Ramghat to Rampur, and established fousdars and collectors of the revenues of it before the arrival of our army at Bisauli, and to maintain these fousdars in the execution of their duty it was only necessary to leave 500 Nudjiff Cawns there and five companies of the Burrah Fultan, in all not amounting to 1500 men, who kept the country in perfect quietness until our army arrived, and after the march of our army to Pathargarh.

(5) 'I was generally informed, and from my own observation I am led to believe, that he treated them with a great deal of severity; for instance, he deprived them of all the ornamental part of their dress, and did not provide them with such accommodation as I thought their rank entitled them to expect. The reports in camp were various, but were not conveyed to me from such authority as to warrant my offering them to the Board.'

With reference to the last answer Francis asked:—

'Do you know, or have you heard, they were at any time reduced to distress for want even of a subsistence?'

To this question Major Hannay replied:—

'I have heard that their subsistence was scanty, but this is one of the reports I have heard and have not been able to ascertain the truth of to my own satisfaction.

(6) 'I have heard, while I was at Bisauli frequently, that he had violated one of the daughters of Mohibullah Khan, but I never gave credit to it; nay, I believe it impossible from the state of health he was in at that time. I may say further that when I heard this report I was at a good deal of pains to investigate the truth of it, and tracing it back I could carry it no further than it was a report that prevailed among the guard at the door of the zenana, and from the situation of this guard to the zenana it was impossible they could be

acquainted with any circumstances that passed within, as the apartments of the women were at such a distance from the gateway where the guard were placed. There was another motive which induced me to disbelieve the report, which was that a few days after this happened the women were carried to camp, where he would have a much better opportunity of doing it without detection had he been disposed or able.'

Question by Francis:—

'Do you know or believe that the Vizier entered the zenanas of the wives of any of the Rohilla chiefs?

'It is impossible for me to answer with any degree of precision, from the zenanas being spacious places consisting of many apartments, many of which are not occupied by women. I never knew of his going into any of them at Pilibhit; I can positively say he did not, for he never went into the town of Pilibhit. At Bisauli, I have heard that he frequently went into the zenana there, but to the best of my remembrance it was after the women were removed to camp, and that he was fitting up the zenanas for the reception of his own family during the time he was going to Pathargarh.'

Questions by General Clavering:—

'Do you not know that Colonel Champion made representations to the Vizier of cruelties exercised by his troops in the Rohilla country?

'I have heard Colonel Champion say that he had remonstrated to the Vizier against the burning of any villages, but I was not present at any such remonstrance. I further heard him say that he had used his offices with the Vizier to persuade him to treat the captive families of the Rohilla chiefs with more humanity and tenderness, and that upon these occasions the Vizier denied having treated them with severity.

'Do you imagine that Colonel Champion would have made such representations to the Vizier if he had not been persuaded that the facts were true?

'The burning of the villages was evident, and I can say with confidence that Colonel Champion would not have made application to the Vizier for the remedy of evils which he did not believe to exist.

'Whether you do not think that the Commander of the army was in a situation to be better informed of transactions of that nature than yourself?

'With respect to the burning of the villages and matters of that nature, with all deference to the Commander-in-Chief, I humbly conceive that I had as good opportunity of being acquainted as any one; with respect to the treatment of the captive families, I conceive he must have had better opportunities of information than me, as he might have received letters from them on the subject which I did not.'

Question by Colonel Monson:—

'What induced the Vizier to enter the zenana at Bisauli after the women had been removed from it?

'To look for treasure was his first motive, and to set up the zenana for his own women was his secondary.'

Some quotations have already been made from the evidence given by Major Balfour before the House of Commons on the 11th May, 1786[1]. The following extracts contain everything else of importance which he then said regarding the treatment of the Rohillas. After he had stated that he had been in the service of the East India Company for more than twenty years, and had served with Colonel Champion in the Rohilla campaign, his examination proceeded as follows:—

'Do you conceive that the Rohilla war was carried on with extraordinary circumstances of cruelty?

'I do not, by any means.

'Were reports spread in the English camp that Shuja-ud-daula had committed several acts of cruelty during that war?

'There were reports spread; but I afterwards understood that there were no good foundations for them. One notorious circumstance was reported, that he had ravished a woman of rank, and that she had stabbed him and afterwards stabbed herself; that was very generally believed. I had afterwards an opportunity, by residing a long time in the country, to know that it was an absolute untruth.

'Were many towns or villages destroyed during the campaign?

'On the army's first entering the country, there were several villages destroyed; but after our engagement with the Rohilla army, which happened eight days after entering the country, I did not know of any villages being destroyed, nor of any towns at all being destroyed.

'Were the inhabitants of the country, the husbandmen and mechanics, prevented from following their occupations by the war, or were they disturbed in their possessions?

'On our first entering the country, the inhabitants fled on all sides; but after the action with the Rohillas, in which Hafiz Rahmat was killed, and the Rohilla army defeated, I understood that the Vizier

[1] See p. 186.

sent out his own Aumils to protect the inhabitants and encourage them in peaceable occupations.

'Did you march back through the Rohilla country after the treaty of Laldhang?

'I did; I first accompanied Faizullah Khan to his capital. I remained with him there for about six weeks, till he was established in his jagheer.

'When you marched back to Oudh, at the end of those six weeks, what was the state of the cultivation of Rohilkhand at that time?

'It was very much the same as at the time when we entered it, which was about eight months before. The conquest of the country might occasion a temporary interruption to the cultivation of lands, but the ryots were returning to their villages and things were going on as formerly.

'When did you command in Rohilkhand?

'I got the command there in March 1778, and commanded there until April 1781.

'Was Bareilly your head quarters at that time?

'It was.

'What was the state of Hafiz Rahmat's family when you commanded in Rohilkhand?

'Such of them as resided there (I cannot be certain how many of them) had houses and gardens allowed them, such as they chose, and they were indulged with renting such lands, small villages, as they wished to have for their own immediate convenience, for supplying their necessaries, at a lower rent than what other lands were usually let for; and it was my particular instructions from the Resident at the Vizier's court to treat them with every respect and attention, and to see that the same was shown to them by others.

'Were they under confinement during any part of 1780?

'Never in confinement, during any part of the time that I commanded in Rohilkhand.

'Are the principal towns in Rohilkhand in ruins?

'Not the towns. Many of the residences of the Rohilla chiefs, from being uninhabited, by their expulsion from the country, were going to ruin, but I confine this entirely to their palaces.'

The whole of the recorded evidence of the English officers who took part in the war, in regard to the cruelties said to have been committed by the Vizier, has now been given. I will next quote the statements made by the Vizier himself.

On the 28th November, 1774, Hastings received from him a letter filled with complaints against Colonel Champion, and accusing the English of having committed violent outrages on the people of the country[1]. He referred in the following terms to the charges of cruelty to the family of Hafiz Rahmat:—

'Some time ago you received letters from some gentlemen concerning the affairs of the family of Hafiz Rahmat Khan and Inayat Khan. The English gentlemen first began this method; I therefore have written all the above particulars for your information. The affair of Hafiz Rahmat Khan's family is as follows: The Colonel sent a message to me that the family of Hafiz Rahmat were dying with hunger; that a storm had one day thrown down the purdas of the tent of Hafiz Rahmat Khan's family, and left the men and women exposed. I went to visit the Colonel, and returned an answer to his message that I sent provisions from my own sircar daily for their support; and that with respect to the purdas which were thrown down by the violence of the wind, I could not help it, that I had no authority over the winds to still them; and that if I had not supplied them with provisions what means had they taken to preserve their existence. My friend, the family of Hafiz Rahmat Khan is well supplied with provisions, and three thousand rupees per month is appointed for this purpose. I have no power with God to prevent the violence of the wind. Consider well these particulars. Let prisoners be ever so well treated and supplied with necessaries, still confinement is uncomfortable. Whoever has lost a father and brother in war, has fallen from the dignity of a throne and become a prisoner, will undoubtedly suffer much misery. I have written this long account that you may be informed of every affair. I have related them all more particularly to Colonel Macleane who will inform you of them. Mr. Middleton will also write you on these subjects. I am very much pleased with Mr. Middleton's good conduct: he is a sensible and intelligent man, and a sincere well-wisher of mine; I therefore consult him on all affairs, and have been spoken to on this subject by the Colonel, who says that Mr. Middleton was appointed to collect the money due to the Company, and that he has no business to interfere in any other matter[2].'

The native historians of the time do not add much to our knowledge, but Mustajab Khan, the son of Hafiz Rahmat Khan, has noticed in the Gulistan-i-Rahmat the treatment of some of the Rohilla chiefs and of his father's family

[1] See *sup.* p. 202, and p. 211.

[2] Clavering, Monson, and Francis, in a Minute dated 25th February, 1775, wrote regarding this letter from the Vizier that they had 'some reason to think it was fabricated and advised by Colonel Macleane,' and it was afterwards insinuated that this was done with the knowledge of Hastings. He indignantly denied all knowledge of the circumstances under which the letter was written. See Appendix D.

during and after the war. Respecting excesses or cruelties committed in the course of the campaign he does not say a word. We are told that after the defeat of the Rohillas two of the sons of Hafiz Rahmat, Mohabbat Khan and Zulfikar Khan, went to the Vizier's camp. They were honourably received and admitted to an audience by Shuja-ud-daula, 'who pretended to lament that he had been compelled to take up arms against their father, and assured them with a solemn oath that he would make a handsome provision for them.' A few days later, according to the same work, Mohabbat Khan was called on by the Vizier to point out the spot where the treasure of Hafiz was buried, to which he replied that his father had no treasure but the affection of his subjects; the Vizier then required the ladies of the family to deliver up their ornaments, and ordered the women to be removed to tents in order that their rooms might be searched for the supposed treasure; soldiers were posted at the tents, ostensibly to protect them from thieves, but in reality to prevent any persons from escaping; the Vizier afterwards sent a message to Mohabbat Khan to the effect that he had been prevented by illness from receiving his visits, but that he hoped to see him in a few days; on the arrival of Shuja-ud-daula at Bisauli, soon afterwards, he was reminded of his promises, 'but, as he never intended to fulfil those engagements, he put an end to remonstrances by confining Fatehullah Khan and Mohibullah Khan, the sons of Dundi Khan, and then confiscated their property'; the whole family of Hafiz Rahmat Khan were sent to Allahabad, where most of them remained until the following January, when Shuja-ud-daula died; his successor, Asuf-ud-daula, 'stopped the allowance of one thousand rupees per month which had been made by his father to Mohabbat Khan, and even the paltry allowance of one hundred rupees per diem for the support of the families confined in the fort of Allahabad was so irregularly paid that they were not unfrequently in distress for food'; some months afterwards, in consequence of the interference of the British Government, the family of Hafiz were released and went to Lucknow.

'After much discussion, the Nawab agreed to grant an annual pension of one lakh of rupees for the support of the families of Hafiz Rahmat Khan and Dundi Khan, in the proportion of 65,000 rupees to the former and 35,000 rupees to the latter; Fattehullah and Mohibullah, the sons of Dundi Khan, joined the Nawab Najf Khan at Delhi, in the hope that he would provide for them; but being disappointed, they fixed their residence at Rampur, while the majority of Hafiz Rahmat's sons remained at Lucknow, subsisting on the small allowance procured for them by the British Government [1].'

The only remaining evidence on this subject is contained in Hamilton's History. It possesses a special value because, as I have already explained, it may be assumed to represent the views of Faizullah Khan. Mohibullah Khan and Fattehullah Khan, the sons of Dundi Khan, were, it will be remembered, the only Rohilla chiefs named by Colonel Champion as having been ill-treated by the Vizier.

'Mohibullah Khan and his brother Fattehulla, depending much upon the assurances which they had received from the Vizier previous to the battle of Kattra, although they had forfeited all title to this dependence by joining their friends in the engagement, retired to Bisauli, their own city, and there remained. The Begum, widow of Saidullah Khan, who resided at Aonla, on learning the death of Hafiz Rahmat, and the defeat of the Rohilla forces, immediately despatched a messenger to Shuja-ud-daula, "requesting to know his pleasure with respect to her, whether he meant that she should surrender up her effects, or rely upon his generosity." In reply to this the Vizier immediately ordered two of his confidential servants to wait upon the Begum, "to assure her of his favourable intentions towards her, and to request her not for a moment to admit any doubt or apprehension into her mind, nor by ill-grounded fears to disseminate confusion and terror in the city of Aonla: that her annual allowance which, under the Rohilla chiefs, had never exceeded 50,000 rupees per annum, should be increased to something more proportionable to her rank and situation, and that she might hope for everything from his future kindness." Confiding in these declarations, the Begum remained at Aonla, and thereby preserved the tranquillity of the city, where there was no more

[1] Gulistan-i-Rahmat, pp. 121–130.

appearance of disturbance or disorder than if nothing extraordinary had happened. The family of Hafiz Rahmat, with a torpid apathy which is not easy to be accounted for, took no measures either for flight or defence, but continued quietly in the fort of Pilibhit, apparently little moved by the late (to them) dreadful catastrophe. Zulficar Khan, Hafiz's eldest son, who had fled to Bareilly immediately after the battle, when he heard of Mohammed Yar Khan being at Aonla, went and joined him at that place. . . . The family of Hafiz Rahmat, on hearing of the Vizier's approach [to Pilibhit], were rather pleased than alarmed at the intelligence, as their greatest dread arose from the apprehension of some of the Rohillas taking their opportunity to retaliate upon them the former exactions of their deceased chief, against which they hoped under the shelter of the English and the Vizier, to find a permanent protection. "In short," says the [Rohilla] narrator, "misfortune and infatuation was their lot, in that they did not think of taking refuge in the intrenchments at the foot of the hills, which were at so inconsiderable a distance, and where, under the guardianship of Faizullah Khan, their honour and their property would have remained secure and untouched, and they would have experienced every kind of attention and regard from that benignity for which he is so justly famed." The event, indeed, soon evinced the folly of their inactivity. The garrison had already abandoned the place; so that, upon the allied troops appearing before it, it was surrendered without any resistance, and the family of Hafiz Rahmat, together with such treasure, jewels, &c., as remained from the wreck of his fortune, fell into the hands of the Vizier without stipulation or condition; and the next day all the women and children were put into palanquins and other covered carriages, and sent off under a strong guard to Aonla, whither the Vizier accompanied them. . . . The two brothers, Mohibullah Khan and Fattehullah, when they beheld the fate of Hafiz Rahmat's family, began to entertain some doubts of the Vizier's intentions with respect to themselves, especially as they were conscious that by their breach of a private agreement previously understood (in joining Hafiz Rahmat in the battle, notwithstanding their acceptance of the overtures from the Vizier) they must in some measure be considered as having forfeited that protection to which they might otherwise have laid claim. They therefore now resolved to divide the hazard, by one of the brothers proceeding to pay his respects to the Nabob, whilst the other should remain at Bisauli (where their families and treasures were deposited), and act as circumstances might direct. Accordingly, Fattehullah Khan proceeded to the Vizier's camp at Bareilly, and there, before he would venture to appear, solicited the mediation of Salar Jang (the Vizier's uncle) in his favour. Some of his friends endeavoured to dissuade the Rohilla from taking this step, and advised him rather to apply to the British commander, "as it was well known that when the English word was pledged it could be relied on, whereas no faith could be placed either in the Vizier himself or any of his officers." Fattehullah, however, rejected this salutary counsel, and procuring an introduction to the Vizier the next day, immediately after being dismissed from audience, he was ordered into confinement. In the interim, Mohibullah Khan waited at Bisauli, under much anxiety to hear of his brother's success, and would have availed himself of the intelligence he received concerning his reception, by removing with the most valuable part of his treasure to join his countrymen at Laldhang; but his intention was at once frustrated by the unexpected appearance of Najf Khan, who arrived at Bisauli the same evening, and either guessing the Rohilla's design, or being furnished with previous instructions, placed guards around his house, so that all hope of escape was extinguished; and thus both the brothers experienced the natural effects of their indecisive and trimming policy. Had they boldly rejected the Vizier's insidious offers in the first instance, and openly and gallantly shared the fortunes of their countrymen in their last retreat, their honour would still have remained untouched and their persons free; but by acceding to the Vizier's offers, and afterwards appearing against him in battle, they entailed upon themselves universal odium, and at the same time incurred his implacable resentment. The day before the arrival of the allied army at Bisauli, Mohammad Yar Khan [the brother of Faizullah Khan] came in, and being presented to the Vizier was very favourably received, nor did he ever afterwards suffer any molestation either in his person or family. Numbers of the other Rohillas, who had not accompanied their countrymen in their flight, on hearing this, came in, and found a similar reception.

'Much has been said of the excessive cruelties practised on the family of Hafiz Rahmat; the above, however, is all that is mentioned by the Rohilla narrator upon this subject, and notwithstanding every possible inquiry, the writer has never been able to discover a single document from which he might ascertain any one particular of this alleged ill-usage, unless the inconvenience necessarily attendant upon confinement and removal are to be treated as such [1].'

The following quotations are taken from the Sair-ul-Mutakherin, the author of which, Syad Gholam Husein Khan, states that he was intimately acquainted with the family of Hafiz Rahmat. They chiefly refer, however, to a later period :—

'Shuja-ud-daula, after his signal victory, being become the master of the country, spread his victorious troops far and near, with orders to put to the sword every Rohilla that should appear in arms or did not submit; and meanwhile he turned his thoughts towards quieting the country, bringing it under order and control, and annexing it to his own dominions. The rest of the Rohilla nation, struck with terror

[1] Hamilton, pp. 244–252.

and dismay submitted, and all their chiefs reluctantly sent their obeisance.'

After referring to the resistance offered by Faizullah Khan, and to the treaty by which Rampur and a part of Rohilkhand was restored to him, the historian thus continues :—

'Thither he retired with the remains of his demolished nation, and there he applied himself to the improvement of the country, and there he now lives with dignity and splendour. The rest of the Rohilla princes, so far from being so much favoured by fortune, were left unnoticed, and some who were suspected of knowing of concealed hoards and treasures, suffered every hardship in a long confinement. I, the poor man, have seen at Lucknow most of the sons of Hafiz Rahmat and Dundi Khan, and it is from their own mouths I have learned their own history. It was a little after Shuja-ud-daula's death, and at the beginning of the reign of his son Asuf-ud-daula. It was at Lucknow that I became fully acquainted with them all, and also with a number of the principal persons that had a share in that expedition. But the most illustrious and valuable amongst these Rohilla princes was undoubtedly Mohabbat Khan, younger brother to Inayat Khan, which latter had once endeared himself to Shuja-ud-daula, by being his companion of arms in his expedition against Azimabad. This young prince seemed, by his figure as well as by his character, to be worthy of dominion, or at least to deserve a better fortune, but times were too hard and insensible, or at least too blind to pay a due attention to so much merit, and he was suffered to linger upon a small pension, quite inadequate to his rank in life (1000 or 1200 rupees per month), and that too at the very time when Faizullah Khan was complimented with a country that cannot yield less than twenty lakhs of rupees; he, whose paternal possessions in the life-time of the Rohilla power never did afford above five lakhs a year; a strange perverseness this! And a strange infatuation of the times indeed [1].'

[1] Sair-ul-Mutakherin, vol. iii. p. 263. See *inf.* Chap. xvii, where an extract from the same work is given with the remarks made by Hafiz Rahmat's son on the death of Shuja-ud-daula. On the 10th August, 1776, the Resident at Lucknow reported that all the members of the families of the Rohilla chiefs had been released, and that the Vizier had engaged to give them a monthly allowance of 8333 rupees. They quarrelled among themselves to such an extent that it was difficult to make any distribution of the money. 'On issuing some money,' the Resident writes, 'to Mohabbat Khan, I was surprised to find a complaint made by another branch of the family that they were starving. When I applied to Mohabbat Khan for an explanation of his not having made a just distribution of the sum, as it was declaredly granted for their general support, he asked me with astonishment how I could expect it, as the complainants were his avowed enemies, and he would himself sooner starve than assist them.' Fifth Report, App. No. 45; Forrest's Selections, vol. ii. p. 553.

Having now brought together all the evidence that I have been able to find in regard to the manner in which the Rohilla war was conducted, I must return for a moment to Mill's History. Although he had not seen the whole of the papers to which reference has been made in the present narrative, the greater part of the correspondence between Hastings and Colonel Champion and Middleton, and the evidence taken before the House of Commons was in his hands. With those papers before him, he deliberately omitted all mention of the fact that Hastings, in language as strong as it was possible to find, had repeatedly expressed his detestation of the cruelties attributed to the Vizier, and had issued the instructions which seemed to him most likely to stop them. Not content with this suppression of the truth, Mill, in the passage that I have quoted[1], has stated that Hastings defended the atrocities of the Vizier, and in proof of his assertion he has professed to quote the very words of Hastings himself. I do not use language too strong for the occasion when I say that a more baseless calumny was never recorded by one calling himself an historian.

The words which Mill has cited are to be found, not in any reply to the representations of Colonel Champion while the war was in progress, but in a Minute written by Hastings on the 10th January, 1775, in answer to a letter, attacking him in unmeasured terms, which had been sent to the Court of Directors by Clavering, Monson, and Francis, who then formed the Majority in the Council. According to a custom very usual with him, Mill has separated from the context the particular words that suited his purpose, and suppressing the rest, he gives his garbled extract as the proof of a false and atrocious charge.

In the letter from the Majority of the Council they had referred in the following terms to the cruelties said to have been committed by the Vizier:—

'Para. 18. The united armies obtained a complete victory over the Rohilla chiefs on the 23rd April. From that time we must refer you

[1] See p. 176.

to the letters recorded in your Consultations for the further operations of the Vizier, his barbarous and unnecessary devastation of the country, the cruelty with which he treated his unhappy prisoners, and particularly the brutal outrages offered to their wives and daughters, though of the first rank. In the letters of Colonel Champion you will find a detail of these proceedings, which he calls *wanton enormities* (uncontradicted, though palliated by the Governor's private agent), which we doubt not will fill you with horror. We enclose copies of three of them, in order to excite and fix your attention to the rest. One paragraph in that of the 15th of June is so striking that we cannot forbear inserting it here:—"I am most heartily disposed to believe that the Board did not suspect their orders could have such consequences as have fallen out; they could not have foreseen so sudden and so total an expulsion and downfall of a whole race of people; they could not have supposed that a war, exalted and supported by British arms, could pay so very little deference to the advices and counsel of a British Commander; nor was it possible to conceive that a man who had himself tasted the gall of misfortune should be so totally unmindful of the unbounded and unparalleled grace shown to him, as to delight in denying a single ray of benevolence to others; such, however, has been the case; and in due intimation of it I have discharged that which was incumbent upon me. I too can say that the Nabob, as the agent of oppression, is alone culpable; but whilst all Asia know that the English give him the rod, and whilst they in vain look up to them as those who ought, if not direct the application at least to prevent an ill use being made of that rod, will they not reasonably conclude that the scourges which the agent gives are connived at? Will they not say that every English chief is another Sujah[1]?"

'Para. 19. These details, gentlemen, would probably never have reached your knowledge, if we had not called for Mr. Hastings' private correspondence with Colonel Champion and Mr. Nathaniel Middleton. Even now, that correspondence is laid before us in so broken and imperfect a state, and so many letters belonging to it confessedly withheld, that we do not for ourselves hesitate to conclude that facts and circumstances still more atrocious than any that appear are suppressed[2].'

The following extract gives the reply of Hastings[3]:—

'Para. 18. An appeal to the passions is an insult to the understanding. Such are the allegations of "barbarous and unnecessary devastation of the country,"—the "cruelty with which the Vizier

[1] This has been already quoted. See p. 197.

[2] Fifth Report, App. No. 45; Letter to Court of Directors, dated 30th November, 1774.

[3] The numbers of the paragraphs in this extract correspond to those in the letter of the Majority of the Council quoted above.

treated his unhappy prisoners,"—"the brutal outrages offered to their wives and daughters, though of the highest rank,"—"his wanton enormities," and the declamatory quotation from one of Colonel Champion's letters on the same subject. I believe it will appear from the evidence of Mr. Nathaniel Middleton's letters, and from the examination of Colonel Leslie and Major Hannay, strongly corroborated even by the letters and depositions of Colonel Champion, the Vizier's principal accuser, that he has been unjustly traduced in the reports which have prevailed of the enormities committed by him in the course of the war. *I believe it to be a truth that he began by sending detachments to plunder. This I pronounce to have been both barbarous and impolitic, but too much justified by the practice of war established among all the nations of the East, and, I am sorry to add, by our own, in an instance which the Vizier has a right to quote in vindication of the charge against him, of a detachment employed in the war, in which we were engaged with him in the year* 1764, *to burn and ravage the country*[1]. It fell to the lot of Colonel, then Major Champion to execute this commission, and how well he discharged it, and how little his feelings were at that time affected by the same scene of barbarities and "wanton enormities" against which he has lately so pathetically exclaimed, will appear from the following copy of a letter from him on the subject, to the late President, Mr. Vansittart, which I quote, not meaning to reproach him with having done the duty assigned him, but to prove that the principle which dictated to Colonel Champion the severe charges with which he has laboured to load the Vizier in the late campaign, was either personal animosity or the desire of persuading the Board to grant him the power which he repeatedly solicited—to control, and, in effect, to command the Vizier. I pretend not to look into the hearts of others, but I exercise the right allowed to all mankind of judging of intentions by facts, and I appeal to Colonel Champion's correspondence with the Select Committee and the Board for the grounds on which I form my judgment, and on which every man who reads them may judge for himself. The letter above alluded to is as follows:—Extract of a letter from Major Champion to Henry Vansittart, Esq., dated 20th June, 1764.

"*Two separate parties have been sent into the enemy's country, the one of which went as high up as Buxar, and according to the direction given me, there are destroyed upwards of a thousand villages. Had not the rain, &c., prevented us, which occasioned our return, we should have done very considerable more damage*[1]. I am now marching in the borders of the Deva to the boundary of the Sircar country, to endeavour to bring in the zemindars, as not one of them of any considerable note is yet come in, nor has a rupee been collected from this country."

'The cruelty with which the Vizier treated his unhappy prisoners forms the second charge against him. It is not even asserted (except

[1] The words in italics have been quoted by Mill.

in the instance which I shall proceed to in the third charge) that they suffered by actual violence, but that they were ill subsisted, and I believe this to be true. Mr. Nathaniel Middleton, whose letters contain the strongest character both of candour and truth, says that the Vizier did allow them too moderate a subsistence and that ill served; his commands, though frequently repeated, being, in this as in every other instance, ill obeyed. The third charge is indeed of the blackest die, "of brutal outrages offered to the wives and daughters of the Rohillas, though of the highest rank." The only authority which the gentlemen of the Majority had for this horrid accusation, at least I recollect no other, was a letter from Mr. Nathaniel Middleton, who mentioned it only as an instance of the falsehoods which had been propagated to injure the Vizier, adding that the unhappy victims of his brutal lust, who could not survive their shame, but had put an end to their own lives, were still living and that the Vizier had never seen them. Colonel Champion's answer to the question proposed to him by the Board on this subject, namely, "Whether he had heard the report and believed there were grounds for it," is a striking instance of the little inclination he had to show favour to the Vizier, but amounts to the strongest conviction of the falsehood of this abominable history. He said, "he did hear such a report, but as to the grounds, he had none sufficient to prove the accusation, but the report was made to him." The charge of oppressing his new subjects has also been laid against the Vizier, and totally refuted by the depositions of Colonel Champion, Colonel Leslie, and Major Hannay, who all declare that the country enjoyed, even in the height of the war, a state of perfect tranquillity.'

'Para. 19. This contains a charge against me for suppression. In answer, I say that these details, if declamations are details, have appeared long ago in Colonel Champion's letters to the Select Committee, complaining of the cruelties exercised by the Vizier, and in the repeated calls which they made upon him to produce the instances of them, which he replied to by repeating the same declamations, but producing no instances, at least none which in my judgment can warrant the smallest part of his invectives against him[1].'

Hastings then gives Colonel Champion's letter of the 12th June, 1774, which has been already quoted[2].

In the passages which have been quoted from the Minute of Hastings, he has stated the facts with truth, justice, and moderation.

I have now brought together all the evidence that I have been able to find in regard to the atrocities said to

[1] Minute of Appeal, Fifth Report, App. No. 45; Forrest's Selections, vol. i. p. 180.

[2] See p. 195.

have been committed in the Rohilla war. It may be summed up in a few sentences.

The statement that atrocities were defended or excused by Hastings had its origin in a baseless falsehood. He did all in his power to cause the war to be conducted with humanity, and, considering all the circumstances of the case, his efforts were successful.

From the time when the army of the Vizier entered Rohilkhand to the conclusion of the treaty of peace with Faizullah Khan, nearly six months elapsed. In the first week of this period, while hostilities were in progress, and in the three or four days which followed the defeat of the Rohillas, many villages were burned, and whatever property could be carried off was plundered.

This occurred in a small tract of country between the Oudh frontier and Pilibhit. There was no serious loss of life or personal suffering, because the villages had been, for the most part, entirely deserted by their inhabitants, who, according to their established custom on the approach of danger, had fled to the Tarái and forest, taking with them their cattle and such valuables as they could easily remove.

The rest of Rohilkhand, a country nearly as large as Belgium, was rapidly occupied without opposition, after the defeat of the Rohillas, and there is no reason to suppose that in any part of it, or at any time, any serious excesses were committed by the troops of the Vizier. Long before the submission of Faizullah Khan, the Hindu inhabitants, who constituted nearly the whole population, were, for the most part, following their usual occupations. There is nothing to show that they were anywhere exposed to any extraordinary hardship or ill-treatment beyond that inevitable in a time of war.

In regard to the Rohillas, whose numbers were comparatively very small, the story of their cruel extermination is absolutely false, nor is there a particle of evidence that any atrocities were committed upon them at any time during the war. Excepting the men who fell in battle, there is no evidence that any Rohilla was put to death, or was treated with any inhumanity.

The only Rohillas who were compelled to leave Rohilkhand, other than the principal chiefs, were the soldiers actually under arms with Faizullah Khan. Under one of the conditions of the final treaty of peace, they crossed the Ganges into the friendly territory of Zabita Khan, their countryman. The rest of the Rohillas were unmolested, or went into Rampur, the Rohilla State assigned by treaty to Faizullah Khan, their recognised chief.

The Rohilla chiefs were generally treated with consideration and lenity. Two of them only, the sons of Dundi Khan, who had broken engagements which they had entered into with the Vizier, were, not unjustly, punished with temporary confinement and confiscation of their property; but they suffered no serious ill-treatment and they were soon released.

The ladies of the families of Hafiz Rahmat and Dundi Khan, with their dependents, suffered much distress and inconvenience from their removal into camp, and from the absence of proper arrangements for their comfort and for their maintenance, and their jewels and personal ornaments were taken from them. The stories that they were, in any case, subjected to personal outrage or gross insult are absolutely false, without any vestige of foundation.

There never was an Indian war in which excesses were not committed. To restrain from all violence troops like those of Shuja-ud-daula would have been impossible, even if their commanders had desired it. Hastings was stating a notorious fact when he said that it was unfortunately true not only that these excesses were the general practice in Eastern warfare, but that the Vizier might find examples of conduct on the part of British troops similar to that of which he had been accused. We all know how, even in more modern times, wars in India have been carried on. The horrors of the Mutinies of 1857 are still fresh in our memories. Even in European countries, and in the present century, terrible atrocities have been committed;

the strong will and stern discipline of Wellington could not always prevent in Spain cruelties towards a friendly people almost as abominable as any that have been perpetrated in India. If Hastings had not firmly resisted the lust of plunder which, as I have shown, pervaded the English army in Rohilkhand, I fear that it would not be the crimes of the Vizier alone that we should now be discussing. I do not doubt that this, like every other war, brought with it an amount of misery far worse than that of which any direct evidence is now before us, but at the same time it seems to me clear that Shuja-ud-daula would have been justified in saying that the campaign in Rohilkhand had been carried on with an absence of violence and bloodshed and generally with a degree of humanity altogether unusual in Indian warfare. Nor can I doubt that this result was mainly due to the remonstrances of Hastings. 'History,' writes Mr. Forrest, 'furnishes no more striking example of the growth and vitality of a slander. The Rohilla atrocities owe their birth to the malignity of Champion and Francis; their growth to the rhetoric of Burke; and their wide diffusion to the brilliancy and pellucid clearness of Macaulay's style[1].' The only defect I can find in this perfectly just judgment is that in pronouncing it Mr. Forrest has forgotten the History of James Mill[2].

[1] Forrest's Selections, Introduction, p. xxxi.

[2] See Appendix D: 'Note on some missing evidence relating to the conduct of the Rohilla War.'

CHAPTER XVI.

THE OBJECTS WITH WHICH THE ROHILLA WAR WAS UNDERTAKEN.

The charge that the acquisition of money was the sole object of the war.—The statements in Mill's History.—Burke's First Charge against Hastings.—Macaulay's Essay.—Mill's suppression of the facts.—Accounts given by Hastings himself of the causes of the war.—His Defence before the House of Commons.—Despatch to the Court of Directors.—Minute by Hastings.—Appeal of Hastings to the Court of Directors.—Minute by Barwell.—The acquisition of money one of the reasons which induced Hastings to take part in the war.—His own admission of the fact.—The policy of Hastings wise and justifiable.—Security against Maratha invasion the primary object of the war.—The arrangements with the Vizier contained nothing unreasonable.—The peculiar conditions under which Hastings was placed.

I HAVE not hitherto noticed in detail one of the most serious charges brought against Hastings in connection with the Rohilla war, and have reserved it for separate consideration.

It has often been asserted that the acquisition of money was the sole object for which the war was undertaken. This charge was brought by Burke and Francis and others of that time, it was repeated in Mill's History, and it was at last dressed up by Macaulay with a power of rhetoric which has made it universally known and almost universally believed.

'A meeting,' Mill writes, 'was concerted between the Vizier and the Governor, which took place at Benares at the beginning of September. The terms are memorable in which the cause and object of this interview are mentioned by the English chief. In his report to the Council at Calcutta, on the 4th of October, 1773, he says: "The Vizier was at first very desirous of the assistance of an English force to put him in possession of the Rohilla country, lying north of his dominions and east of the Ganges. This has long been a favourite object of his wishes; and you will recollect that the first occasion of my last visit was furnished by a proposal of this kind[1]." The Governor-General was so far from revolting at this proposition, or hesitating to close with it, that he stimulated the Vizier to its execution. *Money* was the motive to this eager passion for the ruin of the Rohillas. "As this had long," says the English ruler, "been a favourite object of the Vizier, the Board judged with me that it might afford a fair occasion to urge the improvement of our alliance, by obtaining his assent to a more equitable compensation for the expenses attending the aid which he occasionally received from our forces." The situation of the Company, he says, urged it upon them "as a measure necessary to its interest and safety. All our advices," he continues, "both public and private, represented the distresses of the Company at home as extreme. The letters from the Court of Directors called upon us most loudly for ample remittances, and a reduction of our military expenses. At the same time, such was the state of affairs in this Government, that for many years past the income of the year was found inadequate to its expense; to defray which a heavy bond debt, amounting at one time to 125 lakhs of rupees had accumulated." It was accordingly stipulated that 40 lakhs of rupees, upon the accomplishment of the enterprise, should be advanced to the English by the Vizier, and a monthly allowance, equivalent to the computed expense, be provided for the troops engaged in that service. "By this," says the Governor, "a saving of near one-third of our military expenses would be effected during the period of such service; the stipulation of 40 lakhs would afford an ample supply to our treasury; the Vizier would be freed from a troublesome neighbourhood, and his dominions be much more defensible." In all this, we may allow, there was enough for convenience and profit, both to the President and the Vizier[2].'

In this passage Mill has closely followed the method adopted by Burke in the following passage, taken from the first of the Charges against Hastings, presented to the House of Commons on the 4th of April, 1786:—

'That the object avowed by the said Warren Hastings, and the motives urged by him, for employing the British arms in the utter ex-

[1] The manner in which Mill ends his quotation at this point is characteristic. The next sentence in the report of Hastings is as follows: 'He had certainly just grounds of resentment against the chiefs of this nation, who had not only failed in their engagement to pay him forty lakhs of rupees for his protection against the Marathas, but had actually supplied them with money when they appeared in arms against him.'

[2] History of British India, Book v. chap. 1.

tirpation of the Rohilla nation, are stated by himself in the following terms:—The acquisition of forty lakhs of rupees to the Company, and of so much specie added to the exhausted currency of our provinces; that it would give wealth to the Nabob of Oudh, of which we should participate; that the said Warren Hastings should always be ready to profess that he did reckon the probable acquisition of wealth among his reasons for taking up his arms against his neighbours; that it would ease the Company of a considerable part of their military expense, and preserve their troops from inaction and relaxation of discipline; that the weak state of the Rohillas promised an easy conquest of them; and finally, that such was his idea of the Company's distress at home, added to his knowledge of their wants abroad, that he should have been glad of any occasion to employ their forces, which saved so much of their pay and expenses.'

I will not quote the passage in which, in his famous essay, Macaulay has translated into his own brilliant English the clumsy sentences of Mill. That he never investigated the facts for himself is clear. With the exception of a few erroneous statements taken from the speeches or Charges of Burke, everything that he has written on the subject is traceable to Mill, nor can I blame him for believing that Mill's authority might be accepted as conclusive. His version of the story of the Rohilla war is not history but rhetoric, and I do not propose to criticise it.

The grave and deliberate allegations of Mill stand on a different footing from the rhetoric of Macaulay and the passionate invective of Burke. I have cited all that he has said in proof of his statement of the reasons for which the war was undertaken. Although it is brief, it appears to be conclusive. The sole authority quoted is that of Hastings himself; he is judged and condemned by his own words; there is nothing to lead the reader to suppose that Hastings ever gave any other explanation of his motives.

Out of the voluminous papers written by Hastings on the subject, Mill has referred to only one, the Appeal to the Court of Directors, dated the 3rd December, 1774. It fills thirteen closely printed pages, as large as those of a modern blue-book and from these Mill has selected and pieced together the seventeen lines by which he supports the assertion that according to Hastings' own admission the object of the Rohilla war was money. A more complete suppression of the facts of history could hardly be found.

Whether the alliance of the English with the Vizier in the war against the Rohillas was right or wrong, the foregoing narrative will have shown that it was not the result of any hasty resolution, but was the outcome of a long series of occurrences extending over several years. This cannot be shown more clearly than in the words of Hastings himself.

In reply to the Charges of Burke, in his Defence before the House of Commons, in 1786, he entered at great length into the transactions connected with the Rohilla war, and I quote from it the following passages:—

'The dominions of the Nabob Shuja-ud-daula, our ally, lay open and exposed to that of the Rohillas, both consisting of one vast plain, without any natural line of division or obstruction between them; and both were shut in by the same common boundary, the Ganges, closing them in the northern extremity with impenetrable mountains. The Marathas had successively attempted to possess themselves of this country; and, but for the assistance of the Nabob's forces united with those of the Company, they would have succeeded. The Rohillas, though thus effectually and seasonably protected by the Nabob Shuja-ud-daula, had openly negotiated with the Marathas, and had shown manifest dispositions to unite with them against their defender. The same scenes might be renewed the next year, and repeatedly, with equal danger to the Nabob Shuja-ud-daula, whether the Marathas obtained complete possession of the country, or the Rohillas joined with them to carry their ravages into his. The Company's interests, which were at all times involved in the security of the Nabob Vizier's dominions, had acquired a strong additional tie by his recent engagements with them. The Rohillas had afforded him a just cause for war, and for all the consequences of it, by their repeated breach of engagement, and he had a right to our concurrence and assistance in the prosecution of it. These were the grounds for undertaking the war . . . . I shall recite the particulars of the origin, design, progress, conclusion, and effects of the Rohilla war.

'In May 1771, the King quitted Allahabad, and threw himself into the arms of the Marathas. In a few months afterwards he granted them sunnds, or charters, for the provinces of Kora, Karra, and Allahabad, or the lands immediately situated above the conflux of the rivers Ganges and Jumna, which we had before given to him. In January 1772, General Sir Robert Barker met the Nabob Shuja-ud-daula at Faizabad, who proposed various plans to counteract the ambitious designs of the Marathas, who were then preparing to invade Rohilkhand. The General, by his own authority, ordered a battalion of sepoys for the defence of the lines at Cawnpore. The Governor, Mr. Cartier, and the Select Committee, on the 12th February, 1772, approved of the General's conduct, and authorised him to enter into negotiations on the part of the Company in support of the Nabob's views. On the 28th January, 1772, the General wrote to the Select Committee that the Nabob wished to protect the Rohillas and to treat with them, "which could not be done," he said, "without the consent of the English," for their letters "were written to him in a style as if he was one and the same with the English, and he doubted that without such a concurrence, they meant to do nothing with him alone." The dangerous consequences portended from these alarming symptoms are strongly described in the following extract from a letter of the General to the Select Committee, dated the 25th of February, 1772:—"I should imagine that if the Marathas succeed in their attempts of crossing the river, and make a rapid progress through the Rohilla country towards the Vizier's territories, as they have already given out that they intend cantoning at Lucknow, you will judge it necessary to advance a brigade nearer to His Excellency's dominions, for in this case the approach of the Marathas will be very quick." On the 28th February the General wrote that the Marathas had made good their passage of the river, and given a total defeat to the Rohillas posted at the fords to oppose them; that he had therefore ordered the brigade at Dinapore to march immediately towards the Vizier's dominions, excusing his taking such a step without the authority of the Board, by "the exigency of the service." In this part of the Fifth Report of the Secret Committee, from which I draw this recital, I miss the reply which was written to Sir Robert Barker's letter, but I recollect that the Committee disapproved of the march of the brigade and countermanded it. On the 9th of April the General wrote that "the Marathas had applied to the Nabob Shuja-ud-daula to be the mediator of their differences with the Rohillas, to which he was much inclined," and "was not to be diverted from this scheme," though the General had strenuously opposed it, and pressed him "rather to form an alliance with the Rohillas;" the Nabob insisting "that he had no choice, for he must either join the Marathas in the total reduction of the Rohillas, or bring on a compromise between those powers; for the alternative was an attack on his dominions after the reduction of the Rohillas, unless" (for so the sense follows in the construction) "the English forces would join to support him in the undertaking," preferably recommended by the General; and that "he had therefore sent Captain Gabriel Harper to Hafiz Rahmat, and would do his endeavours to procrastinate this treaty until he received the Committee's instructions."

'On the 13th of April, 1772, I succeeded to the office of President of the Council of Fort William, and from that day only I date my share of responsibility for the acts of the Government of Bengal.

'On the 30th of the same month, the Select Committee for the first time entered into a consideration of the General's repeated references, and the sentiments recorded by them on that occasion most decidedly mark *their*—may I be allowed to change the person and say *my*—strenuous adherence to the cautious and defensive system enjoined by the Company.

'We approved the General's "endeavours to dissuade the Vizier from entering into any negotiations which might lead to an alliance with the Marathas, since we might by this means be precluded from taking such measures as the Company's exact orders might render necessary. But we could not approve of a promise being made to him of the junction of our forces in the prosecution of an offensive war; the more especially, as the Court of Directors, in their letters by the Lapwing, had promised to furnish us with clear and precise instructions respecting our carrying hostilities against the Marathas at a distance from our own borders, which," we added, "might be soon expected, but which never came. We expressed some uneasiness at Captain Harper's deputation, and desired that he might be recalled as soon as he conveniently could be, as we did not choose to appear as principals in these negotiations." In the meantime, the measures pursued by Sir Robert Barker had taken their course, and while I disavow any concern in them, I may add that they proved fortunate in their event. Captain Harper returned on the 21st of May, after having prevailed on Hafiz Rahmat to agree to a personal meeting with the Vizier; the consequence of which was, that on the 17th of June a treaty of alliance was concluded and reciprocally interchanged between the Rohilla chiefs and the Nabob Shuja-ud-daula; and a separate agreement on the part of the Rohillas to pay forty lakhs of rupees to the Nabob Vizier for the expulsion of the Marathas, "whether effected by peace or war;" ten lakhs to be paid on the immediate effect of his march, "enabling the families of the Rohillas to leave the woods and return to their habitations," the rest in three years.

'Both deeds were executed in the presence of Sir Robert Barker, and his signature affixed to both as a witness to them. But the same act made him the guarantee of both; and virtually, by his representation, extended the same obligation to the Company; for it has been shown that he was the instrument of the negotiation, and that the Rohillas themselves had refused to treat with the Nabob alone, that is, without the junction of the English name and faith with his.

'Thus it appears that by a regular and natural gradation of events, the Government of Bengal found itself entangled in the first movements of a war which it had sought to avoid, but which was in its principle and object defensive, and though extending beyond the line of its prescribed operations, had been recently marked out as an exception by the Court of Directors, in their General Letter of the 28th August, 1771, which is that to which the Select Committee alluded in their instructions to Sir Robert Barker of the 30th of April; and that whether the measures which led to this crisis of affairs were right or wrong, or whether the events which produced it might or ought to have been directed in another direction, I myself have no concern in either question. The movements of the machine (if I may be allowed the figure) had received their first impulse from other hands, before the charge of it could be affirmed in any sense to have devolved to mine, and were independent of me. In this state, progress, and direction, I received the share allotted to me in its management; and to these, even in the subsequent conduct of it, my judgment was necessarily compelled to bind itself, whether I approved the part or disapproved it.'

That 'gradation of events,' of which Hastings spoke, and of which he has here given a summary, affords stronger evidence of the causes which led to the Rohilla war than any other evidence that could be adduced. But as Mill has professed to explain those causes on the authority and in the words of Hastings himself, I will follow his example, and will show, in further detail, what Hastings has really said upon this subject.

Several important papers in which, at various stages of his connection with the affairs of Rohilkhand, Hastings stated the reasons for the action which he thought it necessary to take, have already been noticed in this work[1]. I will now give others. Some of them are so long that they cannot be quoted in extenso, but I shall at least omit nothing which might in any way be supposed to support views different from my own.

[1] See in particular the letter to Colonel Champion, dated 17th June, 1774. *Sup.* p. 147. In an interesting letter to his friend Anderson, dated 13th September, 1786, after his return to England, Hastings, referring to his reasons for undertaking the war, wrote as follows:—'In the originating connection and subsequent war with the Rohillas, he did what all States ought to do. The invasion of their country threatened ruin to that of our ally, whom he joined in repelling it, the Rohillas giving a solemn pledge in writing for the payment of twenty lakhs in consideration of the expense and risk incurred in their protection. They obtained their safety and refused to pay the price of it. We made war on them, on just grounds surely, unless any other process than that of the sword can be devised for recovering the rights of nations, defeated them with the death of their ungrateful and perfidious leader, and annexed their dominion to that of Oudh, which from that period became defensible throughout.' Gleig, vol. iii. p. 303. The original draft of this letter, in Hastings' own handwriting, is in the British Museum MSS. 29,170, vol. xxxix.

One of the most valuable of these papers is a despatch sent to the Court of Directors, immediately after the close of the war, written before the change of Government which transferred almost all authority into the hands of Clavering, Monson, and Francis, and before any discussion had begun regarding the propriety of the war or the reasons for which it was undertaken :—

'As we have undoubted though not regular intelligence of the Rohilla war being actually ended by a treaty between the Vizier and Faizullah Khan, we think it proper to recapitulate the causes on which this war was founded, and the advantages which have resulted from it.

'You were informed by our advices of 1772 and 1773 of the necessity which induced us to carry our arms beyond the prescribed line of your instructions into the Rohilla country, for its defence against the Marathas, whose rapid progress and unbounded ambition at that time threatened all Hindostan, and who had actually reduced the greater part of that country, through which the access was open to the Vizier, by the only quarter of his dominions wanting a defensible barrier. Our records at the time when this subject was debated will sufficiently manifest the extreme diffidence and reluctance with which we at last resolved to pass the line of the Vizier's dominions with our forces. The actual orders of the Company confined us within the limits of our own and his possessions; yet they had promised to furnish us with instructions wherein a greater latitude of action on particular occasions would be allowed and recommended. These very promises certainly implied the possibility of cases happening wherein more extensive measures were thought advisable and necessary. But the unsettled state of the Company's affairs at home has, we suppose, prevented us from receiving the promised directions for our conduct, and left us without a guide at a very critical conjuncture, which seemed to call for extraordinary measures, and an immediate exertion of our strength, to give a timely check to the accumulating progress of the Maratha power. Such were the circumstances and the occasion which first dictated to us the measure of passing the prescribed bounds. On this occasion, as declaredly on all others, we acted as if ignorant of the reports and advices from Europe, which informed us that the Company was precluded from resolving on any clear line of action; that supervisors were appointed to supersede the actual Government of Bengal; that a new administration was to be formed; and that the right of the Company and the nation to the territorial possessions was still in debate. We considered ourselves as acting for the national benefit, and assumed an extraordinary but a dangerous degree of responsibility for the sake of promoting the attaining of that object. It was therefore resolved to expel the Marathas from the Rohilla country. The Vizier, whose aid had been solicited by the Rohillas, undertook their defence against the Marathas. An agreement was entered into for this purpose, and a solemn treaty ratified between the Vizier and Hafiz Rahmat Khan, in behalf, and with the express authority of all the other Rohilla chiefs, in the presence of General Sir Robert Barker, the Commander-in-Chief of our forces, by whom it was attested; wherein, this service being effected, the Rohilla chiefs bound themselves to pay to the Vizier the sum of forty lakhs of rupees. The Vizier accordingly took the field, joined by one of our brigades, and fulfilled his engagement by expelling the Marathas from the Rohilla possessions. Notwithstanding which, Hafiz Rahmat, and the rest of the Rohillas, peremptorily refused to acquit themselves of their part of the agreement; and they not only thus infringed the treaty, by withholding the stipulation agreed upon, but treacherously assisted the Marathas against the Vizier with supplies of money, while he was actually engaged, by virtue of the treaty, in expelling them from the Rohilla country. This laid the foundation of the present war against the Rohillas, and was the first motive which induced us to join our aid to the Vizier in chastising them for their perfidy and breach of faith.

'The agreement for entering with the Vizier upon this new measure appeared to us a fit occasion for establishing the Company's alliance with him upon the footing of more adequate advantage to them. Hitherto they had held the labouring oar. The heavy burden of an enormous military expense, under which they were ready to sink, they had constantly supported, while the Vizier, by the tenor of the treaty then existing, without contributing to ease the Company of this weight, experienced the principal and only immediate advantages resulting from it; those acquired by the Company being remote, and consisting merely in the safety of his country, which was a barrier to theirs. Although we still continued without the lights which had been promised by the Court of Directors for the guidance of our conduct, yet in their letter of the 28th of August, 1771, they expressed in stronger terms than ever they had done before their intention, in certain cases, of authorising our departure from the defensive principles hitherto recommended and enjoined. These considerations determined us to avail ourselves of the present opportunity of aiding the Vizier against the Rohillas, as the means of obtaining the proposed advantages to the Company.

'With this view the President was deputed to give the Vizier a meeting at Benares, and to conclude a new form of alliance, in which he was authorised to comprehend the Rohilla enterprise, on such adequate and permanent terms as should indemnify the Company for the expenses at all times incurred in the Vizier's assistance, and to such other more immediate conditions as were suitable to their extraordinary service. A treaty was accordingly concluded, which in the original draft included both these objects, namely, the agreement for the fixed monthly subsidy of 210,000 rupees, for the expenses of our troops when employed in his service, and the payment of forty lakhs of rupees for the projected reduction of the Rohillas. But the Rohilla expedition was at that time set aside, from the irresolution of the Vizier, while the subsidy which had been conceded in consideration of our consent to this proposal still remained an Article of the new treaty. The Vizier afterwards renewed his proposition to attack the Rohillas, and it was again debated in several successive meetings of the Board, as recorded in our proceedings of the 26th November, 1773, with the reasons at large which determined us ultimately to resolve on a compliance with the Vizier's requisition. A brigade was accordingly ordered into his country for that purpose. Every circumstance that could possibly favour this enterprise, by an uncommon combination of political considerations and fortuitous events, operated in support of the measure. 1st. Justice to the Vizier, for the aggravated breach of treaty by the Rohilla chiefs. 2nd. The honour of the Company, pledged implicitly by General Barker's attestation for the accomplishment of this treaty, and which, added to their alliance with the Vizier, engaged us to see redress obtained for the perfidy of the Rohillas. 3rd. The completion of the line of defence of the Vizier's dominions by extending his boundary to the natural barrier formed by the northern chain of hills and the Ganges, and their junction. 4th. The acquisition of forty lakhs of rupees to the Company, and of so much specie added to the exhausted currency of their provinces. 5th. The subsidy of 210,000 rupees per month, for defraying the charges of one-third of our army employed with the Vizier. 6th. The urgent and recent orders of the Company for rescinding charges, and procuring means to discharge the heavy debt at interest, heightened by the advices of their great distress at home. 7th. The absence of the Marathas from Hindostan, which left an open field for carrying the proposed plan into execution. 8th, and lastly. The intestine divisions and disunions in their State, which by engaging them fully at home, would prevent interruptions from their incursions, and leave a moral certainty of success to the enterprise.

'These were the inducements which determined us to adopt this new plan of conduct, in opposition to which one powerful objection, and only one, occurred; namely, the personal hazard we ran in undertaking so uncommon a measure, without positive instructions, at our own risk, with the eyes of the whole nation on the affairs of the Company, and the passions and prejudices of almost every man in England inflamed against the conduct of the Company and the characters of their servants; notwithstanding which, we yielded to the strong necessity impressed upon us by the inducements abovementioned, in spite of the suggestions and the checks of self-interests, which set continually before our eyes the dread of forfeiting the favour of our employers, and becoming the objects of popular invective, and made us rejoice at every change in the Vizier's advices,

R 2

which protracted the execution of the measures. At length however his resolution coinciding with our opinions, the enterprise was undertaken, and, if our intelligence be confirmed, it is now finally closed with that success which we had foreseen from the beginning. We shall then again return to the state of peace from which we emerged when we first engaged in the Rohilla expedition, with the actual possession, or acknowledged right, which the power of this Government can amply and effectually assert, of near seventy lakhs of rupees, acquired by the monthly subsidy and the stipulation; and it rests with you to pass the ultimate judgment on our conduct[1].'

On the 24th October, 1774, three days after Clavering, Monson, and Francis had taken their seats in Council, Hastings recorded a 'Minute on the revenues and politics of the country,' desiring (he said) to assist the new Members by 'laying before them a succinct view of each subject.' In this Minute, he referred in the following terms to the arrangements which had been made with the Vizier:—

'The alliance with the Nabob Shuja-ud-daula, the Vizier of the empire, is the only foreign connection in which this Government can be with propriety said to be engaged. This took place originally by the treaty formed by Lord Clive, at Allahabad, in the year 1765. By a new treaty with the Vizier, dated the 8th September, 1773, in consequence of an interview which I had with him at Benares, the monthly subsidy for the extraordinary expense of our forces employed in his assistance, was fixed at the sum of 210,000 rupees for one brigade, and the provinces of Cora and Allahabad were ceded to him for the sum of fifty lakhs of rupees, of which twenty lakhs were to be immediately due, and were accordingly paid; fifteen lakhs were to be paid at the expiration of a year, and the remaining fifteen at the expiration of two years. At the same time the Vizier had solicited the aid of our troops, to reduce the Rohilla country lying on the north of his dominions between the Ganges and the mountains of Tibet. The immediate plea for these hostilities was the breach of faith, with which the Rohilla chiefs were charged in the supplies of money afforded by them to the Marathas, against whom they had solicited and obtained the Vizier's assistance under a solemn engagement to pay him forty lakhs of rupees on the departure of the Marathas, and for the refusing afterwards to fulfil that engagement.

'This enterprise, the design of which furnished the first occasion of my meeting with the Vizier, formed an article in the original draft of our treaty, but it was afterwards omitted at his desire, and I promised that it should take place if it suited the affairs of the Company

[1] Letter to the Court of Directors, 17th October, 1774, Fifth Report, App. No. 41.

at any other time, when he should find himself in a condition to resume it. Accordingly, in the month of January 1774, the Vizier made a formal requisition of the assistance of a brigade of the Company's forces for the defence of his dominions, and for the prosecution of his former purpose of invading the country of the Rohillas. For this service he engaged to pay the Company, beside the stipulated monthly subsidy, forty lakhs of rupees when it should be concluded. The Vizier's request was granted: the 2nd Brigade was ordered on the service, and Colonel Champion, the Provisional Commander-in-Chief, appointed to the command. Having been joined by the Vizier and his troops, he entered the Rohilla borders on the 17th of April, and on the 23rd of the same month attacked and defeated the army of the Rohillas commanded by Hafiz Rahmat, their leader, who was killed in the action. This victory was decisive, no other enemy appeared in the field; and the Vizier, having obtained possession of the greatest part of the country, both armies marched on the 7th of May to the city of Bisauli, where quarters were prepared for them, and it was intended they should pass the rains there: but the remaining leaders of the Rohillas, having assembled forces under the command of Faizoolah Khan at Najabgar, a town on the northern frontier of the country, the Vizier apprehending their acquiring too great strength, and that the Marathas might return to interrupt the operations before they were brought to a conclusion, prevailed on Colonel Champion to put the brigade again in motion about the latter end of July, and to march with him against the enemy, although the rains were then at their height. The troops enjoyed remarkable good health, and proceeded without opposition to Pathargarh; the enemy flying before them to the skirts of the hills whither the combined armies have followed them. They have lain for a considerable time within a short distance of each other, Colonel Champion waiting for orders from the Select Committee to pursue the enemy beyond the line to which he conceived himself limited by his instructions: the necessary orders were sent, and we have been for some time past in daily expectation of hearing that the war was brought to a conclusion, either by the attack and defeat of the enemy, or by negociation. The last letters from Colonel Champion which you, gentlemen, have read, were dated the 2nd instant, and advise that Faizoolah Khan had delivered himself up, but that the negociation was still continued.

'The advantages proposed from the expedition were:—1st, an addition of territory, and of course of wealth, to the Vizier, in which the Company will always participate; 2nd, the completion of the defensive line of his dominions by freeing them from an inconvenient neighbour and by taking into them the whole space included between the Ganges and the northern mountains; 3rd, the employment of a third part of our force, and a saving at the same time of its expenses; and lastly, the stipulation of forty lakhs to be paid on the conclusion of the undertaking. The retreat of the Marathas to their ancient territories, and the violent dissensions which had arisen in their State, were arguments strongly favouring the time which was chosen for beginning the war; and the justice of it is supported by the undoubted refusal of Hafiz Rahmat to fulfil the conditions of his treaty with the Vizier, of which the original, witnessed by General Sir Robert Barker, is in our possession. . . .

'The bounds which I had prescribed to myself in this paper, and which I have already exceeded, will not admit of my entering into a discussion of the benefits depending on the alliance of the Company with the Vizier. These will appear at large on various parts of our records, to which I shall hereafter distinctly refer. They may be reduced to the following abridgement; a secure barrier, a constant occupation for a part of our army, a reduction of our military expenses, and an accumulating fund of future wealth. He cannot long subsist without our protection, and is incapable of himself becoming an object of our jealousy or apprehension [1].'

My next quotation is from the 'Appeal to the Court of Directors,' written by Hastings on the 3rd of December, 1774, in reply to the virulent attacks made upon him by Francis and his colleagues. It is very long, and my extracts from it would have been shorter but for the fact that this is the only paper quoted by Mill as the authority for his charge against Hastings.

'As the Rohilla war has been the declared source of the most violent measures adopted by the Majority of the Council, I shall briefly recapitulate the grounds and objects of that enterprise, and then proceed to answer the various arguments which have been urged in condemnation of it.

'In the beginning of the year 1772, the Marathas invaded the country of the Rohillas, which after a short but ineffectual opposition at Sukkertole was left at large exposed to their ravages. The Vizier, alarmed at their approach to the only part of his dominions which was easily accessible by such an enemy, applied with such earnestness to Sir Robert Barker, who was at that time with him, for the assistance of an English force, and the General thought the necessity so urgent, that of his own authority he sent orders to the 1st Brigade, which was stationed at Dinapore, to march instantly into the province of Oudh. The Board disapproving this irregular proceeding refused their confirmation of it, and the brigade having reached the length of Benares remained there till the beginning of June and then returned to its former station. The Vizier availing himself of this move-

[1] Fifth Report, App. No. 45; Forrest's Selections, vol. i. p. 116.

ment, offered his protection to the Rohillas and entered into a general treaty of alliance with the chiefs of that nation, and a separate one with Hafiz Rahmat Khan their principal, who, in their name and with their authority, engaged to pay him forty lakhs of rupees for that support whenever the Marathas evacuated the country. Translations of both the treaties are recorded at length in the Consultation of the 23rd July, 1772; and the original of the latter is in the actual possession of the Secretary, attested by General Barker, who was present at the ratification of both. On the approach of the rainy season, the Marathas evacuted the country, and the Vizier demanded the stipulated recompense from the Rohillas, but they evaded payment.

'In the latter end of 1772, the Marathas having extorted from the King a grant of the districts of Kora and Karra, which had been ceded to him by the Company for the express purpose of maintaining his dignity, were preparing to take possession, and as this acquisition would have made them masters of the whole tract of country lying between the rivers Ganges and Jumna, and bordering upon the province of Oudh, the Vizier again applied for assistance to repel such dangerous neighbours. The Proceedings of the late Council, in their Secret Department of the 1st February, 1773, treat this subject very largely, and show how much they considered not only the safety of the Vizier but even of the Company's possessions, to be endangered by this formidable encroachment of the Maratha State. It was ultimately concluded to comply with the requisition of the Vizier, by sending the 1st Brigade for the protection of his dominions against any attempt which the Marathas might make on them, and also determined to prevent their design on Kora, by taking prior possession for the Company, who had certainly the best title to it, when the King could no longer keep it. It was not supposed that the Marathas would quietly submit to the loss of a territory which they had used the most perfidious means to obtain, and every precaution was therefore necessary to guard against their efforts to recover it. The Company's orders of the 28th August, 1771, expressly allowed the necessity of departing on some occasions from the limited plan which they had for a long time enjoined, and in consequence the Rohilla country, north of the Ganges, was included within the line of action prescribed to the General in his instructions; because, if the Marathas, either by the defeat, or which was as likely to happen, by the desertion of the Rohillas to their cause, should gain a footing in that country, nothing could oppose their entering into the province of Oudh, and laying it waste, in spite of any attempt of our forces united with the Vizier's to prevent them. It was not to be supposed that the Marathas, whose ambition for some years past had aspired to universal conquest, and who had extended their arms from the centre of the Balaghaut to the northern extremity of Hindostan, should sit down contented when they had added the Doab, Kora, and Allahabad to their dominions; on the contrary, there was every reason to apprehend, and it was publicly reported in their own camp, that they would next carry their operations into the country of the Vizier, and even into the Company's own possessions. On the grounds which I have described, it was agreed to maintain the province of Kora against the Marathas, and afterwards to extend our arms beyond the prescribed line of the dominions of our ally into the Rohilla country by a discretional latitude allowed the General as above mentioned, which he accordingly made use of by marching the brigade as far as Ramghat; and we have the strongest reason to believe that it was attended with every immediate advantage which we had projected from such a measure, as the Marathas lay during the whole campaign of 1773 in the neighbourhood of our army, but without daring either to cross the river or to approach the borders of Kora; and before the setting in of the rains of that year, their domestic troubles obliged them to return into their own proper dominions.

'Of the resolution to enter the Rohilla country for its defence against the Marathas, the Court of Directors were first advised by the general letter of the 31st of March, 1773, which arrived in England long before the departure of the transports.

'The effectual protection thus afforded the Rohillas, and the departure of the Marathas, having established beyond all contest the right of the Vizier to the forty lakhs which had been stipulated for this important service, and which by the terms of the engagement were really due the preceding year on the retreat of the Marathas from their country, he demanded payment of Hafiz Rahmat Khan, who refused it. The Vizier also accused him of having secretly encouraged the Marathas, and sent them a supply of money, and, if I mistake not, General Sir Robert Barker in some of his letters mentions the same circumstance. The plea of justice thus coinciding with the principles of sound policy, which dictated to the Vizier the necessity of securing himself against the intrigues and perfidy of the Rohillas, who from their situation were most capable of hurting him in his contests with more powerful enemies, and from their natural weakness and the jealousy inseparable from it, would even seek for their safety in fomenting or joining in attempts against him, he formed the design of invading and reducing their country. As his own strength was unequal to such an undertaking, he solicited the aid of this Government for effecting it, and made an offer of fifty lakhs of rupees to be paid on its accomplishment. *As* this proposal was urged in the warmest terms, both in person to Sir Robert Barker, and in his letter to me, and *this had long been a favourite project of the Vizier, the Board judged with me that it might afford a fair occasion to urge the improvement of our alliance by obtaining his assent to a more equitable compensation for the expense attending the aid which he occasionally received from our forces*[1], and to free the Company from the embarrassment to which they might be subjected by retaining the property and possessions of the remote districts of Kora and Allahabad. For this purpose, it was agreed that I should write the following letter to the Vizier, which I beg leave to quote at length, because it fixes the source of those engagements which took place by a progressive train of measures, and terminated in the Rohilla war; and will mark, at least, that this was not the effect either of a precipitate and unweighed resolution, or a tame acquiescence in the Vizier's schemes of ambition, but the result of long deliberation, originally devised and consistently employed as an instrument of promoting the interests of the Company, of perpetuating the dependence of their ally, and converting it to a channel of utility[2]. . . .

'The allurement thus held out to the Vizier succeeded. He proposed, in reply, a meeting with me at Benares, which took place accordingly. *I found him still equally bent on the design of reducing the Rohillas, which I encouraged, as I had before done, by dwelling on the advantages which he would derive from its success*[3], but objecting with great force the orders of the Company, restricting us from such remote schemes of conquest, to which I therefore could not assent, without such conditions obtained in return for it as might obviate their displeasure, and win their sanction to so hazardous and unauthorised a measure. I told him that the Company had drawn themselves into great distress by the enormous load of their military expenses, one entire brigade being kept up for the sole purpose of maintaining a connection with him, since it was useless and unnecessary to the protection of our own provinces; that if he wished, therefore, to avail himself of our aid, either in preventing or even in repelling the designs of his enemies, he must first agree to bear a more equal share of the burden of this expense, by paying the whole charge of the forces lent him for this service while they were so employed. To this, after much contention, he assented, and the sum of 210,000 rupees, which the General computed to be the amount of the expense, was fixed as the monthly subsidy to be paid for the brigade, whenever it should pass the borders of the province of Behar on his requisition. Having obtained this point, which I considered in the light of a perpetual military fund, I easily yielded my assent to the Rohilla plan, on the stipulation of forty lakhs for its accomplishment, ten lakhs being deducted from his first offer, on account of the difference which had taken place in the subsidy.

'This agreement was no sooner made than he suddenly repented, desired to decline the war with the Rohillas till a more favourable conjuncture, when he should be less embarrassed by other engage-

[1] The words in italics have been quoted by Mill.

[2] The letter from Hastings to the Vizier has already been quoted. See *sup.* p. 87.

[3] Words in italics quoted by Mill.

ments, agreeing however to the monthly subsidy whenever his future occasions should oblige him to require the aid of our forces. Thus the Rohilla plan remained rather suspended than wholly abandoned, although it was left optional in our Government to reject or assent to it on a future occasion. Messrs. Lawrell and Vansittart, who were with me at the time, and to whom I made a daily communication in writing of the substance of every conversation which passed between the Vizier and myself, will vouch for the literal truth of this narrative, as corresponding with what I then repeated to them, and I believe it will appear from it, that although I had not engaged the Government by any express obligation to comply with any future application of the Vizier to support his pretensions on the Rohillas, yet as the most essential article of the treaty had originated from this design, and had been yielded to in consideration of my agreement to engage in it, it would have been dishonourable to decline the undertaking, when proposed under circumstances as favourable to its success, and to the general interests of the Company, as they were when I first offered to engage in it.

'Soon after my return to Calcutta the Vizier renewed the proposal for invading the Rohillas, and repeated his desire of engaging in it on the conditions before agreed on. A variety of arguments concurred to favour it at this particular time; none to oppose it. The Marathas were so much occupied by their own dissensions that they could not even defend their possessions in the Doab, much less were they likely to interrupt the operations against the Rohillas. The King had no means of interference but by his General, Najf Khan, for whose attachment we had stronger security in his interest, and in his fear of his rival Abdul Ahmad Khan, than his master had in his allegiance. The Rohillas were too weak to resist so powerful an attack, and as their country was open and undefended either by defiles, woods, or fortresses, and in its greatest extent did not exceed 200 miles, its entire subjection did not require any length of time. To these inducements, which apply only to the success of the undertaking, other motives equally powerful engaged our attention to it *as a measure necessary to the interests and safety of the Company. All our advices, both public and private, represented the distress of the Company at home as extreme. The letters of the Court of Directors called upon us most loudly for ample remittances and a reduction of our military expenses. At the same time, such was the state of affairs in this Government that for many years past the income of the year was found inadequate to its expense, to defray which a heavy bond debt, amounting at one time to 125 lakhs of rupees had accumulated*[1]. The Board had bestowed much labour and time in the retrenchment of their expenses, but much remained yet to be done, and the resolutions which they had already formed required time to produce any visible effect. By allowing the Vizier the military aid which he required, *a*

[1] Words in italics quoted by Mill.

saving of near one-third of our military expenses would be effected during the period of such a service, the stipulation of forty lakhs would afford an ample supply to our treasury, and to the currency of the country, *the Vizier would be freed from a troublesome neighbourhood, and his dominions would be made more defensible*[1], while his alliance with the Company subsisted, by being completely shut in between the river Ganges and the mountains, and his dependence on the Company would be increased by that extension of his possessions, as he himself was incapable of defending even his ancient possessions without our support. . . .

'We might have suffered the Marathas under cover of the King's grant to take possession of Kora and Allahabad, to have allied themselves with the Rohillas or established themselves in that territory, and lain with their armies unmolested on the borders of the open country of our ally the Vizier, till they had completed every preparation for invading it. Such a forbearance might perhaps have been vindicated by the plea that the Company had promised at the distance of two years preceding it to furnish us with their instructions for a different conduct, and that, wanting those instructions, we took for our rule their latest orders on the subject, which enjoined us to confine our views to the bare security of our own possessions and those of our allies. This might have been a sure way to guard our characters against legal imputation, although in fact it would have been inconsistent with the security required; but it is not by such cold and prudential cautions that the British name has acquired such a lustre in India, nor that the British Empire in Bengal is likely to be perpetuated, neither is this the conduct which the Company demands of us. Their orders are enforced by a more liberal spirit, and allow in such cases as are not reducible to fixed and invariable positions, a discretional latitude for the zeal of their servants to exert itself for their security. . . .

'The Board has repeatedly declared in their general letters to the Court of Directors, their intention to adhere to the defensive line recommended to them, and confine their military operations within the limits of the Vizier's territories; and such were their determinations when these letters were written, but at those times they had not fully experienced the inconveniences which attended our engagements with the Vizier in the prosecution of that system, nor had the remedy occurred which since presented itself in the conditions offered for prosecuting the Rohilla enterprise, and which has been successfully applied. Our treaty of alliance obliged us to support the Vizier, when his possessions were threatened with invasion, at a heavy increased military expense, and the exportations of our currency, with our troops; for three successive years these inconveniences had recurred, and it is impossible to say how often they might recur. At last an occasion took place when, by a slight deviation from the defen-

[1] Words in italics quoted by Mill.

sive plan, our alliance with the Vizier might be converted into solid advantages, the employment of our troops made to save near a third part of our military expenses, and the success of their operations to bring a large flow of currency, not only into the Company's territories, but into their treasury. In effect, the very same reasons which before urged us to shirk every military expedition, namely the expense attending it and the exportation of our currency, now operated in the contrary direction, and recommended the employment of our army for the purpose of reducing our expenses and adding to our currency. . . . My sentiments were the same invariably from the beginning, as will be seen from my report to the Board of my proceedings at Benares, and my Minute entered in the consultation above referred to. Private letters are not commonly admissible as authorities, but on this occasion I cannot produce a stronger both of my own fixed opinion from the first movement of this proposition, and of the apprehension which influenced the Board, and I confess myself also against it, than the following extract of a letter which I wrote to Mr. Sulivan by the first despatch after my return from Benares: "I was glad to be freed from the Rohilla expedition, because I was doubtful of the judgment which would have been passed upon it at home, where I see too much stress laid upon general maxims and too little attention given to circumstances which require an exception to be made from them; besides this, an opinion still prevails of the Vizier's great power and his treacherous designs against us, and I cannot expect that my word shall be taken as a proof of their non-existence. On the other hand, the absence of the Marathas and *the weak state of the Rohillas promised an easy conquest of them*, and I own that *such was my idea of the Company's distress at home, added to my knowledge of their wants abroad*, that I should have been glad of any *occasion to employ their forces that saved so much of their pay and expenses*[1]."

'When the measure was determined upon, and we had come to a general agreement, I was averse to introduce any new subject of debate, and therefore easily acquiesced in the expression of a wish entertained by the Board which might be construed as inconsistent with the resolution we had taken. My sentiments of the propriety of the expedition had undergone no change, but I will not deny that I felt myself influenced by the same fears which operated on the other Members of the Council, that the propriety of the measure might not be seen in the same light by our constituents, which we knew, from the temper of the times, might not only draw upon us their severe resentment, but aggravate the load of popular odium which has of late fallen on their servants, and, if I mistake not, these reasons were assigned in express terms upon our proceedings. The engagements between the Vizier and the Rohillas which have been already quoted,

[1] The words printed in italics were quoted by Burke in the First Article of Charge, presented to the House of Commons, 4th April, 1786.

sufficiently evince the justice of the attack upon them; they agreed to make him an acknowledgment of forty lakhs of rupees upon certain conditions; he performed these conditions, and they refused to pay any part of the money they had promised. . . . The Marathas did not possess nor had any claim upon any part of the Rohilla country on the north of the Ganges when we undertook to assist the Vizier in the conquest of it. They might with more reason have attacked us for opposing them in their designs on the Kora district, of which they had obtained a grant from the King. But, in fact, a timid conduct would have been more likely to have involved us in a war with them, than either of those measures; had they been allowed to subdue the Kora district and the country of the Rohillas, the Vizier's territories would have been open to their incursions, their numerous horse might have plundered it in spite of the efforts of our infantry, and their continued ravages might have obliged him to come to an accommodation with them as was once apprehended, on terms which would have afforded them an easy entrance into our own provinces. In short, we are much better secured against their attacks than we should otherwise have been, and the better we are secured the less will they be disposed to attack us. . . .

'Merely for the defence of our own provinces, two brigades upon the present establishment are sufficient; a third is necessary to add to our influence among the powers of Hindostan, to support our alliance with the Vizier, and to answer other exigencies, which may happen at a more remote period of time. Upon the late occasion, when the Rohilla expedition was undertaken, our apprehension of an invasion from the French had entirely ceased; the dissensions among the Marathas fully employed them at home, and are mentioned among the secondary inducements in favour of the undertaking. There was no other enemy from whom we could have the least apprehension of danger; such was the occasion to be embraced for effecting our purpose by a temporary employment of a third part of our forces, and under such circumstances even without reckoning upon the acquisition which was the immediate object of the enterprise, to reduce the Company's military expenses by employing that proportion of their troops which was superfluous for the purpose of their own defence, was a great and manifest advantage; but when the stipulated acquisition of forty lakhs and the political advantages resulting from the measure are superadded, the visionary idea of danger, which did not exist even in imagination at the time the expedition was undertaken, can have no weight as an objection; especially as from our knowledge of the open and defenceless state of the Rohilla country we were morally certain that the undertaking would soon be brought to an issue. By our ancient treaty with the Vizier we are bound to assist him with our forces within his paternal dominions, and the distance between their borders, and the remotest part to which our troops have marched is only 200 miles. I will only add that so long as no immediate danger threatens our own provinces, it is my earnest wish that one of our three brigades might be constantly employed with the Vizier, as well to save so large a proportion of the expense to the Company, as to prevent the ill consequences of total inactivity to the army. The addition of territory acquired to the Vizier instead of raising him to be a dangerous neighbour serves to render him more dependent upon us than before, as he has more occasion for our assistance to enable him to maintain it and to support him against the claims of other powers. If his increase of wealth be an object of jealousy, let it be considered how largely the Company share in it. From September 1773 to September 1775, the sum we have to receive from him by our late engagement amounts to 130 lakhs of rupees.

'I have already remarked that the first proposition for the Rohilla war was made by the Vizier in a letter which I received from him in June 1773, that it was employed afterwards in the negotiations at Benares as an instrument for winning his consent to the payment of the full expenses of our troops employed in his service, and that it was not finally resolved on till the 26th November, after the most ample discussion in the Select Committee and in the Council: it was therefore not precipitately resolved on[1].' . . .

I shall make one more quotation. It is taken from a Minute written in Calcutta, on the 21st November, 1774, by Barwell, the only Member of the new Government who had been a colleague of Hastings when the resolution was taken to assist the Vizier in his conquest of Rohilkhand :—

'Mr. Francis is pleased to say that whatever he may think of the Governor-General's opinion, he is astonished that I should declare for acting, if necessary, in defence of the Vizier's late acquisitions, which he thinks is contradictory to sound policy and to the Company's orders. I have already given reasons for my opinion, and I do not flatter myself with being able to add anything of greater force to effect an alteration in his; however, I will endeavour to remove his surprise at my sentiments, by showing they are grounded on principles similar to his own, and that I think the measure I support perfectly consonant to sound policy and the spirit of the Company's instructions. It often happens with States that their situations are such that by extending their frontier they bring their line of defence to more prescribed, to more defined, narrow, and compact limits; and it is an uncontroverted maxim in politics that natural boundaries are always the most secure. The territories of the Vizier, before his late acquisition, undoubtedly stood in this predicament. Towards that part of the Rohilla country he had no barrier of any kind; he was not only exposed to the in-

[1] Fifth Report, App. No. 45; Forrest's Selections, vol. i. p. 140.

cursions of these people, but also to those of the Marathas, who either by force or agreement were sure to obtain from the Rohillas a passage through their country to attack him, and we consequently were subject from the same cause to be annually called out in his defence. This is not mere speculation; for two successive years, previous to the treaty of Benares, were we in the field to protect him from that quarter, and that upon the old stipulation of 115,000 rupees per month for our whole expenses. The Vizier endeavoured to form an alliance with these people, to obviate, if possible, the danger from their hostile enterprises: they entered into a treaty with him, broke it afterwards, and called in his enemies to protect them. In this situation, who can deny that it was the soundest policy in the Vizier to attempt their reduction? How far it was similar policy in us to assist him is another question; but it appears to me, that if the tranquillity and security of the Vizier's dominions be the object of our alliance with him, we cannot more effectually secure that object than by aiding to remove a constant cause of uneasiness and disturbance to him, and procure for him natural barriers to his dominions on the quarter where they were the most exposed. That the country in question affords this barrier is certain. It shelters him absolutely to the north by the Thibet mountains, and to the south and west by the Ganges, a river hazardous at all times for an enemy to cross. That it was on these ideas the Rohilla expedition was undertaken appears manifestly from the records of the Council and Select Committee, where that country is always mentioned standing in the predicament here defined; and in effect its defence against the Marathas was taken up on these very grounds two years past, without any particular stipulation for the service, or contract for forty lakhs on its success. I trust I have sufficiently explained to the Board, and particularly to Mr. Francis, who is surprised at my declaring for the defence of the Rohilla country, the motives upon which I ground my opinion. I think I have clearly shown it was sound policy in the late Board to undertake the expedition; that the defence and security of the Vizier's dominions rendered it eligible; that it had received mature consideration before it came recommended from the Chair; and that if what I have already pointed out are the objects of our alliance with the Vizier, often approved by the Company, the late Administration could not have acted more conformably to their interests and intentions[1].'

The preceding narrative, and the numerous quotations that have been made from the papers written by Hastings, show clearly how far the desire of obtaining money to relieve the financial difficulties of the Company must be counted among the reasons which induced him to take

[1] Fifth Report, App. No. 45; Forrest's Selections, vol. i. p. 135.

part in the war. To deny that this was a consideration which had great influence on his decision would be as little in accordance with fact as any of the unfounded statements that I have attributed to his accusers. However important the political advantages that he expected from the war may have appeared to him, he would not have embarked in it if he had not at the same time believed that it would be financially advantageous to the Company. This is a fact which he repeatedly avowed and justified.

On the 30th of November, 1774, the Majority of the Council wrote to the Court of Directors:—

> 'We return,' they said, 'to the President's Minute, which soon explains the true motives and object of the war. "The situation of the Rohilla country must make the possession of it always a desirable object to the Vizier." As the truth of this assertion is not to be disputed, we shall only observe upon it, that the most barefaced ambition is seldom so explicit. "He would obtain, by this acquisition, a complete compact State, shut in effectually from foreign invasions; it would give him wealth of which we should partake; and security without any dangerous increase of power: and would undoubtedly, by bringing his frontier nearer to the Marathas, for whom singly he is no match, render him more dependent on us." In these lines it appears to us that there is but one intelligible proposition, viz., that by the conquest of the Rohillas the Vizier would obtain wealth of which we should partake. The expectation of sharing in the spoils of a people, who have given us no cause of quarrel whatsoever, is plainly avowed to be a motive for invading them. We believe there may have been instances of wars undertaken on principles as unwise and as unjust as these, but we doubt whether there ever was an example of the Chief of a great State professing to reckon the probable acquisition of wealth among his reasons for taking up arms against his neighbours [1].'

To this Hastings made the following reply:—

> 'This method of separating the parts of a proposition, and refuting them singly, without adverting to their relation with each other, is new and embarrassing. I own that the conveniency of possessing the Rohilla country was not a sufficient reason for invading it. I never said it was: but if they had afforded a just provocation for invading their country, and we saw advantages in invading it, though neither cause was alone sufficient to produce that effect, yet both united would

[1] Fifth Report, App. No. 45.

certainly justify it, and the most rigid speculator would approve so fair a conclusion. I hope I shall stand acquitted in the breasts of all reasonable men for maintaining the opinions quoted against me in the conclusion of this paragraph; but I adopt it even in the words of my opponents; and if I am "the Chief of a great State" alluded to by them, I shall be always ready to "profess that I do reckon the probable acquisition of wealth among my reasons for taking up arms against my neighbours." I never in any period of my life, though long engaged in public affairs, gave my consent for taking up arms in an unjust cause, and I never shall, but in cases of very notorious enormity, give my consent to take up arms in an unprofitable one[1].'

In his First Charge in the House of Commons, Burke quoted the words 'he had reckoned the probable acquisition of wealth among his reasons for taking up arms against his neighbours,' and in his Answer to the Charge, Hastings again repeated them.

'I declare,' he said, 'most cheerfully and unreservedly, that I avow the principle ascribed to my declarations; and have no doubt that whenever I have had occasion to repeat them, my words have accorded invariably, and at all periods of time, with my general sentiments, which were and are an abhorrence of offensive wars undertaken on the exclusive principles of ambition, profit, or policy. But I will also avow that I would, without scruple, engage in an offensive war for the sake of retaliating an injury actually done, or of meeting the certain intentions of it. . . . I presume that the principle which I have thus stated will be approved by the judgments of all rational men, as it is strictly conformable to the practice of all States in all ages. Wretched and contemptible indeed would be the condition of that Government which should preclude itself from contracting alliances or other engagements with foreign States, and invite the attacks of its less principled neighbours, by establishing it as a rule of fixed and invariable policy never to commit hostilities but in the immediate resistance of actual invasion; and equally irreconcilable with the common sense of mankind would be that policy which should restrict the efforts of a just war to the chastisement of wrong, and reject every advantage acquired by it.'

Whatever view be taken of the propriety of engaging in the Rohilla war, enough has, I think, been said to show that the story of Hastings letting out the English troops for hire to slaughter an unoffending people, without cause or

[1] Minute of Appeal, 10th January, 1775, Fifth Report, App. No. 45; Forrest's Selections, vol. i. p. 184.

S

provocation, for the sole and infamous purpose of putting money into the pockets of his masters, is not true. It was invented by the malignity of Francis, it was adopted by Burke with an indignation of which the motives were honourable but which were blind and unreasoning, it was written down as history by Mill when the evidence of its falsehood was in his hands, and it was then thrown by Macaulay into the rhetorical shape in which it has ever since compelled acceptance from the majority of Englishmen. Before the war was undertaken, while it was in progress, after it had been successfully completed, but when no hostile imputations connected with it had been made, and afterwards when Hastings had to defend himself against the attacks of his enemies, he never varied in the explanation of his policy.

That policy was based on the necessity of guarding against the risk of ruin to ourselves and to our ally. The primary object of the war was to obtain security against the danger which at that time overshadowed all other considerations, that of invasion by the Marathas, who were not far from achieving that universal dominion over India which they openly declared to be their aim. To guard against this danger, Hastings, like Clive, his great predecessor, believed that no measure of precaution could be so efficacious as the maintenance of the territories of the Nawab Vizier of Oudh as a barrier between Bengal and the constantly troubled countries of Northern India. He believed that to secure this object it was necessary that the only road by which Oudh was easily accessible to the inroads of the Maratha armies should be closed. The only means by which this could be done was by the union of Rohilkhand with Oudh, and by the expulsion of the band of turbulent and faithless Afghans who, not many years before, had established themselves in the very quarter from which danger threatened. It had been proved by experience that to obtain the desired security by an alliance with the Rohillas was impossible. A treaty had been entered into between the Rohilla chiefs and the Vizier, by which the Vizier bound himself to protect Rohilkhand against the Marathas, and the Rohillas, on their part, engaged to pay to him, in consideration of that protection, the sum of £500,000. Although the treaty was one to which we were not avowedly a party, it had been concluded with the strenuous co-operation and advice of our Commander-in-Chief, it had been attested by his signature, and it had been approved by our Government. We had given to the Vizier the active and effectual assistance of our army in enabling him to carry out his obligations, and had expelled the Marathas from Rohilkhand. The Rohillas, on their side, refused to fulfil their engagements, and paid nothing to the Vizier. All this afforded, in the belief of Hastings, ample justification to the Vizier for undertaking the war, and ample justification to us for giving him the help without which he might probably have been unsuccessful.

It would be useless to discuss at any length the question whether, judged by the standard of international morality accepted at the present day, the policy of Hastings was right. Conclusions that are obviously true in regard to the relations of organised states and civilised communities are often altogether inapplicable to semi-barbarians such as the Marathas and Rohillas of the time of Hastings. 'To suppose' (says Mr. J. S. Mill, in his 'Dissertations and Discussions') 'that the same international customs, and the same rules of international morality can obtain between one civilized nation and another, and between civilized nations and barbarians, is a grave error, and one which no statesman can fall into, however it may be with those who, from a safe and irresponsible position, criticize statesmen. . . . In the first place, the rules of ordinary international morality imply reciprocity. But barbarians will not reciprocate. They cannot be depended on for observing any rules. Their minds are not capable of so great an effort, nor their will sufficiently under the influence of distant motives.'

If, however, we were to ignore considerations of this kind, and assume that Hastings was morally bound, in his dealings with the Vizier and the Rohillas, to conform to a standard of conduct as high as that recognised by civilised nations in their dealings with each other, I believe that, even tried by this high test, his action was entirely justifiable. If a similar case were now to arise, we should have to answer the following question:—Where a state or its ally is in danger of invasion and ruin by another state, and the only practicable mode of preventing such invasion is by forcibly seizing the territory of an intermediate state, which is either too weak or too treacherous to prevent its territory from being used for hostile purposes by the invaders, is the threatened state justified in forcibly seizing that territory? The authority of great jurists and great statesmen might be quoted in support of an affirmative answer, and the justice of that answer might be enforced by historical precedents and analogies.

If this be true, it must, *a fortiori*, be true if the case be judged by a lower standard. But the relations subsisting between Hastings, the Vizier, the Marathas, and the Rohillas were too essentially unlike the relations of European states to make such a discussion profitable. The question of morality, if it is to be argued, can only be stated thus:—Is a British governor justified in making war upon a confederacy of barbarous chiefs, who, not long before, had imposed their rule on a population foreign to themselves in race and religion; through whose country the only road lies open for attacks by savage invaders upon a British ally, whose security is essential to the security of British possessions; who are too weak and too treacherous to be relied on to close this road; and who have injured that ally by breaking a treaty with him negotiated and attested by a British General, and approved by the British Government? Upon such a question there can hardly be much difference of opinion. The only reasonable answer is that, in such a case, the supreme duty of a governor is to make the dominions under his care secure from foreign attack; that if Hastings believed that the security of the British provinces depended on that of

Oudh, he was bound to take measures of precaution against a common danger; and that if he found it impossible to reconcile the protection of Oudh and of British territory with the maintenance of the dominion of the Rohilla chiefs, he was right in the conclusion that their dominion must cease. It may doubtless be contended that Hastings overrated some of the elements of danger, or committed other errors of judgment, but at all events there is no room for moral reprobation. By ignoring the difficulties and complexities of the situation, it is easy to argue broadly that it is wrong to engage in war without provocation, that the Rohillas had not provoked us, and that the attack upon them was therefore unjustifiable. In the opinion of Hastings the conduct of the Rohillas in breaking their treaty with our ally, and in carrying on negotiations with the common enemy, constituted provocation, and that term can hardly be limited to the case of actual aggression. However this may be, maxims of this sort could afford no assistance to a governor dealing with the question whether Oudh and the British provinces should be allowed to remain exposed to invasion, or how invasion might best be averted.

Financial advantage was, as Hastings wrote to Colonel Champion in a letter that has already been quoted, 'an accessary argument[1].' Having satisfied himself that the establishment of the Vizier's government in Rohilkhand was necessary, he had to settle the terms on which our co-operation should be afforded. Without that co-operation there was obviously no certainty of success. I have shown that Hastings was glad to make use of this opportunity to place the financial conditions of his alliance with the Vizier on a footing more favourable to the Company than that which he found existing, and which he with reason looked upon as inequitable and injurious to the interests of his own Government. Assuming with Hastings that the resolution to establish the Vizier's government in Rohilkhand was politically wise, there was nothing un-

[1] See *sup.* p. 147.

reasonable in the stipulation that in addition to the actual charges of the English brigade, the Vizier, in 'consideration of the Company relinquishing all claim to share in the Rohilla country, although it is to be conquered by their joint forces,' should pay forty lakhs of rupees on the successful completion of the war. The military preparations in 1772, and the campaign of 1773 in Rohilkhand, had caused heavy military expenditure which the payments made by the Vizier were far from covering. That the charges of the expedition should fall upon the party which would reap the greater benefit was a proposition which was doubted by no one, and Francis and his colleagues made it afterwards a subject of accusation against Hastings that the sum which the Vizier had agreed to pay was after all insufficient to cover the expenditure. When power fell into their hands, they took the earliest opportunity which they could find for upsetting the arrangement made by Hastings, and on the death of Shuja-ud-daula, in January 1775, they called on his successor to increase his contributions. 'We experienced in the last campaign,' they wrote to the Resident at Lucknow, 'that the subsidy paid by his father was considerably less than the real expense of the brigade, which served to involve us in difficulty and distress.'

Such considerations as these, however, have no real bearing on the question of the conduct of Hastings. If the English Government had itself borne the whole expense of its operations, and had received nothing from the Vizier, the motives with which the war was undertaken would have been less open to misrepresentation, but they would not, as Hastings himself said, have thereby become more or less just or honourable[1]. If the war was made the opportunity of bringing profit to the stronger

[1] 'Here I cannot omit making one general reflection, which occurs in reading the address of the Majority, which is that their grand and principal objection to the measures of the late Administration seems to be that we allowed the Company to acquire any pecuniary advantages from our political arrangements. The ceding of Kora and Allahabad is objected to as a *sale*, because fifty lakhs of rupees were stipulated to the Com-

power, it did not differ in this respect from many more serious contests. It is true that we might sometimes have been better pleased if Hastings, in his despatches and minutes, had said less regarding the financial advantages of his agreement with the Vizier, and the same observation may be made in regard to many other transactions in which he and other Indian Governors of those times were concerned. But the circumstances under which he was placed ought not to be forgotten. He had frequently to justify to the Directors at home measures of policy opposed to their orders, or of which their approval was doubtful, and it was natural that he should, when it was possible to do so, lay stress on those conditions which would be most likely to reconcile them to his proceedings. The East India Company of those days was essentially mercantile, and the Directors were ready to pardon much that they thought politically inexpedient if it could be shown to be pecuniarily profitable. In the words of Macaulay, they 'never enjoined or applauded any crime. Far from it. Whoever examines their letters, written at that time, will find there many just and humane sentiments, many excellent precepts; in short, an excellent code of political ethics. But every exhortation is modified or nullified by a demand for money. "Govern leniently, and send more money; practise strict justice and moderation towards neighbouring powers, and send more money;" this is, in truth, the sum

pany on that account. If we had given up these without any consideration in return, this objection could not have been made. The subsidy for defraying the whole expense of our forces employed with the Vizier is reproachfully styled *hiring* them. If the Vizier had only paid the extra expenses it would have been less reproachful; but if we had made the Company pay the whole expenses, in the language of the Majority, it must then have been entirely irreproachable, and we should have acted for the glory of the British nation. Our agreement with the Vizier is dishonourable, because the conditions were *mercenary* and *pecuniary*; that is, the Company were to acquire forty lakhs of rupees from it. Had there been no such acquisition to the Company, the Majority would have withheld their dishonourable epithets. Upon these points I leave the Company to decide between the sentiments of the Majority and the motives which influenced our conduct.' Minute by Hastings, dated 10th January, 1775, para. 69. Fifth Report, App. No. 45; Forrest's Selections, vol. i. p. 188.

of almost all the instructions that Hastings ever received from home[1].' This is a somewhat exaggerated statement, but it is substantially true.

Judged by its results, the policy of Hastings was eminently successful. Many a 'wild Mahratta battle' had still to be fought. Nearly thirty years after the Rohilla war, Maratha armies were still contending with the English for empire in India, and Wellesley and Lake were winning their victories of Assaye and Argaum and Laswari. More than forty years elapsed before the power of the Marathas was finally swept away, but during the whole of this time they never attacked or seriously threatened Rohilkhand. The occupation of that province gave to Oudh and to Bengal that permanent protection against the most dangerous of our Indian enemies which it had been the aim of Hastings to secure.

[1] Essays: Warren Hastings.

CHAPTER XVII.

CLAVERING, MONSON, AND FRANCIS, AND THE NEW GOVERNMENT OF BENGAL.—THE SUBSEQUENT HISTORY OF ROHILKHAND.

The Regulating Act of 1773.—New Constitution given to the Government.—The Members of the new Council.—Character of Francis.—Power passes into the hands of the Majority of the Council.—Description by Hastings of his own position.—The Rohilla war becomes the first object of attack against Hastings.—Subsequent proceedings of the Majority.—Their ignorant interference and malignant charges.—Death of Shuja-ud-daula.—The Majority cancel existing treaties and make fresh demands on his successor.—Orders of the Court of Directors on cession of Kora and Allahabad to the Vizier, on the Rohilla war, and on cancelment of the Oudh treaties.—Death of Monson, and recovery of power by Hastings.—Condition of Oudh and Rohilkhand under Asaf-ud-daula.—Prosperity of Rampur under Faizullah Khan.—Wrongful demands upon him.—Francis leaves India.—Hastings returns to England.—Burke and Francis.—Charges against Hastings in the House of Commons.—The First Charge relating to the Rohilla war.—Burke's motion rejected.—Pitt's proceedings and Impeachment of Hastings.—The subsequent history of Rohilkhand.—Death of Faizullah Khan.—Revolution in Rampur.—The Rohillas attack the British troops, and are defeated.—Rampur restored to the grandson of Faizullah Khan.—Cession of Rohilkhand to the British Government in 1801.—Subsequent prosperity of the province.—Raid of Amir Khan.—Revolt at Bareilly in 1816.—Unbroken tranquillity for forty years.—The Mutinies of 1857.—The British power in Rohilkhand swept away.—Atrocities of Rohilla leaders.—Conspicuous loyalty of the Nawab of Rampur.—Restoration of British power.—Honours and rewards to Yusaf Ali Khan of Rampur.—Prosperity of his State.

IN 1773, a definite Constitution was for the first time given by Parliament to the Government of India. By the Regulating Act of that year (13 Geo. III. c. 63), introduced by the Ministry of Lord North, a Governor-General and a Council of four Members were appointed for the Presidency of Bengal, with vaguely defined powers over Madras and Bombay. The administration was to be carried on by the Governor-General and Council in accordance with the votes of a majority of those present. The Governor had a casting vote, but otherwise had no greater authority than any Member of the Council. The first Governor-General and the Members were named in the Act. Hastings was appointed Governor-General. Barwell, who had been a Member of the former Council, was the only one of the new Members who had any Indian experience. The other three were General Clavering, Monson, and Francis. The sole qualification of Clavering was the possession of parliamentary influence; Monson's qualifications were no better; the character of Francis, by far the most able and vigorous of the three, is known to everyone. In the words of Macaulay, he was 'irritable, rude, and petulant, and his hatred was of intense bitterness and long duration,' 'a man in the highest degree arrogant and insolent, a man prone to malevolence, and prone to the error of mistaking his malevolence for public virtue.' 'He was capable,' Sir James Stephen adds, 'not only of the faults of undying malignity and ferocious cruelty, but also of falsehood, treachery, and calumny[1].' The wit of man could not have devised a more impracticable scheme of Government, nor could it have chosen men more scandalously unfit to administer the affairs of a great country than these three Councillors.

They landed in Calcutta on the 19th October, 1774, and Hastings who, in his own words, 'was averse to parade and never used it,' had in their opinion made no sufficient arrangements for the ceremonies of their reception. Only seventeen guns were fired, no troops were drawn up, and they were received by Hastings at his own house instead of in the official Council Chamber[2]. Their 'warfare of scurrility,' as Hastings called it, immediately began. Barwell

[1] 'Nuncomar and Impey,' vol. i. p. 30.

[2] The influence of these supposed breaches of etiquette on their conduct towards Hastings has perhaps been exaggerated. Any one who wishes to know the whole story of the salutes and the rest, and how Mr. Hastings even omitted to put on a ruffled shirt, will find it in Mr. Busteed's very interesting and amusing book, 'Echoes of Old Calcutta.'

alone gave his support to Hastings; Clavering, Monson, and Francis were always a majority, and in less than a week after their arrival the power of the Government had passed into their hands. The fact that a measure had been initiated or approved by Hastings was in itself sufficient to ensure its condemnation. Twelve years afterwards he gave, in a private letter to his friend David Anderson, a description of his position so graphic, so just, and so characteristic of his indomitable spirit, that it deserves quotation :—

'I was a man unknown, unprotected, and unconnected at home, and possessed no other influence abroad than that which I had acquired by my own knowledge and practice, in the credit which the success of my measures impressed on the people of Hindostan, and in the attachment of my fellow-servants and citizens. Without time allowed for the pretext of provocation, the impatience of my adversaries hurried them to a declaration and to acts of hostility on the third day after their arrival. They persevered in their persecutions, which were gross to personal outrage, till the death of Colonel Monson; and their opposition, which the death of General Clavering did but suspend for an instant, continued till their final annihilation by the departure of Mr. Francis in December, 1780. In so long an interval what had I wherewith to sustain the weight of their oppressions but the superior weight of my own character and the consciousness of superior desert, set against the claim of high names which supported the respect of my adversaries; King, Lords, Commons, and Directors, and half the people of England against me; the power of patronage employed in the seduction of my fellow-servants; and for a while the rule taken out of my hands, to be employed in a warfare against me and in that only. Yet even in that time the confidence of my opponents allowed me to transact the current business, in which they never interrupted me but for occasions of personal attack. I suffered in patience; I did my duty when I could; I waited for better and more lasting means; no act or word of intemperance escaped me; no meanness of submission ever afforded my assailants the triumph, even of a moment, over me; and I have been told that they themselves have been heard to confess themselves foiled, even when they had brought their long prepared plans of attack to the Board, and I was unprepared to resist them. When intervals of accidental authority enabled me to act, and I never had more than intervals, I employed them in forming and setting in motion the greatest and most successful measures of my government. When these were impeded by frequent changes of influence, I still continued to keep them in existence, and again gave them energy when my power returned. My antagonists sickened, lied, and fled. I maintained my ground unchanged; neither the health of my body nor the vigour of my mind for a moment deserted me[1].'

The latest and most important of the affairs with which Hastings had been concerned before the arrival of the new Councillors was the Rohilla war, and it naturally became the first subject for attack. The intelligence that the war was over, and that a treaty had been signed with Faizullah Khan, did not reach Calcutta until the 31st October[2]. It was known that negociations were in active progress, and that an immediate settlement was expected, but such considerations had no weight with the Majority of the Council. On the 25th October they desired the Governor-General to lay before the Council the whole of his public and private correspondence with Middleton and Colonel Champion. Hastings declared that he was ready to produce the whole of his official correspondence with Middleton, and 'such parts even of his private correspondence that he could with propriety show.' With regard to his official correspondence with Colonel Champion, he said that the whole of it should be laid before the Council; he refused, without the consent of Colonel Champion, to produce letters

'of a familiar and friendly communication . . . expressly marked with a distinct mode of address as those which he intended as confidential. I am the more observant of this rule because our correspondence has not been altogether cordial on many points, and we have several times expostulated with each other on these topics with the freedom of private friends, and in a style, which though decent in every degree, is yet different perhaps from the formal addresses of official correspondence.'

The protests of Hastings were unavailing, and he refused to comply with the orders of the Council[3]. He wrote soon afterwards to Lord North, and stated his intention,

[1] Letter dated 13th September, 1786, Gleig, vol. iii. p. 303; British Museum MSS. 29,170, vol. xxxix.

[2] Bengal Secret Consultations, 31st Oct. 1774; Fifth Report, App. No. 44.

[3] Fifth Report, App. No. 45; Consultations, 19th December, 1774, India Office Records.

which was carried out, of submitting to him the whole of his correspondence with Middleton, both public and private, so that a judgment might be formed by an impartial authority regarding the propriety of his conduct, 'and in vindication of his own character from the suggestions occasioned by his refusal to expose these letters to the view of the new Council [1].' On the 26th October, the Majority, in spite of the remonstrances of Hastings and Barwell, ordered that as the Governor-General had refused to produce the whole of his correspondence, Middleton should be immediately removed from the post of Resident with the Vizier, that he should be directed to bring the correspondence with him to Calcutta, and that Colonel Champion should be appointed in his place to carry on all communications with the Vizier. On the 31st October orders were sent to Colonel Champion to demand from the Vizier payment of the forty lakhs of rupees promised for the Rohilla expedition, and of any other sums that might be due on other accounts; at least twenty lakhs were to be paid at once, and the rest within a year at latest; in default of compliance by the Vizier with this requisition, within fourteen days, Colonel Champion was ordered to return with the army into the Company's territories; if the Vizier complied, then the troops were to be withdrawn within the former limits of Oudh. The practical result of these orders was not very serious, because long before they had reached their destination, the conditions of the treaty of peace had been carried out and the troops had left Rohilkhand.

I will not attempt to describe the subsequent proceedings of Francis and his colleagues. Every act of the previous Government, important or trivial, which could be made the means of damaging the reputation of Hastings or giving him annoyance, was seized upon. Nor did they confine their ignorant interference and their malignant attacks to his public measures. Charges of the vilest nature against his personal character, brought by the vilest of men, who rightly believed that their accusations would

[1] British Museum MSS.; Gleig, vol. i. pp. 475, 507.

of the Council seized the opportunity of replenishing the Company's coffers, and their proceedings were more successful in gaining this object than anything with which Hastings had been charged. It was declared that all treaties that had been made with the Vizier of Oudh were cancelled by the death of Shuja-ud-daula, except that arrears of money due under them were to be recovered; the subsidy paid for the English troops in Oudh was to be increased by 50,000 rupees a month, and the sovereignty of the districts in the possession of Raja Chait Sing of Benares, which had paid annually twenty-two lakhs of rupees a year to the Vizier, was to be ceded to the Company. Further, the unfortunate Nawab was compelled, without a shadow of reason, to surrender to the widow of Shuja-ud-daula treasure said to amount to two millions sterling and some of his richest districts. Hastings and Barwell protested in vain against these proceedings; they maintained that we had no right to cancel the former treaties which had been contracted with the State of Oudh and which were still binding on us, that by these acts our Government was guilty of a breach of faith, and that Asaf-ud-daula would be unable to fulfil the obligations placed on him.

On the 3rd March, 1775, the Court of Directors sent to the Governor-General and Council a letter approving the measures taken by Hastings in regard to the resumption from the Emperor of the provinces of Kora and Allahabad and their cession to the Vizier, and confirming the treaty of Benares. They also approved the suspension of the

been ruined by Shuja-ud-daula, and himself reduced to the condition in which I then saw him, nevertheless, on seeing his corpse pass by, he could not contain himself, but shed a flood of tears. He added that he cannot compare the general impression of sorrow felt that day by every one to anything but to what is sometimes observed in the last days of the ten first ones of the Moharram, when it is not possible to observe in a numerous assembly one single face that is not affected with grief. He protested that the whole city of Faizabad was in that predicament, no face being to be met with but was bathed in tears, insomuch that he doubted much whether a single person could be found that day that had not wept abundantly.' Sair-ul-Mutakherin, vol. iii. pp. 263–275.

payments made to the Emperor from the revenues of Bengal. In regard to the Rohilla war, they wrote as follows:—

'By letters received overland from our Select Committee at Fort William, dated the 14th and 19th of May, 1774, we are informed of the defeat and death of Hafiz Rahmat Khan, Chief of the Rohillas, and of the probability of their country being speedily subdued by Shuja-ud-daula; and notwithstanding the pecuniary advantages which the Company have gained by that event, we are exceedingly concerned to find that our arms have been employed in the conquest of the Rohillas, though we must confess the conduct of their chiefs, in refusing to fulfil their solemn stipulations with the Vizier, seems to have drawn upon them the calamities they have suffered. After noticing the cautionary terms settled with Shuja-ud-daula previous to the march of our troops, we can have no doubt of his having fulfilled the conditions of the agreement by which he became entitled to our assistance; and had the object in view been extended no further than to compel payment of the forty lakhs of rupees due to the Vizier and the Company for the protection afforded to the Rohillas, we should have had less objection to the measure, though it would have been much more agreeable to our feelings if the Rohillas had faithfully complied with their engagements, which were entered into for the immediate and mutual defence of the contracting parties, and in which also the interest of the Company was concerned. The treaty of Allahabad compels us to assist the Vizier in defending his dominions in case they shall at any time hereafter be attacked, but in regard to new conquests, or to any warlike enterprises beyond his own territories, we absolutely prohibit you from employing our troops on such expeditions, on any pretence whatever. We much approve the alteration made in the second Article of the treaty of Allahabad, respecting the terms upon which our assistance is in cases of necessity to be granted to Shuja-ud-daula, as those terms were very inadequate to the service to be performed, and consequently very improper[1].'

A few days later the Directors wrote again to the same effect, and repeated in stronger terms their instructions that no expeditions of this kind should again be undertaken.

When these orders were received, the Majority of the Council declared that 'no condemnation could be more severe than that which the Court of Directors have passed on the Rohilla war and on the conduct of the late

[1] Fifth Report, App. No. 46.

Administration[1].' Hastings, on the other hand, interpreted them as an approval of his proceedings[2].

In October 1775, in consequence of the dissensions in the Calcutta Government, all these questions again came before the Court of Directors, but the time for any impartial judgment had passed. Lord North and his Cabinet knew little, and cared less, about the administration of Indian affairs except so far as personal and party interests were involved. It was expedient to conciliate Clavering and his friends because they had influence in Parliament, and there were no such inducements to give support to Hastings. All the pressure that the Government could bring to bear upon the Court of Directors and on the Court of Proprietors was exercised on the side of the Majority of the Council. After much discussion the following Resolution was agreed to by a General Court of Proprietors on the 6th December, 1775:—

> 'That notwithstanding this Court hath the highest opinion of the services and integrity of Warren Hastings, Esquire, and cannot admit a suspicion of corrupt motives operating on his conduct without proof, yet they are of opinion with their Court of Directors, that the agreement made with Shuja-ud-daula for the hire of a part of the Company's troops for the reduction of the Rohilla country, and the subsequent steps taken for carrying on that war, were founded on wrong policy, were contrary to the general orders of the Company, frequently repeated, for keeping their troops within the bounds of the provinces, and for not extending their territories; and were also contrary to those general principles which the Company wish should be supported.'

It was resolved at the same time that Hastings ought to have laid before the Council the whole of his correspondence with Middleton, and that the orders recalling the troops from the Rohilla expedition were proper. On this last point, however, it was added that 'considering the situation of affairs at that time between the Company and Shuja-ud-daula, the Court think that recalling them so hastily might have been attended with inconveniences.' These Resolutions were sent to India on the 15th Decem-

[1] Address to Directors, 21st November, 1775; Forrest's Selections, vol. ii. p. 460.

[2] Ibid. p. 491.

ber, 1775, with a despatch from the Court of Directors approving in almost all respects the views of the Majority of the Council[1].

When this despatch was written, the Directors had heard of the death of the Vizier, but no details had reached them of the subsequent action taken towards his son, and they wrote as follows:—'Although the death of Shuja-ud-daula may render it necessary to make new arrangements with his successor, we cannot agree with our Council that our treaties with the State of Oudh expired with the death of the Nabob. When, however, the Directors learned that the proceedings of the Majority of the Council had given to the Company an increase of twenty-two lakhs of rupees to their annual revenues, and six lakhs more for the expenses of their troops, they entirely changed their opinion. On the 24th December, 1776, they wrote to the Bengal Government in the following terms:—'It is with singular satisfaction we observe at any time the attention paid by our servants to the great interests of their employers; and it is with particular pleasure we here signify our entire approbation of the late treaty concluded with Asaf-ud-daula, successor of Shuja-ud-daula, by which such terms are proposed as seem to promise us solid and permanent advantages[2].'

In September 1776, the death of Monson gave Hastings, through his casting vote, a majority in the Council, and until he left India, in 1785, he retained the power that he had recovered.

I will briefly notice some of the events that occurred in Rohilkhand during the remaining years of Hastings' administration.

[1] Fifth Report, App. No. 46. Writing to Anderson, on the 13th September, 1786, in a letter already quoted, Hastings referred to the action taken by the Directors in the following terms:—'The Directors, as usual, allowed the justice of our proceedings and approved them—but condemned both when Clavering and his associates condemned them.' Gleig, vol. iii. p. 303; British Museum MSS. 29,170.

[2] Fifth Report of the Committee of Secrecy, p. 97. Mill remarks upon this:—'The conduct of the Directors was peculiar.' History, Book v. chap. 2.

For some years after the termination of the Rohilla war, nothing happened to bring the affairs of Rohilkhand prominently before the Bengal Government. When Shuja-ud-daula died, Oudh, according to the standard of those times, was in a flourishing condition, and Rohilkhand was apparently as well off as it had been under the Rohillas, but after the accession of his son everything began to fall rapidly into disorder. Asaf-ud-daula was incompetent, abominably vicious, and contemptible, and the misfortunes of his country were greatly increased by the extortionate demands of Francis and his colleagues. Whether Rohilkhand afterwards suffered more than other parts of the Vizier's dominions is doubtful, and some very competent judges declared that much of the desolation and ruin on which the enemies of Hastings loved to dwell were in fact relics of the time of the Rohillas and of the Maratha invasions. However this may have been, the condition of the country was miserable, and the only part of Rohilkhand which was comparatively well administered and prosperous was the State of Rampur, which had been made over to the Rohilla chief Faizullah Khan.

In 1780, the condition of affairs in India was critical. In the words of Hastings:—

> 'We were engaged in a war with the Marathas; Haidar Ali Khan had overrun the Carnatic and defeated Colonel Baillie's detachment; Sir Hector Munro had been obliged to retreat to Madras; a Maratha army lay contiguous to the southern frontier of Bengal; and at the same instant of time we received intelligence that a very considerable armament had been fitted out by France, which did in fact arrive upon the coast of Coromandel in the month of January following[1].'

The very existence of our empire in India seemed to be threatened, and the defence of Oudh and Rohilkhand was one of the measures that were necessary. Faizullah Khan, under a mistaken, and as Hastings afterwards admitted, an inexcusable interpretation of the treaty under which he held his territory, was called on to furnish a contingent of 5000 men. He objected to comply with this demand,

[1] Defence before the House of Commons, 1786.

and Hastings, on the ground that he had been guilty of a breach of his engagements, agreed to the proposal of the Vizier that he should be dispossessed of his jagir. No action, however, was taken ; the mistake was acknowledged, and, in 1783, Faizullah Khan was glad to make a new agreement, under which, on condition of paying to the Vizier fifteen lakhs of rupees, he was released altogether from the obligation, hitherto ill-defined, under which he was bound to render military service to the Vizier. These proceedings formed the subject of one of the Charges brought against Hastings in 1786, but it was afterwards abandoned.

With this exception, little or nothing that Indian historians have thought worth recording happened in Rohilkhand for twenty years after the close of the Rohilla war. The old controversies, however, were not over.

In December 1780, Francis left Calcutta, and when he reached England he found better opportunities than he had lately found in India for indulging his bitter animosity against Hastings. In February 1785, Hastings himself resigned his office, and in the following June he landed in England. 'Neither lapse of years, nor change of scene,' writes Macaulay, 'had mitigated the enmities which Francis had brought back from the East. After his usual fashion, he mistook his malevolence for virtue, nursed it, as preachers tell us we ought to nurse our good dispositions, and paraded it, on all occasions, with Pharisaical ostentation.' Unfortunately, this mistake was not confined to himself alone. His art and his ability were great, and the noble and passionate mind of Burke, full to overflowing with hatred and indignation against all injustice and oppression, was ready to receive as truth and virtue the malevolence of Francis.

In the fierce struggles in Parliament between the two great parties led by Pitt and Fox, the administration of India had often, between 1780 and 1785, been a subject of contention. Hastings, on his return to England, had been cordially received by the public and by the Court.

It was believed that Pitt and other Ministers desired to support and honour him. Although the Opposition had been inclined to think the opportunity a good one for attacking and embarrassing the Government, it appears doubtful whether they would have taken the measures which they actually adopted if they had not been forced into them by Hastings and his friends. On the 29th of June, 1785, a few days after the arrival of Hastings in England, Burke had given notice, in the House of Commons, 'that if no other gentleman would undertake the business, he would, at a future day, make a motion respecting the conduct of a gentleman just returned from India.' During the rest of the session he took no further action, but on the 18th February, 1786, the first day of the next session, Major Scott, the ardent but not always the judicious friend of Hastings, reminded the House that Hastings had been for some months in England, and he called upon Burke to produce his charges and to fix the earliest possible day for the discussion. This was a challenge that could not be refused[1]. In April, Burke presented to the House of Commons twenty-two Articles of Charge of High Crimes and Misdemeanours against Warren Hastings. The First Charge was to the effect, that in contradiction to the orders of the Court of Directors, Hastings furnished the Nabob of Oudh with a body of troops for the purpose of extirpating the nation of the Rohillas; that the motive of Hastings in undertaking the war was the acquisition of money to the Company; and that when the English commander protested against the inhumanity with which the war was carried on, he was reprimanded by Hastings for

[1] I have found in the British Museum the following note, in the handwriting of Hastings:—'1786. 24 January. Major Scott called on Mr. Burke to declare whether he meant to make his charge and when. Mr. Burke replied with a story of the Duke of Parma, who to a similar demand of Henry IV. answered, "that he had travelled from Amiens to Paris to learn from his enemy when and where was the best day to fight him." In this decent and dignified way was this great work begun.' British Museum MSS. 29,219, vol. i.; Parl. Debates, vol. xiii. The same story, in a somewhat different form, is told by Auber, 'Rise and Progress of the British Power in India,' vol. i. p. 692.

representing a matter with which he had no authority to interfere. Hastings was allowed to make his answer in writing to all the charges; he prepared a paper of great length, which was read to the House; and Colonel Champion, Middleton, and other witnesses were examined at the bar[1].

On the 1st of June, 1786, Burke moved the First Charge relating to the Rohilla war. The reports of the debate are very imperfect, and they contain nothing that throws light upon any part of the subject. It would be useless to refer to them at length, but I quote from Adolphus the following summary:—

'Mr. Burke viewed the question as an appeal from British favour to British justice. The matter must either be criminal or a very false accusation: there was no medium; no alternative; the result must be that Warren Hastings had been guilty of gross, enormous, and flagitious crimes, or himself be a base, calumniatory, wicked, and malicious accuser. There were but three motives which were known to actuate men and excite them to turn accusers; ignorance, inadvertency, and passion. When he considered that Mr. Hastings had been fourteen years at the head of Government in India, and not one complaint sent home against him, he trembled at the enormous power he had to contend with; for such silence could be ascribed to that alone, since it was not in human nature, situated as Mr. Hastings had been, to preserve conduct so pure, even-handed, and unimpeachable, as to afford no room for a single accusation. As to the charges themselves, excepting in some few points, the facts which they contained had been admitted by Mr. Hastings at the bar, in what he had called his defence, but which he had composed and delivered rather in the style of their master than that of the person they were accusing. He entered at length into the circumstances preceding, attending, and following the Rohilla war, and dwelt on it, as an undertaking to extirpate the whole nation for £400,000. The motion was supported by Mr. Powys, Lord North, Mr. Hardinge, and several other members, and, on an adjourned debate, by Mr. Francis and Mr. Anstruther, and most powerfully by Mr. Fox. It was opposed by Lord

[1] The most important parts of the First Charge have already been quoted or noticed. It is much too long and diffuse to be printed *in extenso*. See p. 174. At the trial of Hastings, Major Scott, in his evidence given on the 16th of April, 1788, said that the Answers to the Charge relating to the Rohilla war, and to the King's tribute, as well as the Introduction to the Defence, were written by Hastings himself. As to the general character of the charges, see Preface.

Mulgrave, Mr. Burton, Mr. Grenville, and Mr. Dundas, and on a division rejected by a majority of 119 to 67[1].'

One hundred and eighty-six members only had been present, and the majority that pronounced in favour of Hastings had done so, for the most part, on purely party grounds. As regards the question of the criminality or the innocence of Hastings, it would be absurd to attach the least value to their decision. Proof of this was afforded a few days later. Hastings and his friends were jubilant over their victory, and when, on the 13th of June, Fox brought forward the next

[1] Adolphus, 'History of England,' vol. iv. p. 252. As an illustration of the arguments brought forward to induce the House to agree to the motion, I give the following extract from Fox's speech:—'The Rohillas were a brave people, and, what is singular, the only free people in India. They governed the country of which they were possessed with a mildness of which its very flourishing condition, so as to be called the garden of Hindostan, is an undeniable proof. They were endowed with all those national virtues which Britons have been accustomed to admire, and which form a strong chain of connection between countries which enjoy the blessings of liberty. Ought not such a people to have met with sympathy and regard in the feelings of this nation? Ought not a cause such as theirs to have interested a British bosom? To mark out such a people as the objects of avarice, as the victims of unprovoked resentment, or to abandon them to the rod of tyranny and oppression, what conduct could be more derogatory to the character of a nation which enjoyed the influence of liberty? What mode of procedure could be more disgraceful to the honour and humanity of the British name?' As might have been expected, few of the speakers seem to have had any but the most rudimentary knowledge of the facts. Among those who opposed the motion, Grenville described more accurately than anyone else the policy of Hastings:—'He thought the war was perfectly just as well as politic. The Rohillas were situated in the adjacency of the Vizier's dominions, and the Vizier was our barrier against the Marathas. . . . The question was not so much about the consequences of the Rohilla war as about the original justice of it. What was the precise case? Our ally, whose dominions we had by solemn treaty agreed to guarantee, received an aggression. He was injured by a set of people who had it in their power to be his dangerous enemy. They might join with the Marathas, and from that moment his country was insecure. They owed him a sum of which they refused him the payment. There was both an aggressive and a political alarm. The Vizier had cause not only for resentment but jealousy, and the English having the same political interest, as well as being bound by treaty, were of course obliged to go with him into the war. The justice and policy of the war went hand-in-hand. That war was just which originated in an aggression, and that war was political which seemed to strengthen a frontier, to take off a suspicious and ill-disposed neighbour who had it in his power and who betrayed the inclination to favour the views of an avowed enemy.' Parliamentary History, vol. xxvi. Debate on the Articles against Mr. Hastings.

Charge, respecting the treatment of Chait Singh, no one had any doubt about the result. The supporters of the Ministry had received the usual summons to be in their places to resist the motion. Pitt himself began his speech with approval of the conduct of Hastings and with censure of his opponents, but to the astonishment of everybody, on both sides of the House, he ended by declaring his intention of voting for Fox's motion. 'The House,' says Macaulay, 'was thunderstruck, and well it might be so,' for the reasons which Pitt gave for his sudden change of front were unintelligible then, and they have remained unintelligible ever since. As Mill has observed, 'some article of secret history is necessary to account for this sudden phenomenon.' A sufficient number of Pitt's supporters followed him silently as they had done before, and Hastings was condemned by 119 votes against 79. The result, in the following year, was the Impeachment of Hastings. With it I have now no concern; on the Rohilla charge he had been acquitted, and it was not again revived in Parliament [1].

My account of the Rohilla war, and of the charges against Hastings of which it was the cause, has been completed, but my readers may wish to know something of the subsequent history of Rohilkhand, and I will give a very brief sketch of the principal events that have occurred there since 1783, when Faizullah Khan was relieved from the obligation of rendering military service to the Vizier.

Faizullah Khan was a good and prudent ruler, and the condition of his territory was always far better than that of the rest of the province. He died in July 1794, and was succeeded by his eldest son, Mohammad Ali, a man of overbearing disposition and ungovernable temper. In a short time he became very unpopular, and his brother, Gholam Mohammad, entered into a conspiracy with several of the chiefs and principal officers of the army to depose

[1] A clear account of Pitt's remarkable proceeding, and the most probable explanation of it, is given by Sir Alfred Lyall in his 'Warren Hastings,' p. 193.

him. Mohammad Ali was seized and murdered, and Gholam Mohammad took possession of the State. The Vizier and the English Government refused to recognise this usurpation, and a brigade of British troops was sent under Sir Ralph Abercrombie to punish it. Large numbers of Rohillas flocked to join Gholam Mohammad, and with a force of some 25,000 men he marched into the Vizier's territory towards Bareilly. On the 24th October, 1794, the Rohillas attacked the British at Bhitaura[1]. They completely routed our Native cavalry, which was seized with a disgraceful panic, and we narrowly escaped a serious disaster. After a far more determined contest than that which had brought their dominion to an end, twenty years before, the Rohillas were completely defeated, with a loss on our side of 600 men, and 14 British officers were killed.

Gholam Mohammad soon surrendered; he was banished to Benares, and the Rampur State, considerably reduced in extent, was given to the infant son of Mohammad Ali. A large amount of treasure which Faizullah Khan had accumulated was at the same time confiscated, and it was paid to the Company on account of debts due by the Vizier. Rampur has remained ever since in the possession of Faizullah Khan's descendants.

In 1801 Rohilkhand was ceded by the Nawab Vizier to the British Government, and the immediate result was, we are told, 'as the change from chaos to kosmos[2].' With

[1] Now usually called Fatehganj.

[2] Gazetteer, N. W. P., Bareilly, p. 675. There are interesting accounts of the wretched condition of Rohilkhand under the Oudh Government in Tennant's 'Indian Recreations,' published in 1804. He travelled through Rohilkhand in 1798-99. 'Such an extent of desolate and rich fields (he writes) is nowhere to be met with but in Rohilkhand. Amidst the present solitude and gloom of this province, you see evident traces of its former cultivation.... From the quantity of land under crop the population of Rohilkhand must be very small; not the hundredth acre is in cultivation, a proportion so small that the wild animals are in danger of devouring the people and their subsistence.' He describes, however, the condition of other parts of Northern India through which he travelled as equally miserable. 'The whole face of the country in the Lower Doab, as well as the appearance of the ruined towns wears a melancholy gloom. Remains of its former population and fertility are

the exceptions which I shall notice, the country has ever since enjoyed unbroken tranquillity, its progress has been great, and few parts of our Indian Empire are now more prosperous. The first disturbance of the public peace was in 1805. Early in that year, Amir Khan, the well-known Rohilla leader, was sent across the Ganges by Holkar with a large body of Pindari horse to ravage Rohilkhand. His adventurous raid through the province, the swift pursuit by the English, and his rapid retreat across the Doáb were over in less than a month. In 1816, a serious outbreak occurred at Bareilly. It was caused in the first instance by the imposition of a new house-tax, but the riot with which it began soon became a revolt. The green flag of Islam was raised, large numbers of Rohillas collected, and an attack was made upon the English troops. Several hundred insurgents were killed, but in a few days order was restored.

During the next forty years the peace of the province was undisturbed, but in 1857 came the tremendous catastrophe of the Mutiny of the Bengal Army. On the 31st

continually meeting the eye of the traveller, which he contrasts with the extensive wastes or jungles that now occupy so great a part of the surface.' 'The provinces of Agra and Delhi, once so famous for their population and wealth, are at present in the most wretched state. During half a century they have been the seat of uninterrupted devastation; the lands are nearly laid waste, and the miserable ryots dare not provide anything beyond immediate subsistence, from too well-founded an apprehension that they would draw upon themselves the cruelties of some licentious chief whose trade is pillage, and whose support is the spoils of his miserable neighbour.' 'The British territories are in truth the only part of the country which the natives peaceably possess; the only asylum where they at this time enjoy, in any competent degree, either protection, plenty, or comfort.' See also Major Marsack's evidence before the House of Commons on the 3rd May, 1786. This, however, must be looked on with suspicion. He attempted to levy black-mail on Hastings. A reference is made to this in a private note in the handwriting of Hastings, now in the British Museum:—'1786, 3rd May, Colonel Champion examined and Major Marsack. N.B. Major Marsack had received a summons to attend the Committee of the House on the 3rd April, and on the 1st of that month I received from him a note demanding £10,383 16*s*. for a pretended debt, but offering to refer it to the arbitration of mutual friends. It was followed by a second on the 4th, and a third dated the 6th. I returned no answer, but caused them to be produced in the House in his examination.' British Museum MSS. 29,219, vol. i.

of May the Native troops at Bareilly revolted. Many military and civil officers escaped to the hills of Naini Tal, but every man, woman, and child of European extraction that remained and could be found was murdered. Khan Bahadur, a grandson of Hafiz Rahmat, had been a Subordinate Judge in our service, and he was proclaimed Viceroy of the Emperor[1]. Almost at the same time, the British power was swept away throughout the rest of Rohilkhand. The only other places where Native troops were stationed were Shahjehanpur and Moradabad. At Shahjehanpur, nearly the whole of the English, men, women, and children, were brutally murdered; at Moradabad, most of them escaped to Naini Tal or Meerut; other Christians who remained were killed, or forced to profess the Mohammedan faith. In Bijnor, the Government was assumed by Mohammad Khan, Nawab of Najibabad, the grandson of Zabita Khan, the former Rohilla ruler. Throughout Rohilkhand, except in Rampur, anarchy prevailed. Foremost in the commission of every atrocity were the Pathans, and these descendants of the Rohillas of the last century showed that they had lost nothing of their former barbarism. There was one great exception. Mohammad Yusaf Ali Khan, Nawab of Rampur, the great-grandson of Faizullah Khan, remained conspicuously loyal. For nearly a year he held possession of the Moradabad district on behalf of the British Government, he protected the lives of Christians, and every service that he could give was ungrudgingly rendered.

The worst atrocities were committed at Bareilly, and they were not the work only of the Mohammedan rabble, but were actively encouraged by Khan Bahadur, the Rohilla Governor. One of his first acts was to order the murder of all Europeans, and that every one who sheltered

[1] When the Mutinies of 1857 broke out, the grandsons and other members of Hafiz Rahmat's family were in receipt of large pensions from the British Government. Most of them joined Khan Bahadur, but small allowances were afterwards restored to those who had taken no part in the rebellion; and in 1889 there were still thirty descendants of Hafiz Rahmat on the Indian pension-roll.

them should suffer death. One gallant Englishman was cut to pieces in Khan Bahadur's presence, 'proclaiming in a loud voice that they might destroy him and others, but could never destroy the British Government.'

Nearly a year elapsed before British authority was everywhere restored. Khan Bahadur found his way into Nepal; in 1860 he was surrendered by the Nepalese authorities, and he was hanged at Bareilly. The Nawab of Najibabad was seized at Rampur and sentenced to transportation for life. Several of the other leaders were killed during the rebellion.

Honours which Indian princes always prize, titles and decorations, and the right to an increased number of guns in his salute, were bestowed by the British Government on the loyal ruler of Rampur, and he received a more substantial and more unusual reward in the gift of a strip of British territory adjoining his old dominions, containing more than a hundred and thirty villages with a land revenue of 120,000 rupees a year. The population of the State in 1891 was more than 500,000; nearly one-half were Mohammedans, and of these the majority were Pathans. There can be no doubt that there are now many more Rohillas in Rampur alone than there were a hundred years ago in the whole of Rohilkhand. The little State has always been well administered. Its revenues, which in the time of Faizullah Khan were estimated at fifteen lakhs of rupees, now exceed thirty lakhs a year.

APPENDIX A.

HAFIZ RAHMAT KHAN AS A POET.

(See page 28.)

In an article by M. James Darmesteter in the 'Contemporary Review,' October, 1887, on 'Afghan Life in Afghan Songs,' he writes as follows:—'There are two sorts of poets: the *Sha-ir* and the *Dum*. With the *Sha-ir* we have nothing to do; he is the literary poet, who can read, who knows Háfiz and Saadi, who writes Afghan Ghazals on the Persian model, who has composed a Diván. Every educated man is a *Sha-ir*, though, if he be a man of good taste, he will not assume the title; writing Ghazals was one of the accomplishments of the old Afghan chiefs. Háfiz Rahmat, the great Rohilla captain, Ahmed Sháh, the founder of the Durani Empire, had written Diváns, were "Diván people"—*Ahli Diván*, as the expression runs. The *Sha-ir* may be a clever writer, he may be a fine writer; but he has nothing to teach us about his people. We may safely dismiss him with honour and due respect. The *Dum* is the popular singer and poet, for he combines the two qualities, like our *Jongleur* of the Middle Ages. The *Dums* form a caste; the profession is hereditary.'

M. Darmesteter says in the same article that with rare exceptions the work of the 'literary poets' is worth very little, but that the popular, unwritten songs of the Afghans, though despised and ignored by the reading classes, are of a very different character, simple, true to nature, and sometimes powerful and beautiful.

In his interesting book, *Lettres sur l'Inde* (1888), M. Darmesteter gives an account of his visit to Rampur, and he mentions that, when he was leaving the place, a Rohilla presented him with a collection of poems by Hafiz Rahmat and other Rohilla chiefs. I am indebted to M. Darmesteter for the following further information. The collection presented to him at Rampur, and which is now among the Oriental manuscripts in the British Museum, contains a number of poetical compositions by Afghan chiefs, and one of them is a poem by Hafiz Rahmat, in Pushtu; it has for its subject the hereditary enmity between the Afghans and the Moghals. There appears no reason for doubting that this was written by Hafiz Rahmat; as M. Darmesteter observes, 'les Afghans cultivent volontiers le plagiat mais non pas l'apocryphe.' Hafiz Rahmat, like other Afghan leaders of the last century, seems to have held that the reputation of a chief and soldier was incomplete until he was known as the author of a Diván. Thus, Ahmad Shah, the victor of Panipat, composed a Diván that is still admired; his successors have imitated him, and not long ago a popular singer at Peshawar was heard singing a Ghazal of Shah Shuja.

M. Darmesteter tells me that although he has not himself seen the Diván of Hafiz Rahmat, it is a matter of notoriety among educated Afghans that he left one. I hope that it may still be found in India, but I have been unable to discover it. In Rampur and Bareilly not even the fact that it existed seems now to be remembered.

While, however, this volume was passing through the press, I received from India four Persian Ghazals, said to have been composed by Hafiz Rahmat. I can at present say nothing regarding their authenticity, but this is not doubted by persons whose opinion deserves high consideration, and it seems not improbable that they formed part of the missing Diván.

I quote the following definitions from M. Garcin de Tassy's *Histoire de la Littérature Hindouie*, &c. vol. i. p. 30:—'*Gazal*, sorte d'ode ... ne devant pas être composée de plus de douze vers.' '*Diwan*, un recueil de gazals rangés par ordre alphabétique de la dernière lettre des vers, et par suite le recueil des poésies d'un écrivain. On fait un ou deux gazals, puis quelques-uns encore; enfin, quand on a un nombre suffisant, on les réunit en *Diwan*.'

I have to thank M. Darmesteter for another fact which had escaped my notice. Hafiz Rahmat possessed a collection of books which after his defeat and death was carried off by Shuja-ud-daula to Lucknow. It subsequently formed part of the library of the Kings of Oudh, a catalogue of which was made by Dr. Sprenger. One volume of this was published in 1854. The library contained, Dr. Sprenger writes, 'the whole of the literary treasures of Hafiz Rahmat Khan,' and referring to a collection of books that he found in the arsenal 'in about forty dilapidated boxes,' he says :—'The number of volumes in this collection is very great and among them are some Pushtu works written with great care for the brave and learned Rohilla chief.' The Lucknow library was dispersed or destroyed during the Mutinies of 1857, but a considerable number of the books that it contained have from time to time been recovered.

APPENDIX B.

NOTE TO CHAPTER III.

MILL'S STATEMENTS REGARDING THE ROHILLA GOVERNMENT.

THE statements made by Mill, in his 'History of British India,' regarding the excellence of the Rohilla Government must not be left unnoticed.

'It is completely proved,' he writes, 'that the Rohilla territory was the best governed part of India; that the people were protected; that their industry was encouraged; and that the country flourished beyond parallel. It was by these cares, and by cultivating diligently the arts of neutrality, that is, by pretending, according to the necessity of Indian customs, to favour all parties, not by conquering a larger territory from their neighbours, that the Rohilla chiefs had endeavoured to provide for their independence. After the death of Najib-ud-daula no one among them was remarkably distinguished for talents. Hafiz Rahmat Khan, whose territories lay nearest to those of Shuja-ud-daula, was looked upon as the chief of the tribe, but his character had in it more of caution than of enterprise, and his prudence had stamped upon him the reputation of avarice.'

In a foot-note Mill adds that Najib-ud-daula had impressed both on Indians and Europeans the highest opinion of his character, and he cites from Verelst a passage regarding him which I shall quote presently. The manner in which he has made it appear that he has good authority for his statements is characteristic.

The Afghan chief, Najib-ud-daula, was, as I have mentioned, First Minister of the Empire, and he was master of a large and rich tract of country in the Doáb, between the Ganges and Jumna. His only possessions in Rohilkhand were a small part of what is now the Bijnor district, and although he gave to Hafiz Rahmat and the other chiefs, who were Rohillas like himself, the advantage of his powerful support, he had nothing to do with the actual administration of the province. Among the noted Afghans particularly cautious of risking his treasures by engaging in .putes or war. With all his parsimony he is not very rich, and his on Inayat Khan, a bold giddy youth without education or parts, draws all he can from him to supply his own extravagance[1].'

The object of Mill was to satisfy his readers that Rohilkhand 'flourished beyond all parallel' under the rule of the Rohillas, and proof of the high character and enlightenment of their chiefs would go far to establish that position. Unfortunately for his purpose, no such proof was forthcoming; but he found in Verelst's letters statements which English readers, with imperfect knowledge, would easily accept as sufficient without suspicion that they had no bearing on the subject. The only important chief in Rohilkhand mentioned by Verelst was Hafiz Rahmat, but the account given of him was by no means flattering. It was consequently necessary to suppress the passage that referred to him, and Verelst's statement that Hafiz Rahmat's character was only distinguished by low cunning, intrigue, deceit, and avarice, is travestied in the observation that he had more caution than enterprise, and that his prudence had stamped upon him the reputation of avarice. But, although Verelst had said nothing about other chiefs in Rohilkhand, he had referred to other men of high character in other provinces, who were also classed as Rohillas. This was sufficient for Mill's purpose. The enlightened administration of Najib-ud-daula and Ahmad Khan, and the remarkable virtues of the former, were made to afford proof that Rohilkhand, a country with the government of which they had no concern, was 'by far the best governed part of India.'

[1] Verelst's letters will be found in the Appendices to his 'View of the Rise, Progress, and Present State of the English Government in Bengal,' 1772.

APPENDIX C.

NOTE TO CHAPTERS VI AND VII.

THE CAMPAIGNS OF 1772 AND 1773 IN ROHILKHAND.

THE description that I have given of the campaigns of 1772 and 1773 in Rohilkhand, and especially of the latter, differs so essentially from that of Mill and of others who have obviously accepted his statements without independent inquiry, that some further explanation is desirable.

Mill's account of the manner in which the treaty of 1772 between the Rohillas and the Vizier was concluded, and of the preceding events, is very inaccurate. He says that 'the Rohillas entered into the engagement with the utmost reluctance, in compliance solely, as it would appear, with the importunities of the English,' and he makes the reader suppose that the engagement was one highly injurious to the Rohillas. There is no foundation for such statements. For our knowledge of the facts we are almost entirely dependent on the official and private letters of Sir Robert Barker. He desired from first to last to see an alliance established between the Rohillas and the Vizier, not because he had any liking for the Rohillas, for he always believed them to be utterly faithless, and deserving on their own account of no consideration, but because he thought the maintenance of their power desirable in the interests of the Company. It is clear that an alliance with the Vizier offered to the Rohillas the only means of safety that remained to them. Mill appears to assume that when the treaty was made, the Rohillas, in accordance with 'the universal practice of Indian Governments of fulfilling no obligations which they can violate or evade,' had no intention of observing the conditions by which they had bound themselves, and this 'universal practice' seems to have been considered by him a justification of

U 2

their subsequent breach of faith. That Mill was right in supposing that the Rohillas never intended to fulfil their obligations, if it were possible to avoid them, is very probable, but the treaty was in itself reasonable, and if it had been honestly carried out by the Rohillas, it would have been highly advantageous to them.

Wilson, in a note to his edition of Mill's History, has referred to the account of the arrangements between the Rohillas and the Vizier, given by the son of Hafiz Rahmat in the Gulistán-i-Rahmat. According to it (and a similar story is told in the Gul-i-Rahmat), the Marathas agreed to leave Rohilkhand on receiving forty lakhs of rupees from Hafiz Rahmat, provided that the Vizier made himself responsible for the payment; it states that the other Rohilla chiefs entreated Hafiz Rahmat to consent, promising to contribute their quotas; that he gave a bond accordingly to the Vizier, who in his turn gave his own bond for forty lakhs to the Marathas, and that they then withdrew their armies from Rohilkhand. It is added that when, in the following year, the Marathas renewed their invasion, they informed Hafiz Rahmat that it was their intention to march into Oudh; that they offered to make over to him Shuja-ud-daula's bond on condition of his not opposing them; that Hafiz Rahmat refused their proposal and communicated it to the Vizier, 'and concluded by requesting the return of his bond, as the money for the payment of which Shuja-ud-daula had made himself responsible had not been sent, nor could it be supposed that the Nawab would now consider his engagement binding; as a necessary consequence of which his claim on Hafiz ceased.' It is clear from the public and private correspondence of Sir Robert Barker that there is no foundation for this story. I only notice it because Wilson seems to have supposed that it might be true. As I have said, in the Preface to this work, the Gulistan-i-Rahmat has little historical value. In this case, the author evidently desired to make it appear that his father was guilty of no breach of faith when he afterwards evaded fulfilment of the treaty, and he follows the false account given by Hafiz Rahmat himself in a letter to Hastings, to which I shall presently refer.

Mill's misrepresentations regarding the campaign of 1773 are more serious. According to him, the Marathas were not expelled from Rohilkhand by the troops of the Vizier and the English; the Rohillas were never defended against the Marathas; the treaty between the Vizier and the Rohillas was a fraud; the Vizier never to which Mill had no access, has been mainly derived from the official letters, and frequent quotations from them have been made. Sir Robert Barker reported to his Government in the plainest terms that in 1773 the Marathas were prevented by the forces of the English and the Vizier from overrunning Rohilkhand, and were expelled by those forces from that country; that while the actual defeat of the Maratha invasion was due to the English troops and to the fear with which they were regarded, the Vizier had with their assistance duly performed his engagements towards the Rohillas; that the Rohillas were guilty of a gross breach of faith in refusing, after they had been delivered from the Marathas, to carry out the conditions of the treaty into which they had entered; and that the payments claimed by the Vizier under that treaty were justly due in return for the services rendered by him.

The reference made by Mill to a Minute in which Sir Robert Barker is said to have 'condemned the assistance given to the destruction of the Rohillas' is also entirely misleading and inaccurate, but as this had no connection with the transactions of which I am now speaking, but referred to events of later date, I do not now notice it [1].

The quotation from Sir Robert Barker's evidence before the House of Commons is more precise, for in this case Mill gives the very words of one of the questions and answers. Let us see what this evidence really was. I shall quote from the official report [2] every question and answer referring to the subject:—

'Sir Robert Barker called in and examined.

'Do you know of any formed design of the Rohillas to conquer Sujah Dowlah, and to extirpate his family, and the race of Mahometans that possessed the country of Oude, from that country, during the term of your service?

'I do not.

'Do you know anything of a design of Sujah Dowlah for the purpose of making a conquest of the country of the Rohillas?

'Not till after the forfeiture of the engagement they had made in their treaty of the year 1772, with Sujah Dowlah. There was always a jealousy subsisting between the Rohillas and Sujah Dowlah, but

[1] See note, p. 124.

[2] Minutes of the Evidence taken before a Committee of the House of Commons, being a Committee of the whole House, appointed to consider of the several Articles of Charge of High Crimes and Misdemeanours, presented to the House against Warren Hastings, Esquire, late Governor of Bengal. May 2, 1786.

I do not know of any declared resolution of Sujah Dowlah to reduce their country before that period.

'Has Sujah Dowlah been considered as an ambitious prince, desirous of extending his dominions at the expense of his neighbours, or was he not?

'He was an ambitious prince. I do not know that he declared himself desirous of acquiring possessions, nor making conquests, before that time.

'What was the ground of jealousy between him and the Rohillas?

'It was a matter that arose in his father's time, upon some territories taken from him and possessed by the Rohillas (I am speaking from hearsay as to this last), which he had ever kept in remembrance.

'Were you privy to the treaty between the Rohillas and Sujah Dowlah for the purpose already mentioned?

'If the question means in the year 1772, I was.

'Did you sign it as a witness?

'I did.

'Did you conceive that you bound the Company by that signature to a guarantee of the treaty by war, in case either of the parties had declined to perform their engagements?

'I did not, and my reasons for signing it were these: First, It was requested of me by the Vizier Sujah Dowlah and the Rohillas, the two parties. Second, I knew there would be no treaty unless I did witness it, the Rohillas not having faith enough in the Vizier to take his signature only.

'Did not the Vizier charge the Rohillas with an infraction of that treaty?

'He did.

'In what did that infraction consist?

'In not paying the £400,000.

'Whether the Rohillas were included in the line of defence, or intended to be formed against the Marathas in 1772?

'If the question means that the treaty with the Nabob and Vizier formed that line of defence, it certainly did.

'*Were the Marathas in fact prevented from invading the Rohillas by any acts of Sujah Dowlah, or by his protection of the country?*

'*No*[1].

'Whether the Marathas were not prevented from possessing themselves of the Rohilla country by the British troops joined with those of Sujah Dowlah?

'The Marathas were driven and expelled from the Rohilla country by the British troops and those of the Vizier.

'What grounds had you for writing, in your letter to the Calcutta Council, dated April 6, 1773, "It is well known that neither promises

[1] This question and answer, printed in italics, are the only parts of Sir Robert Barker's evidence which Mill has quoted.

nor oaths have been able to bind this treacherous sect of people (speaking of the Rohillas) to their engagements"?

'It was very evident that oaths did not bind them, by their evasion to pay the forty lakhs, as agreed to with Sujah Dowlah, and their general character was that of a treacherous sect of people.

'When you, with the British army, entered the Rohilla country, in the beginning of 1773, was not Hafiz Rahmat on his march to join the Marathas?

'I do not know that he was; he had been carrying on conferences; there was an intercourse between him and the Marathas, but I do not think he was marching to join them.

'Were not some of the Rohillas, at that time, joined with the Marathas?

'I do not know that there were.

'Whilst you were with Sujah Dowlah, was any demand made by him on the Rohillas for the payment of the forty lakhs?

'Frequently; demands by the Nabob, and representations from myself.

'Did they pay the money in consequence of those demands and representations?

'I do not know that they did.

'Did not you depute Captain Gabriel Harper to Hafiz Rahmat, the Rohilla chief, in May, 1772, previous to the treaty entered into with Sujah Dowlah and the Rohillas?

'I did, at the Vizier's particular and earnest request.

'Did not Hafiz Rahmat meet you and Sujah Dowlah in consequence?

'He did.

'Did not Hafiz Rahmat declare that he looked on Sujah Dowlah and the English as one?

'I do not exactly recollect that expression. He had great faith in the English, and his visit to the Vizier was in consequence of that faith.

'Whether any compulsion was used by you, or any other English gentleman, to induce Hafiz Rahmat to sign the treaty?

'None.

'Did not you, sometime on or about the 24th of March, 1773, send on a proposition from Sujah Dowlah to the Council in Calcutta, "That if the Rohillas should fail in their engagements, Sujah Dowlah would give the Company forty lakhs of rupees to put him in possession of the Rohilla country"?

'I am not certain as to the particular date of that letter, but I wrote to the Board, "That the Nabob offered fifty lakhs of rupees (upon a failure of the Rohillas to their engagement) to put him in possession of that part of the Rohilla country, commonly called Hafiz Rahmat's."

'Do you mean the whole of the Rohilla country, except that now held by Faizullah Khan?

'I meant that part of the Rohilla country held by Hafiz Rahmat.

'Did not Sujah Dowlah and the English punctually perform every part of their engagements with the Rohillas, notwithstanding the evasions of that chief? And did not you, after the completion of the service, and the retreat of the Marathas, enclose a treaty to the Council of Calcutta for the purpose of showing them how literally it had been performed?

'The service was completely performed; I believe I enclosed a treaty some time before that, as soon as it was executed.

'Do you not recollect that you enclosed a second copy of the treaty, and accompanied it with words to this effect: "That you enclosed it, to show how literally it had been performed, notwithstanding the evasion of the chiefs"?

'I think it very probable I did, but at this distance of time I do not recollect that letter.

'Was it not the subject of common conversation, as you might have heard in the army or the service under your command in 1773, that the conduct of the Rohillas was treacherous? And in the morning the army marched under you to Ramghat, in order to force the Marathas to pass the Ganges, "That we were on that day to breakfast with the Rohillas and dine with the Marathas"?

'I do not know what conversation might pass in the army, but I never heard any such thing.

'Did not you mention to the Board in Calcutta, in several letters written in the course of that service, previous to our junction with the Rohillas, your suspicion of the conduct they meant to pursue?

'I mentioned several times the duplicity of their conduct; that they were carrying on conferences both with the Marathas and Sujah Dowlah.

'Did not the army under your command, after having forded the Ganges and recrossed it again into the Rohilla country on the eastern side, remain in camp in the neighbourhood of Ramghat till the Rohillas were freed from all danger of future invasion?

'We did.

'Did not you, when the British army returned, after having completely effected the service on which they were sent, remain a few days behind the army, for the professed purpose of inducing Hafiz Rahmat to comply with his engagements?

'I did.

'Whether in the month of March, 1773, you wrote any letter to the Council at Calcutta, mentioning that some of the Rohilla chiefs had actually joined with the Marathas?

'Of the great number of letters I wrote to the Council, it is impossible for me at this time to recollect. I do not recollect such a letter.

'Upon what grounds do you form the belief that, to avoid the necessity of war, the Rohillas would have surrendered part of their effects, to have possessed the remainder?

'From a knowledge of the people in general. It is their constitution to part with something, when forced to it, rather than risk the remainder.

'What do you mean by the expression "forced to it"?

'I mean an armed force coming to compel them.

'Do you mean that an armed force would have been necessary to have obtained payment of a part, to preserve the remainder?

'I do verily believe it.

'Then you believe that an armed force would have been necessary to have compelled payment even of a part?

'I believe it would, or the appearance of an armed force.

'Do you not believe that such payment might have been obtained by an amicable interposition of the English Governor with the Rohillas?

'I do not think it could, without the appearance of compulsion.

'In what year were the Marathas driven out of the Rohilla country by the united power of the English and the Vizier?

'In the year 1773, I think.

'Had the Marathas overrun the Rohilla country in 1773?

'No; the British arms prevented them.

'If the British arms prevented them from overrunning the country, how could they be driven out?

'They were within the Rohilla country, and did not overrun it.

'How far had they advanced into the Rohilla country?

'They had advanced as far as Azapoor, but it must be observed that their depredations were confined chiefly to the towns on the banks of the Ganges.

'Were they driven out by the British forces only?

'By the terror of the British arms only, because the Vizier was considerably in the rear.

'Did the Rohillas assign any reason, and what, in justification of their not paying the money?

'The Rohillas said, it was true we had driven out the Marathas from their country, and saved them, but they might return the next year, when our joint forces were not in the Rohilla country, to defend them; that we had done little, meaning that we had not destroyed the Maratha armies.

'Were the Rohillas considered as a free and independent nation, competent to make treaties with other States?

'They were independent.

'What was the reputed character of Sujah Dowlah?

'It is very difficult to draw the character of Sujah Dowlah. He was, like all other Indostaners, not observing much faith when it was his interest to do otherwise.

'You have spoken of the Rohillas as a sect; were they the cultivators of the soil of the Rohilla country?

'They were not. The Hindoos compose the greatest part of the people of India; a very large proportion compose the husbandmen, mechanics, and lower order of people.

'Were not the Rohillas merely possessors of the civil and military power?

'I believe they were.'

Out of the whole of this evidence Mill has selected the single question and answer which, detached from the context, could be made to appear to support his narrative. It will be seen that in the answer marked by me in italics, Sir Robert Barker was merely referring to the fact that the Marathas had not been prevented from crossing the Ganges into Rohilkhand, and he has been quoted as the authority for statements totally opposed to those which he actually made.

Both Hafiz Rahmat and the Vizier sent to Hastings their accounts of these two campaigns, and I give them in extenso. The Vizier's narrative, written in reply to that of Hafiz Rahmat, is substantially in complete accordance with the official and private letters of Sir Robert Barker. Hafiz Rahmat, on the other hand, 'makes statements,' as Mr. Forrest has observed,

'totally at variance with the treaty which he signed, and puts forward a palpable falsehood when he states that the English General and the Vizier sent envoys to him, "desiring that I would enter into no terms with the Marathas, and they would give me back my engagement for forty lakhs of rupees, and do everything both for my present and future security." He had the temerity to conclude as follows: "But at length they left everything unfinished, and after temporizing for a long time with the Marathas, returned to their own homes, leaving me still a prey to the Marathas. You are no doubt acquainted with all their proceedings. It is a point which requires justice and consideration." The Nawab, with much greater justice, accuses Rahmat Khan of breach of faith and treachery[1].'

Letter from Hafiz Rahmat Khan, Chief of the Rohillas, to the Governor.

After the usual compliments, and expressing his desire of an interview, he proceeds:—

'The bonds of friendship and affection, and the mutual intercourse which have long subsisted and taken root between us and the English

[1] Forrest's Selections, Introduction, vol. i. p. xvi.

Sirdars may not be unknown to you. Having heard of your fame, I wish that a perfect harmony and concord should be established and confirmed between us, and I hope that you will have the same inclination on your part. It is from these motives as well as in consideration of there being no difference or disagreement between us, that I represent to you the following few circumstances that you may have them in your memory at the time of discussion. Last year when His Majesty and the Maratha Sirdars were at variance with the Nabob Zabita Khan, and when, after confusion was thrown into that Nabob's affairs, His Majesty and the Marathas crossed the Ganges to come into these parts, the Rohilla Sirdars, for the protection of their women, fled to the skirts of the jungles. At this time the Vizier of the Empire and General Barker arrived at Shahabad, and sent Captain Harper to me with a message to come and join them, which they persisted in with great perseverance. As our interests were equal, I therefore went and had an interview with the gentlemen, when an agreement was concluded between us in which I agreed to pay forty lakhs of rupees on account of peshkush to the King and the Maratha Sirdars, and the gentlemen on their part engaged to effect my security, by establishing peace between me and the King and the Maratha Sirdars, declaring that they would, in a day or two after that, march from Shahabad, to fall upon and come to extremities with the Marathas, and to put an end to their operations. Notwithstanding this, the gentlemen never came to any negotiation with the Marathas, so as to put an end to their operations, nor ventured to attack them, but finally returned towards Fyzabad, leaving their engagements unfulfilled. When the rainy season commenced, the Marathas of themselves crossed the Ganges and encamped in the Doáb, threatening me still with hostilities. During the rains I repeatedly called on the Nabob, the General, and Captain Harper, to conclude these affairs with His Majesty and the Marathas, but they came to no determination on the subject, nor took any measures for effecting security. When the rainy season was drawing to an end, and the Marathas had approached near the banks of the Ganges, they then demanded of me sums of money, which after much temporizing I was at last obliged to pay them. Afterwards they went to the Presence, and procured a sunnud for Kora and Allahabad, with which they returned to the banks of the Ganges and made preparations of bridges for crossing it; and at the same time sent a person of their confidence to demand payment of the money which had been stipulated, saying it belonged to them and the King; and also with many inducements requested that I would let them pass through my territories, assuring me that they would commit no depredations or ravages on the ryots, and they would pass through with expedition towards the Soubah of Oudh, or whithersoever they thought proper. They also engaged to remit me a large sum on account of the stipulation, and to do whatever was agreeable and would give satisfaction to the

Rohilla Sirdars. At this juncture the Nabob and the General being arrived near, they sent to me Syed Shaw Muddun and Mahomed Mukrim Cawn, desiring that I would enter into no terms with the Marathas; and they would give me back my engagement for forty lakhs of rupees, and do everything both for my present and future security. Having, therefore, in view the long friendship which had subsisted between the Nabob Vizier and the English gentlemen and myself, I declined all offers made by the Marathas, and came over to them, in revenge for which it is well known that the Marathas recrossed the Ganges and plundered Moradabad and Sumbhul. The gentlemen promised that they would cross and continue on the other side of the Ganges during the rains, and would not return to Fyzabad or Calcutta until they had entirely driven away the Marathas, and fully satisfied themselves both with respect to their own and my security. But at length they left everything unfinished; and after temporizing for a long time with the Marathas returned to their own homes, leaving me still a prey to the Marathas. You are no doubt acquainted with all these proceedings. It is a point which requires justice and consideration. As a friendship has long been established between us, I doubt not but you will at all times and on all occasions wish to preserve it. Other particulars the Major will inform you of.'

The Vizier's Narrative of the behaviour of the Rohillas.

'The case of the Rohillas is as follows: That from the beginning to this time I have treated them with friendship and attention, and on their part I have met with nothing but ill-treatment, treachery, and a breach of faith. Accordingly, when the Marathas marched with a large army against Najib-ud-daula in Sukertaul, and Hafiz Rahmat, Dundi Khan, and the rest at Jellabad, where they reduced them to the greatest straits and difficulties, if I had not assisted them they would all have been ruined and deprived of their women, country, and government. But by the favour of God, I afforded them at that time such assistance that the Marathas were put to flight, and took their route to the Deccan, and the territory, property, and women of the Rohillas remained in security. Again, the year before last, when the Marathas advanced their troops against the Rohillas, Zabita Khan received a total defeat; and Hafiz Rahmat and the others, being unable to oppose them, took shelter with their women at the foot of the hills, where, if I had made ten days' delay, they would all have perished by the bad water and unsalutary air. By the favour of the Almighty, I went with the English troops to Shahabad, and stopped the approach of the Marathas, and sometimes using authority and menaces, and sometimes friendly mediation and temporizing, according to the circumstances, I caused them to pass the Ganges; and relieving from confinement delivered to Zabita Khan the daughter of Ali Mahommad Khan, a principal chief of the Rohillas, and nine of the women and daughters of Najib-ud-daula, and the wife and son of Zabita Khan, together with 400 women the Marathas had taken prisoners. I also called to me Hafiz Rahmat Khan and the others who had taken protection under the hills, and replaced them on their former footing in the possession of their country. My friend General Barker is well acquainted with these circumstances, in whose presence they entered into an engagement for the payment of forty lakhs of rupees, and pledged their faith and religion for its performance. In the sequel they did not remain steady to their agreement, but in the height of the rains, antecedent to every other person, Zabita Khan first went and connected himself with the Marathas, and Hafiz Rahmat Khan sent the holy Koran, which contains the religion of the Mussulmen, to the Marathas as a token of his friendship. He also gave them five lakhs of rupees, and established a friendship and good understanding with them. The whole world are well acquainted that envoys from Hafiz Rahmat were with the Marathas, and treated with them in the above manner. Myself, continuing firm and steady to my engagements, I proceeded in concert with the English troops from Fyzabad to the assistance of the Rohillas, and arrived by successive marches at Ramghat. I previously acquainted Hafiz Rahmat Khan that he should make preparations, and that I should shortly arrive and act in conjunction with him. As Hafiz Rahmat Khan had entered into intrigues with the Marathas notwithstanding I was near him, and the Marathas at a considerable distance, he nevertheless under various pretensions and evasions drew near the Maratha army to such a degree that the morning when I arrived with the English forces, and came upon the Marathas, Hafiz Rahmat Khan was within seven or eight coss of them, when from necessity only he came and waited on me. I am certain that if I had been four gurries later with the English forces, he would have joined the Marathas and fallen upon me, and that only from my near approach he was compelled to come to me. Afterwards, when the Marathas could not face the English forces and myself, and set out for the Deccan, Hafiz Rahmat Khan did not pay me a single daum on account of the agreement executed in presence of the General as aforementioned; nor did he treat me with that respect, or present me with the customary presents which are used amongst mankind as marks of friendship and hospitality. The heavy burden of increased expense which I have sustained, both on account of my own troops and those of the English, are as evident as the sun at noonday. I made no use of menaces concerning taking the money by force, otherwise, had I been so inclined, I could have taken it in the space of a day. I passed the matter over, and took no notice of it, and they on their part pleaded excuses, evasions, and delays. They even encamped at three or four coss distance from mine and the English army, with an intention to come to a battle should I insist on the payment of the money. Of the truth of this every gentleman that was with me can witness. My mentioning it is unnecessary. In short, the Rohillas have been guilty of treachery, baseness, and a breach of faith, and have paid no regard either to their oaths and agreements. I have, notwithstanding, hitherto put up with this behaviour, but can do it no longer. To oblige them to make reparation is expedient and just [1].'

[1] Fifth Report, App. No. 19. Forrest's Selections, vol. i. p. 34.

APPENDIX D.

NOTE ON SOME MISSING EVIDENCE RELATING TO THE CONDUCT OF THE ROHILLA WAR.

In Chapters XIII, XIV, and XV, I have stated all the facts that I could ascertain respecting the atrocities said to have been committed during the Rohilla war. Further evidence, which I have been unable to discover, was once in existence; it is possible that it may still be found, and I hope, though I hardly expect, that the researches of some future explorer of the old records of those times may be more fortunate than my own.

I have given an account (p. 203) of the long letter which Colonel Champion wrote on the 30th January, 1775, in reply to the complaints brought against him by the Nawab Vizier. It is clear that, after the change in the Government, Colonel Champion resolved to do all in his power to further the wishes of the enemies of Hastings into whose hands all power had passed. His letter was laid before the Council on the 14th February, and on the same day Hastings declared his intention of delivering to the Secretary a series of written questions which he desired to propose to Colonel Galliez and other officers who had served in the campaign. On the 16th February he wrote to Colonel Champion informing him that he intended to make a full inquiry into the charges brought by the Vizier, and particularly in regard to the long inaction of the English troops before the final advance against Faizullah Khan. 'As these accusations,' Hastings wrote, 'were addressed to me by the Vizier in my capacity of the First Member of the Administration, it became the duty of my station to submit them to inquiry, and the method I preferred was to give them to your perusal, never doubting but your promised vindication would contain an ample refutation of them; but it does not appear to me that you have refuted them. I now acquaint you that I shall submit these matters to the examination and decision of the Board, and make a very

X

free inquiry into such parts of your conduct as have been arraigned by the Vizier, and I give you this notice to prevent the supposition of my taking advantage of your absence in the prosecution of these inquiries, that you may, if you think it necessary, defer your departure for the opportunity, either of supporting the accusations you have brought against the late Administration and me, or defending yourself from the charges which may appear against you.' In reply to this letter, Colonel Champion wrote that Hastings had kept the Vizier's letter for a month before calling on him for an answer, although it was known that he was on the point of leaving India, and he said that he had no fear of the result of any inquiry[1]. On the 20th March, in accordance with the notice given by him on the 14th February, Hastings laid before the Council the questions which he proposed 'to be put to the field officers and others who served in the late campaign, for the elucidation of several matters which he thinks it will be necessary to ascertain in reply to Colonel Champion's letter.' The questions were addressed to Colonel Galliez, who had succeeded Colonel Champion in the command of the army, and who had commanded the brigade of Native troops during the war, Colonel Leslie, Major Hannay, and other military officers, to Middleton, who had been Resident with the Vizier, to Roberts, the Commander-in-Chief's Persian Interpreter, and to Captain Macpherson, his Aide-de-camp. The questions were numerous; 44 questions, for instance, were proposed to Colonel Galliez, 52 to Major Hannay, and 31 to Middleton. The majority of them referred to the conduct of the war, and especially to the delay that had taken place in attacking Faizullah Khan and bringing the campaign to a close, to the proceedings of Colonel Champion's Banian, who had long been looked on with extreme suspicion, and who had been charged with gross corruption and treachery[2], and some of the questions related to the treatment by the Vizier of his

[1] Consultations, Secret Department, Feb. 24, 1775. India Office Records; British Museum MSS. 28,973, vol. iv.

[2] The private correspondence between Hastings and Middleton, preserved in the British Museum, contains many references to Colonel Champion's Banian or Dewan, Kali Charan. Middleton, in a confidential report, said that the Vizier was in great fear of him. 'I am well convinced that the Dewan has taken great pains, not without a proportionate degree of success, to persuade the Nabob that every measure of importance, even the operations of the army, is more or less influenced by his counsels.' Letter, September 15, 1774.

Rohilla prisoners. On the last subject, with which alone I am now concerned, the following were the questions asked:—

'Where were the Rohilla prisoners at or about the 31st May?

'How were they carried on the march?

'Do you know whether any of the women of the Rohilla chiefs were searched for jewels in the Vizier's presence at or about that time?

'Do you know of any instances of violence or cruelty wantonly exercised upon the Rohilla captives?

'Was it, do you suppose, in consequence of instructions from the Vizier, or with his privacy?

'Was Mohibullah Khan engaged in the war?

'Do you know that he had given the Vizier any cause of resentment against him?

'Have you reason to believe, from the knowledge you had of the Vizier, that he was of a sanguinary or cruel disposition?

'In what light were the English troops considered by the natives and people in general, compared with former campaigns where our troops and the Vizier's have acted in conjunction?

'Did you see any villages set on fire in the Rohilla country after the action of the 23rd of April?

'Do you suppose it was in consequence of instructions from the Vizier or with his privacy?'

The record of the discussion in the Council that followed the presentation of the questions is a good illustration of the manner in which Hastings was treated by his colleagues. No account of it has, I believe, been published, and I give the following extracts:—

'*General Clavering*. I must observe that the persons to whom the Governor-General has chosen to propose questions are almost all of them those whom he knows to be in enmity with Colonel Champion. The questions themselves are most of them very captious and foreign to the objects on which the Governor-General means to ground his own justification. What other answers can be expected of the question upon the character of a gentleman's Banian but that he is an infamous rogue? Were questions of a similar nature to be asked to any man in Calcutta relating to the Governor's own Banian, the answer would most probably be that he was rapacious and tyrannical. I am told that he holds a Court of Caste Cutcherry within the Governor's own house, when, availing himself of the prejudices of the Hindu religion, he tries, judges, and condemns. I am told he fines and imprisons. Wherefore, if a question of the kind be proposed, it is proper that Colonel Champion's agent give full information of the Governor's Banian, and obtain what accounts he can of his transactions in Calcutta. Besides, it is so consistent with justice that the questions proposed on one side by the Governor and on the other by Colonel Champion should be transmitted together, that the facts which are intended to be proved or disproved by them, as far as such kind of evidence can be admitted, may be considered together, and the weight given to them which their credibility may merit.'

'*The Governor-General.* There is no occasion to publish invitations to people to give information against my Banian or myself. The whole world are already too well apprized of the wishes of the gentlemen who rule the administration in this respect. Neither do I know why this is introduced in a Minute in the question before us. As to the Court of Castes, commonly called the Jatmally Cutcherry, it is of as ancient institution as the Government itself, and the process of it is as regular as that of any Court of justice in the country. I have never yet heard a single complaint against any of its decisions, except one in which it appeared that the Court had afforded protection to a woman against intended violence. If any Member of the Board considers the Court to be an improper one, let him propose the abolition of it. I shall be heartily glad to be freed from it. With respect to the General's objections to the questions, I take upon me to say that they are neither captious nor foreign to the object, but directly tend to the purposes which I have declared to Colonel Champion himself in a letter on record I shall aim at in the prosecution of this inquiry. I cannot help it if the gentlemen to whom I have proposed these questions are the Colonel's enemies. I proposed the questions only to those whom I believed capable of giving me information. His agents may propose any questions to be put to those that they esteem his friends. I shall make no objection to it.'

The following orders were then passed by the Council:—

'That copies of the several questions be immediately transmitted to the agents of Colonel Champion, that they may propose any which they shall judge necessary on his part, and send to be put at the same time as the above to the persons proposed in them [1].'

On the 24th March, another letter was received from Colonel Champion, written on board the ship on which he had sailed for England. It was addressed to the Council, and contained a repetition of some of his former statements [2].

On the 20th and 24th April, nearly 250 questions were received, which Colonel Champion wished to propose to a number of officers.

[1] Consultations, March 20, 1775, India Office Records; Forrest's Selections, vol. ii. p. 329. India Office Records.

[2] Consultations, March 24, 1775.

They were sent to the Council by his Attorneys. It is impossible to give any summary of these questions. They referred to every sort of subject; a large proportion of them had no bearing upon any facts of interest connected with the war, but asked for opinions on a multitude of matters, many of them of the most trivial nature and altogether foolish. A few only of the questions related to the treatment of the families of the Rohilla chiefs. It was ordered by the Council on the 24th April,—'That these questions be also put as proposed, and that the Secretary transmit such of them and of all the foregoing ones to each separate person within the provinces as are directed to them, and that the following letter be written to Colonel Galliez with such as are to be put to officers with his Brigade in the Field.' The letter to Colonel Galliez desired him to deliver the letters, and to send the answers as soon as possible[1].

At the meeting of the Council on the 8th of May, 1775, a letter was read from Lieutenant Roberts, Persian Interpreter to the Commander-in-Chief, with reference to the questions which he had been desired to answer. He said that he was bound by an oath of secrecy to Colonel Champion not to reveal the transactions of his office, and he asked whether he was dispensed by the Council from observance of this oath. The record of the discussion which followed has not, I believe, been published, and it is so characteristic that it deserves quotation:—

'The Governor-General begs leave to remark that the Board's authority in this case is the necessary authority, and that if Mr. Roberts has any objections to it he ought to state them.

'Ordered, that Lieutenant Roberts be called upon accordingly.

'*General Clavering.* I must remark on this that Mr. Roberts was Persian Interpreter to Colonel Champion, and, as he declares, under an oath of secrecy, I think in cases wherein the State is concerned, such as that of Mr. Nathaniel Middleton, who was public Resident from this Council, though deemed by the Governor-General as his private Agent, I think in such a case he was absolutely obliged to lay his correspondence before the Board, but I don't think the State the least interested in the question put to Mr. Roberts whether the character of Colonel Champion's Banian be good or bad. I understand he is at present in the employ of the Commissary-General, who, I daresay, would not employ him if he was worse than any other of the tribe, and the questions besides appear only intended to gratify

[1] Consultations, April 20 and 24, 1775. India Office Records.

the spleen of the Governor-General against Colonel Champion. I repeat it, the questions can answer no public purpose whatever but to destroy that confidence which men in station must have in their Secretaries or Persian Translators. I therefore desire that the question may be put to him whether he was not bound not to reveal the confidential secrets of Colonel Champion, but when required to do so in a due course of law.

'*The Governor-General.* I believe it will appear from the preceding Minute, and from every other Minute of General Clavering, that he has had no other motive than to gratify his own spleen against me, and to excite mine, and I shall appeal to the Court of Directors whether I am right in making this observation after such a Minute as has just been delivered in by the General. Mr. Roberts received his appointment not from Colonel Champion but from the Board, and in the office of Persian Translator to the Commander-in-Chief he was not considered as appertaining to any particular person, but to the officer, whoever he might be, that held the command. I consider every question proposed by me should be put to Mr. Roberts and other persons respecting Colonel Champion and the transactions of the late campaign, as bearing a relation to the State either as they affect the character of Colonel Champion in respect to his command or my own. I have reason to believe that Colly Churn did interfere in matters of the State, and therefore I have a right to put the questions which I did propose. With respect to the question proposed by the General I have no objection.

'*General Clavering.* As the Governor-General imagines that the replies he may receive from Mr. Roberts may tend to elucidate any transaction of consequence to the State, I agree to it notwithstanding the Governor-General himself has always objected to Mr. Middleton's being laid before the Board, although he was under no oath whatever; with respect to the Governor's imagining I have conceived personal spleen to him, I must beg he will be persuaded I am actuated by no other motive in my public opposition to him but what concerns the public, and to prevent his employing the authority of his station to oppress Colonel Champion who is now absent, and therefore requires the protection of every member of this Board.

'*The Governor-General.* I am sorry to swell our Minutes with these frequent replies and rejoinders, but I must justify myself from the charge brought against me by the General of using my authority to oppress Colonel Champion. I have no authority. Colonel Champion enjoys the protection of that part of this Government in whom the whole authority virtually resides. Colonel Champion, though absent, is not entitled to my silence either with respect to the accusations which he has thought proper to throw on my conduct or the transactions of the war which I affirm to be misrepresented by him. He knew my intention of entering into the investigation of both before his departure, and had no right to prefer accusations against me on the eve of his return to England if he meant to avail himself of his departure as a plea of exemption from such an investigation.

'*General Clavering*. Colonel Champion has already informed the Board that it was not possible for him to deliver into the Board the voluminous defence which he had been obliged to make in answer to a charge brought against him by the Vizier. A charge which he alleges was fabricated at the Presidency and sent up to Sujah Dowla to be copied over. In this correspondence between Colonel Champion and this Government there appears in almost all the letters, whether from the Governor himself or from the Board, the fullest approbation of his conduct, and further that there appears no other cause for the Governor's private resentment to him than the generous indignation which the Colonel showed at the inhuman and cruel treatment of the Vizier to his prisoners. The Board are now, in consequence of the cruel state in which those poor unhappy people were left, making remonstrances to the present Nabob to endeavour that some alleviation may be shown to their unhappy fate; this is a part that we think worthy of us in vindication of the honour and reputation of the English name.

'*The Governor-General*. I hear with astonishment new charges produced against me and expressed in a style which indicates a design in the General to provoke me to a forgetfulness of my own temper and moderation. If such is the General's design, this Board is not the proper place for it. I am charged with having abetted and encouraged the Vizier in acts of the most inhuman barbarities even to such a degree as to pursue with rancour a man whose only fault was that he opposed those barbarities. I am charged with having fabricated the letter which the Vizier wrote in accusation of Colonel Champion, a charge which I must fix upon the General, unless he can make it appear from Colonel Champion's declarations that he made it. I solemnly deny both. My letters to Colonel Champion and to Mr. Middleton, which are I believe on record, will prove that I took the most effectual measures that could have been taken by me to obtain a relief of the Rohilla prisoners if they had actually suffered the distresses which Colonel Champion declared they did; nor did I know or even suspect the Vizier's intention of writing such a letter at the time that it was written. I cannot offer direct proofs of a negative, but I can offer circumstantial proofs, and for these I refer to my letters both to the Vizier, to Colonel Champion, and to Mr. Middleton, which are on record, that I carefully avoided mentioning either to the Vizier or to Colonel Champion any circumstances that could aggravate the misunderstanding between them except the mention only of such points as I was obliged by my duty to mention, and those with a suppression of every circumstance not material to the subject which might inflame; that my whole conduct to both was conciliatory and not ostensibly but really such, since the strongest letter which was ever written by me to the Vizier was in recommendation of Colonel Champion, and inviting him to bestow his entire confidence in Colonel Champion, was not even communicated to that gentleman.

'*General Clavering*. I have advanced nothing in my former Minute but what appears in the defence that Colonel Champion has made. He has proved I think to the satisfaction of every impartial person that his representations to the Governor of the ill-treatment that the prisoners met with was displeasing to him; he has further proved that he concluded the campaign with the entire satisfaction of the Vizier by receiving a letter of thanks from him. He has traced Colonel Macleane following the Vizier from the Camp to Lucknow where the letter was written; and though it cannot be proved as yet with a certainty that the letter itself was copied from one sent from the Presidency or dictated from the suggestions of Colonel Macleane, I have no doubt but Colonel Champion will prove that likewise to the satisfaction of the world. In regard to what the Governor mentions of any design I may conceive to affront him, I here declare I have none, except he will take as such my professed opposition to almost all the measures of his late administration.

'*The Governor-General*. I shall make a further reply, but I beg that my not continuing this dialogue may not be imputed to an acquiescence in the General's assertions[1].'

On the 25th May, 1775, the Secretary informed the Council that answers to the questions had been received from ten officers, and it was ordered that these should lie for consideration until the other answers had been received. In the report of the proceedings of the Council on the 10th July, 1775, a letter from Colonel Galliez is recorded, in which it is stated that another packet had been forwarded, 'being the last of the questions [Qy. answers to questions] proposed to those officers now in camp, who were present at the battle of St. George.' On this no orders appear to have been passed, and no further notice either of the questions or of the answers has been found in any of the subsequent Proceedings of the Government. The records in the India Office, in the British Museum, and in Calcutta, have been repeatedly searched in vain, but neither Hastings nor his accusers appear to have again referred to the subject. Mr. Forrest, who was good enough at my request to institute a second examination of the Calcutta records in the hope of discovering the missing papers, has suggested to me an explanation of their disappearance which I have little doubt is correct. Francis, after the examination in the Council chamber of

[1] Consultations, 8th May, 1775. India Office Records.

Colonel Leslie and Major Hannay and Colonel Champion, probably came to the conclusion that no capital could be made out of the imaginary atrocities of the Rohilla war, and that other weapons against Hastings must be found. Immediately afterwards, the vile charges of Nandkumar were invented, and in the contest that followed nothing more was heard of the Rohillas. The answers of the officers were probably put aside because they referred to matters in which no one retained much interest, and it was the more probable that this would happen because if replies were ever furnished to all the foolish and irrelevant questions of Colonel Champion they must have formed a mass of papers which few would have been inclined to look at. After Francis returned to England he saw that he could use the Rohilla war as one of the means of rousing against Hastings the generous but reckless and unthinking indignation of Burke. If, as was actually the case, no further attempt was made to produce evidence in support of the charges of cruelty that had been brought, it was certainly because in the task of finding such evidence even the skilful malignity of Francis had failed.

INDEX.

THE END.

Clarendon Press, Oxford.

SELECT LIST OF STANDARD WORKS.

1. DICTIONARIES.

A New English Dictionary on Historical Principles, founded mainly on the materials collected by the Philological Society. Edited by James A. H. Murray, LL.D. Imperial 4to. In Parts, price 12*s.* 6*d.* each.

Vol. I (A and B), half-morocco, 2*l.* 12*s.* 6*d.*
Part IV, Section 2, C—CASS, beginning Vol. II, price 5*s.*
Part V, CAST—CLIVY, price 12*s.* 6*d.*
Part VI, CLO—CONSIGNER, price 12*s.* 6*d.*

Vol. III, Part I, E—EVERY, edited by Henry Bradley, M.A., with the co-operation of Dr. Murray, price 12*s.* 6*d.*

An Etymological Dictionary of the English Language, arranged on an Historical Basis. By W. W. Skeat, Litt.D. *Second Edition.* 4to. 2*l.* 4*s.*

A Middle-English Dictionary, containing Words used by English Writers from the Twelfth to the Fifteenth Century. By Francis Henry Stratmann. A new edition, re-arranged, revised, and enlarged by Henry Bradley. 4to, half-bound, 1*l.* 11*s.* 6*d.*

An Anglo-Saxon Dictionary, based on the MS. collections of the late Joseph Bosworth, D.D. Edited and enlarged by Prof. T. N. Toller, M.A., Owens College, Manchester. Parts I-III. A-SAR. 4to, stiff covers. 15*s.* each. Part IV, § 1, stiff covers, 8*s.* 6*d.* *Just Published.*

An Icelandic-English Dictionary, based on the MS. collections of the late Richard Cleasby. Enlarged and completed by G. Vigfússon, M.A. With an Introduction, and Life of Richard Cleasby, by G. Webbe Dasent, D.C.L. 4to. 3*l.* 7*s.*

A Greek-English Lexicon, by H. G. Liddell, D.D., and Robert Scott, D.D. *Seventh Edition, Revised and Augmented throughout.* 4to. 1*l.* 16*s.*

An Intermediate Greek-English Lexicon, founded upon the Seventh Edition of Liddell and Scott's Greek Lexicon. Small 4to. 12s. 6d.

A Latin Dictionary, founded on Andrews' edition of Freund's Latin Dictionary, revised, enlarged, and in great part rewritten by Charlton T. Lewis, Ph.D., and Charles Short, LL.D. 4to. 1l. 5s.

A School Latin Dictionary. By Charlton T. Lewis, Ph.D. Small 4to. 18s.

A Sanskrit-English Dictionary. Etymologically and Philologically arranged, with special reference to Greek, Latin, German, Anglo-Saxon, English, and other cognate Indo-European Languages. By Sir M. Monier-Williams, D.C.L. 4to. 4l. 14s. 6d.

Thesaurus Syriacus: collegerunt Quatremère, Bernstein, Lorsbach, Arnoldi, Agrell, Field, Roediger: edidit R. Payne Smith, S.T.P. Vol. I, containing Fasc. I–V, sm. fol. 5l. 5s.
Fasc. VI. 1l. 1s. Fasc. VII. 1l. 11s. 6d. Fasc. VIII. 1l. 16s.

2. LAW.

Anson. *Principles of the English Law of Contract, and of Agency in its Relation to Contract.* By Sir W. R. Anson, D.C.L. *Sixth Edition.* 8vo. 10s. 6d.

—— *Law and Custom of the Constitution.* Part I. Parliament. 8vo. 10s. 6d.

Bentham. *An Introduction to the Principles of Morals and Legislation.* By Jeremy Bentham. Crown 8vo. 6s. 6d.

Digby. *An Introduction to the History of the Law of Real Property.* By Kenelm E. Digby, M.A. *Third Edition.* 8vo. 10s. 6d.

Grueber. *Lex Aquilia.* The Roman Law of Damage to Property: being a Commentary on the Title of the Digest 'Ad Legem Aquiliam' (ix. 2). With an Introduction to the Study of the Corpus Iuris Civilis. By Erwin Grueber, Dr. Jur., M.A. 8vo. 10s. 6d.

Hall. *International Law.* By W. E. Hall, M.A. *Third Edition.* 8vo. 22s. 6d.

Holland. *Elements of Jurisprudence.* By T. E. Holland, D.C.L. *Fifth Edition.* 8vo. 10s. 6d.

—— *The European Concert in the Eastern Question;* a Collection of Treaties and other Public Acts. Edited, with Introductions and Notes, by T. E. Holland, D.C.L. 8vo. 12s. 6d.

Holland. *Gentilis, Alberici, De Iure Belli Libri Tres.* Edidit T. E. Holland, I.C.D. Small 4to. half-morocco, 21s.

Holland. *The Institutes of Justinian,* edited as a recension of the Institutes of Gaius, by T. E. Holland, D.C.L. *Second Edition.* Extra fcap. 8vo. 5s.

Holland and Shadwell. *Select Titles from the Digest of Justinian.* By T. E. Holland, D.C.L., and C. L. Shadwell, B.C.L. 8vo. 14s.

Also sold in Parts, in paper covers, as follows:—

Part I. Introductory Titles. 2s. 6d.

Part II. Family Law. 1s.

Part III. Property Law. 2s. 6d.

Part IV. Law of Obligations (No. 1). 3s. 6d.

Part IV. Law of Obligations (No. 2). 4s. 6d.

Markby. *Elements of Law considered with reference to Principles of General Jurisprudence.* By Sir William Markby, D.C.L. *Fourth Edition.* 8vo. 12s. 6d.

Moyle. *Imperatoris Iustiniani Institutionum Libri Quattuor;* with Introductions, Commentary, Excursus and Translation. By J. B. Moyle, D.C.L. *Second Edition.* 2 vols. 8vo. Vol. I. 16s. Vol. II. 6s.

Pollock and Wright. *An Essay on Possession in the Common Law.* By Sir F. Pollock, M.A., and R. S. Wright, B.C.L. (Now the Hon. Mr. Justice Wright). 8vo. 8s. 6d.

Poste. *Gaii Institutionum Juris Civilis Commentarii Quattuor;* or, Elements of Roman Law by Gaius. With a Translation and Commentary by Edward Poste, M.A. 8vo. 18s.

Raleigh. *An Outline of the Law of Property.* By Thos. Raleigh, M.A. 8vo. 7s. 6d.

Stokes. *The Anglo-Indian Codes.* By Whitley Stokes, LL.D.

Vol. I. Substantive Law. 8vo. 30s.

Vol. II. Adjective Law. 8vo. 35s.

First and Second Supplements to the above, incorporating Indian Legislation and Judicial Decisions to May 31, 1891. 8vo, 6s. 6d.

Separately, No. 1, 2s. 6d.; No. 2, 4s. 6d.

Twiss. *The Law of Nations considered as Independent Political Communities.* By Sir Travers Twiss, D.C.L.

Part I. On the Rights and Duties of Nations in time of Peace. New Edition. 8vo. 15s.

Part II. On the Rights and Duties of Nations in time of War. 21s.

---

3. HISTORY, BIOGRAPHY, ETC.

Baker's Chronicle. *Chronicon Galfridi le Baker de Swynebroke.* Edited with Notes by Edward Maunde Thompson, Hon. LL.D. St. Andrews; Hon. D.C.L. Durham; F.S.A.; Principal Librarian of the British Museum. Small 4to, stiff covers, 18s.; cloth, gilt top, 21s.

Bentham. *A Fragment on Government.* By Jeremy Bentham. Edited with an Introduction by F. C. Montague, M.A. 8vo. 7s. 6d.

Bentham. *An Introduction to the Principles of Morals and Legislation.* By Jeremy Bentham. Crown 8vo. 6s. 6d.

Boswell's *Life of Samuel Johnson, LL.D.* Edited by G. Birkbeck Hill, D.C.L. In six volumes, medium 8vo. With Portraits and Facsimiles. Half-bound, 3l. 3s.

Calendar *of the Clarendon State Papers*, preserved in the Bodleian Library. In three volumes. 1869–76.

Vol. I. From 1523 to January 1649. 8vo. 18*s.*

Vol. II. From 1649 to 1654. 16*s.*

Vol. III. From 1655 to 1657. 14*s.*

Calendar *of Charters and Rolls* preserved in the Bodleian Library. 8vo. 1*l.* 11*s.* 6*d.*

Carte's *Life of James Duke of Ormond.* 6 vols. 8vo. 1*l.* 5*s.*

Clarendon's *History of the Rebellion and Civil Wars in England.* Re-edited from a fresh collation of the original MS. in the Bodleian Library, with marginal dates and occasional notes, by W. Dunn Macray, M.A., F.S.A. 6 vols. Crown 8vo. 2*l.* 5*s.*

—— *History of the Rebellion and Civil Wars in England.* To which are subjoined the Notes of Bishop Warburton. 7 vols. medium 8vo. 2*l.* 10*s.*

—— *History of the Rebellion and Civil Wars in England.* Also his Life, written by himself, in which is included a Continuation of his History of the Grand Rebellion. Royal 8vo. 1*l.* 2*s.*

—— *Life, including a Continuation of his History.* 2 vols. medium 8vo. 1*l.* 2*s.*

Earle. *Handbook to the Land-Charters, and other Saxonic Documents.* By John Earle, M.A., Professor of Anglo-Saxon in the University of Oxford. Crown 8vo. 16*s.*

Finlay. *A History of Greece from its Conquest by the Romans to the present time,* B.C. 146 to A.D. 1864. By George Finlay, LL.D. A new Edition, revised throughout, and in part re-written, with considerable additions, by the Author, and edited by H. F. Tozer, M.A. 7 vols. 8vo. 3*l.* 10*s.*

Fortescue. *The Governance of England:* otherwise called The Difference between an Absolute and a Limited Monarchy. By Sir John Fortescue, Kt. A Revised Text. Edited, with Introduction, Notes, &c., by Charles Plummer, M.A. 8vo, half-bound, 12*s.* 6*d.*

Freeman. *The History of Sicily from the Earliest Times.* Vols. I. and II. 8vo. Cloth, 2*l.* 2*s.* *Just Published.*

—— *History of the Norman Conquest of England; its Causes and Results.* By E. A. Freeman, D.C.L. In Six Volumes. 8vo. 5*l.* 9*s.* 6*d.*

—— *The Reign of William Rufus and the Accession of Henry the First.* 2 vols. 8vo. 1*l.* 16*s.*

—— *A Short History of the Norman Conquest of England.* *Second Edition.* Extra fcap. 8vo. 2*s.* 6*d.*

Gardiner. *The Constitutional Documents of the Puritan Revolution,* 1628–1660. Selected and Edited by Samuel Rawson Gardiner, M.A. Crown 8vo. 9*s.*

Gascoigne's *Theological Dictionary ('Liber Veritatum'):* Selected Passages, illustrating the Condition of Church and State, 1403–1458. With an Introduction by James E. Thorold Rogers, M.A. 4to. 10*s.* 6*d.*

Greswell. *History of the Dominion of Canada.* By W. PARR GRESWELL, M.A. Under the auspices of the Royal Colonial Institute. Crown 8vo. With Eleven Maps. 7*s.* 6*d.*

—— *Geography of the Dominion of Canada and Newfoundland.* By the same Author. Crown 8vo. With Ten Maps. 6*s.*

Gross. *The Gild Merchant;* a Contribution to British Municipal History. By Charles Gross, PH.D. Instructor in History, Harvard University. 2 vols. 8vo. Half-bound, 24*s.*

Hodgkin. *Italy and her Invaders.* With Plates and Maps. By T. Hodgkin, D.C.L. Vols. I–IV, A.D. 376–553. 8vo. 3*l.* 8*s.*

—— *The Dynasty of Theodosius;* or, Seventy Years' Struggle with the Barbarians. By the same Author. Crown 8vo. 6*s.*

Hume. *Letters of David Hume to William Strahan.* Edited with Notes, Index, &c., by G. Birkbeck Hill, D.C.L. 8vo. 12*s.* 6*d.*

Kitchin. *A History of France.* With Numerous Maps, Plans, and Tables. By G. W. Kitchin, D.D. In three Volumes. *Second Edition.* Crown 8vo, each 10*s.* 6*d.*

Vol. I. to 1453. Vol. II. 1453–1624. Vol. III. 1624–1793.

Luttrell's (*Narcissus*) *Diary.* A Brief Historical Relation of State Affairs, 1678–1714. 6 vols. 8vo. 1*l.* 4*s.*

Lucas. *Introduction to a Historical Geography of the British Colonies.* By C. P. Lucas, B.A. With Eight Maps. Crown 8vo. 4*s.* 6*d.*

Lucas. *Historical Geography of the British Colonies:*

Vol. I. The Mediterranean and Eastern Colonies (exclusive of India). With Eleven Maps. Crown 8vo. 5*s.*

Vol. II. The West Indian Colonies. With Twelve Maps. Crown 8vo. 7*s.* 6*d.*

Machiavelli. *Il Principe.* Edited by L. Arthur Burd, M.A. With an Introduction by Lord Acton. 8vo. Cloth, 14*s.*

Ranke. *A History of England, principally in the Seventeenth Century.* By L. von Ranke. Translated under the superintendence of G. W. Kitchin, D.D., and C. W. Boase, M.A. 6 vols. 8vo. 3*l.* 3*s.*

Rawlinson. *A Manual of Ancient History.* By George Rawlinson, M.A. *Second Edition.* 8vo. 14*s.*

Rhŷs. *Studies in the Arthurian Legend.* By John Rhŷs, M.A. 8vo. 12*s.* 6*d.*

Ricardo. *Letters of David Ricardo to T. R. Malthus* (1810–1823). Edited by James Bonar, M.A. 8vo. 10*s.* 6*d.*

Rogers. *History of Agriculture and Prices in England,* A.D. 1259–1702. By James E. Thorold Rogers, M.A. 6 vols., 8vo. 7*l.* 2*s.*

—— *First Nine Years of the Bank of England.* 8vo. 8*s.* 6*d.*

—— *Protests of the Lords, including those which have been expunged, from 1624 to 1874;* with Historical Introductions. In three volumes. 8vo. 2*l.* 2*s.*

Smith's *Wealth of Nations.* With Notes, by J. E. Thorold Rogers, M.A. 2 vols. 8vo. 21*s.*

Sprigg's *England's Recovery;* being the History of the Army under Sir Thomas Fairfax. 8vo. 6s.

Stubbs. *Select Charters and other Illustrations of English Constitutional History, from the Earliest Times to the Reign of Edward I.* Arranged and edited by W. Stubbs, D.D., Lord Bishop of Oxford. *Seventh Edition.* Crown 8vo. 8s. 6d.

—— *The Constitutional History of England, in its Origin and Development. Library Edition.* 3 vols. Demy 8vo. 2l. 8s.

Also in 3 vols. crown 8vo. price 12s. each.

—— *Seventeen Lectures on the Study of Medieval and Modern History, delivered at Oxford* 1867–1884. Crown 8vo. 8s. 6d.

Stubbs. *Registrum Sacrum Anglicanum.* An attempt to exhibit the course of Episcopal Succession in England. By W. Stubbs, D.D. Small 4to. 8s. 6d.

Wellesley. *A Selection from the Despatches, Treaties, and other Papers of the Marquess Wellesley, K.G., during his Government of India.* Edited by S. J. Owen, M.A. 8vo. 1l. 4s.

Wellington. *A Selection from the Despatches, Treaties, and other Papers relating to India of Field-Marshal the Duke of Wellington, K.G.* Edited by S. J. Owen, M.A. 8vo. 1l. 4s.

Whitelock's *Memorials of English Affairs from* 1625 *to* 1660. 4 vols. 8vo. 1l. 10s.

4. PHILOSOPHY, LOGIC, ETC.

Bacon. *The Essays.* With Introduction and Illustrative Notes. By S. H. Reynolds, M.A. 8vo, half-bound. 12s. 6d.

—— *Novum Organum.* Edited, with Introduction, Notes, &c., by T. Fowler, D.D. *Second Edition.* 8vo. 15s.

—— *Novum Organum.* Edited, with English Notes, by G. W. Kitchin, D.D. 8vo. 9s. 6d.

—— *Novum Organum.* Translated by G. W. Kitchin, D.D. 8vo. 9s. 6d.

Berkeley. *The Works of George Berkeley, D.D., formerly Bishop of Cloyne; including many of his writings hitherto unpublished.* With Prefaces, Annotations, and an Account of his Life and Philosophy, by Alexander Campbell Fraser, LL.D. 4 vols. 8vo. 2l. 18s.

The Life, Letters, &c., separately, 16s.

Bosanquet. *Logic; or, the Morphology of Knowledge.* By B. Bosanquet, M.A. 8vo. 21s.

Butler's *Works, with Index to the Analogy.* 2 vols. 8vo. 11s.

Fowler. *The Elements of Deductive Logic, designed mainly for the use of Junior Students in the Universities.* By T. Fowler, D.D. *Ninth Edition,* with a Collection of Examples. Extra fcap. 8vo. 3s. 6d.

—— *The Elements of Inductive Logic, designed mainly for the use of Students in the Universities.* By the same Author. *Fifth Edition.* Extra fcap. 8vo. 6s.

Fowler. *The Principles of Morals.* (Introductory Chapters.) By T. Fowler, D.D., and J. M. Wilson, B.D. 8vo, boards, 3s. 6d.

—— *The Principles of Morals.* Part II. By T. Fowler, D.D. 8vo. 10s. 6d.

Green. *Prolegomena to Ethics.* By T. H. Green, M.A. Edited by A. C. Bradley, M.A. 8vo. 12s. 6d.

Hegel. *The Logic of Hegel;* translated from the Encyclopaedia of the Philosophical Sciences. With Prolegomena by William Wallace, M.A. 8vo. 14s.

Hume's *Treatise of Human Nature.* Edited, with Analytical Index, by L. A. Selby-Bigge, M.A. Crown 8vo. 9s.

Locke's *Conduct of the Understanding.* Edited by T. Fowler, D.D. *Third Edition.* Extra fcap. 8vo. 2s. 6d.

Lotze's *Logic*, **in Three Books;** of Thought, of Investigation, and of Knowledge. English Translation; Edited by B. Bosanquet, M.A. *Second Edition.* 2 vols. Cr. 8vo. 12s.

—— *Metaphysic*, in Three Books; Ontology, Cosmology, and Psychology. English Translation; Edited by B. Bosanquet, M.A. *Second Edition.* 2 vols. Cr. 8vo. 12s.

Martineau. *Types of Ethical Theory.* By James Martineau, D.D *Third Edition.* 2 vols. Cr. 8vo. 15s.

—— *A Study of Religion: its Sources and Contents. Second Edition.* 2 vols. Cr. 8vo. 15s.

5. PHYSICAL SCIENCE.

Aplin. *The Birds of Oxfordshire.* By O. V. Aplin. 8vo. 10s. 6d.

Chambers. *A Handbook of Descriptive and Practical Astronomy.* By G. F. Chambers, F.R.A.S. *Fourth Edition*, in 3 vols. Demy 8vo.

- Vol. I. The Sun, Planets, and Comets. 21s.
- Vol. II. Instruments and Practical Astronomy. 21s.
- Vol. III. The Starry Heavens. 14s.

De Bary. *Comparative Anatomy of the Vegetative Organs of the Phanerogams and Ferns.* By Dr. A. de Bary. Translated and Annotated by F. O. Bower, M.A., F.L.S., and D. H. Scott, M.A., Ph.D., F.L.S. Royal 8vo, half-morocco, 1l. 2s. 6d.

—— *Comparative Morphology and Biology of Fungi, Mycetozoa and Bacteria.* By Dr. A. de Bary. Translated by H. E. F. Garnsey, M.A. Revised by Isaac Bayley Balfour, M.A., M.D., F.R.S. Royal 8vo, half-morocco, 1l. 2s. 6d.

De Bary. *Lectures on Bacteria.* By Dr. A. de Bary. *Second Improved Edition.* Translated by H. E. F. Garnsey, M.A. Revised by Isaac Bayley Balfour, M.A., M.D., F.R.S. Crown 8vo. 6s.

Fisher. *A Class Book of Elementary Chemistry.* By W. W. Fisher, M.A., F.C.S. Crown 8vo. 4s. 6d.

Chemistry in Space. By Van't Hoff. Translated and edited by J. E. Marsh, B.A. Crown 8vo. 4s. 6d.

Goebel. *Outlines of Classification and Special Morphology of Plants.* A new Edition of Sachs' Text-Book of Botany, Book II. By Dr. K. Goebel. Translated by H. E. F. Garnsey, M.A. Revised by Isaac Bayley Balfour, M.A., M.D., F.R.S. Royal 8vo, half-morocco, 1l. 1s.

Sachs. *Lectures on the Physiology of Plants.* By Julius von Sachs. Translated by H. Marshall Ward, M.A., F.L.S. Royal 8vo, half-morocco, 1*l.* 11*s.* 6*d.*

—— *A History of Botany.* Translated by H. E. F. Garnsey, M.A. Edited by I. Bayley Balfour, M.A., M.D., F.R.S. Crown 8vo. 10*s.*

Fossil Botany. *Being an Introduction to Palaeophytology from the Standpoint of the Botanist.* By H. Graf zu Solms-Laubach. Translated by H. E. F. Garnsey, M.A. Edited by I. Bayley Balfour, M.A., M.D., F.R.S. Royal 8vo, half-morocco, 18*s.*

Annals of Botany. Edited by Isaac Bayley Balfour, M.A., M.D., F.R.S., Sydney H. Vines, D.Sc., F.R.S., and W. G. Farlow, M.D.

- Vol. I. Parts I–IV. Royal 8vo, half-morocco, gilt top, 1*l.* 16*s.*
- Vol. II. Parts V–VIII. 2*l.* 2*s.*
- Vol. III. Part IX. 1'1*s.* 6*d.*; X. 13*s.* 6*d.*; XI. 18*s.*; XII. *In the Press.*
- Vol. IV. Part XIII. 12*s.* 6*d.*; XIV. 13*s.* 6*d.*; XV. 10*s.* 6*d.*; XVI. *In the Press.*
- Vol. V. Part XVII. 10*s.* 6*d.*

Biological Series. (*Translations of Foreign Biological Memoirs.*)

I. *The Physiology of Nerve, of Muscle, and of the Electrical Organ.* Edited by J. Burdon-Sanderson, M.D., F.R.SS. L. & E. Medium 8vo. 1*l.* 1*s.*

II. *The Anatomy of the Frog.* By Dr. Alexander Ecker, Professor in the University of Freiburg. Translated, with numerous Annotations and Additions, by G. Haslam, M.D. Med. 8vo. 21*s.*

III. *Contributions to the History of the Physiology of the Nervous System.* By Professor Conrad Eckhard. Translated by Miss Edith Prance. *In Preparation.*

IV. *Essays upon Heredity and Kindred Biological Problems.* By Dr. A. Weismann. Translated and Edited by E. B. Poulton, M.A., S. Schönland, Ph.D., and A. E. Shipley, M.A. *Second Edition.* Crown 8vo. 7*s.* 6*d.*

Prestwich. *Geology, Chemical, Physical, and Stratigraphical.* By Joseph Prestwich, M.A., F.R.S. In two Volumes.

- Vol. I. Chemical and Physical. Royal 8vo. 1*l.* 5*s.*
- Vol. II. Stratigraphical and Physical. With a new Geological Map of Europe. Royal 8vo. 1*l.* 16*s.*
- New Geological Map of Europe. In case or on roller. 5*s.*

Rolleston and Jackson. *Forms of Animal Life.* A Manual of Comparative Anatomy, with descriptions of selected types. By George Rolleston, M.D., F.R.S. *Second Edition.* Revised and Enlarged by W. Hatchett Jackson, M.A. Medium 8vo. 1*l.* 16*s.*

Oxford

AT THE CLARENDON PRESS

LONDON: HENRY FROWDE

OXFORD UNIVERSITY PRESS WAREHOUSE, AMEN CORNER, E.C.